CONGRESSIONAL ELECTIONS

Campaigning at Home and in Washington

Third Edition

Paul S. Herrnson
UNIVERSITY OF MARYLAND

CQ PRESS

A Division of Congressional Quarterly Inc.
Washington, D.C.

CQ Press
A Division of Congressional Quarterly Inc.
1414 22nd Street, N.W.
Washington, D.C. 20037

(202) 822-1475; (800) 638-1710

www.cqpress.com

Printed in the United States of America

Cover design: Kachergis Book Design, Pittsboro, North Carolina

04 03 02 01 00   5 4 3 2 1

Library of Congress Cataloging-in-Publication Data

Herrnson, Paul S.
    Congressional elections : campaigning at home and in Washington /
Paul S. Herrnson. — 3rd ed.
        p.   cm.
    Includes bibliographical references and index.
    ISBN 1-56802-534-3 (paper)
    1. United States. Congress—Elections. 2. Electioneering—United
States. 3. Campaign funds—United States. 4. Political action
committees—United States. I. Title.
JK1976.H47   2000
324.973'0929—dc21   00-020410

In Memory of
Harry Perlman

Contents

Preface

When CQ Press invited me to write a third edition of this book I was delighted. For one thing, the invitation suggested that the first two editions had been well received, which is music to the ears of any author. More important, the invitation gave me the opportunity to analyze further the important changes that have taken place in congressional elections. These include the massive growth in "soft money" fund-raising and expenditures, the escalation of party agenda-setting efforts, the legalization of party independent expenditures, the surge in party and interest group "issue advocacy" advertising, the increasingly partisan campaign activities of tax-exempt interest groups, and the expanded roles of members of Congress as contributors to and fund-raisers for other candidates.

This edition, like the previous two, is about congressional elections and their implications for Congress and, more generally, for American government. Most congressional elections are contests between candidates who have vastly unequal chances of victory. Incumbents generally win because of their own efforts and because many challengers find themselves in a catch-22 situation. Without name recognition, challengers and candidates for open seats have trouble raising funds, and without funds they cannot enhance their name recognition or attract enough support to run a competitive race. This conundrum hints at a fundamental truth of congressional elections: candidates wage two campaigns— one for votes and one for money and other resources. The former takes place in the candidate's district or state. The latter is conducted primarily in the Washington, D.C., area, where many political consultants, political action committees (PACs), other interest groups, and the parties' national, senatorial, and congressional campaign committees are located. The timing of the two campaigns overlaps considerably, but candidates and their organizations must conceptualize the campaigns as separate and plot a different strategy for each.

Although this book focuses on congressional election campaigns, considerable attention is given to voters, candidates, governance, and campaign reform. I have gathered information from candidates, campaign aides, political consultants, party strategists, PAC managers, journalists, and other political insiders to describe their goals, strategies, decision-making processes, and roles in congressional campaigns. I also have assessed the influence that the efforts of these individuals and groups have on election outcomes.

The conclusion I draw is that the norms and expectations associated with congressional campaigns affect who runs, the kinds of organizations the candidates assemble, how much money they raise, the kinds of party and interest group support they attract, the strategies and communications techniques they use, and whether they win or lose. The need to campaign for votes and resources, in turn, affects how members of Congress carry out their legislative responsibilities and the kinds of reforms they are willing to consider. These observations may seem intuitive, but they are rarely discussed in studies of voting behavior and are usually overlooked in research that focuses on the role of money in politics. Given their importance, it is unfortunate that congressional campaigns have received so little attention in the scholarly literature.

The candidates, consultants, parties, and interest groups that have participated in congressional elections in the late 1990s are all systematically analyzed. The analysis in this edition is based primarily on interviews with and questionnaires from nearly 400 House and Senate candidates and other political insiders in the 1998 elections. It also relies on campaign finance data furnished by the Federal Election Commission, information on televised campaign advertisements assembled by the Campaign Media Analysis Group (CMAG), and exit surveys taken by the Voter News Service. Memoranda and interviews provided by campaign organizations, party committees, PACs, and other interest groups further contribute to the study. Generalizations derived from the analysis are supported with concrete examples from case studies of individual campaigns. Insights also are drawn from my own participation in congressional campaigns and from the questionnaires and interviews provided by more than 450 candidates and campaign aides who competed in the congressional elections held between 1992 and 1996. The evidence supports the thesis that the campaigns candidates wage at home for votes and in Washington for money and campaign assistance have a significant effect on the outcomes of congressional elections. It shows that the activities of party committees, interest groups, campaign volunteers, and journalists are also important.

The findings for soft money, including issue advocacy ads, have important implications for public policy, especially campaign finance reform. They show that "outside campaigning" by parties and interest groups can overwhelm candidates' own campaign efforts. Policy makers should be particularly concerned about the role of unregulated money in congressional elections.

Scholars using this book as a classroom text might be interested in reviewing the questionnaires I used to collect information from congressional campaigns. They were valuable research tools for students in my congressional elections seminars, who used them to guide their field research on campaigns. The questionnaires, my syllabus, class assignments, and other course materials are available on the Internet at *http://herrnson.cqpress.com*. The Web site also lists other Internet resources that students and scholars researching congressional elections should find useful. Information about the methods I used to conduct the research discussed in this book also appear on the Web site.

The publication of *Congressional Elections* would not have been possible without the cooperation of many individuals and institutions. I am indebted to the hundreds of people who consented to be interviewed, completed questionnaires, or shared election targeting lists and other campaign materials with me. Their participation in this project was essential to its success.

I also wish to thank the Pew Charitable Trusts, which funded some of the research on which this book is based. The Department of Government and Politics at the University of Maryland provided a stimulating environment in which to work. David Magleby and Kelly Patterson collaborated with me on the 1998 Congressional Campaign Study, which was used to collect some of the campaign data analyzed in this edition. Kenneth Goldstein supplied the CMAG data and helped prepare them for analysis. Peter Roybal of Congressional Quarterly made available information on the candidates' backgrounds, and Jock Friedly of *The Hill* furnished material on political scandals. Robert Biersack provided insights into the nuances of the campaign finance data. Owen Abbe and Peter Francia provided valuable assistance during various stages of the research. Chris Bailey, William Bianco, Jim Gimpel, Thomas Kazee, Sandy Maisel, Stephen Salmore, Frank Sorauf, Ric Uslaner, and Clyde Wilcox made valuable comments on earlier editions of the book. John Green, Jim Thurber, and many of the aforementioned individuals made helpful suggestions for the third edition. Kelly Patterson and an anonymous reviewer for CQ Press went over the manuscript in detail, making many useful recommendations. CQ Press's Brenda Carter, Gwenda Larsen, and Christopher Karlsten played a vital role in preparing the manuscript. I am delighted to have the opportunity to express my deepest appreciation to all of them.

Finally, a few words are in order about the person to whom this book is dedicated. My uncle, Harry Perlman, did not live to see the completion of this book, but his contributions to it were critical. The construction jobs he gave me were the most important form of financial aid I received while pursuing my college education. His ideas about politics and philosophy helped me to appreciate the virtues of democratically held elections and to recognize the inferiority of other means of transferring political power. His unwavering belief that people can be taught to value what is good about their political system and to recognize its shortcomings was a source of inspiration that helped me complete this book.

CONGRESSIONAL ELECTIONS

Introduction

Elections are the centerpiece of democracy. They are the means Americans use to choose their political leaders, and they give those who have been elected the authority to rule. Elections also furnish the American people with a vehicle for expressing their views about the directions they think this rule ought to take. In theory, elections are the principal mechanism for ensuring "government of the people, by the people, [and] for the people."[1]

An examination of the different aspects of the electoral process provides insights into the operations of our political system. Separate balloting for congressional, state, and local candidates results in legislators who represent parochial interests, sometimes to the detriment of the formation of national policy. Private financing of congressional campaigns, which is consistent with Americans' belief in capitalism, favors incumbents and increases the political access of wealthy and well-organized segments of society. Participatory primaries, which require congressional aspirants to assemble an organization in order to campaign for the nomination, lead candidates to rely on political consultants rather than on party committees for assistance in winning their primaries and general elections. These factors encourage congressional candidates and members of Congress to act more independently of party leaders than do their counterparts in other democracies.

Congressional elections are affected by perceptions of the performance of government. Americans' satisfaction with the state of the economy and with the nation's foreign policy, as well as with their own standard of living, provides a backdrop for elections and a means for assessing whether presidents, individual representatives, and Congress as an institution have performed their jobs adequately. Issues related to the internal operations of Congress—such as the perquisites enjoyed by members—can affect congressional elections. Conversely, congressional elections can greatly affect the internal operations of Congress, the performance of government, and the direction of domestic and foreign policy. Major political reforms and policy reversals generally follow elections in which there have been substantial congressional turnover.

One of the major themes developed in this book is that campaigns matter a great deal to the outcome of congressional elections. National conditions are significant, but their impact on elections is secondary to the decisions and actions of candidates, campaign organizations, party committees, organized interests, and other individuals and groups. This comes as no surprise to those who toil in campaigns, but it is in direct contrast to what many scholars would argue.

In order to win a congressional election or even to be remotely competitive, candidates must compete in two campaigns: one for votes and one for resources. The campaign for votes is the campaign that generally comes to mind when people think about congressional elections. It requires a candidate to assemble an organization and to use that organization to target key groups of voters, select a message they will find compelling, deliver that message, and get supporters to the polls on election day.

The other campaign, which is based largely in Washington, D.C., requires candidates to convince the party operatives, interest group officials, political consultants, and journalists who play leading roles in the nation's political community that their races will be competitive and worthy of support. Gaining the backing of these various individuals is a critical step in attracting the money and campaign services that are available in the nation's capital and in other wealthy urban centers. These resources enable the candidate to run a credible campaign back home. Without them, most congressional candidates would lose their bids for election.

In this book I present a systematic assessment of congressional election campaigns that draws on information from a wide variety of sources. Background information on the more than 14,000 major-party contestants who ran between 1978 and 1998 furnished insights into the types of individuals who try to win a seat in Congress and the conditions under which they run. Personal interviews and survey data provided by more than 830 candidates and campaign aides who were involved in the 1992, 1994, 1996, and 1998 House and Senate elections permitted analysis of the organization, strategies, tactics, issues, and communications techniques used in congressional campaigns. They also provided insights into the roles that political parties, political action committee (PACs), and other groups play in those contests.

Case studies of sixty House campaigns conducted in the elections of 1992 through 1998 illustrate with concrete examples the generalizations drawn from the larger sample. These include many typical elections, such as Republican representative Ed Royce's 1998 victory over Democratic challenger Asuncion "Cecy" R. Groom in California's 39th congressional district, as well as a few unusual contests, such as those that have enabled GOP representative Constance Morella of Maryland to dominate a congressional district composed primarily of Democratic voters.

Many competitive contests, such as Democratic incumbent David Price's thirteen-point victory over Republican Thomas Roberg in North Carolina's 4th congressional district and Democrat Tammy Baldwin's six-point win over Republican Josephine Musser in an open-seat race in Wisconsin's 2nd congressional district, are also discussed. The former race took some unusual turns because the district had been redrawn twice after the 1996 election. The boundaries were changed when the Supreme Court ruled that a nearby district had been racially gerrymandered. The latter race highlights the importance of volunteers in congressional campaigns.

Some races are included because they illustrate the role of scandal or technology in campaigns. Three-term incumbent Jay Kim, R-Calif., lost his 41st congressional district primary to challenger Gary Miller in 1998 after pleading guilty to violating campaign finance laws during his first House race. The open-seat House contest in Washington State between Democrat Brian Baird and Republican Don Benton is examined because of the impact that Baird's innovative Web site had on the campaign.

Also included are contests that involved large amounts of campaign spending by political parties and interest groups. The open seat Senate contest in Kentucky between Republican representative James Bunning and Democratic representative Scott Baesler is analyzed because their parties and numerous interest groups spent huge sums of soft money on so-called issue advocacy ads to promote the election of one candidate over the other. The three-way House race in New Mexico's 3rd congressional district between first-term Republican incumbent Bill Redmond, Democratic nominee Tom Udall, and Green Party candidate Carol Miller is discussed for similar reasons.

Other campaigns are covered because they include members of the Republican House freshman class of 1994, who came to Washington wearing "Majority Maker" buttons on their lapels. Many of their 1996 and 1998 reelection campaigns were extremely competitive and the focus of intense party and interest group activity.

Most of the discussion focuses on House candidates and campaigns because they are easier to generalize about than Senate contests. Differences in the sizes, populations, and political traditions of the fifty states and the fact that only about one-third of all Senate seats are filled in a given election year make campaigns for the upper chamber more difficult to discuss in general terms. Larger, more diverse Senate constituencies also make Senate elections less predictable than House contests. Nevertheless, insights can be gained into campaigns for the upper chamber by contrasting them with those waged for the House.

Interviews with party officials, conducted over the course of the 1992 through 1998 elections, give insights into the strategies used by the Democratic and Republican national, congressional, and senatorial campaign committees. Similar information provided by the managers of a representative group of PACs is used to learn about PAC contribution strategies. Campaign contribution and spending data furnished by the Federal Election Commission (FEC) are used to examine the role of money in politics. Information about televised campaign commercials furnished by the Campaign Media Analysis Group is used to assess the impact of party and interest group issue advocacy. Web sites, newspapers, press releases, and advertising materials distributed by candidates, parties, and interest groups furnish examples of the communications that campaigns disseminate. Exit surveys taken by the Voter News Service provide insights into public opinion. Collectively, these sources of information, along with scholarly accounts published in the political science literature and insights drawn from my own participation in congressional and campaign politics, have permitted a comprehensive portrayal of contemporary congressional election campaigns.

In the first five chapters I examine the strategic context in which congressional election campaigns are waged and the major actors that participate in those contests. Chapter 1 provides an overview of the institutions, laws, party rules, and customs that constitute the framework for congressional elections. The framework has a significant impact on who decides to run for Congress; the kinds of resources that candidates, parties, and interest groups bring to bear on the campaign; the strategies they use; and who ultimately wins a seat in Congress. I also focus on the setting for the congressional elections held during the 1990s, with special emphasis on 1998.

Chapter 2 contains a discussion of candidates and nominations. I examine the influence of incumbency, national conditions, and the personal and career situations of potential candidates on the decision to run for Congress. I also assess the separate contributions that the decision to run, the nomination process, and the general election make toward producing a Congress that is overwhelmingly white, male, middle-aged, and drawn from the legal, business, and public service professions.

The organizations that congressional candidates assemble to wage their election campaigns are the subject of the third chapter. Salaried staff and political consultants form the core of most competitive candidates' campaign teams.

These professionals play a critical role in formulating strategy, gauging public opinion, fund-raising, designing communications, and mobilizing voters.

Political parties and interest groups—the major organizations that help finance elections and provide candidates with important campaign resources—are the subjects of the next two chapters. Chapter 4 includes an analysis of the goals, decision-making processes, and election activities of party committees. I discuss many recent innovations, including party independent expenditures and issue advocacy. In Chapter 5 I concentrate on the goals, strategies, and election efforts of PACs and other interest group organizations. Among the innovations it covers are business- and union-sponsored issue advocacy ads and the political activity of groups that enjoy tax-exempt status.

The sixth chapter examines the fund-raising process from the candidate's point of view. The campaign for resources requires a candidate to formulate strategies for raising money from individuals and groups in the candidate's own state, in Washington, D.C., and in the nation's other major political and economic centers. It is clear from Chapters 4, 5, and 6 that Washington-based elites have a disproportionate effect on the conduct of congressional elections.

In Chapters 7 through 9 I concentrate on the campaign for votes. A discussion of voters, campaign targeting, issues, and other elements of strategy make up Chapter 7. Campaign communications, including television, radio, direct mail, and field work, are the focus of Chapter 8. The subject of winners and losers is taken up in Chapter 9. In it I analyze what does and does not work in congressional campaigns.

In Chapter 10 I address the effects of elections on the activities of individual legislators and on Congress as an institution. The final chapter takes up the highly charged topic of campaign reform. I recommend specific reforms and discuss the obstacles that must be overcome before meaningful campaign reform is enacted.

CHAPTER ONE

The Strategic Context

Congressional elections, and elections in the United States in general, are centered more on the candidates than are elections in other modern industrialized democracies. In this chapter I discuss the candidate-centered U.S. election system and explain how the Constitution, election laws, and the political parties form the system's institutional framework. I explain how the nation's political culture and recent developments in technology have helped this system flourish.

The influence that the political setting in a given election year has on electoral competition and turnover in Congress is also covered. The setting includes some predictable factors such as the decennial redrawing of House districts, some highly likely occurrences such as the wide-scale reelection of incumbents, and transient, less predictable phenomena, such as congressional scandals. All these features of the setting affect the expectations and behavior of potential congressional candidates, the individuals who actually run for Congress, political contributors, and voters.

THE CANDIDATE-CENTERED CAMPAIGN

Candidates, not political parties, are the major focus of congressional campaigns, and candidates, not parties, bear the ultimate responsibility for election outcomes. These characteristics of congressional elections are striking when viewed from a comparative perspective. In most democracies, political parties are the principal contestants in elections, and campaigns focus on national issues, ideology, and party programs and accomplishments. In the United States, parties do not actually run congressional campaigns nor do they become the major focus of elections. Instead, candidates run their own campaigns, and parties contribute money or election services to some of them. Parties also may advertise or mobilize voters in behalf of candidates. A comparison of the terminology commonly used to describe elections in the United States and that used in Great Britain more than hints at the differences. In the United States, candidates are said to *run* for Congress, and they do so with or without party help. In Britain, on the other hand, candidates are said to *stand* for election to Parliament, and their party runs most of the campaign. The difference in terminology only slightly oversimplifies reality.

Unlike candidates for national legislators in most other democracies, congressional candidates are self-selected rather than recruited by party organizations.[1] All of them must win the right to run under their party's label through a participatory primary, caucus, or convention, or by scaring off all opposition. Only after they have secured their party's nomination are major-party candidates assured a place on the general election ballot. Until then, very few receive significant party assistance. Independent and minor-party candidates can get on the ballot in other ways, usually by paying a registration fee or collecting several thousand signatures from district residents.

The nomination process in most other countries, in contrast, begins with a small group of party activists pursuing the nomination through a "closed" process that allows only formal, dues-paying party members to select the candidate.[2] Whereas the American system amplifies the input of primary voters and in a few states caucus participants, these other systems respond more to the input of local party activists and place more emphasis on peer review.

The need to win a party nomination forces congressional candidates to assemble their own campaign organizations, formulate their own election strategies, and conduct their own campaigns. The images and issues that they convey to voters in trying to win the nomination carry over to the general election. The efforts of individual candidates and their campaign organizations have a larger impact on election outcomes than the activities of party organizations and other groups.

The candidate-centered nature of congressional elections has evolved in recent years as parties and interest groups have developed issue advocacy advertisements and mobilized voters in competitive races. However, the basic structure of the system remains intact. That structure has a major impact on virtually every aspect of campaigning, including who decides to run, the kinds of election strategies the candidates employ, and the resources that are available to them. It affects the decisions and activities of party organizations, PACs, other interest groups, and journalists. It also has a major influence on how citizens make their voting decisions and on the activities that successful candidates carry out once they are elected to Congress. Finally, the candidate-centered nature of the congressional election system affects the election reforms that those in power are willing to consider.

THE INSTITUTIONAL FRAMEWORK

In designing a government to prevent the majority from depriving the minority of its rights, the framers of the Constitution created a system of checks and balances to prevent any one official or element of society from amassing too much power. Three key features of the framers' blueprint have profoundly influenced congressional elections: the separation of powers, bicameralism, and federalism. These aspects of the Constitution require that candidates for the House of Representatives, Senate, and presidency be chosen by different methods and constituencies. House members were and continue to be elected directly by the people. Senators were originally chosen by their state legislatures but have been selected in statewide elections since the passage of the Seventeenth Amendment in 1913. Presidents have always been selected through the electoral college. The means for filling state and local offices were omitted from the Constitution, but candidates for these positions were and continue to be elected independently of members of Congress.

Holding elections for individual offices separates the political fortunes of members of Congress from one another and from other officials. A candidate for the House can win during an election year in which his or her party suffers a landslide defeat in the race for the presidency, experiences severe losses in the House or Senate, or finds itself surrendering its hold over neighboring congressional districts, the state legislature, the governor's mansion, and various local offices. The system encourages House, Senate, state, and local candidates to communicate issues and themes that they perceive to be popular in their districts even when these messages differ from those advocated by their party's leader. The system does little to encourage teamwork in campaigning or governance. In 1990 many Republican congressional candidates took a "no new taxes" pledge, a pledge that was diametrically opposed to the tax increase signed into law by their party's standard-bearer, President George Bush. Eight years later, several Democratic congressional candidates opposed "fast track" legislation that would have given their party's leader, President Bill Clinton, greater clout and leeway in negotiating trade agreements with other nations. These acts would be labeled party disloyalty and considered unacceptable under a parliamentary system of government with its party-focused elections, but they are entirely consistent with the expectations of the Constitution's framers. As James Madison wrote in *Federalist* no. 46,

A local spirit will infallibly prevail . . . in the members of Congress. . . .
Measures will too often be decided according to their probable effect, not on
the national prosperity and happiness, but on the prejudices, interests, and
pursuits of the governments and people of the individual States.

When congressional candidates differ from their party's presidential nominee
or national platform on major issues, they seek political cover not only from
the Constitution but also from state party platforms, local election manifestos,
or fellow party members who have taken similar positions.

Of course, congressional candidates usually adopt issue positions that are
held by other party candidates for the House, Senate, or presidency. In 1932
most Democrats embraced Franklin D. Roosevelt's call for an activist government to battle the Great Depression. In 1994 most Republican candidates for
the House, as well as some candidates for the Senate and some state legislatures,
embraced the issues outlined in their party's Contract with America.[3] In 1996
most Democratic candidates for the House and Senate supported the positions
articulated in their party's Families First Agenda and the Democratic platform.
In 1998 most candidates supported the issue stances articulated in their party's
policy memos and press releases.

Federal and state laws further contribute to the candidate-centered nature of
congressional elections. Originally, federal law regulated few aspects of congressional elections, designating only the number of representatives a state was
entitled to elect. States held congressional elections at different times, used different methods of election, and set different qualifications for voters. Some
states used multimember at-large districts, a practice that awarded each party a
share of congressional seats proportional to its share of the statewide popular
vote; others elected their House members in odd years, which minimized the
ability of presidential candidates to pull House candidates of their own party
into office on their coattails. The financing of congressional campaigns also
went virtually unregulated for most of the nation's history.

Over the years, Congress and the states passed legislation governing the election of House members that further reinforced the candidate-centered nature
of congressional elections at the expense of parties. The creation of geographically defined, single-member, winner-take-all congressional districts was particularly important in this regard. These districts, which were mandated by the
Apportionment Act of 1842, encouraged individual candidates to build locally
based coalitions. Such districts gave no rewards to candidates who came in
second, even if their party performed well throughout the state or in neighboring districts.[4] Thus, candidates of the same party had little incentive to work
together or run a party-focused campaign. Under the multimember district or

general ticket systems that existed in some states prior to the act and continue to be used in most European nations, members of parties that finish lower than first place may receive seats in the legislature. Candidates have strong incentives to run cooperative, party-focused campaigns under these systems because their electoral fortunes are bound together.

The timing of congressional elections also helps to produce a candidate-centered system. Because the dates are fixed, with House elections scheduled biennially and roughly one-third of the Senate up for election every two years, many elections are held when there is no burning issue on the national agenda. Without a salient national issue to capture the voters' attention, House and Senate candidates base their campaigns on local issues or on their personal qualifications for holding office. Incumbents stress their experience, the services they provide to constituents, or seniority, whereas challengers attack their opponents for casting congressional roll-call votes that are out of sync with the views of local voters, for pandering to special interests, or for "being part of the problem in Washington." Open-seat races focus mainly on local issues, the candidates' political experience, or character issues.

In contrast, systems that do not have fixed election dates, including most of those in western Europe, tend to hold elections that are more national in focus and centered on political parties. The rules regulating national elections in those systems require that elections be held within a set time frame, but the exact date is left open. Elections may be called by the party in power at a time of relative prosperity, when it is confident that it can maintain or enlarge its parliamentary majority. Elections also may be called when a burning issue divides the nation and the party in power is forced to call a snap election because its members in parliament are unable to agree on a policy for dealing with the crisis. In contrast to congressional elections, which are often referenda on the performance of individual officeholders and their abilities to meet local concerns, these elections focus on national conditions and the performance of the party in power.

Because the boundaries of congressional districts rarely match those for state-wide or local offices and because terms for the House, the Senate, and many state and local offices differ from one another, a party's candidates often lack incentives to work together. House candidates consider the performance of their party's candidates statewide or in neighboring districts to be a secondary concern, just as the election of House candidates is usually not of primary importance to candidates for state or local office. Differences in election boundaries and timing also encourage a sense of parochialism in party officials that is similar to that in their candidates. Cooperation among party organizations can be achieved only by persuading local, state, and national party leaders that it is in their mutual best interest. It is often heightened during elections that precede the decennial taking of the census, when politicians at all levels of government focus on the imminent redrawing of election districts.

Although the seeds for candidate-centered congressional election campaigns were sown by the Constitution and election laws, it was not until the middle of the twentieth century that the candidate-centered system firmly took root. Prior to the emergence of this system, during a period often called the "golden age of political parties," party organizations played a major role in most election campaigns, including many campaigns for Congress. Local party organizations, often referred to as old-fashioned political machines, had control over the nomination process, possessed a near monopoly over the resources needed to organize the electorate, and provided the symbolic cues that informed the electoral decisions of most voters.[5] The key to their success was their ability to command the loyalties of large numbers of individuals, many of whom were able to persuade friends and neighbors to support their party's candidates. It was not until the demise of the old-fashioned machine and the emergence of new campaign technology that the modern candidate-centered system finally blossomed.

Reforms intended to weaken political machines played a major role in the development of the candidate-centered system. One such reform was the adoption of the Australian ballot by roughly three-quarters of the states between 1888 and 1896.[6] This government-printed ballot listed every candidate for each office and allowed individuals to cast their votes in secret, away from the prying eyes of party officials. The Australian ballot replaced a system of voting in which each party supplied supporters with its own easily identifiable ballot that included only the names of its own candidates. The Australian ballot, by ensuring secrecy and simplifying split-ticket voting, made it easy for citizens to focus on candidates rather than parties when voting. This type of ballot remains in use today.

State-regulated primary nominating contests, which were widely adopted during the Progressive movement of the early 1900s, deprived party leaders of the power to handpick congressional nominees and gave that power to voters who participated in their party's nominating election.[7] The merit-based civil service system, another progressive reform, deprived the parties of patronage. No longer able to distribute government jobs or contracts, the parties had difficulty maintaining large corps of campaign workers.[8] Issues, friendships, the excitement of politics, and other noneconomic incentives could motivate small numbers of people to become active in party politics, but they could not motivate enough people to support a party-focused system of congressional elections.

Congressional candidates also lacked the patronage or government contracts needed to attract large numbers of volunteer workers or to persuade other candidates to help them with their campaigns. By the mid–twentieth century the "isolation" of congressional candidates from one another and from their own party organizations was so complete that a major report on the state of political parties characterized congressional candidates as the "orphans of the political system." The report, which was published by the American Political Science Association's Committee on Political Parties, went on to point out that congressional candidates "had no truly adequate party mechanism available for the conduct of their campaigns, . . . enjoy[ed] remarkably little national or local support, [and] have mostly been left to cope with the political hazards of their occupation on their own."[9]

Voter registration and get-out-the-vote drives and redistricting were about the only areas of election politics in which there was, and remains, extensive cooperation among groups of candidates and party committees. But even here the integration of different party committees and candidate organizations—and especially those involved in congressional elections—was and continues to be short of that exhibited in other democracies.

The Federal Election Campaign Act of 1974 and the amendments, regulatory rulings, and court decisions that have shaped federal campaign finance law (collectively known as the FECA) further reinforced the pattern of candidate-centered congressional elections.[10] The original 1974 law placed strict limits on the amount of money parties could contribute to or spend directly on behalf of their congressional candidates. Many of these limits remain in place (see Table 1-1, p. 16). It further limited the parties' involvement in congressional elections by placing ceilings on individual contributions and an outright ban on corporate, union, and trade association contributions to the accounts the parties use to contribute to or expressly campaign for federal candidates (see Table 1-2, p. 18). Moreover, the FECA provided no subsidies for generic, party-focused campaign activity.[11]

The law's provisions for political parties stand in marked contrast to the treatment given to parties in other democracies. Most of these countries provide subsidies to parties for campaign and interelection activities.[12] The United States is the only democracy in which parties are not given free television and radio time.[13] The support that other democracies give to parties is consistent with the central role they play in elections, government, and society, just as the lack of assistance afforded to American parties is consistent with the candidate-centered system that has developed here.

Lacking independent sources of revenue, local party organizations are unable to play a dominant role in the modern cash-based system of congressional campaign politics.[14] The national and state party committees that survived the reform movements and changes in federal election laws lack sufficient funds or staff to dominate campaign politics. Perhaps even more important, party leaders have little desire to do so. They believe a party should bolster its candidates' campaigns, not replace them with a campaign of its own.[15]

Nevertheless, the evolution of campaign finance law has enabled parties to play a greater role in recent congressional elections. The 1979 amendment to the FECA exempted from federal contribution and spending limits voter registration drives, get-out-the vote efforts, and other grass-roots activities sponsored by state and local party committees. It also allowed these organizations to distribute slate cards and other materials that list federal candidates without reporting these activities to the FEC. The amendment, combined with various FEC rulings and court decisions, created a legal loophole that permits campaign spending that is technically outside of the federal campaign finance system but is used to influence the outcome of federal elections. The funds that flow through this loophole, commonly referred to as "soft" money (as opposed to the "federal" or "hard" money that is spent inside the system), include contributions that come from sources and in amounts banned under the federal system. Some soft money contributions are collected from corporations, unions, and wealthy individuals in amounts in excess of $1 million.[16]

Most soft money is raised and spent by political parties, but other groups, some of which are closely affiliated with party committees, also collect and distribute soft money in order to influence federal elections. Party soft money expenditures surpassed $220 million during the 1998 contests.[17] The soft money activity of interest groups cannot be accounted for fully because it does not have to be reported to the FEC; however, it is estimated that groups spent between $170 million and $240 million on the 1998 elections.[18] Soft money has become one of the most controversial components of the election system, and its elimination has become a major goal of political reformers.

Another change in the campaign finance system that has increased the role of interest and party-affiliated groups in elections concerns the use of funds collected by tax-exempt organizations for political use.[19] These groups, classified as 501(c)(3) and 501(c)(4) organizations in the federal tax code, do not pay taxes because they purportedly exist for charitable, educational, or other civic purposes rather than earning profits. In recent years, however, some tax-exempt groups have carried out activities designed to influence congressional and other elections. Among these groups are GOPAC, which was part of former House Speaker Newt Gingrich's political operation; Americans for Tax Reform, a group that has close ties with the Republicans; and Vote Now '98, a voter registration group that focuses on demographic groups that are traditionally loyal to Democrats.[20]

A series of court decisions, including one that was handed down in the midst of the 1996 election season, increased the activities that parties, PACs, and

TABLE 1-1

Campaign Contribution and Spending Limits in Congressional Elections

	Contributions		Hard money			Soft money
			Coordinated expenditures		Independent expenditures	Issue advocacy and other expenditures
	To a House candidate	To a Senate candidate	On behalf of a House candidate	On behalf of a Senate candidate	To expressly help or harm a candidate	To help or harm a candidate without expressly advocating the candidate's defeat
Individuals	$1,000	$1,000	Prohibited	Prohibited	No limit	No limit
Political action committees	$5,000	$5,000	Prohibited	Prohibited	No limit	No limit
Corporations, unions, trade associations, and other groups	Prohibited	Prohibited	Prohibited	Prohibited	Prohibited except by qualified non-profit organizations	No limit
Party congressional campaign committees	$5,000	Can make a portion of another party committee's coordinated expenditures	$10,000 (adjusted for inflation)	Can make a portion of another party committee's coordinated expenditures	No limit	Must be allocated in proportion to hard money expenditures in a given state

Party senatorial campaign committees	$5,000	$17,500	Can make a portion of another party committee's coordinated expenditures	2¢ per voter for Senate candidates (adjusted for inflation)	No limit	Must be allocated in proportion to hard money expenditures in a given state
Party national committees	$5,000	$5,000	Can make a portion of another party committee's contributions	Can make a portion of another party committee's coordinated expenditures	No limit	Must be allocated in proportion to hard money expenditures in a given state
State and local party committees	$5,000	$5,000	$10,000 (adjusted for inflation)	2¢ per voter for Senate candidates (adjusted for inflation)	No limit	Must be allocated in proportion to hard money expenditures in a given state

Notes: Individuals and PACs can make the maximum contribution in each stage of the election (primary, runoff, and general election). The same is true of party committees' contributions in House races, but the committees rarely contribute to primary or runoff candidates. The senatorial campaign committees can contribute a total of $17,500 per Senate candidate in all three stages of the election. PACs must have been registered for at least six months, received contributions from more than fifty contributors, and made contributions to at least five federal candidates. Otherwise, they are subject to the same limits as those imposed on individual contributors. Corporations, labor unions, and federal government contractors are prohibited from making independent expenditures, but qualified nonprofit social welfare organizations that do not engage in business activities and have no shareholders other than employees or creditors can make independent expenditures. The limits for coordinated expenditures made on behalf of House candidates in states with only one House seat are twice the normal amount. A party committee can make agency agreements allowing other party organizations to make some or all of its coordinated expenditures. National party soft money expenditures cannot exceed 35 percent of the total party expenditures in presidential election years and 40 percent of the total party expenditures in midterm election years. The limits for state and local party soft money expenditures vary according to the composition of a state's ballot. Some of these limits are under challenge in the courts. For example, the federal district court in Colorado has ruled that there can be no limit on party coordinated expenditures for federal candidates.

TABLE 1-2
Annual Federal Contribution Limits for Individuals, Party Committees, Political Action Committees, and Other Interest Groups

	Hard money contributions				Soft money contributions			
	To national party committees	To state party committees	To political action committees	Total annual contributions	To a House or Senate candidate	To national party committees	To state party committees	Total annual contributions
Individuals	$20,000	$5,000	$5,000	$25,000	Prohibited	No limit	Subject to state law	No limit
Political action committees	$15,000	$5,000	$5,000	No limit	Prohibited	No limit	Subject to state law	No limit
Corporations, unions, trade associations, and other groups	Prohibited	Prohibited	Prohibited	Prohibited	Prohibited	No limit	Subject to state law	No limit
Party congressional campaign committees	No limit	No limit	$5,000	No limit	Prohibited	No limit	Subject to state law	No limit
Party senatorial campaign committees	No limit	No limit	$5,000	No limit	Prohibited	No limit	Subject to state law	No limit
Party national committees	No limit	No limit	$5,000	No limit	Prohibited	No limit	Subject to state law	No limit
State and local party committees	No limit	No limit	$5,000	No limit	Prohibited	No limit	Subject to state law	No limit

Notes: Total annual contributions also include contributions to all federal candidates (see Table 1-1). "National party committees" refers to the parties' national committees, congressional campaign committees, and senatorial campaign committees.

other interest groups can use to influence federal elections.[21] These rulings allow these organizations to spend unlimited sums of hard or soft money on issue advocacy ads that resemble ads that in the past could only be financed with hard money.[22] Most issue advocacy ads are nearly identical to hard money ads in that they praise or criticize federal candidates by name or feature their likenesses. The major visible differences between the two types of ad are that issue advocacy ads *cannot expressly* call for a candidate's election, and they tend to be more negative than hard money ads.[23] The courts also asserted the parties' right to make unlimited independent expenditures on campaign communications that *expressly* advocate the election or defeat of a federal candidate—by using phrases like "vote for" or "vote against"—as long as these expenditures are made with hard money and without the candidate's knowledge or consent. Party and interest group independent expenditures, issue advocacy campaigns, and voter mobilization efforts have significantly increased these organizations' influence in congressional elections. It is unlikely that these efforts will do away with the candidate-centered nature of congressional elections, but they have significantly altered it.

POLITICAL CULTURE

Historically, American political culture has supported a system of candidate-centered congressional elections in many ways, but its major influence stems from its lack of foundation for a party-focused alternative. Americans have traditionally held a jaundiced view of political parties. *Federalist* no. 10 and President George Washington's farewell address are evidence that the framers and the first president thought a multitude of overlapping, wide-ranging interests preferable to class-based divisions represented by ideological parties. The founders designed the political system to encourage pragmatism and compromise in politics and thus to mitigate the harmful effects of factions. Although neither the pluralist system championed by the framers of the Constitution nor the nonpartisan system advocated by Washington has been fully realized, both visions of democracy have found expression in candidate-centered campaigns.

Congressional elections test candidates' abilities to build coalitions of voters and elites from diverse individuals. The multiplicity of overlapping interests, lack of a feudal legacy, and relatively fluid social and economic structure in the United States discourage the formation of class-based parties like those that have developed in most other democracies.[24] The consensus among Americans for liberty, equality, and property rights and their near-universal support for the political system further undermine the development of parties aimed at promoting major political, social, or economic change.[25]

Americans' traditional ambivalence about political parties has found expression during reform periods. The Populist movement of the 1890s, the Progressive movement that came shortly after it, and the rise of the New Left in the 1960s all resulted in political change that weakened the parties. Turn-of-the-century reformers championed the Australian ballot, the direct primary, and civil service laws for the explicit purpose of taking power away from party bosses.[26] Similarly, the reform movement that took hold of the Democratic Party during the 1960s and 1970s opened party conventions, meetings, and leadership positions to the increased participation of previously underrepresented groups. The reforms, many of which were adopted by Republican as well as Democratic state party organizations, made both parties more permeable and responsive to pressures from grass-roots activists. They weakened what little influence party leaders had over the awarding of nominations, giving candidates, their supporters, and issue activists more influence over party affairs.[27]

Post–World War II social and cultural transformations undermined the parties even further. Declining immigration and increased geographic mobility eroded the lower-class ethnic neighborhoods that were an important source of party loyalists. Increased educational levels encouraged citizens to rely more on their own judgment and less on party cues in political matters. The development of the mass media gave voters less-biased sources of information than the partisan press. The rise of interest groups, PACs, and other forms of functional and ideological representation created new arenas for political participation and new sources of political cues.[28] The aging of the parties, generational replacement, and the emergence of new issues that cut across existing fault lines led to the decline of party affiliation among voters and to more issue-oriented voting.[29] These developments encouraged voters to rely less on local party officials and opinion leaders for political information.[30] Cultural transformations created a void in electoral politics that individual candidates and their organizations came to fill.

Current attitudes toward the parties reflect the nation's historical experience. Survey research shows that most citizens believe that parties "do more to confuse the issues than to provide a clear choice on the issues," and "create conflict where none exists." Half of the population believes that parties make the political system less efficient and that "it would be better if, in all elections, we put no party labels on the ballot."[31]

Negative attitudes toward the parties are often learned at an early age. Many schoolchildren are routinely instructed to "vote for the best candidate, not the party." This lesson appears to stay with some of them into adulthood. Typically less than 10 percent of all registered voters maintain that the candidate's political party is the biggest factor in their vote decision. Candidates and issues rank higher.[32]

Although American history and culture extol the virtues of political independence and candidate-oriented voting, the electoral behavior of citizens does provide an element of partisanship in congressional elections. Almost two-thirds of all voters were willing to state that they identified with the Democratic or Republican Party in 1998, which is typical of the last two decades. About 71 percent of all self-identified independents held attitudes and exhibited political behaviors similar to those of partisans. Although few registered voters state that they cast their votes chiefly on a partisan basis, in 1998 more than three-quarters of them cast their congressional ballots along party lines. Such high levels of party-line voting are common in modern American politics, and partisanship is among the best predictors of voting behavior in congressional elections, ranking second only to incumbency. The fact that over 85 percent of the voting population perceives, retains, and responds to political information in a partisan manner means that elections are not entirely candidate-centered.[33] Yet the degree of partisanship that exists in the contemporary United States is still not strong enough to encourage a return to straight-ticket voting or to foster the development of a party-focused election system.

CAMPAIGN TECHNOLOGY

Political campaigns are designed to communicate ideas and images that will motivate voters to cast their ballots for particular candidates. Some voters are well-informed, have strong opinions about candidates, issues, and parties, and will vote without ever coming into contact with a political campaign. Others will never bother to vote, regardless of the efforts of politicians. Many voters need to be introduced to the candidates and made aware of the issues in order to become excited enough to vote in a congressional election. The communication of information is central to democratic elections, and those who are able to control the flow of information have tremendous power. Candidates, campaign organizations, parties, and other groups employ a variety of technologies to affect the flow of campaign information and win votes.

Person-to-person contact is one of the oldest and most effective approaches to winning votes. Nothing was or is more effective than having a candidate, or a candidate's supporters, directly ask voters for their support. During the golden age of parties, local party volunteers assessed the needs of voters in their neighborhoods and delivered the message that, if elected, their party's candidates would help voters achieve their goals.[34] Once these organizations lost their control over the flow of political information they became less important, and candidate-assembled campaign organizations became more relevant players in elections.

The dawning of the television age and the development of modern campaign technology helped solidify the system of candidate-centered congressional elections.[35] Television and radio studios, printing presses, public opinion polls, high-speed computers, and sophisticated targeting techniques are well suited to candidate-centered campaign organizations because they, and the services of the political consultants who know how to use them, can easily be purchased. Congressional candidates can assemble organizations that meet their specific needs without having to turn to party organizations for assistance, although many candidates request their parties' help.

New technology has encouraged a major change in the focus of most congressional election campaigns. It has enabled campaigns to communicate more information about candidates' personalities, issue positions, and qualifications for office. As a result, less campaign activity is now devoted to party-based appeals. Radio and television were especially important in bringing about this change because they are well suited to conveying images and less useful in providing information about abstract concepts, such as partisan ideologies.[36] The overall effect of the electronic mass media is to direct attention away from parties and toward candidates.

The increased focus on candidate imagery that is associated with the "new style" of campaigning encourages congressional candidates to hire professional technicians to help them convey their political personas to voters.[37] Press secretaries, pollsters, issue and opposition researchers, and media experts are commonplace in most congressional campaigns. Local party activists became less important in congressional elections as the importance of political consultants grew and the contributions of semiskilled and unskilled volunteers diminished. The emergence of a national economy of campaign finance and the rise of a cadre of fund-raising specialists with the skills, contacts, and technology to raise money from individuals and PACs further increased the candidate-centered character of election campaigns because they provided candidates with the means for raising the contributions needed to purchase the services of political consultants.

Changes in technology transformed most congressional campaigns from labor-intensive grass-roots undertakings, at which local party committees excelled, to money-driven, merchandised activities requiring the services of skilled experts. Most local party committees were unable to adapt to the new style of campaign politics.[38] Initially, party committees in Washington, D.C., and in many states were also unprepared to play a significant role in congressional elections. However, the parties' national, congressional, and senatorial campaign committees and several state party organizations proved more adept at making the transition to the new-style politics. They began to play a meaningful role in congressional election campaigns during the late 1970s and early 1980s.[39]

THE POLITICAL SETTING

Candidates, campaign managers, party officials, PAC managers, and others who are active in congressional elections consider more than the institutional framework, available technology, and culturally and historically conditioned expectations of voters when planning and executing electoral strategies. They also assess the political setting, including the circumstances in their district, their state, or the nation as a whole. At the local level, important considerations include the party affiliation, tenure, and intentions of the incumbent or other potential candidates, and the partisan history of the seat. Relevant national-level factors include whether it is a presidential or midterm election year, the state of the economy, presidential popularity, international affairs, and the public's attitude toward the government. In 1992 the populist anti-Washington sentiments that crystallized in the independent presidential candidacy of Ross Perot were significant. Similarly, hostile sentiments directed at congressional Democrats and President Clinton led to the Republican takeover of Congress in 1994. Disapproval of the two federal government shutdowns and some elements of the "Republican revolution" helped make many 1996 congressional elections competitive. Clinton's scandalous relationship with former White House intern Monica Lewinsky injected an element of uncertainty into several 1998 campaigns, playing a decisive role in the outcome of at least one House contest. The issue was pivotal in Democratic challenger Rush Holt's narrow victory over Republican incumbent Michael Pappas in New Jersey's 12th congressional district.

Of course, one's perspective on the limits and possibilities of the political setting depends largely on one's vantage point. Although they talk about the competition and are, indeed, wary of it, congressional incumbents, particularly House members, operate in a political setting that works largely to their benefit. As explained in later chapters, incumbents enjoy significant levels of name recognition and voter support, are able to assemble superior campaign organizations, and can draw on their experience in office to speak knowledgeably about issues and claim credit for the federally financed programs and improvements in their state or district. Incumbents also tend to get favorable treatment from the press. Moreover, most can rely on loyal followers from previous campaigns for continued backing: supporters at home tend to vote repeatedly for incumbents, and supporters in Washington and the nation's other wealthy cities routinely provide incumbents with campaign money.

Things look different from the typical challenger's vantage point. Most challengers, particularly those who possess some political experience, recognize that most of the cards are stacked against an individual who sets out to take on an incumbent. Little in the setting in which most congressional campaigns take place favors the challenger. Most challengers lack the public visibility, money, and campaign experience to wage a strong campaign. Moreover, because those who work in and help finance campaigns recognize the strong odds against challengers, they usually see little benefit in helping them. As a result, high incumbent success rates have become a self-fulfilling prophecy. Senate reelection rates ranged from 55 percent to almost 97 percent between 1950 and 1998. Between 1986 and 1998 less than 3 percent of all Senate incumbents had no major-party opponent, and half of those involved in contested races won by 60 percent or more of the two-party vote. Only 11 percent of all senators seeking reelection during 1996 and 1998 were defeated.[40] Between 1950 and 1998, House incumbents enjoyed reelection rates of better than 92 percent; the 1996 and 1998 elections returned to Congress 94 percent and 98 percent, respectively, of those who sought to keep their jobs. Even during the tidal wave that swept away thirty-four Democrats in the House in the 1994 elections, just over 90 percent of all House incumbents who sought to remain in office did so.[41] With some important exceptions, most experienced politicians wait until an incumbent retires before running for office. Thus, many House seats fail to attract meaningful competition.

Elections for open seats are highly competitive. They attract extremely qualified candidates who put together strong campaign organizations, raise huge amounts of money, and mount lively campaigns. Even House candidates of one party campaigning for seats that have been held by the other party for decades can often attract substantial resources, media attention, and votes.

There are many explanations for the relative lack of competition in House elections. Some districts are so dominated by one party that few individuals of the other party are willing to commit their time, energy, or money to running for office. In many cases, the tradition of one-party dominance is so strong that virtually all the talented, politically ambitious individuals living in the area join the dominant party. When an incumbent in these districts faces a strong challenge, it usually takes place in the primary, and the winner is all but guaranteed success in the general election.[42]

Uncompetitive House districts are sometimes the product of the redistrict-ing process. In states where one party controls both the governorship and the state legislature, partisan gerrymandering is often used to maximize the num-ber of House seats the dominant party can win. In states where each party controls at least some portion of the state government, compromises are fre-quently made to design districts that protect congressional incumbents. Party officials and political consultants armed with computers, election returns, and demographic statistics can "pack" and "crack" voting blocs in order to promote either of these goals.[43] The result is that large numbers of congressional districts are designed to be uncompetitive.

The desire of incumbents to retain their seats has changed Congress in ways that help discourage electoral competition. Most of those who are elected to Congress quickly understand that they will probably never hold a higher office because there are too few of such offices to go around. Like most people, they do everything in their power to hold on to their jobs. Congress has adapted to the career aspirations of its members by providing them with resources that can be used to increase their odds of reelection. Free mailings, WATS lines, district offices, and subsidized travel help members gain visibility among their con-stituents. Federal "pork-barrel" projects also help incumbents win the support of voters.[44] Congressional staffs help members write speeches, respond to con-stituent mail, resolve problems that constituents have with executive branch agencies, and follow the comings and goings in their bosses' districts.[45] These perquisites of office give incumbents tremendous advantages over challengers. They also work to discourage those experienced politicians who could put forth a competitive challenge from taking on an entrenched incumbent.

The dynamics of campaign finance have similar effects. Incumbents have tremendous fund-raising advantages over challengers, especially among PACs and wealthy individual donors. Many incumbents build up large war chests to discourage potential challengers from running against them. With the excep-tion of millionaires and celebrities, those challengers who decide to contest a race against a member of the House or Senate typically find they are unable to raise the funds needed to mount a viable campaign.

Given that the cards tend to be so heavily stacked in favor of congressional incumbents, most electoral competition takes place in open seats. Open-seat contests draw a larger than usual number of primary contestants. They also attract significantly more money and election assistance from party commit-tees, individuals, PACs, and other groups than do challenger campaigns.[46] Spe-cial elections, which are called when a seat becomes vacant because of an incumbent's resignation or death, are open-seat contests that tend to be par-ticularly competitive and unpredictable. They bring out even larger numbers of primary contenders than normal open-seat elections, especially when the seat that has become vacant was formerly held by a longtime incumbent.

The concentration of competition in open-seat elections and the decennial reapportionment and redistricting of House seats have combined to produce a ten-year, five-election cycle of political competition. Redistricting leads to the creation of many new House seats and the redrawing of the boundaries of numerous others. It encourages an increase in congressional retirements, leads more nonincumbents than usual to run for the House, and thereby increases competition in many House elections.[47]

Another cyclical element of the national political climate that can influence congressional elections is the presence or absence of a presidential election. Presidential elections have higher levels of voter turnout than midterm elections, and they have the potential for coattail effects. A presidential candidate's popularity can become infectious and lead to some increase in support for the party's congressional contestants. A party that enjoys much success in electing congressional candidates during a presidential election year is, of course, likely to lose some of those seats in the midterm election that follows.[48] An unpopular president can further drag down a party's congressional contestants.[49] Presidential election politics had a strong impact on the election of 1932, in which the Democrats gained ninety seats in the House and thirteen seats in the Senate. The Democratic congressional landslide was a sign of widespread support for the Democratic presidential candidate, Franklin D. Roosevelt, as well as a repudiation of the incumbent president, Herbert Hoover, and his policies for dealing with the Great Depression.[50] Although coattail effects have declined since the 1930s, Ronald Reagan's 1980 presidential campaign is credited with helping the Republicans gain thirty-three seats in the House and twelve seats in the Senate.[51] Bill Clinton's presidential elections were conspicuous for their lack of coattails. Democrats lost ten House seats and broke even in the Senate in 1992; they gained only ten seats in the House and lost two seats in the Senate in 1996. Coattail effects are rarely visible when a presidential candidate wins by margins as small as Clinton's 43 percent of the popular vote in 1992 and 49 percent in 1996.

Congressional candidates who belong to the same party as an unpopular president also run the risk during midterm elections of being blamed for the failures of their party's chief executive.[52] The Republicans' forty-nine-seat House and four-seat Senate losses in 1974 grew out of a sense of disgust about the Nixon administration's role in the Watergate break-in and President Gerald Ford's decision to pardon Nixon.[53] The Democrats' loss of fifty-two seats in the House and eight seats in the Senate in 1994 was caused largely by voter animosity toward Clinton, dissatisfaction with his party's failure to enact health care reform or a middle-class tax cut, and the Republicans' successful portrayal of the White House and the Democratic-controlled Congress as corrupt and out of step with the views of most voters. The Democrats' net gain of five House seats in 1998 bucked a sixty-year trend in which the president's party always suffered losses in midterm elections.[54]

The economy, foreign affairs, and other national issues have some effect on congressional elections. The president's party often loses congressional seats in midterm elections when economic trends are unfavorable, although the relationship between economic performance and congressional turnover has been weakening in recent years.[55] Foreign affairs may have contributed to the Democrats' congressional losses in 1972 during the Vietnam War.[56] Americans, however, tend to be less concerned with "guns" than with "butter," and so international events generally have less of an effect on elections than domestic conditions.

Other national issues that can affect congressional elections are civil rights, social issues, and the attitudes of voters toward political institutions. The civil rights revolution, the women's movement, urban decay, the emergence of the hippie counterculture, and the protests they spawned influenced voting behavior during the 1960s and 1970s.[57] Political scandal, and the widespread distrust of government that usually follows, can lead to the defeat of politicians accused of committing ethical transgressions, but as the 1974 and 1994 elections demonstrate, individual members of Congress who are not directly implicated in scandal can also suffer because of it.

National issues are likely to have the greatest effect on congressional elections when candidates take unambiguous stands on them.[58] Presidential politics are likely to have the greatest influence on congressional elections when voters closely identify congressional candidates with a party's presidential nominee or an incumbent president. House and Senate candidates generally respond strategically to national politics in order to improve their electoral fortunes. When their party selects a popular presidential candidate or has a popular incumbent in the White House, congressional candidates ally themselves with that individual in order to take advantage of the party cue. When their party selects an unpopular nominee or is saddled with an unpopular president, congressional candidates seek to protect themselves from the effects of partisanship by distancing themselves from the comings and goings of the executive branch. The partisan campaigns that Democratic congressional candidates ran during the New Deal era and in 1996 and that Republicans mounted during the height of Ronald Reagan's presidency exemplify the former strategy. The independent, nonpartisan campaigns that many congressional Republicans carried out in 1990, 1992, and 1996 and Democrats carried out in 1994 and 1998 are representative of the latter.

RECENT CONGRESSIONAL ELECTIONS

The political settings that shaped the opportunities presented to politicians, parties, interest groups, and ultimately voters in the 1980s and 1990s had some important similarities. All but the 1994 midterm elections took place during a period of divided control, which made it difficult to credit or blame only one party for the government's performance or the nation's affairs. Most of the elections also took place under the shadow of a weak economy and were haunted by the specter of huge budget deficits. The 1998 election was an important exception, occurring as the two parties debated how to spend projected budget surpluses.

Civil rights and racial and gender discrimination were issues in many campaigns during the 1990s as a result of the highly publicized studies of the unequal salaries and advancement prospects for women and African Americans, and the brutal beatings of African American motorist Rodney King by white police officers in Los Angeles and of Haitian immigrant Abner Louima in New York City. The Senate Judiciary Committee's treatment of Anita Hill and her allegations of sexual harassment against Supreme Court nominee Clarence Thomas during his confirmation hearings called further attention to racial and gender issues. Women's issues were also highlighted by the Clinton/Lewinsky scandal and by the allegations of sexual harassment that led Bob Packwood, R-Ore., to resign from the Senate. Gay rights found its place on the agenda as the nation debated the military's long-standing policy against homosexuals serving in the military. The issue stayed prominent, partially as a result of the gruesome slaying of gay university student Matthew Shepard in Laramie, Wyoming.

A final arena in which civil rights issues were fought was redistricting. In 1986 the Supreme Court ruled that any gerrymandering of a congressional district that purposely diluted minority strength was illegal under the 1982 Voting Rights Act.[59] Most states interpreted the ruling cautiously, redrawing many of the districts after the 1990 census with the explicit purpose of giving one or more minority group members better-than-even chances of being elected to the House. Several groups opposed the majority-minority seats, claiming they were unconstitutional. Their successful lawsuits led to the redrawing of many congressional districts in Florida, Georgia, Louisiana, North Carolina, and Texas after the 1992 elections. They also nullified the results of several primary contests and forced three run-off elections to be held in Texas in December 1996. Both Virginia's 3rd congressional district, which was drawn to promote the election of an African American, and New York's 12th congressional district, which was designed to elect a Hispanic, were overturned in federal court after the 1996 elections. The redistricting that followed the 1990 census even influenced some 1998 House elections. North Carolina's majority-black 1st congressional district, redrawn following the 1996 elections, was declared unconstitutional during the 1998 primary season and redrawn again, forcing that state to postpone all its House primaries for four months. The irony of these decisions is that they may not be final. The 2000 redistricting process will undoubtedly inspire new legal challenges.

Dissatisfaction with the political establishment in Washington also occupied a prominent position on the political agenda at the close of the twentieth century. Gridlock and the federal government's inability to solve problems associated with drug abuse, crime, the environment, rising health care costs, the unsatisfactory performance of the nation's schools, the deficit, and a myriad of other seemingly intractable issues resulted in voter frustration with national politicians. Much of this hostility was directed toward Congress, and many incumbents responded with a strategy that had served them well in the past—running for reelection by campaigning against Congress itself.[60]

Political scandal and the anti-Washington mood gave open-seat and challenger candidates for Congress many powerful issues to use in campaigns during the 1990s. The Keating Five scandal, which implicated five senators in improperly lobbying federal bank regulators on behalf of Charles Keating, who was a major campaign supporter, ignited anti-Congress sentiments in 1990. Congressional pay raises and the scandal-tainted resignations of House Speaker Jim Wright, D-Texas, and House Democratic Whip Tony Coelho, D-Calif., added fuel to the fire during that same year. In 1992 the flames of anti-Congress sentiment were further fanned by the House banking scandal, which revealed that 325 current or former House members had made 8,331 overdrafts at the House bank; by the House Post Office scandal, which implicated some high-ranking House members and staff in exchanging stamps for money; and by the savings and loan crisis, which left American taxpayers footing a bill for failed banking institutions that is estimated to reach $180 billion.[61] Not surprisingly, support for the national legislature reached an all-time low prior to the 1994 elections, with polls estimating that roughly three-fourths of all Americans disapproved of Congress's performance.[62]

Political scandal, congressional perquisites, the federal deficit, and government gridlock are easily identifiable issues that can be used effectively against congressional incumbents and others who are identified with the Washington establishment. In 1994 conditions were ripe for the Republicans to pick up a significant number of congressional seats. Public hostility toward Washington, Democratic control of both the executive and legislative branches of the national government, and the Democrats' historical association with the growth of federal programs and the bureaucracy put that party in a precarious position.

Moreover, Clinton's early missteps on health care reform, gays in the military, and tax cuts, and allegations of ethical misconduct by the president and his administration, served to energize Republican candidates and their supporters while demoralizing Democrats and their allies. Under Gingrich's leadership, the Republicans capitalized on these circumstances by running a nationalized anti-Washington campaign that drew on the Contract with America.[63]

Following their takeover of Congress in 1994, House Republicans passed most elements of their contract.[64] The public supported congressional reform, crime control, welfare reform, a balanced budget amendment, and other contract provisions that would promote a smaller, less expensive government. However, it objected to GOP plans to grant $240 billion in tax cuts to the wealthiest elements in society while reducing future Medicare funding by $270 billion, and cutting appropriations for Medicaid, education, and environmental protection. The federal government shutdowns, which were largely blamed on Gingrich, increased public misgivings about the Republican Congress. Just as the missteps of Democrats laid the foundation for a nationalized political campaign in 1994, those of Republicans laid the foundation for one in 1996. Democrats sought to capitalize on the Republicans' difficulties by campaigning against what they labeled "the extremist Republican Congress" and offering their Families First Agenda, which included several modest policy proposals that were designed to appeal to middle-income and blue-collar families.

The setting for the 1998 elections was promising for incumbents of both parties. Most Americans benefited from a strong economy marked by rising incomes, low inflation, a high employment rate, a booming stock market, and the first federal budget surplus in three decades. Violent crime was down, as was the percentage of the population on welfare. Despite being bombarded daily with the tawdry details of the Clinton/Lewinsky scandal, the public directed relatively little hostility at Washington. Public approval of Congress reached a record 57 percent in February 1998 and remained well above 40 percent throughout the campaign season. Clinton's poll ratings also reached historic highs despite the scandal, hovering around 65 percent. More important for members of Congress, 58 percent of the public maintained that most incumbents deserved reelection—almost twice as many as in 1992 and about 67 percent more than in 1994.[65] Moreover, most individual representatives and senators read polls that were even more favorable than the public's evaluations of Congress as a whole. Constituents typically have much higher opinions of their own representatives than they do of Congress as an institution and its other members.[66] The 1998 elections took place in an environment that favored the status quo, gave neither party a strong advantage, and benefited incumbents in general.

TABLE 1-3

Number of Unchallenged and Defeated House Incumbents

	1982	1984	1986	1988	1990	1992	1994	1996	1998
Incumbent unchallenged by major-party opposition in general election	49	63	71	81	76	25	54	20	94
Incumbent defeated									
In primary	10	3	3	1	1	19	4	2	1
In general election	29	16	6	6	15	24	34	20	6

Sources: Compiled from various editions of *CQ Weekly.* The primary and general election results are from Norman J. Ornstein, Thomas E. Mann, and Michael J. Malbin, *Vital Statistics on Congress, 1997–1998* (Washington, D.C.: Congressional Quarterly, 1998), 61.

Note: The 1982 and 1992 figures include incumbent-versus-incumbent races.

Public approval of Congress did not prevent the parties from seeking to create a setting that would benefit their candidates. Party leaders tried to focus public attention on issues that favored their party. For the Democrats, those issues included education, job creation, health care, the environment, and Social Security. For the Republicans, tax cuts, government downsizing, family values, and other moral issues were central. Many Republicans tried to capitalize on Clinton's personal indiscretions. Both parties claimed credit for the nation's strong economy, but the Democrats had an advantage on the issue.

The political setting for the congressional elections of 1992 through 1996 produced more serious challenges to national legislators, particularly House members, than had occurred in the previous decade (see Table 1-3). Nineteen House incumbents lost their primaries in 1992—a post–World War II record— and another thirty-four lost in the general election two years later—the most since the post-Watergate housecleaning of 1974.

The results of the 1998 elections deviated significantly from the moderate-to-high levels of incumbent losses recorded in the rest of the decade. Jay Kim, R-Calif., was the only House member to lose a primary, and only six others were defeated in the general election. Moreover, ninety-four incumbents enjoyed the luxury of running unopposed by a major-party candidate, one fewer than the record set in 1950. Florida was notable for the lack of competition in its elections: the names of fourteen of the state's twenty-three-member House delegation were left off the ballot because these incumbents faced no opposition, and another four faced only a token minor-party opponent. High reelection rates for incumbents and the increased costs associated with campaigning discouraged many would-be challengers nationwide from running for Congress.[67] Voter satisfaction with local and national affairs may also have been important. In Florida, for example, some potential candidates either opted not to run or withdrew from the race because they felt that voter approval of the status quo left them with few issues on which to mount a campaign.[68]

Nevertheless, the long-term trend toward increasing competition in contested House elections, including open-seat contests, persists. The trend is apparent when the candidates are divided into categories based on the "marginality" of the districts in which they ran. During the post-redistricting elections of 1982, 38 percent of all House candidates in major-party contested races ran in marginal districts. Included in this group are the 15 percent of the candidates classified as "incumbents in jeopardy," on the basis of their having lost the general election or won by a margin of 20 percent or less of the two-party vote; the 15 percent of the candidates who opposed them—labeled "hopeful challengers"; and the 8 percent of the candidates—classified as open-seat "prospects"—who ran in contests that were decided by 20 percent or less of the two-party vote (see Table 1-4).[69] The 1992 post-redistricting House elections were slightly more competitive than those in 1982 because a greater number of retirements led to an increase in the number of marginal open-seat races.

Recent elections witnessed even more competitive contests. Whereas only 31 percent of the candidates in major-party contested races in 1984 had run in marginal districts, 43 percent did so in 1994. Similarly, 35 percent of 1998 House candidates in major-party contested races waged close campaigns; only 21 percent had done so ten years earlier.

The growth in competitive races was not merely the result of an increase in open-seat contests following House retirements. There was also an increase in the competitiveness of contested incumbent-challenger races, especially in the South and in districts where recently elected House members struggled to defend their seats.[70] Incumbency remained a valuable asset, especially in discouraging opposition, but those incumbents who faced major-party challengers were more likely to be involved in marginal races than their counterparts had been ten years ago.

The Senate elections held in the first half of the 1990s were not much different from those held in the previous decade in regard to the challenges presented to incumbents (see Table 1-5). Only two members of the upper chamber were defeated in a primary between 1990 and 1996. In 1992 the Cook County recorder of deeds, Carol Moseley-Braun, defeated Sen. Alan Dixon in the Illinois Democratic primary. In the 1996 Republican Senate primary in Kansas,

TABLE 1-4

Competition in House Elections

	1982	1984	1986	1988	1990	1992	1994	1996	1998
Incumbents									
In jeopardy	15%	13%	9%	8%	15%	14%	17%	15%	14%
Shoo-ins	27	34	35	39	32	25	27	29	31
Challengers									
Hopefuls	15	13	9	8	15	14	17	15	14
Likely losers	27	34	35	39	32	25	27	29	31
Open-seat candidates									
Prospects	8	5	7	5	5	13	9	8	7
Mismatched	7	1	4	3	1	9	5	4	3
(N)	(750)	(736)	(720)	(712)	(696)	(794)	(766)	(812)	(680)

Source: Compiled from Federal Election Commission data.

Notes: Figures are for major-party candidates in contested general elections, excluding incumbent-versus-incumbent races (which occasionally follow redistricting), runoff elections, and contests won by independents. Incumbents in jeopardy are defined as those who lost or who won by 20 percent or less of the two-party vote. Shoo-ins are incumbents who won by more than 20 percent of the two-party vote. Hopeful challengers are those who won or who lost by 20 percent or less of the two-party vote. Likely loser challengers are those who lost by more than 20 percent of the two-party vote. Open-seat prospects are those whose election was decided by 20 percent or less of the two-party vote. Mismatched open-seat candidates are those whose election was decided by more than 20 percent of the two-party vote. Some columns do not add to 100 percent because of rounding.

TABLE 1-5

Number of Unchallenged and Defeated Senate Incumbents

	1982	1984	1986	1988	1990	1992	1994	1996	1998
Incumbent unchallenged by major-party opposition in general election	0	1	0	0	5	1	0	0	0
Incumbent defeated									
In primary	0	0	0	0	0	1	0	1	0
In general election	2	3	7	4	1	4	2	1	3

Sources: Compiled from various issues of *CQ Weekly.* The primary and general election results are from Norman J. Ornstein, Thomas E. Mann, and Michael J. Malbin, *Vital Statistics on Congress, 1997–1998* (Washington, D.C.: Congressional Quarterly, 1998), 62.

TABLE 1-6

Competition in Senate Elections

	1982	1984	1986	1988	1990	1992	1994	1996	1998
Incumbents									
In jeopardy	26%	17%	20%	17%	20%	22%	23%	21%	15%
Shoo-ins	20	27	20	24	25	16	14	9	28
Challengers									
Hopefuls	26	17	20	17	20	22	23	21	15
Likely losers	20	27	20	24	25	16	14	9	28
Open-seat candidates									
Prospects	10	10	12	12	3	21	14	35	9
Mismatched	0	3	6	6	7	3	11	6	6
(N)	(66)	(64)	(68)	(66)	(60)	(68)	(70)	(68)	(68)

Source: Compiled from Federal Election Commission data.

Notes: Figures are for major-party candidates in contested general elections. Incumbents in jeopardy are defined as those who lost or who won by 20 percent or less of the two-party vote. Shoo-ins are incumbents who won by more than 20 percent or less of the two-party vote. Hopeful challengers are those who won or who lost by 20 percent or less of the two-party vote. Likely loser challengers are those who lost by more than 20 percent of the two-party vote. Open-seat prospects are those whose election was decided by 20 percent or less of the two-party vote. Mismatched open-seat candidates are those whose election was decided by more than 20 percent or less of the two-party vote. Some columns do not add to 100 percent because of rounding.

Rep. Sam Brownback defeated Sen. Sheila Frahm, who had been appointed to take Robert Dole's Senate seat after Dole left the Senate to run for president. Moreover, when the classification scheme used for House candidates is applied to the Senate it becomes clear that the incumbent-challenger contests of the early and middle 1990s were somewhat more competitive than those that preceded them and those that took place in 1998 (see Table 1-6).

What did change were the numbers and competitiveness of open seats. During the 1980s, 18 percent or fewer Senate candidates were involved in open-seat contests. In 1992, this number jumped to 24, and in 1996 it reached 41 percent—a record that is likely to stand for some time. Moreover, only 14 percent of the 1996 open-seat contestants ran in races that were decided by more than 20 percent of the vote. As a group, the 1998 open-seat Senate elections were less competitive than those held earlier in the decade.

The competitiveness of recent congressional elections and the large number of open seats in both chambers ensured the appearance of many new faces in

Congress during the 1990s. Almost 57 percent of the members of the 106th Congress took their seats after the 1992 elections. As a group, those sworn into the 102d through 106th Congresses were more diverse than previous classes. The House opened its first session of the 106th Congress with thirty-one more women, eleven more African Americans, and nine more Hispanics than had served in the 101st. Change generally comes more slowly to the upper chamber. Nevertheless, the number of female senators increased by six, and the election of Ben Nighthorse Campbell, R-Colo., in 1992 gave Native Americans demographic representation in the Senate.

Despite this diversity, the vast majority of newcomers had at least one thing in common with one another and with their more senior colleagues: they came to Congress with significant political experience under their belts. Thirty-seven of the forty new House members elected to the 106th Congress had previously held another public office, served as a party official, worked as a political aide or consultant, or run for Congress at least once before getting elected. And, of the three freshmen who had not held an elective or unelective political post, one—Rep. Jim DeMint, R-S.C.—was elected to take the seat of a close friend and confidant—former representative Bob Inglis. All but one of the senators elected for the first time in 1998 had held at least one elective office. The exception was Sen. John Edwards, D-N.C., who had no previous political experience before joining the Senate.

SUMMARY

The Constitution, election laws, campaign finance regulations, and participatory nominations provide the institutional foundations for the candidate-centered congressional election system. The nation's history and individualistic political culture, which inform Americans' traditional ambivalence toward political parties, shore up that system. Candidates who can afford to hire political consultants to learn about and contact voters have benefited from technological advancements, which have allowed the system to assume its contemporary pro-incumbent, professionally oriented, money-fueled form.

How campaigns are conducted in the future will be influenced by changes currently under way in the strategic environment in which congressional elections are waged. Recent changes in campaign finance law, for example, especially those that allow parties and interest groups to broadcast issue advocacy ads, have increased these organizations' abilities to influence the tenor and outcomes of congressional elections.

CHAPTER TWO

Candidates and Nominations

Can I win? Is this the right time for me to run? Who is my competition likely to be? These are the kinds of questions that have always gone through the minds of prospective candidates. During the golden age of political parties, party bosses helped individuals make up their minds whether or not to run for Congress. In many places the bosses' control over the party apparatus was so complete that, when in agreement, they could guarantee the nomination to the person they wanted to run. Moreover, receiving the nomination was usually tantamount to winning the election because strong political machines were usually located in one-party areas.[1]

After the golden age, party leaders had less control over the nomination process and less ability to ensure that the individuals they recruited would, in fact, win the nomination. Contemporary parties are no longer the primary recruiters of congressional candidates. Parties continue to play a role in encouraging some individuals to run for office and in discouraging others. But they serve more as vehicles that self-recruited candidates use to advance their careers than as organizations that can make or break those careers. Party recruitment has been largely replaced by a process referred to as candidate emergence.[2]

In this chapter I examine who decides to run for Congress, how potential candidates reach their decisions, and the influence that different individuals and groups have on these decisions. I also examine the impact of political experience on a candidate's prospects of winning the nomination and the influence of nominations and general elections on the representativeness of the national legislature.

STRATEGIC AMBITION

The Constitution, state laws, and the political parties pose few formal barriers to running for Congress, enabling virtually anyone to become a candidate. Members of the House are required to be at least twenty-five years of age, to have been U.S. citizens for at least seven years, and to reside in the state they represent. The requirements for the Senate are only slightly more stringent. In addition to residing in the state they represent, senators must be at least thirty years old and have been U.S. citizens for at least nine years. Some states bar prison inmates or individuals who have been declared insane from running for office, and most states require candidates to pay a small filing fee or to collect anywhere from a few hundred to several thousand signatures prior to having their names placed on the ballot. As is typical for election to public offices in many democracies, a dearth of formal requirements allows almost anyone to run for Congress. Well over seventeen hundred people declare themselves candidates in most election years.

Although the formal requirements are minimal, other factors, related to the candidate-centered nature of the electoral system, favor individuals with certain personal characteristics. Strategic ambition, which is the combination of a desire to get elected, a realistic understanding of what it takes to win, and an ability to assess the opportunities presented by a given political context, is one such characteristic that distinguishes most successful candidates for Congress from the general public. Most successful candidates must also be self-starters, since the electoral system lacks a tightly controlled party-recruitment process or a well-defined career path to the national legislature. And, because the electoral system is candidate-centered, the desire, skills, and resources that candidates bring to the electoral arena are the most important criteria separating serious candidates from those who have little chance of getting elected. Ambitious candidates, sometimes referred to as *strategic, rational,* or *quality* candidates, are political entrepreneurs who make rational calculations about when to run. Rather than plunge right in, they assess the political context in which they would have to wage their campaigns, consider the effects that a bid for office could have on their professional careers and families, and carefully weigh their prospects for success.[3]

Strategic politicians examine many institutional, structural, and subjective factors when considering a bid for Congress.[4] The institutional factors include filing deadlines, campaign finance laws, prohibitions for or against preprimary endorsements, and other election statutes and party rules. The structural factors include the social, economic, and partisan composition of the district, its geographic compactness, the media markets that serve it, the degree of overlap between the district and lower-level electoral constituencies, and the possibilities that exist for election to some alternative office. One structural factor that greatly affects the strategic calculations of nonincumbents and is prone to fluctuate more often than others is whether an incumbent plans to run for reelection.

Potential candidates also assess the political climate in deciding whether to run. Strategic politicians focus mainly on local circumstances, particularly whether a seat will be vacant or the results of the previous election suggest that an incumbent is vulnerable.[5] National forces, such as a public mood that favors Democrats or Republicans or challengers or incumbents, are usually of secondary importance. The convergence of local and national forces can have a strong impact on the decisions of potential candidates. The widespread hostility the public directed at Congress and its members played a major role in influencing who ran in the 1992, 1994, and 1996 primaries and general elections.[6] These forces motivated many House incumbents to retire and encouraged many would-be House members to believe that a seat in Congress was within their reach.[7] Favorable circumstances and these candidates' positive self-assessments encouraged them to think they could win the support of local, state, and national political elites, raise the money, build the name recognition, and generate the momentum needed to propel them into office.[8] In 1998 the nation's overall prosperity and the public's positive feelings toward incumbents had the opposite effect.

Incumbents

For House incumbents the decision to run for reelection is usually an easy one. Congress offers its members many reasons to want to stay, including the ability to affect issues they care about, a challenging environment in which to work, political power, and public recognition. It is also an ideal platform for pursuing a governorship, cabinet post, or even a seat in the oval office. Name recognition and the advantages inherent in incumbency—such as paid staff and the franking privilege (which have an estimated worth of $1.5 million per year)—are two factors that discourage strong opposition from arising.[9] Furthermore, House members recognize that the "home styles" they use to present themselves to constituents create bonds of trust that have important electoral implications.[10]

Incumbents undertake a number of additional preelection activities to build support and ward off opposition. Many raise large war chests early in the election cycle in order to intimidate potential opponents.[11] Many also keep a skeletal campaign organization intact between elections and send their supporters campaign newsletters and other political communications. Some even shower their constituents with greeting cards, flowers, and other gifts.[12] Their congressional activities, preelection efforts, and the fact that they have been elected to Congress at least once before make most incumbents fairly secure in the knowledge that they will be reelected.

Under certain situations, however, incumbents recognize that it may be more difficult than usual for them to hold on to their seats. Redistricting, for example, can change the partisan composition of a House member's district or it can force two incumbents to compete for one seat.[13] A highly publicized ethical transgression usually weakens an incumbent's reelection prospects. A poor economy, an unpopular president or presidential candidate, or a wave of anti-government hostility also has the potential to undermine legislators who represent marginal districts. These factors can influence incumbents' expectations about the quality of the opposition they are likely to face, the kinds of reelection campaigns they will need to wage, the toll those campaigns could take on themselves and their families, and their desire to stay in Congress.

When the demands of campaigning outweigh the benefits of getting reelected, strategic incumbents retire. Elections that immediately follow redistricting are often preceded by a jump in the number of incumbents who retire, as was the case in 1952, 1972, 1982, and 1992 (see Figure 2-1). Elections held during periods of voter frustration, congressional scandal, or incivility within Congress itself are also preceded by high numbers of retirements.[14] A combination of redistricting, anti-incumbent sentiments, and a decline in comity in the House led 15 percent of all House members to retire in 1992—a post–World War II record. Whereas the numerous hard-fought elections that took place in 1994 inspired many congressional retirements in 1996, retirements declined in 1998. The relatively high appraisals of Congress that preceded the 1998 elections, and the efforts of party leaders, who wanted to minimize the number of open seats they had to defend, helped reduce the number of House retirements to thirty-three, less than 8 percent of House members.

Elections that occur following upheaval within Congress itself are also marked by large numbers of congressional retirements. The political reforms passed during the mid-1970s, which redistributed power from conservative senior House members to more liberal junior ones, encouraged many senior members to retire from the House.[15] The Republican takeover of the House in 1994 also encouraged large numbers of Democrats, and some Republicans, to retire. For the Democrats, retirement was preferable to waging a reelection campaign that, if successful, would result in their continuing to suffer the powerlessness associated with being in the minority. For the Republicans, it was preferable to enduring the indignity of being defeated for a committee chairmanship or some

FIGURE 2-1

Number of Retirements by House Incumbents, 1950–1998

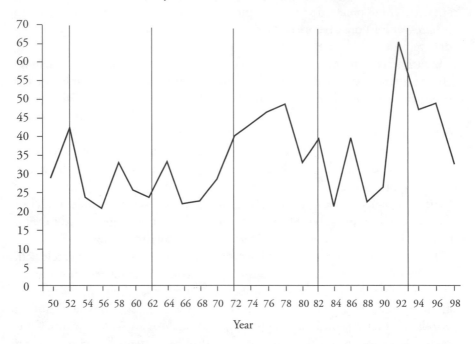

Year

Sources: Compiled from various issues of *CQ Weekly* and Norman J. Ornstein, Thomas E. Mann, and Michael J. Malbin, *Vital Statistics on Congress, 1997–1998* (Washington, D.C.: Congressional Quarterly, 1998), 63.

other leadership post. Rep. Norman Mineta, D-Calif., former chair of the Public Works and Transportation Committee, retired nine months into the 104th Congress, reportedly for the former reason. Rep. Carlos Moorhead, R-Calif., who was the senior Republican member of two committees going into the 104th Congress and ended up chairing neither of them, was influenced by the latter.[16]

The retirements that took place prior to the 1998 elections showed different patterns. Only Rep. William Paxon, R-N.Y., retired for reasons associated with a loss of power. He was forced to resign his leadership post after word leaked out of his role in the aborted coup d'état against Speaker Newt Gingrich. Twelve other House members retired to run for governor or the Senate, and many others retired for personal reasons. It is impossible to anticipate all of the motives for retirements in 2000, or any other year for that matter. Nevertheless, the term limits pledges that some recently elected members took when they first ran for Congress will account for the departures of some relatively junior legislators. The term limits that House Republicans set for committee chairmanships, and the fallout from the races for those posts, will probably account for others.

The individuals who are most likely to retire from Congress are senior members who decide they would rather enjoy the fruits of old age than gear up for an election campaign, members who are implicated in some kind of scandal, members in the minority party who tire of their lack of influence, and members who find their districts largely obliterated by redistricting.[17] The period just before the 1998 elections was marked by several retirements that were motivated by these reasons. Reps. Harris Fawell, R-Ill., Henry Gonzalez, D-Texas, and Esteban Torres, D-Calif., were among the House's senior members who chose to retire. The latter two retirements were in part motivated by the goal of creating family dynasties in Congress: Gonzalez succeeded in helping his son Charlie claim his seat; Torres's son-in-law and top aide, James Casso, lost the Democratic primary race to California assemblywoman Grace Napolitano, who went on to win the general election. Rep. Joseph Kennedy, D-Mass., who first contemplated a run for governor, chose to retire after adverse publicity about his first marriage lengthened an already long list of personal scandals involving him and his family. The retirements of Democratic Caucus chairman Vic Fazio, D-Calif., and Democratic Study Group chairman David Skaggs, D-Colo., both of whom had been expected to rise in their party's House leadership ranks, were purportedly influenced by their disenchantment with being in the minority. No members of the 105th Congress opted to retire because of the effects of redistricting. However, after the 2000 census several members likely will follow the example of Rep. Cleo Fields, D-La. First elected in 1992, Fields retired from the House in 1996 after a three-judge federal panel disassembled his district, which had held an African American majority. Strategic retirements create major opportunities for nonincumbents and contribute to the high retention rates for incumbents who stand for reelection.

Nonincumbents

The conditions that affect the calculations of strategic incumbents also influence the decision making of nonincumbents who plan their political careers strategically.[18] Redistricting has a tremendous impact on these individuals. More state and local officeholders run for the House in election cycles that follow redistricting than in other years (see Figure 2-2).[19] Many of these candidates anticipate the opportunities that arise from the creation of new seats, the redrawing of old ones, or the retirements that often accompany elections after redistricting. The effects of redistricting and the anti-incumbent mood that gripped the nation encouraged roughly 350 candidates who had officeholding

FIGURE 2-2

Number of House Primary Candidates by Political Experience, 1978–1998

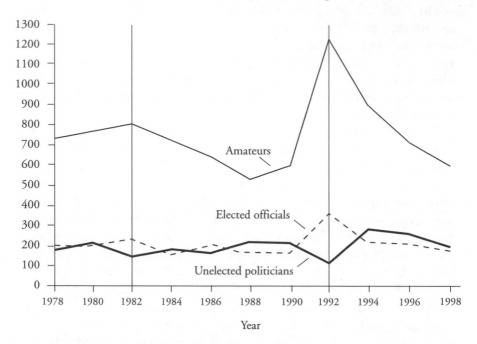

Sources: Compiled from various issues of *CQ Weekly.*

Note: Includes nonincumbent candidates for major-party nominations only.

experience to run in 1992. Voter hostility toward the nation's capital and the possibility for change encouraged 210 elected officials and former officeholders to run in 1994 and another 209 to run in 1996. The public's positive assessments of the 105th Congress had the opposite effect in 1998, when only 162 current and former officeholders ran for Congress.

Candidates who have significant campaign and political experience but who have never held elective office also respond to the opportunities that emerge in specific election years. These "unelected politicians" comprise legislative and executive branch aides, political appointees, state and local party officials, political consultants, and individuals who have previously lost a bid for Congress. Most of these politicians think strategically. Prior to deciding to run, they monitor voter sentiment, assess the willingness of political activists and contributors to support their campaigns, and keep close tabs on who is likely to oppose them for the nomination or in the general election.

Unelected politicians differ from elected officials and former officeholders in their perceptions of what constitutes a good time to run. For example, individuals with elective experience were more likely than unelected politicians to view the post-redistricting elections of 1992 favorably. The major reason for this difference is that the candidacies of the elected officials weighed heavily in the strategic calculations of the unelected politicians. Unelected politicians appreciate that most elected officials possess more name recognition and fundraising advantages than they do. Unelected politicians typically balk at the opportunity to contest a primary against an elected official, even when other circumstances appear favorable. However, if a candidate with elective experience does not come forward, individuals with other significant forms of political experience will usually run. Relatively few experienced nonincumbents viewed the early days of the 1998 election cycle as promising for their causes. The pro-incumbent political environment discouraged unelected politicians from running. Few were willing to run in a bad year for challengers or against a candidate with officeholding experience.

Political amateurs are an extremely diverse group, and it is difficult to generalize about their political decision making. Only a small subgroup of amateurs, referred to as *ambitious amateurs,* behave strategically, responding to the same opportunities and incentives that influence the decisions of more experienced politicians. Most amateurs do not spend much time assessing these factors. *Policy amateurs,* comprising another subgroup, are driven by issues, whereas *experience-seeking* or *hopeless amateurs* run out of a sense of civic duty or for the thrill of running itself.[20]

Record numbers of amateurs ran in the 1982 and 1992 elections. A few were ambitious challengers, who, after weighing the costs of campaigning and the probability of winning, declared their candidacies. Many policy and experience-seeking amateurs were also compelled to run in the early and middle 1990s. These elections provided political landscapes that were ideal for running advocacy-oriented or anti-incumbency campaigns. Calls for change and relentless government-bashing in the media provided reform-minded candidates from both parties with ready-made platforms. The Contract with America and supporting issue papers, campaign manifestos, and Republican recruitment efforts helped inspire more GOP than Democratic candidates to run in 1994—the first time in decades. The legislation proposed and enacted by the Republican-led 104th Congress inspired many policy-oriented Democratic and GOP candidates to run in 1996. The possibilities for turnover in these elections attracted all types of amateurs.

The 1998 elections, in contrast, did not offer nonincumbents the same opportunities as did the previous three elections. Nevertheless, many political

FIGURE 2-3

House Primary Candidacies of Politicians by Party and Experience,
1978–1998

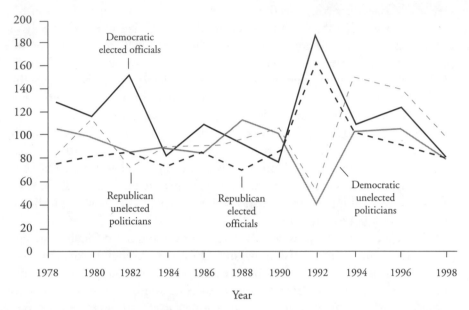

Sources: Compiled from various issues of *CQ Weekly*.

Note: Includes candidates for major-party nominations only.

amateurs ran for the House, demonstrating that they are less sensitive to fluctuations in the opportunities presented by the political environment than are
candidates who possess significant political experience.

What appears to be a year of opportunity for strategic politicians of one
party is often viewed as a bad year by their counterparts in the other. Democrats with experience in lower office considered 1978 and 1982 to be good
years to run for the House; Republicans with comparable levels of experience
did not (see Figure 2-3). In 1978 many Democrats believed that the lingering
effects of the Watergate scandal and the retirements of forty-nine House members improved their electoral prospects. In 1982 many Democrats expected to
benefit from the sluggish economy and declining popularity of President
Reagan.[21]

Republicans, in contrast, judged 1980 to be a good year. Double-digit inflation and the failures of Jimmy Carter's presidency encouraged many experi-

enced Republicans to run for Congress while discouraging qualified Democratic candidates.[22] The 1990 elections also attracted many highly qualified Republican candidates while discouraging the candidacies of similarly qualified Democrats. Many of these GOP members apparently thought that the Keating Five scandal (which implicated four Democrats and only one Republican), the congressional pay raise, the forced retirements of House Speaker Jim Wright and House Majority Whip Tony Coelho, and the diffuse hostility that voters were directing at Congress could be used to whip up sentiment against Democratic incumbents.

The 1992 election was somewhat unusual in that strategic politicians of both parties judged it to hold tremendous possibilities. The effects of redistricting, a weak economy, congressional scandal, and voter antipathy encouraged record numbers of Democratic and Republican officeholders to run for Congress. The 1994 election witnessed a significant decline in candidates with elective experience from both parties, but especially Democrats. Democratic and Republican unelected politicians, however, saw greater opportunities that year, perhaps because of the decline in the number of politicians with elective experience who chose not to run.

The Republican takeover of Congress had a significant effect on candidate emergence in the 1996 elections. The number of Republican candidates with elective or significant unelective experience decreased slightly after 1994 because many individuals in the GOP's candidate pool undoubtedly believed that their party had captured virtually every vulnerable Democrat-held seat in the tidal wave of that year. Many Democratic elected officials also opted not to run in 1996. Demoralized by their party's low standing in the polls, the president's unpopularity, the House Republicans' initial legislative success, and the risk of political defeat, many declined to run against GOP freshmen, including some who were vulnerable to a strong challenge. Democratic unelected politicians filled the void in some of these districts; political amateurs did likewise in others.

Experienced politicians of both parties responded similarly to the political conditions present early in the 1998 election cycle. Nearly identical numbers of elected officials from both parties ran for Congress. The numbers of unelected politicians who ran were also nearly the same for both parties. Because 1998 did not appear to be a good year for challengers of either party, many opted not to run.

Typically most of the best-qualified office seekers wait until a seat opens, either through the retirement or the death of the incumbent, before throwing their hats into the ring.[23] Once a seat becomes vacant, it acts like a magnet, drawing the attention and candidacies of many individuals. Usually several

TABLE 2-1

The Effect of Seat Status on Nonincumbent Candidates for House
Nominations in 1998

	Democrats			Republicans		
	Elected officials	Unelected politicians	Political amateurs	Elected officials	Unelected politicians	Political amateurs
Open seat	48%	20%	20%	46%	21%	25%
Democratic incumbent seeking reelection	2	14	20	49	62	61
Republican incumbent seeking reelection	49	66	60	5	16	14
(N)	(81)	(80)	(292)	(81)	(98)	(305)

Sources: Compiled from various issues of *CQ Weekly.*

Note: Some columns do not add to 100 percent because of rounding.

strategic politicians will express interest in an open seat. Open seat races, defined as contests in which there was no incumbent at the beginning of the
election season, accounted for 8 percent of 1998 elections. Forty-eight percent
of the Democratic elected officials who ran for the House in 1998, and 46 percent of their Republican counterparts, ran in open-seat races(see Table 2-1).[24]

Incumbency discourages competition in primary elections, especially within
the incumbent's party. Only 2 percent of the Democratic elected officials who
ran for the House in 1998 were willing to challenge one of their party's incumbents for the nomination. Their Republican counterparts were similarly gun
shy about attempting to commit political fratricide: only 5 percent were willing to challenge a GOP House member in the primary.

The candidacies of elected officials usually contrast with those of unelected
politicians and amateur candidates. Unelected politicians and political amateurs are more willing to engage in internecine warfare with one of their party's
House incumbents or to run in a primary for a seat that is controlled by an
incumbent from the opposing party. These candidates have fewer political costs
to weigh than do elected officials when considering whether to enter a congressional primary. Prospective candidates who do not hold an elective office do
not have to give up a current office in order to run for Congress, as do most

officeholders whose positions are coterminous with congressional elections.[25] They also do not have to be concerned about the effect a defeat could have on an established political career.

Others Involved in the Decision to Run

The drive to hold elective office may be rooted in an individual's personality and tempered by the larger political environment, but potential candidates rarely reach a decision about running for Congress without touching base with a variety of people.[26] Nearly all candidates single out their family and friends as being highly influential in their decision to enter or forgo the race.[27] More than one young, talented, experienced, and well-connected local politician who wanted a seat in Congress has remarked only half in jest that family members would probably shoot them if they decided to run. Family concerns, financial considerations, and career aspirations have kept many ambitious and highly regarded local politicians from running for Congress.

Political parties, labor unions, other organized groups, and political consultants can also affect a prospective candidate's decision, but they have far less impact than the people who are directly involved in an individual's daily life. Potential candidates usually discuss their plans with these groups only after mulling for a long time the idea of running. Sometimes, would-be candidates approach local party leaders, fellow party members in the House or the Senate, or officials from their party's state, national, congressional, or senatorial campaign committee to learn about the kinds of assistance that would be available should they decide to run. On other occasions the party initiates the contact, seeking to nurture the interest of good prospects.

Barred from simply handing out the nomination, party leaders can influence a prospective candidate's decision to run in a variety of ways. State and local party leaders can help size up the potential competition and try to discourage others from contesting the nomination.[28] In some states party leaders can help a candidate secure a preprimary endorsement, but this does not guarantee nomination.

Members of Congress and the staffs of the Democratic and Republican congressional and senatorial campaign committees often encourage prospective candidates to run. Armed with favorable polling figures and the promise of party assistance in the general election, they search out local talent. Promising individuals are invited to meet with members of Congress and party leaders in Washington and to attend campaign seminars. They are also given lists of PACs and political consultants who possess some of the resources and skills needed to conduct a congressional campaign.[29] That is where national party involvement usually ends. When more than one candidate signs up to run for a nomination, the national parties usually remain neutral unless a primary challenger seriously threatens an incumbent.

Party recruitment is especially important and difficult when local or national forces favor the opposing party. Just as a strong economy or popular president can encourage members of the president's party to run, it can discourage members of the opposition party from declaring their candidacies, most notably when an incumbent of the opposing party is seeking to remain in the seat. Sometimes the promise of party support can encourage a wavering politician to run under what at the outset appear to be less than optimal conditions.

Recruiting candidates to run for traditionally uncompetitive seats is not a major priority, but party committees work to prevent those seats from going uncontested. According to staffers from both parties' congressional and senatorial campaign committees, getting candidates to run for these seats is an important part of building for the future. These candidacies can strengthen state and local party committees by giving them a campaign on which to focus and deepening the farm team from which candidates emerge. They also help prepare a party for opportunities that might arise when an incumbent retires, House districts are redrawn, or a scandal or some other event changes the partisan dynamics in the district. GOPAC, a political committee that was headed by Newt Gingrich prior to his becoming Speaker of the House, played a major role in recruiting Republicans to run for office, including many who helped the GOP win its House majority in 1994.

Labor unions, PACs, and other organized groups typically play more limited roles in candidate recruitment than parties. A few labor PACs and some trade association committees, such as the Committee on Political Education (COPE) of the American Federation of Labor–Congress of Industrial Organizations (AFL-CIO) and the American Medical Association's AMPAC, take polls to encourage experienced politicians to run.[30] Others, such as the National Federation of Independent Business's PAC, sponsor campaign training seminars to encourage individuals who support the group's position to run for the House. Some PACs, such as the pro-women EMILY's List, WISH List, and Women's Campaign Fund, search out members of specific demographic groups and offer them financial and organizational support.[31] Labor unions focus most of their candidate-recruitment efforts, and campaign activities in general, on Democrats. Ideological PACs are among the most aggressive in searching out candidates, and many offer primary assistance to those who share their views. Few corporate PACs become involved in recruiting candidates because they fear offending incumbents.

Finally, political consultants can become involved in a potential candidate's decision making. In addition to taking polls and participating in candidate-training seminars, consultants can use their knowledge of a state or district to assist a would-be candidate in assessing political conditions and sizing up the potential competition. Politicians who have had long-term relationships with consultants usually seek their advice prior to running for Congress.

PASSING THE PRIMARY TEST

There are two ways to win a major-party nomination for Congress: in an un-contested nominating race or by defeating an opponent. It is not unusual for incumbents to receive their party's nomination without a challenge. Even in the 1992 elections, which were marked by a record number of nonincumbent candidacies, 52 percent of all representatives and 42 percent of all senators who sought reelection were awarded their party's nomination without having to defeat an opponent.

Incumbent Victories in Uncontested Primaries

Victories by default occur mainly when an incumbent is perceived to be invulnerable. The same advantages of incumbency and preelection activities that make incumbents confident of reelection make them seem invincible to those contemplating a primary challenge. Good constituent relations, policy representation, and other job-related activities are sources of incumbent strength. A hefty campaign account is another.

The loyalties of political activists and organized groups also discourage party members from challenging their representatives for the nomination. While in office, members of Congress work to advance the interests of those who supported their previous election, and in return they routinely receive the support of these individuals and groups. With this support comes the promise of endorsements, campaign contributions, volunteer campaign workers, and votes. Would-be primary challengers often recognize that the groups whose support they would need to win the nomination are often among the incumbent's staunchest supporters.

Senior incumbents benefit from the clout—real and perceived—that comes with climbing the ranks of congressional leadership. Rep. Larry Combest, R-Texas, completed his seventh term in Congress in 1998 and is typical of most senior incumbents, who are routinely awarded their party's nomination without a fight. One of the major reasons that no one is willing to challenge Combest is that he is well-suited to Texas's 19th district. A fourth-generation farmer and staunch conservative, Combest shares the views of those in his rural, agricultural district. He is against taxes and government regulation but does not let ideology keep him from advancing his district's interests, including fighting for federal price support for his constituents' crops.[32]

Combest also enjoys widespread support because he excels at other aspects of his job: he maintains three district offices to provide constituent services, returns to the district on a regular basis, and votes in accordance with his constituents' views. As a long-time member of the Agriculture Committee, and its chairman in the 106th Congress, he wields tremendous influence over agriculture policy. Prospective GOP challengers, and the Republican activists whose support they would need to defeat Combest in a primary, recognize the district's interests would suffer should he leave Congress. Moreover, Combest is a prodigious fund-raiser. Despite having always won with more than 60 percent of the vote since he was elected in 1984—he routinely polls better than 75 percent— and despite having run unopposed in two of his last four elections, he raised almost $530,000 in 1998. His fundraising prowess helps to scare off primary opposition.[33]

Finally, Combest has the support of many interest groups and is covered like a hero in the local press. One West Texas paper, the *Andrews News,* wrote that "if we had about 50 more congressmen like Combest, we might eventually straighten out the mess in the Washington beltway." The support Combest has received from the press and local advocacy groups deprives would-be primary challengers of much of the organizational and financial support and media coverage they would need to defeat him.[34] Not surprisingly, none of the Republican politicians who would normally be included on a list of Combest's rivals or potential successors has challenged him for the nomination.

Junior incumbents rarely have the same kind of clout in Washington or as broad a base of support as senior legislators, but because they tend to devote a great deal of time to expanding their bases of support they too typically discourage inside challenges.[35] Junior members also may receive special attention from national, state, and local party organizations. Both the Democratic Congressional Campaign Committee (DCCC) and the National Republican Congressional Committee (NRCC) hold seminars immediately after the election to instruct junior members on how to use franked mail, town meetings, and the local press to build voter support. Prior to the start of the campaign season these party committees advise junior members on how to defend their congressional roll-call votes, raise money, and discourage opposition.[36]

State party leaders also give junior members of Congress advice and assistance. Prior to the 1992 elections, first-term representative James Moran, D-Va., received what is perhaps the most important form of help state party leaders can bestow upon a candidate: a supportive district. Democrats in Virginia's capital redrew the state's congressional map with an eye toward improving Moran's reelection prospects. They added heavily Democratic areas to the district, let it be known that they considered this Moran's seat, and even invited one of his potential rivals to run in another congressional district.[37]

Local party activists, who form the pool of potential candidates from which inside opposition usually emerges, are generally more inclined to help junior legislators than challenge them because these activists often worked to elect that individual in the first place. Their loyalties tend to be especially strong when the seat is competitive or was held by the opposition party for a long period of time. As several Democrats in Moran's district explained, teamwork was essential in winning the seat, and the same team that helped elect Moran discouraged other Democrats from running against him during the 1990s.[38]

Considerations of teamwork rarely protect House members who are vulnerable because of scandal. These incumbents face stronger challenges from within their own party than do others. Experienced politicians are often willing to take on an incumbent who is toiling under the cloud of scandal.

Contested Primaries with an Incumbent

When incumbents do face challenges for their party's nomination, they almost always win. Of the 103 House members who were challenged for their party's nomination in 1998, only one, Jay Kim, was defeated. Typically, only those members of Congress who have allegedly committed an ethical transgression, lost touch with their district, or suffer from failing health run a significant risk of falling to a primary challenger.

What kinds of challengers succeed in knocking off an incumbent for the nomination? The answer is candidates who have had significant political experience. Only 2 percent of the Democrats and 5 percent of the Republicans who sought to defeat an incumbent in a primary in 1998 had been elected officials. Yet, an elected official was the only primary challenger to wrest a party nomination away from an incumbent that year (see Table 2-2). Elected officials typically succeed where others fail because they are able to take advantage of previous contacts to gain the support of the political and financial elites who contribute to or volunteer in political campaigns. They can readily make the case that they have represented some of the voters in the district and know what it takes to get elected. Some of these candidates consciously use a lower-level office as a steppingstone to Congress.[39]

Gary Miller's primary victory over Kim and two other Republican candidates is typical of a nomination contest in which a challenger knocks off an

TABLE 2-2
Political Experience and Major-Party Nominations for the House in 1998

	Primary challenges to an incumbent		Primary contests to challenge an incumbent		Primary contests for an open seat	
	Demo- crats	Repub- licans	Demo- crats	Repub- licans	Demo- crats	Repub- licans
Level of experience						
Elected officials	3%	6%	14%	15%	35%	28%
Unelected politicians	15	25	21	20	14	16
Political amateurs	82	68	65	65	51	56
(N)	(71)	(63)	(287)	(269)	(113)	(134)
Primary winners						
Elected officials	0%	100%	19%	21%	55%	47%
Unelected politicians	0	0	25	20	21	24
Political amateurs	0	0	56	59	24	29
(N)	(0)	(1)	(150)	(157)	(33)	(34)
Primary success rates						
Elected officials	0%	25%	70%	82%	46%	43%
Unelected politicians	0	0	62	58	44	38
Political amateurs	0	0	45	53	14	13

Sources: Compiled from various issues of *CQ Weekly.*

Notes: Figures are for nonincumbents only. Some columns do not add to 100 percent because of rounding.

incumbent. Kim, who had been in Congress for three terms and served on the International Relations Committee and Transportation and Infrastructure Committee, would have enjoyed easy reelection in 1998 had it not been for the campaign finance scandal that dogged most of his congressional career. Southern California's suburban 41st district favors Republicans and gave Kim 59 percent of the vote or better in the three general elections in which he competed.

In the early months of his first term, however, the scandal tarnished the image of this self-made millionaire and Korean immigrant. Reports in the *Los Angeles Times,* the *Orange County Register,* and the other local media outlets documented a long trail of sloppy bookkeeping and lax compliance with campaign finance disclosure requirements. Kim's hold on his seat began to weaken.[40] In 1994 four opponents challenged him in the Republican primary: Valerie Romero, an automobile dealer; Ronald Curtis, a mining company executive and Vietnam Veteran; Todd Thakar, an attorney who did not live in the district;

and Robert Kerns, owner of several businesses, including an oil company and toxic cleanup firm.[41] Romero waged the most effective fight against Kim, winning the endorsement of former Pomona mayor Charles Bader. Nevertheless, Kim prevailed with 41 percent of the vote because his opponents divided the remainder.[42]

Kim's problems escalated during his third term. His campaign treasurer, Seokuk Ma, pleaded guilty in April 1997 to charges that he had concealed illegal contributions, and it became clear that the Congressman would also be implicated.[43] Sixteen months later, Kim pleaded guilty to accepting $250,000 in illegal foreign contributions to his 1992 campaign. Kim's difficulties encouraged three Republicans to challenge him in California's new open primary: Miller, who had previously served on the Diamond Bar City Council, been mayor of Diamond Bar City, and spent four years in the California Assembly; Peter Pierce, a deputy district attorney; and Jack Healy, who withdrew from the race but whose name remained on the ballot.[44] Kim's sentence of house arrest in Arlington, Virginia, made it impossible for him to return to California to campaign and led to his being blasted heavily in the media. Miller used Kim's conviction to attract publicity and motivate his own supporters. He recruited volunteers to canvas the district's precincts by informing them, "You are cordially invited to kick a criminal out of Congress."[45] Because Miller and Kim took many of the same issue stances, the vote was largely a choice between two ideologically similar candidates, one who had legal difficulties and another who did not. Miller prevailed in the contest, collecting almost twice as many votes as did Kim, who finished second.[46]

Open Primaries

Opposing-incumbent primaries are those primaries in which an incumbent of the opposing party has decided to seek reelection. A second type of open nomination, called an open-seat primary, occurs in districts in which there is no incumbent seeking reelection. Both types of primaries attract more candidates than contests in which a nonincumbent must defeat an incumbent in order to win the nomination, but opposing-incumbent primaries are usually the less hotly contested of the two.

In opposing-incumbent primaries political experience is usually a determining factor. Elected officials do well in such primaries. In 1998 elected officials made up about 15 percent of the candidates and about 20 percent of the winners. Democratic elected officials enjoyed a nomination rate of 70 percent, and their Republican counterparts had a success rate of 82 percent. Relatively more unelected politicians of both parties ran in opposing-incumbent primaries in

1998. Democrats enjoyed a slightly greater success rate than that achieved by Republicans, but neither group of unelected politicians did as well as their party's elected officials. Political amateurs overwhelmed other candidates both in numbers and in the percentages that won primaries, but as one would expect, their overall success rates in the primaries were lower than those of more experienced candidates.

The Republican primaries held in Virginia's 8th congressional district during the 1990s are typical of most opposing-incumbent nominating contests in that the local heavyweights sat them out to pursue safer options. In 1992 U.S. District Attorney Henry Hudson and former House member Stan Parris, arguably two of the best potential Republican candidates, opted not to seek the nomination to challenge the Democratic incumbent, James Moran. Hudson instead chose to become head of the U.S. Marshal's Office, and Parris, who Moran had defeated in 1990, accepted an appointment to the St. Lawrence Seaway Commission. These developments favored Kyle McSlarrow, a GOP conservative activist, who went on to defeat Bill Cleveland, a Capitol Hill police officer, and Joe Vasipoli, a member of the Alexandria City Council, for the nomination.[47] The next three Republican contests in the 8th district attracted even weaker candidates than those who had run in 1992. In 1994 McSlarrow ran unchallenged. John Otey, a defense contractor, won the 1996 nomination without opposition. In 1998 Demaris Miller, a research psychologist, whose husband unsuccessfully had challenged Sen. John Warner for the 1996 Senate nomination, won unopposed.[48]

Open-seat primaries are the most competitive of all nominating contests. They typically attract many highly qualified candidates, often pitting one elected official against another. Relatively large numbers of candidates with officeholding experience ran for open seats in 1998. Elected officials of both parties had moderately high success rates. Many unelected politicians also did well. Large numbers of political amateurs also ran, but with considerably less success than that achieved by more experienced candidates.

The Democratic and Republican primaries in Wisconsin's 2nd congressional district, like most open-seat primaries, were hard-fought contests that featured many qualified candidates.[49] The races began in February 1997 when Republican incumbent Scott Klug announced that he would not run for a fifth term, leading to the first open-seat contest in the district in forty years. The district had been held by Democratic representative Robert Kastenmeier for thirty-two years before he was defeated by Klug. National and state leaders of both parties considered the seat highly competitive.

The Democrats drew some of the most qualified politicians in the district. State representative Tammy Baldwin, state senator Joe Wineke, and Dane County executive Rick Phelps started their campaigns shortly after Klug's announcement. Patrick O'Brien, a homemaker, joined the race later to give voters the opportunity to vote for a nonpolitician.

Baldwin began to prepare for a House campaign in 1996, when she attended a candidate-training session sponsored by the Women's Campaign Fund and met with representatives of the National Organization of Women and EMILY's List, a PAC that plays a major role in the financing of Democratic women's campaigns. The support of these organizations has been critical to the election to Congress of many female Democrats.

All three of the experienced primary candidates expended a great deal of energy on fund-raising, making the contest one of the nation's most costly. Phelps, who had secured Kastenmeier's endorsement, spent more than $607,000 in the primary, while Wineke spent $346,000. Baldwin surpassed them both, spending $642,000. O'Brien, never a contender in the race, spent a mere $300.

The Democrats debated education, health care, Social Security, taxes, and other prominent issues, but they took similar stances on them. One sharp distinction among them was gender. As the only woman in the race, Baldwin portrayed herself as a champion of women's issues. She frequently pointed out that Wisconsin had never sent a woman to Congress and broadcast television ads stating that "Tammy Baldwin will take on the issues that most congressmen won't." Another distinction among the candidates was that only Baldwin was gay. Neither she nor any of the other Democratic candidates made an issue of her sexual orientation, but her status as the only woman and the only gay candidate in the primary enabled her to tap into national donor networks. Baldwin further distinguished herself from her opponents by making special efforts to mobilize students and other young people, who traditionally have low rates of voter participation.[50] Baldwin's unique assets—superiority on gender issues, a savvy media campaign, money, and the support of younger voters—combined with an attractive appearance to help her garner 37 percent of the vote, two percent more than the share won by Phelps, who finished second.

The Republican primary was more hotly contested and significantly more bruising than the Democratic race. Six candidates competed for the nomination. However, like the Republican incumbent they hoped to replace, none had ever held elective office before running for Congress. Only State Insurance Commissioner Jo Musser and former congressional aide Nicholas Fuhrman had significant political experience. The other candidates were Sauk County beer distributor Donald Carrig, University of Wisconsin history professor John Sharpless, DeForest chiropractor Meredith Bakke, and former Madison firefighter Ron Greer. Like the Democratic primary, the Republican contest was expensive. Carrig spent $712,000, including $457,000 from his own pocket.

Musser spent $414,000, of which almost $290,000 came from personal funds. Spending by Carrig and Musser exceeded that of the other candidates by a large margin: Bakke and Greer spent $247,000 and $187,000, respectively, while Fuhrman spent $144,000 and Sharpless, $73,000.

The Republicans debated many of the same issues as had the Democrats, and with the exception of Greer, all sought to portray themselves as the rightful heir to Klug, though he would endorse no one. Greer separated himself from the rest of the pack in another way: he aggressively attacked Baldwin and the gay community, mailing a fund-raising letter that labeled her "a left-wing lesbian." The letter and Greer's public pronouncements against homosexuals won him some support in conservative circles but drew the condemnation of the other Republican candidates. Finally, Greer got extra attention from Republican primary voters and the press because he was the only African American in the race. His aggressive tactics and the similarities among the other candidates enabled Greer to come close to winning the nomination. He captured 20 percent of the vote, 395 ballots behind Musser, the winner.

NOMINATIONS, ELECTIONS, AND REPRESENTATION

The electoral process—which transforms private citizen to candidate to major-party nominee to House member—greatly influences the makeup of the national legislature. Those parts of the process leading up to the general election, especially the decision to run, play an important role in producing a Congress that is not demographically representative of the U.S. population. The willingness of women and minorities to run for Congress during the last few decades and of voters to support them have helped make the national legislature somewhat more representative in regard to gender and race. Still, in many respects Congress does not mirror American society.

Occupation

Occupation has a tremendous effect on the pool of House candidates and on their prospects for success. Individuals who claim law, politics, or public service (many of whom have legal training) as their profession are a minuscule portion of the general population but make up 37 percent of all nomination candidates, 46 percent of all successful primary candidates, and 50 percent of all House members (see Table 2-3). The analytical, verbal, and organizational skills required to succeed in the legal profession or in public service help these individuals undertake a successful bid for Congress.[51] The high salaries that

TABLE 2-3

Occupational Representativeness of 1998 House Candidates and Members of the 106th Congress

Occupation	General population	Nomination candidates	General election candidates	House members
Agricultural or blue-collar workers	26%	5%	5%	3%
Business or banking	12	20	22	24
Clergy or social work	—	1	1	—
Education	2	8	10	13
Entertainer, actor, writer, or artist	1	2	2	2
Law	—	18	25	32
Medicine	1	4	4	4
Military or veteran	1	1	—	—
Politics or public service	—	19	21	18
Other white-collar professionals	17	9	8	3
Outside work force	35	3	1	—
Unemployed	4	—	—	—
Unidentified, nonpolitical occupation	—	10	—	—
(N)	(248,718,000)	(1,339)	(776)	(435)

Sources: General population figures are from U.S. Department of Commerce, Bureau of the Census, *Statistical Abstract of the United States* (Washington, D.C.: U.S. Government Printing Office, 1992), xii, 18, 392–394; candidate occupation data are from various issues of *CQ Weekly.*

Notes: Figures include all 1998 major-party House candidates and all members of the 106th Congress, including Rep. Bernard Sanders, I-Vt. The figures for the general population are from 1990. Dashes = less than 0.5 percent. Some columns do not add to 100 percent because of rounding.

members of these professions earn give them the wherewithal to take a leave of absence from work so they can campaign full time. These highly paid professionals can also afford to make the initial investment that is needed to get a campaign off the ground. Moreover, their professions place many attorneys and public servants in a position to rub elbows with political activists and contributors whose support can be crucial to winning a House primary or general election.

Business professionals and bankers are not as overrepresented among nomination candidates, major-party nominees, or House members as are public servants and lawyers, but persons in business tend to be successful in congressional elections. Many possess money, skills, and contacts that are useful in politics. Educators (particularly college professors) and other white-collar professionals also enjoy a modicum of success in congressional elections. Of these, educators are the most successful group of candidates. They rarely possess the wealth of lawyers and business professionals, but educators frequently have the verbal, analytical, and organizational skills needed to get elected.

Just as some professions are overrepresented in Congress, others are underrepresented. Disproportionately few persons employed in agriculture or blue-collar professions either run for Congress or are elected. Even fewer students, homemakers, and others who are considered outside the work force attempt to win a congressional seat.

Closely related to the issue of occupation is wealth. Personal wealth is a significant advantage in an election system that places a premium on a candidate's ability to spend money. Roughly 7 percent of House members have assets worth $2 million or more, a far greater proportion than the less than one-half of 1 percent of the general population who enjoy similar wealth.[52]

Gender

A record fifty-eight women were elected to the House in 1998, just a fraction—less than one-sixth—of the number of men. The major reason for the underrepresentation of women in the legislative branch is that fewer women than men run for Congress (see Figure 2-4). Less than 14 percent of all contestants for major-party nominations in 1998 were female. Women are underrepresented among congressional candidates for many reasons. Active campaigning demands greater time and flexibility than most people can afford, particularly women. Women continue to assume primary parenting responsibilities in most families, a role that is difficult to combine with long hours of campaigning. Only since the 1980s have significant numbers of women entered the legal and business professions, which often serve as training grounds for elected officials and political activists. Women also continue to be underrepresented in state legislatures and other elective offices, which commonly serve as steppingstones to Congress.[53]

Once women decide to run, gender does not affect their election prospects.[54] Women are just about as likely as men to advance from primary candidate to nominee to House member.[55] As more women come to occupy lower-level offices or to hold positions in the professions from which congressional candidates usually emerge, the proportion of women candidates and members of Congress can be expected to increase.

FIGURE 2-4

Gender Representativeness of 1998 House Candidates and Members of the 106th Congress

Percent

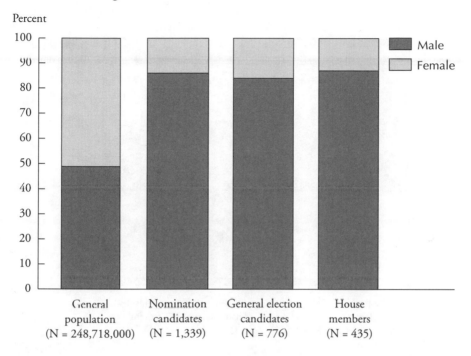

Male
Female

General population (N = 248,718,000)   Nomination candidates (N = 1,339)   General election candidates (N = 776)   House members (N = 435)

Sources: General population figures are from U.S. Department of Commerce, Bureau of the Census, *Statistical Abstract of the United States* (Washington, D.C.: U.S. Government Printing Office, 1992), xii, 18, 392–394; candidate gender data are from various issues of *CQ Weekly*.

Notes: Figures include all 1998 major-party House candidates and all members of the 106th Congress, including Rep. Bernard Sanders, I-Vt. The figures for the general population are from 1990.

Age

Congressional candidates are also somewhat older than the general population, and this is only partly due to the age requirements imposed by the Constitution. The average candidate for nomination is three and one-half times as likely to be forty to fifty-four years of age as twenty-five to thirty-nine (see Figure 2-5). Moreover, successful nomination candidates tend to be older than those whom they defeat. The selection bias in favor of those who are forty to seventy-four continues into the general election; as a result, Congress is made up largely of persons who are middle-aged or older.

FIGURE 2-5

Age Representativeness of 1998 House Candidates and Members
of the 106th Congress

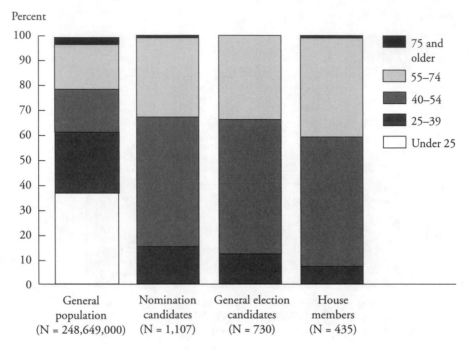

Percent

Legend:
- 75 and older
- 55–74
- 40–54
- 25–39
- Under 25

| General population (N = 248,649,000) | Nomination candidates (N = 1,107) | General election candidates (N = 730) | House members (N = 435) |

Sources: General population figures are from U.S. Department of Commerce, Bureau of the Census, *Statistical Abstract of the United States* (Washington, D.C.: U.S. Government Printing Office, 1992), xii, 18, 392–394; candidate age data are from various issues of *CQ Weekly*.

Notes: Figures include all 1998 major-party House candidates and all members of the 106th Congress, including Rep. Bernard Sanders, I-Vt. The figures for the general population are from 1990. Some of the Ns differ from those in Figure 2-4 because of missing data.

The underrepresentation of young people is due to an electoral process that allows older individuals to benefit from their greater life experiences. People who have reached middle age typically have greater financial resources, more political experience, and a wider network of political and professional associates to help them with their campaigns. Moreover, a formidable group of people who are forty to seventy-four years old—current representatives—also benefit from considerable incumbency advantages.

FIGURE 2-6

Religious Representativeness of 1998 House Candidates and Members of the 106th Congress

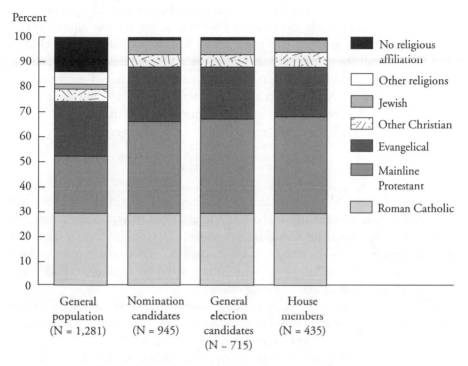

Percent

Legend:
- No religious affiliation
- Other religions
- Jewish
- Other Christian
- Evangelical
- Mainline Protestant
- Roman Catholic

General population (N = 1,281) · Nomination candidates (N = 945) · General election candidates (N - 715) · House members (N = 435)

Sources: General population figures are compiled from Virginia Sapiro, Stephen J. Rosenstone, and the National Election Studies, *American National Election Study, 1998: Post-Election Survey* (Ann Arbor: University of Michigan, 1999); candidate religion data are from various issues of *CQ Weekly*.

Notes: Figures include all 1998 major-party House candidates and all members of the 106th Congress, including Rep. Bernard Sanders, I-Vt. Some of the Ns differ from those in Figure 2-4 because of missing data.

Religion

Religion has an impact on candidate emergence, sometimes providing politicians with a policy concern, such as abortion or human rights, that gives them the motivation to run. Yet it has little effect on how candidates do once they enter the candidate pool. Most religions, including Roman Catholicism and evangelical Christianity, are represented among nomination candidates, major-party nominees, and House members in proportions that match their representation in the general population (see Figure 2-6). Only mainline Protestants and Jews run for and win congressional seats in numbers that exceed their proportions of the population. Several other religions, including Islam, Hinduism, and Buddhism, which together make up 5percent of the population, are virtually invisible among congressional candidates and national legislators.

Individuals who claim no religious identification are the most underrepresented "belief" group in Congress. People who do not participate in church activities typically have fewer political and civic skills than those who do, which may discourage them from running for Congress.[56] Atheists and agnostics also may believe that it would be impossible for them to get elected given the large role that organized religion plays in politics in many parts of the country. The result is they have little presence in politics or national government.

Race and Ethnicity

Race and ethnicity, like religion and gender, have a greater effect on candidate emergence than on electoral success.[57] Whites are heavily overrepresented in the pool of nomination candidates, whereas persons of other races are underrepresented (see Figure 2-7). This situation reflects the disproportionately small numbers of minorities who have entered the legal or business professions or who occupy state or local offices.

Once minority politicians declare their candidacies, they have fairly good odds of winning. The recent successes of minority House candidates are largely due to redistricting processes that were intended to promote minority representation.[58] A few House members, such as Republican Conference Chairman J. C. Watts Jr., an African American who was elected in 1994 to represent Oklahoma's 4th congressional district, won seats that were not specifically carved to promote minority representation in Congress. Still, most minority candidates are elected in districts that have large numbers of voters belonging to their racial or ethnic group, and once they win these seats they tend to hold them. Only one of the incumbents who had occupied a majority-minority seat was not reelected in 1996 and 1998, after the courts mandated that their districts be redrawn.[59] The success of these members can be attributed to their ability to build multiracial coalitions and the advantages that incumbency confers on them.[60]

Party Differences

Public servants and members of the legal profession comprise a large portion of each party's candidate pool, but more Republican candidates come from the business world and more Democratic candidates are lawyers and public ser-

FIGURE 2-7

Racial and Ethnic Representativeness of 1998 House Candidates and Members of the 106th Congress

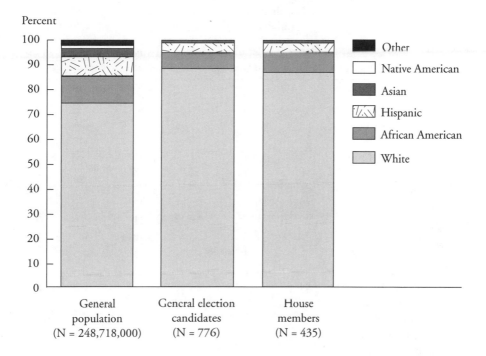

Percent

Legend:
- Other
- Native American
- Asian
- Hispanic
- African American
- White

General population (N = 248,718,000)
General election candidates (N = 776)
House members (N = 435)

Sources: General population figures are from U.S. Department of Commerce, Bureau of the Census, *Statistical Abstract of the United States* (Washington, D.C.: U.S. Government Printing Office, 1992), xii, 18, 392–394; candidate race data are from various issues of *CQ Weekly.*

Notes: Figures include all 1998 major-party House candidates and all members of the 106th Congress, including Rep. Bernard Sanders, I-Vt. The figures for the general population are from 1990.

vants (see Table 2-4). The GOP's overrepresentation of business professionals continues through each stage of the election and in the House, as does the Democrats' overrepresentation of lawyers and career politicians. Attorneys and career public servants from both parties do well in elections, but they are more strongly represented in the Democratic than the Republican Party. Business executives, in contrast, have a bigger presence in the ranks of Republican legislators. Even though Republicans have historically been viewed as the defenders

TABLE 2-4

1998 Major-Party Nomination and General Election Candidates and House Members of the 106th Congress

	Nomination candidates		General election candidates		House members	
	Demo-crats	Repub-licans	Demo-crats	Repub-licans	Demo-crats	Repub-licans
Occupation						
Agricultural or blue collar workers	5%	5%	5%	5%	2%	5%
Business or banking	14	25	15	30	15	32
Clergy or social work	1	1	1	1	1	—
Education	10	7	12	8	15	11
Entertainer, actor, writer, or artist	2	2	2	2	1	2
Law	22	15	30	21	35	30
Medicine	3	5	3	6	3	4
Military or veteran	—	1	—	1	—	—
Politics or public service	21	17	25	17	24	13
Other white-collar professionals	8	9	6	9	4	2
Outside work force	2	3	1	2	—	—
Unidentified, not politics	11	10	—	—	—	—
(N)	(642)	(696)	(379)	(396)	(211)	(223)
Gender						
Male	83%	88%	80%	88%	82%	92%
Female	17	12	20	12	18	8
(N)	(642)	(696)	(379)	(396)	(211)	(223)
Age						
25–39	12%	19%	9%	15%	6%	8%
40–54	53	50	55	52	52	52
55–74	34	30	35	32	41	39
75 and older	1	1	1	1	1	—
(N)	(522)	(584)	(359)	(370)	(211)	(223)

(Table continues)

TABLE 2-4
(continued)

	Nomination candidates		General election candidates		House members	
	Demo-crats	Repub-licans	Demo-crats	Repub-licans	Demo-crats	Repub-licans
Religion						
Roman Catholic	32%	26%	33%	26%	36%	22%
Mainline Protestant	32	41	34	43	29	49
Evangelical	20	25	18	23	19	20
Jewish	10	3	10	2	10	—
Other Christian	4	6	4	6	3	8
No religious affiliation	1	—	2	—	3	—
(N)	(433)	(511)	(342)	(372)	(211)	(223)
Race and Ethnicity						
White	82%	93%	82%	94%	74%	98%
African American	9	3	11	3	17	—
Hispanic	6	2	6	2	7	1
Other	2	1	1	—	1	—
(N)	(642)	(696)	(379)	(396)	(211)	(223)

Sources: Compiled from various issues of *CQ Weekly.*

Notes: Figures are for all major-party nomination candidates, all major-party general election candidates, and all major-party members of the 106th Congress (which excludes Rep. Bernard Sanders, I-Vt.). Dashes = less than 0.5 percent. Some columns do not add to 100 percent because of rounding. Candidates under twenty-five years of age and those affiliated with "other" religions are omitted from the table because none ran in 1998.

of the rich, members of both parties are found among Congress's wealthiest legislators.[61]

More women run for Democratic than Republican nominations for Congress. This gender gap reflects the greater number of women who identify with the Democratic Party and that party's greater acceptance of female candidates. Democratic women are also more successful in winning the nomination and getting elected to the House than are their GOP counterparts.

Democratic primary candidates tend to be somewhat older than their Republican counterparts, reflecting the different orientations of the individuals in the parties' candidate pools. Democratic primary candidates are more likely to come from the ranks of politicians and to consider a congressional election as a somewhat risky opportunity to take a step up the career ladder. Members of the Republican candidate pool are more apt to have careers in the private sector. Many run for Congress before they have taken major strides in their profession, recognizing that if they wait too long they may have advanced too far professionally to want to sacrifice their career in order to run.[62] The initial age difference between Democratic and Republican candidates lays the foundation for an uneven trend toward a middle-aged Congress. The age difference between the parties gets smaller as the candidates progress through the primaries and the general election.

The parties also draw candidates from different religious, racial, and ethnic groups. Republican primary contestants are mainly Protestant and white, as are the GOP's nominees and House members. The Democratic Party attracts candidates from a wider array of groups, including significant numbers of Roman Catholics, Jews, and African Americans. These patterns reflect the parties' electoral coalitions.

THE SENATE

The Senate historically has been less demographically representative than the House, but it, too, has been moving toward more accurately mirroring the U.S. population in some important ways. After the 1990 elections, the Senate had only two women. It also had two Asian American members (both from Hawaii), but no Native Americans or African Americans. Over 60 percent of its members were at least fifty-five years of age. Senate members came from a variety of occupations, but roughly 47 percent were lawyers. Another 25 percent were drawn from the business and banking communities, and 8 percent were journalists. An additional 8 percent were educators, and 6 percent were from the agricultural sector.[63] The remainder held a variety of positions, with 4 percent claiming politics or public service as their profession. In short, descriptions of the Senate as a bastion for white, wealthy, middle-aged, professional men were very close to the mark.

Part of the reason that the Senate has been slower to change than the House is that Senate terms are six years, and only one-third of the upper chamber is up for election at a time. Other reasons have to do with the heightened demands of Senate campaigns. As statewide races, Senate primary and general election campaigns require larger amounts of money, more extensive organizations, and more complex strategies than do House campaigns. Successful Senate candidates generally possess more skill, political connections, and campaign experience than do their House counterparts. The fact that so many members of the Senate had extensive political experience prior to their election suggests that the dearth of women and minorities in lower-level offices may help to explain why the upper chamber is changing more slowly than the lower. In order to gain seats in the Senate, members of traditionally underrepresented groups have had first to place citizens in positions that serve as steppingstones to that body. As more women, African Americans, and members of other underrepresented groups are elected or appointed to local, state, and federal offices, their numbers in the Senate will probably increase.

Nevertheless, a single election can have a great effect on the Senate's makeup. After the polls closed in 1992, five more women had secured seats in the upper chamber, including the Senate's first African American woman, Illinois Democrat Carol Moseley-Braun. In addition, the Senate prepared to swear in its first Native American, Ben Nighthorse Campbell. The 1994, 1996, and 1998 elections did not have as big an impact on the demographic makeup of the Senate as that of 1992. The 1994 election added two more women to the upper chamber. The 1996 election resulted in a net increase of one female senator, bringing the total to nine, and the 1998 election resulted in the loss of the Senate's only African American—Moseley-Braun.

Even though traditionally underrepresented groups have increased their numbers in the Senate, this does not mean that the upper chamber has become a place of employment for individuals with a diverse array of backgrounds. Fifty-three senators in the 106th Congress were drawn from the legal profession. Another twenty-one came from the business and banking communities, six from education, and seven from public service. An additional four had been journalists, and two had worked in agriculture. The remainder had held positions ranging from surgeon to social worker. Over 65 percent were fifty-five years of age or older.[64]

Most senators had significant political experience prior to getting elected, often having held more than one office. Forty-four of the senators in the 106th Congress had previously served in the U.S. House of Representatives, twelve had been governors of their states, twenty-seven had held some other statewide office, nine had been state legislators, and twelve had served in a local office. Eleven had served as party officials, political aides, or presidential appointees or had run for the Senate.[65] Only four senators—John Edwards, D-N.C., Bill Frist, R-Tenn., Orrin Hatch, R-Utah, and Frank Lautenberg, D-N.J.—were elected to the Senate without having previously held elective office or some other significant political position.

Although senators are more likely than representatives to have to defend their nominations, Senate primaries tend to be less competitive than those for the House. Between 1982 and 1996 Alan Dixon and Sheila Frahm were the only two senators who sought to be renominated and were defeated. The relative ease with which members of the Senate retain their party's nomination can be attributed to a number of factors besides the tremendous demands that Senate primary contests make on challengers. For one thing, senators and Senate candidates are highly strategic. Like their counterparts in the House, members of the Senate use their office to help their state receive its share of federal projects, to garner positive coverage in the press, and to build support among voters. Senators, like representatives, also build huge campaign treasuries to discourage potential opponents. Finally, most members of the Senate are shrewd enough to recognize when it is time to step down, as demonstrated by the voluntary retirements in 1992 of Sens. Alan Cranston, D-Calif., Dennis DeConcini, D-Ariz., and Don Riegle, D-Mich., all of whom had been implicated in the Keating Five scandal. In 1998 Sens. Dale Bumpers, D-Ark., Daniel Coats, R-Ind., Wendell Ford, D-Ky., and John Glenn, D-Ohio, opted for voluntary retirement. Former Republican senator Dirk Kempthorne's decision to leave the Senate to wage a successful campaign for Idaho's governorship further demonstrates that these politicians are also astute enough to recognize other opportunities. The effect of scandal, aging, infirmity, declining public support, and strategic ambition on Senate turnover tends to be felt more through retirements than primary defeats.

Moreover, the most qualified opponent that a senator is likely to face in a primary is a current House member or some other elected official.[66] Because these individuals are also highly strategic, only a few are willing to risk their current positions by picking a primary fight. Most prefer to wait until a seat becomes open.

When an incumbent does announce his or her retirement, or a member of the opposite party appears vulnerable, political parties and interest groups help to shape the field of Senate candidates by encouraging potential candidates to declare their candidacies. These organizations promise the same types of support, under the same kinds of circumstances, to potential Senate candidates as they offer to House candidates. Party organizations rarely become involved in contested Senate primaries even though they may promise a candidate from hundreds of thousands to millions of dollars in campaign support upon winning the nomination. The parties' senatorial campaign committees are singled out by candidates as the most influential organizations in the candidate-recruitment process. Nevertheless, the decision to run for the Senate, like the decision to run for the House, is a personal one. Family and friends, issues, and a desire to improve government or become a national leader are more influential in the decisions of candidates to run for the Senate than are political organizations.[67]

SUMMARY

Virtually anyone can run for Congress because there are few legal requirements for serving, and neither party committees nor interest groups have the power to simply hand out a congressional nomination. Strategic politicians, mainly individuals who have held office or have some other significant unelective experience, carefully assess political conditions before deciding to run. Most incumbents—who are the most strategic of all politicians—choose to run again, but personal considerations, a loss of political clout in Congress, redistricting, scandal, or a wave of voter hostility toward the federal government or their party can encourage an incumbent to retire. These factors also have an impact on the candidacy decisions of strategic nonincumbents, but the opening of a congressional seat is even more important than other political conditions in spurring on their candidacies. Amateur politicians tend to be less discriminating and are considerably less likely to win their party's nomination.

Candidate emergence, nomination, and election processes have a major impact on who serves in Congress. Most members of the contemporary House and Senate are white, middle- or upper-class males. Most are middle-aged or older and belong to a mainstream religion. The vast majority also have had significant previous political experience prior to getting elected. The number of national legislators who belong to underrepresented groups has increased in recent years, but change comes slowly to Congress, especially in the Senate.

CHAPTER THREE

The Anatomy of a Campaign

Most House and Senate candidates relied on state and local party committees to wage their campaigns during the parties' golden age. An individual candidate's "organization" was often little more than a loyal following within the party. By the mid-1950s, few congressional candidates could count on party organizations to obtain their nominations and wage their campaigns. Senate campaigns became significantly more professional during the 1950s and 1960s; House campaigns followed suit during the 1970s.[1] The decline of the political machine and the legal and systemic changes that fostered it led to the development of the modern campaign organization.[2]

Most contemporary congressional campaigns are waged by highly specialized, professional organizations. Few campaign organizations are fully self-sufficient. Most employ paid staff and volunteers to carry out some of the tasks associated with running for Congress and hire political consultants to perform specialized campaign activities, such as formulating strategy, taking polls, and producing campaign ads. But consultants do more than carry out isolated campaign tasks. Political consulting has become highly professional, replete with its own standards, professional associations, and trade magazines. Consultants help budding politicians learn what to expect and what will be expected of them during the campaign. Consultants' opinions of what is strategically and tactically advisable and ethical have a major impact on candidate conduct.[3] In this chapter I describe campaign organizations, focusing on the political consultants and other personnel who work in them and on how campaigns spend their money.

CAMPAIGN ORGANIZATIONS

Candidates need to achieve several interrelated objectives to compete successfully in an election, including raising money, formulating a strategy, and communicating with and mobilizing voters. Specialized skills and training are required to meet many of these objectives. Senate campaigns, which are larger and must typically reach out to more voters, employ more paid staff and consultants than do their House counterparts.

The biggest factor in House campaigns is incumbency. Assembling a campaign organization is an easy task for incumbents. Most merely reassemble the personnel who worked on their previous campaign. A substantial number of incumbents keep elements of their organizations intact between elections. Some of these organizations consist only of a part-time political aide or fund-raiser. Others are quite substantial, possessing the characteristics of a permanent business. They own a building and have a large professional staff, a fund-raising apparatus, an investment portfolio, a campaign car, an entertainment budget, and a team of lawyers, accountants, and consultants on retainer. House incumbents typically spend more than $200,000 on organizational maintenance during the two years leading up to an election.[4] Some congressional leaders, such as Minority Leader Richard Gephardt, D-Mo., put together "Cadillac" campaigns that spend more than $1 million on staff, rent, office equipment, supplies, and other resources used for organizational maintenance.[5]

Few House challengers or open-seat candidates possess even a temporary organization capable of contesting a congressional election until just before their declaration of candidacy. Nonincumbents who have held an elective post usually possess advantages over those who have not in assembling a campaign organization. Some have steering committees, "Friends of 'Candidate X'" clubs, or working relationships with political consultants from previous campaigns. Candidates who have never held an elective office but have been active in politics usually have advantages over political amateurs in building an organization. Previous political involvement gives party committee chairs, political aides, and individuals who have previously run for office some knowledge of how to wage a campaign and ties to others who can help them. The organizational advantages that incumbents possess over challengers are usually greater than those advantages that experienced nonincumbents have over political amateurs.[6]

Almost nine out of ten House members' campaign organizations are managed by a paid staffer or some combination of paid staffer and outside consultant (see Table 3-1).[7] Very often the campaign manager is the administrative assistant or chief of staff in the House member's congressional office. Adminis-

TABLE 3-1
Staffing Activities in House Elections

	All	Incumbents		Challengers		Open-seat candidates	
		In jeopardy	Shoo-ins	Hope-fuls	Likely losers	Pros-pects	Mis-matched
Campaign management							
Paid staff	59%	69%	70%	71%	30%	83%	67%
Consultant	15	18	16	19	12	17	—
Political party	2	2	—	7	1	4	—
Interest groups	2	2	4	2	2	—	—
Volunteer	21	8	13	12	43	4	33
Not used	4	—	1	—	14	—	—
Press relations							
Paid staff	56%	74%	62%	62%	33%	79%	44%
Consultant	15	20	15	26	4	25	11
Political party	3	2	2	7	2	—	—
Interest groups	3	—	5	2	6	—	—
Volunteer	20	—	13	14	41	4	44
Not used	6	4	2	—	16	—	—
Issue and opposition research							
Paid staff	33%	43%	43%	36%	21%	25%	11%
Consultant	28	39	27	36	8	62	44
Political party	8	6	2	22	7	4	—
Interest groups	5	2	4	3	9	12	—
Volunteer	18	10	5	16	41	—	33
Not used	12	8	18	—	19	—	—
Fund-raising							
Paid staff	58%	65%	65%	69%	35%	75%	78%
Consultant	21	29	28	17	7	50	11
Political party	4	6	2	7	2	8	—
Interest groups	4	—	4	2	7	4	—
Volunteer	20	6	16	16	34	12	22
Not used	6	—	—	—	20	—	—
Accounting/FEC reporting							
Paid staff	45%	63%	62%	43%	21%	42%	44%
Consultant	17	29	22	12	7	21	22
Political party	3	6	—	5	2	—	—
Interest groups	3	2	1	5	4	—	—
Volunteer	32	2	17	41	52	42	33
Not used	4	—	1	—	14	—	—

(Table continues)

TABLE 3-1
(continued)

	All	Incumbents		Challengers		Open-seat candidates	
		In jeopardy	Shoo-ins	Hope-fuls	Likely losers	Pros-pects	Mis-matched
Polling							
Paid staff	5%	6%	7%	9%	1%	4%	11%
Consultant	55	86	54	76	18	88	56
Political party	3	2	4	2	3	4	—
Interest groups	2	—	2	3	2	—	—
Volunteer	9	4	4	10	18	—	—
Not used	28	6	29	7	57	4	33
Media advertising							
Paid staff	18%	16%	22%	19%	18%	17%	11%
Consultant	55	80	61	74	19	71	56
Political party	1	2	1	2	—	4	—
Interest groups	4	4	4	—	9	4	—
Volunteer	12	—	1	7	33	4	33
Not used	11	4	12	2	23	4	—
Get-out-the-vote drives							
Paid staff	27%	33%	32%	33%	7%	62%	33%
Consultant	10	14	7	5	13	12	—
Political party	23	29	23	26	20	17	11
Interest groups	11	14	12	9	9	12	—
Volunteer	50	49	46	60	41	67	67
Not used	9	—	7	2	22	4	—
Legal advice							
Paid staff	10%	6%	18%	5%	8%	8%	—
Consultant	21	29	32	21	9	25	11
Political party	11	14	6	24	4	21	—
Interest groups	7	8	4	9	7	12	—
Volunteer	29	22	17	34	42	21	44
Not used	24	18	22	16	33	17	44
Average number of activities performed by paid staff or consultants	5.2	7.0	6.2	5.9	2.6	6.9	5.0
(N)	(313)	(49)	(82)	(58)	(91)	(24)	(9)

Source: The 1998 Congressional Campaign Study.

Notes: Figures are for major-party candidates in contested general elections. The categories of candidates are the same as those in Table 1-4. Figures for interest groups include labor unions. Dashes = less than 0.5 percent. Some columns do not add to 100 percent because some activities were performed by more than one person or group or because of rounding.

trative assistants and other congressional staffers routinely take leaves of absence from their jobs to work for their boss's reelection, sometimes as volunteers who consider the bonuses or high salaries they receive as congressional aides when they are not on leave as compensation enough. Incumbents who are shoo-ins (who won by more than 20 percent of the vote) are just as likely as those who are in jeopardy of losing their seats (who lost or won by less than 20 percent of the vote) to hire a paid staffer to handle day-to-day management and a general consultant to assist with campaign strategy. Most hopeful challengers (who won or lost by 20 points or less) have professionally managed campaigns, but only 42 percent of all likely loser challengers (who lost by more than 20 percent of the vote) are managed by a paid staffer or general consultant. Many of these campaigns rely on volunteer managers, but some have no managers at all, relying on the candidates themselves to run their own campaigns.

Open-seat campaigns are similar to those waged by incumbents. Virtually all open-seat prospects (whose races were decided by margins of 20 percent or less) rely on a paid staffer or general consultant to manage their campaigns, and some use both. Many open-seat candidates who are considered mismatched (whose election was decided by more than 20 percent of the vote) also have professional managers, but a substantial portion of them rely on volunteers for campaign management. Few campaigns are managed by personnel provided by a political party or interest group, regardless of their competitiveness.

Professional staff carry out press relations in most campaigns. Nearly three-quarters of all incumbents in close races hire a paid staffer, frequently a congressional press secretary who is on a leave of absence, to handle their relations with the media. A significant number of incumbents, particularly those involved in competitive contests, hire campaign consultants to issue press releases and handle calls from journalists. Challengers and open-seat candidates are less likely than incumbents to depend on paid staff to handle their press relations. However, about 90 percent of all open-seat prospects and almost 90 percent of all hopeful challengers rely on paid staff or professional consultants for this purpose.

Issue and opposition research is often carried out by a combination of professional staff, outside consultants, and volunteers. Nonincumbents in one-sided races, likely losers who generally have less money than incumbents and candidates running for competitive open seats, rely more heavily on volunteers to conduct research. Many hopeful challengers also depend on party organizations, particularly the Democratic and Republican congressional campaign committees, for research. Since at least the mid-1980s the NRCC, which is the wealthier and more heavily staffed of the two campaign committees, has furnished more candidates with opposition and issue research than has its Democratic counterpart.

Fewer incumbents than nonincumbents depend on their party's congressional campaign committee for research materials because their congressional staffs routinely provide much of the information they need. One of the perquisites of office is having a staff that can write memos on the major issues facing the nation and the district. These are normally drafted to help House members represent their constituents, but the political payoffs from them are significant. In fact, both congressional campaign committees offer training seminars for House members to inform them of how legally to utilize their congressional staff for political purposes.

Fund-raising is a campaign activity that requires skill and connections with individuals and groups that are able and willing to make political contributions. Many campaigns use some mix of a paid campaign staffer, a professional finance director, and volunteers to raise money. Incumbent campaigns rely heavily on professional paid staff and professional consultants, regardless of the competitiveness of their races. Some keep direct-mail experts and fund-raisers who specialize in big donors on the payroll to collect contributions between elections. They also hire staff with accounting skills to file their Federal Election Commission reports. Fewer likely loser challenger campaigns have a salaried employee or professional consultant in charge of raising funds or accounting. But competitive challengers and most open-seat candidates rely heavily on paid aides and professional consultants for fund-raising. One of the ironies of congressional elections is that most challengers, who have the greatest need to raise and spend money, cannot afford to pay an experienced fund raiser.

Polling and advertising are two specialized aspects of campaigning that are handled primarily by political consultants who are hired on a contractual basis. Most candidates running for marginal seats hire an outside consultant to conduct polls. Substantial numbers of incumbents who were shoo-ins and mismatched open-seat candidates did not take polls in 1998. But an even greater number of challengers in lopsided races, who could have benefited from accurate public opinion information, did not take them. Most likely losers opt not to conduct a survey in order to save money for some other campaign activity. Consultants typically consider this an ill-advised approach to campaigning. In the words of one pollster, "It's like flying without the benefit of radar."

Incumbents are the most likely to have professionally produced campaign communications. The vast majority of incumbents hire a media consultant or use some combination of media consultant and campaign aide to produce television commercials, radio advertisements, and direct mail. Challengers and open-seat candidates in closely contested races are about as likely to hire professional media consultants as are incumbents who find themselves in similar circumstances. Challengers in one-sided contests, who face the biggest hurdles in conveying a message and developing name recognition among voters, are by far the least likely to employ the services of a media consultant.

Campaign staff, parties, PACs, and other groups figure prominently in the field activities of virtually all campaigns. Incumbents depend as much, if not more, on these organizations than do challenger and open-seat candidates. Where these campaigns differ is that incumbents in close races rely somewhat less on volunteers than do their nonincumbent counterparts. Democratic House candidates also receive significantly more help with mobilizing voters from unions, reflecting their party's historical ties with the labor movement.

Most House campaigns depend on volunteers for legal counseling. More incumbents than nonincumbents keep an election-law expert on the payroll or on retainer, but the differences between competitive incumbents and competitive open-seat candidates are not that large. Challengers and open-seat candidates in one-sided contests rely on volunteers the most for legal counsel. The fact that only 24 percent of all House campaigns were waged without the assistance of an attorney reflects the complexity of modern elections and the legal codes that govern them.

The overall professionalism of contemporary House campaigns is reflected in the fact that the average campaign uses paid staff or political consultants to carry out roughly five of the preceding nine activities (see the bottom of Table 3-1). The typical incumbent in jeopardy and open-seat prospect uses skilled professionals to carry out seven of these activities. Hopeful challengers use an average of about six. Nonincumbents in one-sided contests, particularly challenger races, are substantially less reliant on professional help. Nonincumbents who are officeholders and unelected politicians assemble more professional campaign organizations than do political amateurs.[8]

The organization that Rep. Ed Royce assembled to conduct his 1998 reelection campaign in California's 39th congressional district is typical of those put together by most shoo-in incumbents. A Republican and former state senator, Royce since 1992 has represented a wealthy, predominantly white district that has a high proportion of white-collar workers. The district has been safe for Republicans for decades. Following his initial victory, Royce has always won with at least 62 percent of the vote.

Royce began the 1998 election with the same campaign team he had used during the last few elections. David Gilliard of Gilliard, Banning, and Associates, a Sacramento full-service consulting firm, carried out most of the campaign's election activities. Gilliard was responsible for strategy, direct mail, press relations, and media development. Jim Terry, a veteran of several California statehouse campaigns, worked part-time as the campaign's on-site manager. The campaign did no specialized issue or opposition research, and it took no polls.

The congressman did most of his own fund-raising. Volunteers filed his FEC reports, helped arrange fund-raising events, handed out literature, distributed yard signs, and handled other grass-roots activities. The campaign did not establish its own headquarters, choosing instead to work out of the Orange County Republican headquarters. This strategy enabled it to coordinate its get-out-the-vote efforts with those of other Republican campaigns as part the GOP's "Victory '98" voter mobilization program. Had Royce perceived the race to be more competitive, he would have put together a larger campaign team, established his own headquarters, and campaigned more aggressively.[9]

The campaign team that Royce's opponent, Cecy Groom, put together was underfunded and understaffed, as is typical of most campaigns waged by likely-loser challengers. Groom, a Filipino immigrant who had served twelve years on her local school board, including two terms as president, recognized that she was facing an uphill battle. She had declared her candidacy just two months before the district's open primary and had to compete for the nomination with another Democrat, who had already received the local Democratic Party's endorsement. The contested primary helped increase her name recognition in the district, but it cost her valuable campaign dollars, of which she had few to spare.[10]

Groom staffed her campaign largely with amateurs. Originally run by a paid but inexperienced manager, her campaign went through three managers before she took over the role herself. Groom hired American Mutual Admiration Company of Redondo Beach for strategic advice and direct mail. She contracted Media One to customize generic ads that were originally produced by the DCCC. Groom relied on about 150–200 friends, Democratic activists, and other volunteers for the rest of her campaign efforts, including fund-raising, direct-mail, press relations, research, and get-out-the-vote drives. The Filipino community was active in Groom's campaign, as are most ethnic communities when one of their own runs for office. The Groom campaign took no polls, marshaling its meager resources solely to communicate its message.[11]

The 1998 campaign waged by Rep. David Price, D-N.C., contrasts sharply with those of Groom and Royce but is typical of campaigns run by House incumbents in jeopardy. Price was first elected in 1986, when he defeated GOP representative Bill Cobey. He then lost to challenger Fred Heineman in the Republican tidal wave of 1994 and later reclaimed his seat from Heineman in 1996. In 1998 Price faced Republican challenger Thomas Roberg, a wealthy North Carolina businessman.

The state's 4th congressional district includes Chapel Hill, Durham, parts of Raleigh (the state capital), some smaller cities, and several suburban and rural areas. During the last two decades, large population influxes and frequent redistricting (a result of federal court rulings involving two nearby black-majority districts) have made it difficult for those holding the seat to build name recognition and bonds of trust with their constituents. For these reasons, the district is one of the nation's most competitive.

Price believed that Roberg would be a strong challenger in 1998. Shortly after Roberg joined the race, Price stated, "He's the most presentable opponent I've ever had. He's personable and articulate. He has lots of money and he's very determined. He's good with sound bites, but his weakness is that he tends to slip up once he has to delve beyond the surface of the issues."[12] In anticipation of Roberg's challenge, Price hired some of the nation's leading political consultants. Saul Shorr, of Shorr and Associates of Philadelphia, produced the campaign's television and radio commercials; the Tyson Organization of Fort Worth provided the phone banks used for voter contact; and Cooper-Secrest of Alexandria, Virginia, did Price's polling. "Mac" McCorkle of McCorkle Policy Consulting, based in Durham, North Carolina, provided general strategic advice.[13]

The campaign's paid staff—all from the 4th district—included a press secretary, treasurer, two field operatives, and two individuals who assisted with fundraising, research, and other activities. Jean Louise Beard took a leave of absence from Price's congressional office to serve as the campaign's finance director. William Moore, chief of staff in Price's congressional office, also provided significant input into the campaign. The campaign's staff was assisted by approximately 150 volunteers, including many from the National Treasury Employees' Union and the AFL-CIO. The volunteers stuffed envelopes, staffed phone banks, hosted fund-raising events in their homes, and accompanied the candidate as he knocked on doors in their neighborhoods. To mobilize voters, the Price organization worked closely with the campaign of Democratic Senate challenger John Edwards and with the North Carolina Democratic Party's coordinated campaign.[14]

Roberg's campaign was similar to many campaigns waged by hopeful challengers. Roberg had not previously run for elective office, but he was not a political neophyte. His four years of chairing the Wake County Republican Party had familiarized him with the rigors of campaign politics. Roberg assembled a fairly professional campaign, relying heavily on the political talent available in the Raleigh area. He initially hired Rotterman and Associates for general consulting. The firm was responsible for formulating overall campaign strategy, managing media relations, and helping to organize events. Teller Opinion did the campaign's polling, while Todd Strumke, a local ex-Marine, brought order to its day-to-day operations. Dick Ellis, a former television and radio announcer who had substantial political experience, helped with press relations, organized events, and played an important role in producing the ads the campaign used during the last five weeks of the campaign. The NRCC and the Heritage Foundation provided some issue research, and the NRCC gave the campaign opposition research on Price. The candidate's wife also did a substantial amount of opposition research and performed other vital campaign duties. Roughly 350 volunteers, many of whom knew Roberg from his days as Wake County party chair, helped with fund-raising, staffed telephone banks, and carried out other grass-roots efforts. The campaign's treasurer was also a volunteer.[15]

As is the case with many nonincumbent campaigns, the Roberg organization was plagued by internal dissension. The biggest disagreement was between the candidate and his general consultants over the tone of their television and radio ads. Roberg wanted to use a mix of issue-oriented ads and attack ads, and the Rotterman team favored waging a predominantly negative campaign. About three weeks before election day the candidate fired his consultants. He relied on Ellis and his other staff to design the rest of his media ads.[16]

The campaigns waged by Democrat Tammy Baldwin and Republican Jo Musser in Wisconsin's 2nd congressional district are representative of those undertaken by most open-seat prospects. Both campaigns were professionally staffed. Baldwin hired veteran campaign manager Paul Devlin to oversee her campaign and seven other full-time staff to handle press relations, raise money, coordinate field and volunteer activities, and carry out other relatively nontechnical campaign duties. She also enlisted the services of several national consulting firms: the Feldman Group of Washington, D.C., handled polling; Will Robinson of McWilliams, Cosgrove, Smith, and Robinson, also of Washington, provided media advertising and general consulting services; Terris and Jaye of San Francisco handled direct mail; and the Tyson Organization did the mass phoning for the campaign's get-out-the-vote effort. Baldwin's operation also benefited from an extraordinary three thousand volunteers. Following the campaign strategy used successfully by Rep. Walter Capps, D- Calif., and by Lois Capps, his wife and successor in the state's 22nd congressional district, the Baldwin campaign sought to reach out to students. It eventually recruited seventeen hundred students from the University of Wisconsin to help with its get-out-the-vote drive and other grass-roots efforts.[17] The candidate and the campaign's staff, consultants, and volunteers performed like a well-oiled political machine, as is often the case when an experienced politician runs for higher office.

Musser's campaign also had a full coterie of paid staff, political consultants, and volunteers. However, like Roberg's campaign, it never jelled into a cohesive working unit. Musser employed six full-time aides to carry out campaign activities, such as management, press relations, fund-raising, and field operations.

David Welch and Associates, with offices in Pennsylvania and West Virginia, provided media advertising services and general consulting advice, while American Viewpoints of Alexandria, Virginia, took Musser's polls. The campaign also recruited 375 volunteers. Its major problems were that it lacked clear lines of authority and was plagued by dissension, as evidenced by the fact that it went through four campaign managers before veteran manager Ruth DeWitt came on board four weeks before the primary.

CAMPAIGN BUDGETS

The professionalism of contemporary congressional campaigns is reflected in how they budget their money. House candidates spend 53 percent of their campaign funds on communicating with voters and 40 percent on fund-raising, staff salaries, travel, and other miscellaneous expenses (see Figure 3-1).[18] Polling and other research account for about 7 percent of campaign costs. The substantial amounts budgeted for electronic media reveal the important role played by modern communication techniques in most House campaigns. The typical campaign spends approximately 17 percent of its budget on television and 7 percent on radio. Of course, the precise amount that a campaign spends on TV depends largely on how closely the boundaries of the district match those of the local media market. The next-largest expense comes from direct mail, which accounts for almost 10 percent of its total costs. Newspaper ads account for almost 4 percent. The remaining 15 percent is spent largely on campaign literature, registration and get-out-the-vote drives, billboards, yard signs, and other field activities.

One of the most interesting facts about congressional elections is that the various kinds of candidates differ little in their approaches to budgeting. The largest differences are that nonincumbents allocate about 12 percent more than do incumbents for campaign communications and compensate by scrimping on overhead and polling. Challengers also spend more on campaign literature than do incumbents and open-seat candidates. Candidates in contests decided by 20 percent or less of the two-party vote allocate a larger portion of their funds to television than do candidates in one-sided races.

Of course, candidates tailor their campaign budgets to suit their districts. Both the Price and Roberg campaigns budgeted almost half of their resources for electronic communications, taking advantage of the relatively inexpensive media market that encompasses the district. Price spent 48 percent of his budget on television and none on radio; Roberg spent 31 percent of his money on TV and 18 percent on radio.[19] Neither the Royce nor the Groom campaign

FIGURE 3-1

The Budget of a Typical House Campaign

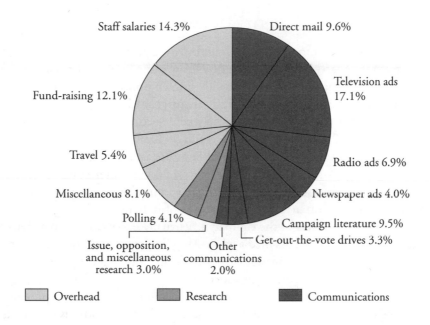

Staff salaries 14.3% Direct mail 9.6%

Television ads 17.1%

Fund-raising 12.1%

Travel 5.4%

Radio ads 6.9%

Miscellaneous 8.1% Newspaper ads 4.0%

Polling 4.1% Campaign literature 9.5%

Get-out-the-vote drives 3.3%

Issue, opposition, and miscellaneous research 3.0% Other communications 2.0%

☐ Overhead ☐ Research ☐ Communications

Source: The 1998 Congressional Campaign Study.
Notes: Figure is for major-party candidates in contested general elections. N - 294.

spent any money on network television because of the inefficiency of advertising in Los Angeles's media market, which is extremely expensive and spans many congressional districts. Each campaign spent about 10 percent of its budget on cable television. Direct mail constituted most of the campaigns' communication expenditures.[20]

The overall similarity in campaign budgets is remarkable given the different sums that incumbent, open-seat, and challenger campaigns spend. The widespread availability of campaign technology, the tremendous growth of the political consulting industry, and the extensive dissemination of information through the American Association of Political Consultants, *Campaigns & Elections* magazine, and campaign seminars sponsored by those organizations, political parties, and interest groups have fostered a set of shared expectations about how a campaign should spend its funds. These expectations are reinforced when campaign personnel negotiate their salaries and draw up budgets, when political consulting firms set their rates, and when party officials and PAC managers scrutinize campaign budgets prior to making a contribution.

SENATE CAMPAIGNS

Senate campaigns are more expensive, run by more professional organizations, and attract more party assistance than do House campaigns. Senate candidates rely primarily on paid staffs and nationally known political consultants to develop their strategies and carry out their campaigns. Most Senate incumbents keep a substantial organization intact between elections. The typical senator spent more than $2.1 million in overhead and $950,000 on fund-raising in the period leading up to the 1998 election.[21] Sen. Barbara Boxer, D-Calif., spent the most, nearly $4 million on staff salaries, rent, computer equipment, and associated office expenses, plus an additional $3.9 million on fund-raising.[22]

Senate campaigns often have combinations of individuals sharing responsibilities for various aspects of the campaign. Virtually every campaign assigns a paid aide to work with a mass media advertising firm to develop the candidate's communications. Opposition research is typically conducted by a campaign aide, often in conjunction with a private consultant or party official. Campaign staff, consultants, volunteers, party committees, and interest group representatives make substantial contributions to Senate candidates' fund-raising efforts. Most Senate campaigns also hire one or more field managers to participate in coordinated voter mobilization efforts that draw on the resources of national, state, and local party committees. Democratic Senate candidates also coordinate their field work with labor unions, and most Senate candidates of both parties rely on volunteers to help with their voter registration and get-out-the-vote efforts.

The major difference in spending between Senate and House contests is in the allocation of media expenditures. The average Senate campaign spends about 30 percent of its money on television advertising, as opposed to the one-fifth spent by the typical House campaign. Senate campaigns also allocate far smaller portions of their budgets to radio advertising, campaign literature, newspaper ads, billboards, and yard signs than do House contestants. The differences in communications expenditures reflect both the greater practicality and the necessity of using television advertising in statewide races.

SUMMARY

Contemporary congressional elections are primarily waged by candidate-centered organizations that draw on the expertise of political consultants for polling, mass media advertising, and other specialized functions. Few candidates depend on parties and interest groups to carry out many campaign activities; the important exception is voter mobilization. Incumbents and open-seat candidates in competitive races wage the most professional campaigns; challengers in lopsided contests rely on the most amateur organizations. Despite these variations in organizations and tremendous disparities in funding, campaigns are more alike than different in how they budget their resources. The match between district boundaries and media markets and the preferences of individual candidates and their campaign aides have bigger effects on campaigns' budgetary allocations than does either incumbency or the closeness of the race.

CHAPTER FOUR

The Parties Campaign

Political parties in the United States have one overriding goal: to elect their candidates to public office. Policy goals are secondary to winning control of the government. Nevertheless, the parties' electoral influence has waxed and waned as the result of legal, demographic, and technological changes in American society and reforms instituted by the parties themselves. During the golden age of political parties, local party organizations dominated elections in many parts of the country. They picked the candidates, gauged public opinion, raised money, disseminated campaign communications, and mobilized voters, most of whom had strong partisan allegiances. "The parties were, in short, the medium through which the campaign was waged."[1]

By the 1950s, most state and local party organizations had been ushered to the periphery of the candidate-centered system. Party organizations at the national level had not yet developed into repositories of money and campaign services for congressional candidates. Most contenders for the House and Senate were largely self-recruited and relied on campaign organizations that they themselves had assembled to wage their bids for office. Professional consultants helped fill the void left by deteriorating party organizations, providing advice about fund-raising, media, polling, and campaign management to clients who were willing to pay for it.[2]

During the late 1970s and early 1980s, first Republican and then Democratic national party organizations in Washington, D.C., began to adapt to the contemporary candidate-centered system.[3] This system emphasizes campaign activities requiring technical expertise and in-depth research. Many candidates, especially nonincumbents running for the House, lack the money or professional know-how needed to run a modern congressional campaign. Candidates' needs created the opportunity for party organizations to assume a more important role in congressional elections.[4] The national parties responded to these needs, not by doing away with the candidate-centered election system but by assuming a more important role in it.[5] In this chapter I discuss the role that party organizations play in congressional elections, including their influence on the agendas around which campaigns are fought, the kinds of assistance they give to House and Senate candidates, the strategies that inform their giving, how they select candidates for support, and the effects of their assistance on candidates' campaigns.

NATIONAL AGENDA SETTING

Contemporary House elections are usually fought on local issues, and Senate elections typically focus on statewide concerns. When congressional candidates discuss national issues, they usually emphasize their local implications. Since the early 1980s, Democratic and Republican congressional leaders have produced lengthy issues handbooks and "talking points" for congressional candidates that focus on national issues and include instructions on how to use party rhetoric and statistics compiled in Washington to address local concerns.[6] Many candidates found these materials useful, but the materials were not intended to produce nationalized campaigns and did not do so.

Nevertheless, congressional elections are not always dominated by local issues. In 1932 the Great Depression dominated the national political agenda and the outcomes of many House and Senate races. In 1974 the Democrats nationalized the elections on Watergate, the Nixon administration's ethical lapses, and reform issues. During the 1994 elections, House Republicans set a national agenda that had two foci. The first focus was on the ethical and policy failures of the Clinton administration and House Democrats. Republican leaders published pamphlets criticizing the president's policy performance and leadership and the "special interest" culture they asserted had developed in the House under forty years of Democratic control.[7] These publications provided the anti-Washington rhetoric used by many GOP candidates and inspired the high-tech television commercials that made Democratic congressional candidates appear to metamorphose, or "morph," into President Bill Clinton. The publications also provided much of the substance for discussions broadcast over conservative radio shows and on *GOP-TV,* the Republicans' cable television show.

The House Republicans' second focus was on the Contract with America, the ten-point program developed under the direction of then–minority whip Newt Gingrich. The contract included a call for a balanced budget amendment, welfare reform, term limits, and seven other planks based on popular ideas. More than 370 Republican House members and candidates affixed their signatures to the contract at a formal ceremony that took place on the Capitol steps, and many campaigned on contract issues.[8] Even though only one-third of the public had heard of the contract prior to the election, the document and supporting research provided GOP candidates with valuable talking points. The Republicans' nationalized campaign helped them win control of both houses of Congress for the first time in forty years.

The elections of 1996 were less nationalized than those of 1994. Led by President Clinton, the Democrats sought to paint congressional Republicans as "extremists" who wanted to cut appropriations for Medicare, Medicaid, and education to pay for tax breaks for the rich; who would turn corporate polluters loose on the environment; and who had shut down the federal government to force their will on the American people. Congressional Democrats portrayed themselves as the champions of working Americans in their Families First Agenda. The agenda focused on moderate policy proposals in areas such as health care, education, and the environment. The Republicans had hoped in 1996 to set a campaign agenda focused on the bills they had passed as part of the Contract with America. However, they were put on the defensive by public reaction to the government shutdowns and the Democrats' early media campaign. These developments led many GOP candidates to try to "denationalize" their elections by emphasizing their independence from Speaker Gingrich.

Other factors also prevented the 1996 election from becoming fully nationalized. A situation of divided government—a Democratic president and a Republican-controlled Congress—made it difficult for either party to claim full credit or to place full blame on the other party for the government's performance. The modesty of the Democrats' policy proposals and divisions within both parties' ranks prevented partisan lines from crystallizing as clearly as they had in 1932, 1974, and 1994. More important, the GOP's acceptance of a compromise budget that was heavily influenced by the Clinton administration and the president's signing of the Republican welfare bill helped to blur partisan distinctions.

The 1998 elections also were held under conditions of divided government, making it difficult for either party to promote a nationalized campaign agenda. Given that President Clinton was besieged by impeachment proceedings and a tawdry sex scandal, most Democratic House and Senate candidates worked to distance themselves from Washington and to run on issues of concern to local voters. Nevertheless, Democratic congressional leaders tried to focus the attention of voters and the media on education, the environment, Social Security, jobs and the economy, and Medicare and other health-care-related issues— issues that traditionally work to their party's advantage. They also distributed

TABLE 4-1
The Most Important Issues to Voters in the 1998 Elections

	All	Democrats	Republicans	Independents
Education	22.8%	30.5%	14.6%	21.6%
Jobs and the economy	16.2	20.7	11.2	16.4
Social Security	12.2	16.1	9.5	10.7
Health care	7.5	10.7	3.9	6.5
Taxes	15.0	10.5	20.2	15.5
Morals and ethics	20.4	6.6	34.0	22.7
Clinton/Lewinsky	5.9	4.9	6.6	6.7
(N)	(4,765)	(1,840)	(1,610)	(1,130)

Source: Voter News Service exit surveys.

policy memos and talking points on these issues to arm candidates with useful facts, figures, and sound bites.

The Republicans had heated debates over whether to try to nationalize the election.[9] Gingrich, the party's conservative wing, and most members of the class of 1994 favored a nationalized media campaign. Many others preferred a localized approach that would allow candidates to choose from many traditional GOP issues—such as balancing the budget, advocating tax cuts, reducing the size and scope of the federal government, waging war on crime and drugs, and promoting traditional family values—and tailor them to their individual districts.[10] Ultimately, Gingrich's side won out and the party invested $22 million in "Operation Breakout," a Washington-driven issue advocacy campaign.[11] The first wave of issue advocacy ads highlighted Republican accomplishments, such as the balanced budget. The second wave contrasted popular Republican issue stances with unpopular Democratic policy positions. The final wave reminded voters of the president's sex scandal and impeachment.

The Democrats had a slightly greater impact on the political agenda than did the Republicans. Exit polls showed that voters identified education as the most important election issue in 1998, followed by moral and ethical issues, jobs and the economy, taxes, Social Security, and health care (see Table 4-1).[12] More Democratic than Republican voters selected education, jobs and the economy, Social Security, and health care as their top concerns—issues that have traditionally favored the Democratic Party. In contrast, more Republican than Democratic voters chose taxes and morality and ethics, which traditionally have been positively associated with the GOP. Despite its extensive coverage in the press, few voters considered the Clinton/Lewinsky scandal the most important issue in the race. Independent voters, who define the battleground in most close contests, slightly favored issues associated with the Democrats' agenda. The fact that the Democrats' traditional issues topped the national agenda helped them to pick up House seats in a midterm election—an unusual feat for the president's party.

THE NATIONAL, CONGRESSIONAL, AND
SENATORIAL CAMPAIGN COMMITTEES

Party organizations in the nation's capital have developed into major sources of campaign money, services, and advice for congressional candidates. The Democratic National Committee (DNC) and the Republican National Committee (RNC) focus most of their efforts on presidential elections but also pay attention to gubernatorial, statehouse, and a small number of mayoral elections. They also set the national campaign agenda and strengthen state and local organizations. The national committees' involvement in House and Senate elections tends to be relatively limited. It includes conducting candidate training seminars; furnishing candidates with party platforms, campaign manifestos, and talking points; and coordinating with congressional, senatorial, state, and local party campaign committees to mobilize partisan voters. Congressional candidates in search of money, election services, or assistance in running their campaigns rarely turn to their national committee for help.[13]

The parties' congressional and senatorial campaign committees, sometimes referred to as the "Hill committees," have developed into major support centers for House and Senate candidates.[14] The congressional campaign committees focus their efforts on House races, and the two senatorial campaign committees focus on Senate contests. All four Hill committees set fund-raising records in 1998, as did the parties' national, state, and local organizations. The DCCC amassed a budget of just over $42 million, and its Republican rival raised almost $93 million. The two senatorial committees—the Democratic Senatorial Campaign Committee (DSCC) and the National Republican Senatorial Committee (NRSC)—raised approximately $61.5 million and $91.2 million, respectively.[15]

The chairs, vice chairs, and members of the Hill committees are all members of Congress who are selected by their colleagues in the House or Senate. For the most part, the members of each committee act like a board of directors, setting priorities and giving the committee staff the support it needs to participate in campaigns. However, one area where members play an essential role is fundraising. Congressional and senatorial campaign committee chairs, vice chairs, and other party leaders have always raised money from individuals, PACs, and other interest groups, but in recent years they have tapped into a new source—their colleagues in the House and Senate.[16]

During the 1998 elections, congressional leaders of both parties established quotas for contributions by incumbents. The House Republicans set the highest quotas, ranging from $2,500 per year for first-term members to $7,500 per year for party leaders and committee chairs. The NRCC also established rates for participation in Operation Breakout, which topped out at $100,000 for party leaders and committee chairs. Although some legislators, such as Rep. Philip Crane, R-Ill., grumbled about being dunned for contributions, the competition for majority control of the House and the Republicans' desire to amass the sixty Senate seats needed to bring cloture on Democratic filibusters gave Hill committee chairs persuasive arguments for fund-raising.

Democratic leaders coaxed members of Congress, congressional retirees, and other politicians to donate from their election accounts and the "leadership" or "member" PACs they sponsor more than $2.9 million in hard money to the DCCC, $923,500 to the DSCC, $21,691 to the DNC, and almost $1.3 million to state and local Democratic party committees.[17] Republican leaders were even more successful, raising from members of the House and Senate, congressional retirees, and leadership PACs more than $9.0 million in hard money for the NRCC, $1.3 million for the NRSC, $470,500 for the RNC, and more than $2.1 million for state and local GOP organizations. Members of Congress and other party leaders also helped the parties to raise millions of dollars in hard and soft money during the 1998 elections. This massive redistribution of wealth demonstrates that Hill committee leaders can get national legislators to look beyond their own campaigns to consider ways to help party organizations and the candidates they assist. A sense of enlightened self-interest encouraged members to raise money for national, state, and local party organizations. Once involving only a few party leaders and senior members, in 1998 this redistribution of wealth involved hundreds of lawmakers, including some first-term legislators who aspire to leadership posts.

In addition to their members, the congressional and senatorial campaign committees are composed of many highly skilled political professionals. During the 1998 elections the DCCC and DSCC employed 126 and 45 full-time staff, and their Republican counterparts had 55 and 80 full-time employees. The staffs oversee the committees' daily operations, are influential in formulating party strategies, and play a major role in the implementation of those strategies. The staffs are divided along functional lines; different divisions are responsible for administration, fund-raising, research, communications, and campaign activities.[18] As major centers of political expertise and campaign support, the Hill committees are expensive to operate. They typically spend between 45 percent and 55 percent of their budgets on voter lists, computers, media studios, staff salaries, fund-raising, loan repayments, and other overhead.

STRATEGY, DECISION MAKING, AND TARGETING

The Hill committees have a common overriding goal of maximizing the number of seats their parties hold in Congress.[19] They become heavily involved in some elections, giving selected candidates large contributions and making substantial expenditures on their behalf, including expenditures on issue advocacy ads. They also give these candidates strategic, research, technical, and transactional assistance. The last form of help enables candidates to raise the money and other resources needed to conduct a congressional campaign. Finally, the Hill committees participate with the national committees and state and local party organizations in generic, party-focused election activities that are designed to help candidates for Congress and other offices get elected.

The campaign committees try to focus most of their efforts on competitive House and Senate contests. Protecting incumbents in jeopardy is a major priority. Pressures from nervous incumbents can skew the distribution of committee resources from competitive challenger and open-seat candidates toward members of Congress who hold safe seats. The funds available to a committee can also affect the way it distributes its resources. Other institutional forces that affect committee decision making are the aspirations of its chair and other members. The two individuals who had the most significant roles in modernizing the NRCC and DCCC, former representatives Guy Vander Jagt and Tony Coelho, used their chairmanships as vehicles for advancement in the ranks of the House leadership, as did successor chairs Bill Paxon, R-N.Y., Vic Fazio, D-Calif., and Martin Frost, D-Texas.[20] Reps. Patrick Kennedy, D-R.I., and Thomas Davis, R-Va., committee chairs in the 106th Congress, showed signs of following their predecessors' example.

National political and economic conditions are additional factors that influence which candidates get campaign resources. When the president is popular and the economy is strong, the campaign committees of the president's party usually invest more resources in challenger and open-seat races. Conversely, the out-party committees use more of their resources to support incumbents. When national conditions do not favor the president's party, the patterns are reversed: the in-party committees take a defensive posture that favors incumbents, and the out-party committees go on the offensive, using more of their resources to help nonincumbents.[21] The unpredictable nature of national political conditions and economic trends and of events that take place in states and congressional districts means that committee decision making and targeting are necessarily imperfect. As a result, some safe incumbents and uncompetitive nonincumbents inevitably receive committee assistance, whereas some competitive nonincumbents get little or no help.

The conditions surrounding the elections held in the early and mid-1990s made strategic decision making and targeting difficult, especially for the two House campaign committees.[22] Redistricting, always fraught with ambiguities, was complicated by racial redistricting issues that delayed many 1992 House elections while districts were being redrawn. It also introduced complications into later elections for the same reason. Court battles over majority-minority House districts in Florida, Georgia, Illinois, New York, North Carolina, and Virginia required that the boundaries of numerous neighboring districts be moved before the 1998 elections.

Redrawn districts or newly created seats are only two of several factors that complicate the committees' tasks. The president's popularity often shifts up and down, making it difficult for the committees to decide whether to pursue an offensive or a defensive strategy. Congressional scandals and the hostility that voters often direct toward Congress result in some incumbents unexpectedly finding themselves in jeopardy. These circumstances give some challengers a correspondingly unexpected boost. The late retirements of some House members and the primary defeats of others further complicate the committees' efforts.

Because of the uncertainty surrounding post-redistricting elections, the NRCC and DCCC in the early 1990s drew up huge "watch" lists of "opportunity" or competitive races. During the 1992 elections, each committee's watch list initially included approximately 300 elections. The committees shortened the lists over the course of the campaign season, but going into the last week of the election each list still had more than 150 opportunity races—more than three times the number included at that point in the 1990 election. During the 1994 and 1996 elections the committees initially focused on about 160 seats apiece before they pared their lists down to about 75 races.[23] In early 1998 the parties concentrated on about 100 races each before honing in on around 65 competitive contests.[24]

Individual candidates are selected for placement on the committees' watch lists on the basis of several criteria. The competitiveness of the district and incumbency are the first two considerations. Candidates running in districts that were decided by close margins in the last election or who are competing for open seats are likely to be placed on a committee's watch list. The strength of the candidate is another consideration in the case of nonincumbents. Those who have had political experience or have celebrity status are likely to be targeted for assistance. Challengers and open-seat contestants who assemble professional campaign organizations are also likely to receive support. Having a professional organization assures the committee that the resources it contributes will be used properly; this is especially true if campaign committee officials are familiar with the consultants who have been hired.[25]

A variety of idiosyncratic factors also come into play when the committees select the candidates who will be given the most support initially. An incumbent who is accused of committing an ethical transgression, perceived to be out of touch with people in the district, in poor health, or in trouble for some other reason is a likely candidate for extra committee help. These difficulties often provoke a response by the other party's campaign committee, resulting in the incumbent's opponent also benefiting from extra party money and campaign services. Although party leaders work aggressively to recruit women and minorities to run for Congress, neither party uses gender or race as a criterion for determining who gets campaign assistance. Ideology is also not used to select candidates for support. Women, minorities, liberals, and conservatives are assisted only to the degree that their races are expected to be competitive.[26] As Kentucky senator Mitch McConnell, NRSC chair in the 105th and 106th Congresses, explains,

> In doing my job as the chairman of the senatorial committee, the only criteria is, How close are you? I can't joust with windmills; and I'm not going to fund landslides. And we make the decision every day by the numbers. I get tracking polls from the states where we're competitive across the country. I have no particular bias in favor of or against any of our candidates. The only issue is, How close are you?[27]

The committees' lists of competitive elections are revised throughout the election season. Regional coordinators who monitor congressional races within designated parts of the country advise their colleagues in Washington about the latest developments in individual elections. As a result, some candidates drop in priority and are cut off from party help and others gain more committee attention and support. Because of the tremendous uncertainty surrounding recent House elections, both the Democratic and Republican congressional campaign committees have begun to distribute their resources incrementally. Rather than drop a large quantity of money or extensive election services in a candidate's lap early in the campaign season, the committees distribute them piecemeal in response to the candidate's ability to meet a series of discrete fundraising and organizational goals. Incumbents usually meet these quickly, but the goals pose more formidable hurdles for challengers and open-seat candidates. Nonincumbents who meet their goals in a timely fashion are usually within reach of victory at the end of the election season and receive substantial party support. Of course, a party committee's ability to give them these contributions is limited by available funds.

CAMPAIGN CONTRIBUTIONS AND COORDINATED EXPENDITURES

Party contributions to candidates in congressional elections are restricted by the Federal Election Campaign Act. National, congressional, and state party campaign committees can each give $5,000 to a House candidate at each stage of the election process: primary, runoff, and general election (see Table 1-1).[28] The parties' national and senatorial campaign committees can give a combined total of $17,500 in an election cycle to a candidate for the Senate. State committees can contribute an additional $5,000 to Senate candidates.

Parties can also spend larger sums to expressly help individual candidates. These outlays, referred to as "coordinated expenditures" because they can be made in direct coordination with a candidate's campaign, typically are for campaign services that a Hill committee or some other party organization gives to a candidate or purchases from a political consultant on the candidate's behalf. Coordinated expenditures often take the form of polls, TV commercials, radio ads, fund-raising events, direct-mail solicitations, or issue research. They differ from campaign contributions in that both the party and the candidate share control over them, giving the party the ability to influence some aspects of how the campaign is run. Originally set in 1974 at $10,000 for all national party organizations, the limits for coordinated expenditures on behalf of House candidates are adjusted for inflation and reached $32,550 in 1998.[29] The limits for national party coordinated expenditures in Senate elections vary by state population and are also indexed to inflation. In 1998 they ranged from $65,100 per committee in the smallest states to $1,517,937 in California.

State party committees are authorized to spend the same amounts in coordinated expenditures in House and Senate races as are the parties' national organizations, but some state party committees do not have the funds to do so. In races in which a state party lacks resources and a parties' congressional or senatorial campaign committee deems it important for the party to spend as much money as possible, the state and national party organizations form "agency agreements" that transfer the state party's quota for coordinated expenditures to the national party.[30] In situations in which a state party has enough money to make the maximum legal contribution and coordinated expenditure in a targeted congressional race but has other priorities, such as a gubernatorial election or state legislative elections, national party organizations may induce the state party to spend their hard money in the congressional election by offering them a "money swap." In many of these agreements, national party organizations make campaign contributions to state or local candidates or soft money transfers to state party organizations in sums that are equal to or slightly greater than the amounts they request state parties to spend in congressional races. Other money swaps involve exchanges of larger sums.[31] Money swaps have become more common than agency agreements in recent elections, but both methods enable Washington-based party organizations to coordinate a national spending strategy in congressional elections.[32]

From the mid-1970s through the early 1990s, most party activity in congressional elections took the form of cash contributions or coordinated expenditures on polling, fund-raising, research, and other campaign services. The 1996 contests were the first in which the parties made independent expenditures with hard money and spent significant sums of hard and soft money on issue advocacy advertisements. During the 1998 elections, the parties cut back on their hard money contributions and coordinated expenditures in order to spend even more hard and soft money on issue advocacy advertising. This strategic adjustment enabled the parties to direct more of their total resources to close elections. Democratic Party and Republican Party contributions and coordinated expenditures in congressional elections dropped by roughly 17 percent and 20 percent, respectively, from their 1996 levels.

Nevertheless, the parties' total contributions and coordinated expenditures remained significant. The Democrats distributed $945,589 in contributions and almost $4.6 million in coordinated expenditures in the 1998 House races; the Republicans distributed more than $2.1 million and $6.3 million in these contests (see Table 4-2). The parties were close to parity in their spending and coordinated expenditures in the 1998 Senate races, the GOP outspending the Democrats by only $185,149.

Coordinated expenditures are the vehicle of choice for most party activity in congressional elections. Their higher limits than those for cash contributions, the possibility for creating agency agreements, and the control they afford party committees in candidates' campaigns make coordinated expenditures an attractive avenue for party involvement. Coordinated spending also enables the parties to take advantage of economies of scale when purchasing and distributing campaign services. Because the parties purchase the services of political consultants in large quantities, they pay below-market rates, which enables them to provide candidates with services whose true market value exceeds the FECA's coordinated expenditure limits.[33]

TABLE 4-2
Party Spending in the 1998 Congressional Elections

	House		Senate	
	Contributions	Coordinated expenditures	Contributions	Coordinated expenditures
Democratic				
DNC	$6,894	$0	$0	$1,394,776
DCCC	413,281	2,969,951	11,500	0
DSCC	68,000	0	232,500	8,424
State and local	457,414	1,628,426	27,833	8,006,963
Total Democratic	$945,589	$4,598,377	$271,833	$9,410,163
Republican				
RNC	$417,431	$224	$25,063	$3,867,605
NRCC	768,718	5,069,215	14,024	0
NRSC	45,000	0	231,359	36,775
State and local	878,183	1,230,597	233,800	5,458,519
Total Republican	$2,109,332	$6,300,036	$504,246	$9,362,899

Source: Federal Election Commission, "FEC Reports on Political Party Activity for 1997–98," press release, April 9, 1999.

Note: Figures include party spending in all congressional elections, including primaries, runoffs, and uncontested races.

The four Hill committees determine the parties' congressional campaign spending strategies, are the source of most party funds spent in congressional elections (some funds are transferred to state or national party committees before they are contributed to congressional candidates), and deliver most of the parties' campaign services.[34] The campaign committees distribute most of their money to candidates in close elections (see Table 4-3). The Democrats' allocation patterns for House candidates in 1998 indicated they followed a modified defensive strategy. The party directed 43 percent of its money to incumbents. The remaining 57 percent was committed to challengers and candidates for open seats. The minority party usually takes a more aggressive posture than does the majority party. However, in midterm elections, when one of its members occupies the White House, the minority party usually expects to lose seats and spends considerable resources on incumbents. The DCCC's strategy in 1998 reflected early concerns among Democratic legislators that investigations into improprieties in DNC fund-raising and the Clinton/Lewinsky scandals would demoralize the party's base and drive down Democratic turnout. Demo-

TABLE 4-3

The Allocation of Party Money in the 1998 Congressional Elections

	House		Senate	
	Democrats	Republicans	Democrats	Republicans
Incumbents				
In jeopardy	31%	22%	52%	42%
	(45)	(49)	(6)	(4)
Shoo-ins	12	7	—	5
	(105)	(107)	(9)	(10)
Challengers				
Hopefuls	30%	38%	33%	35%
	(49)	(45)	(4)	(6)
Likely losers	6	12	1	5
	(107)	(105)	(10)	(9)
Open-seat candidates				
Prospects	21%	21%	8%	12%
	(23)	(23)	(3)	(3)
Mismatched	—	—	5	—
	(11)	(11)	(2)	(2)
Total ($, thousands)	$5,161	$7,098	$9,652	$9,189
	(340)	(340)	(34)	(34)

Source: Compiled from Federal Election Commission data.

Notes: The categories of candidates are the same as those in Table 1-4. Figures include contributions and coordinated expenditures by all party committees to major-party candidates in contested general elections. They do not include soft money expenditures. Dash = less than 0.5 percent. Some columns do not add to 100 percent because of rounding. The numbers of candidates are in parentheses.

cratic members of Congress recalled that in the midterm elections of 1994, when President Clinton had angered many voters, some incumbents had lost their seats and the party had lost control of Congress. Later in the 1998 election season, when it appeared that the scandals would not undercut Clinton's high popularity ratings and that the public was becoming disenchanted with the Republican onslaught on the president, some of the pressure to devote substantial resources to incumbents abated.[35]

Democratic money was fairly well targeted in 1998. The party committees delivered 31 percent of their funds to incumbents in jeopardy, 30 percent to hopeful challengers, and 21 percent to open-seat prospects. The party's ability to distribute 82 percent of its funds to candidates in elections that were decided by twenty or fewer percentage points was a vast improvement over that of previous years, such as 1992, when it distributed only 53 percent of its funds to candidates in close races.[36] The improved targeting was due to three factors: fewer Democratic incumbents clamoring for party resources; more information on the progress of individual campaigns—information that was collected by a team of three regional field coordinators deployed by the DCCC; and greater resistance by DCCC decision makers to pressures from nervous but safe incumbents.

In contrast to the Democrats' strategy, the plan adopted by Republican party committees in the 1998 House elections was moderately aggressive. Clinton's ethical problems and the expectation that the usual rhythm of past midterm elections would prevail, with the president's party suffering losses, emboldened the GOP early in the election season. In mid-July Speaker Gingrich went so far as to predict that his party would gain as many as forty seats.[37] Others were not quite so optimistic, but many Republicans went on record as stating that their party would pick up between ten and twenty seats.[38] It was not until October that members began to voice concerns about Republican core voters failing to turn out in the upcoming elections. Some GOP legislators believed that a strategy focusing on Clinton's problems would not substitute for tax cuts and other legislative accomplishments, of which there were few, in motivating Republicans to vote.[39] The GOP delivered 59 percent of their funds to hopeful challengers and open-seat prospects and only 22 percent to incumbents in jeopardy. Republican party organizations, which also deployed field coordinators and traditionally distribute their resources effectively, sent only about 19 percent of their funds to candidates in uncompetitive contests, whose chances of victory were unlikely to change even with additional party money.

It is relatively easy for the parties to target their money in Senate elections. DSCC and NRSC officials have to assess their candidates' prospects in only thirty-three or thirty-four races per election, and those races take place within borders that do not shift every ten years because of redistricting. Polling data are also available for all of the races. As a result, virtually all the parties' funds are spent in close elections. In 1998 the Democrats spent all but 6 percent of their money in competitive contests, favoring incumbents in jeopardy, followed by hopeful challengers. The Republicans distributed all but 10 percent of their funds to candidates in close elections, favoring incumbents in jeopardy over hopeful challengers. Both parties perceived open-seat elections to be where some hard-fought battles would take place, and each devoted roughly 12 percent of its resources to them.

In addition to distributing campaign contributions and coordinated expenditures directly to candidates, the Hill committees have recently begun to en-

TABLE 4-4

Party-Connected Contributions in the 1998 Congressional Elections

	House		Senate	
	Democrats	Republicans	Democrats	Republicans
Leadership PAC contributions	$2,602,063	$5,997,906	$374,735	$1,741,214
Candidate contributions	2,172,061	2,111,190	115,513	162,989
Contributions from retirees and members not up for reelection	363,820	138,670	122,288	124,848
Total	$5,137,944	$8,247,766	$612,536	$2,029,051

Source: Compiled from Federal Election Commission data.

Note: Figures are for contributions from leadership PACs, candidates, retired members, and members of Congress not up for reelection in 1998 to candidates in all congressional elections, including those in primaries, runoffs, and uncontested races.

courage the flow of "party-connected" contributions from incumbents' leadership PACs and reelection accounts to needy candidates, such as nonincumbents and some new members. Leadership PACs have been involved in congressional elections since Rep. Henry Waxman, D-Calif., founded the first one in 1978, but they were few in number and distributed relatively little money before the late 1980s.[40] Their numbers had grown to 113 by 1998, when they distributed more than $10.7 million. Although leadership PACs are technically political action committees rather than party organizations—and although candidate-to-candidate contributions are not the same as party contributions—those who make these contributions share several of the party committees' objectives, and many rely on party cues when making them.[41] Their ties to the congressional parties, their reliance on them for information, and the fact that, with few exceptions, all of their contributions flow to members of their party warrant the labeling of these contributions as party-connected.

During the 1998 elections former and current members of Congress—mostly incumbents seeking reelection—and a small number of other prominent politicians contributed more than $16 million from their campaign accounts or leadership PACs to 691 primary and general election candidates (see Table 4-4).[42] The biggest contributors were party leaders and policy entrepreneurs. Reps. Nancy Pelosi, D-Calif., and Christopher Cox, R-Calif., led their respective parties in individual contributions, giving almost $115,000 and $108,000 from their own war chests. Majority Leader Richard Armey of Texas, Speaker

TABLE 4-5

The Distribution of Party-Connected Contributions in the 1998
Congressional Elections

	House		Senate	
	Democrats	Republicans	Democrats	Republicans
Incumbents				
In jeopardy	40%	32%	46%	23%
Shoo-ins	18	12	18	23
Challengers				
Hopefuls	20%	27%	12%	29%
Likely losers	2	5	4	5
Open seats				
Prospects	20%	22%	17%	14%
Mismatched	9	2	3	5
Total (thousands)	$4,808	$8,010	$609	$2,010

Source: Compiled from Federal Election Commission data.

Notes: Figures are for contributions from leadership PACs, candidates, retired members, and members of Congress not up for reelection in 1998 to major-party candidates in contested general elections. Categories and numbers of candidates are the same as those in Table 4-3. Some columns do not add to 100 percent because of rounding.

Gingrich, and Appropriations Committee Chairman Robert Livingston of Louisiana led the GOP in leadership PAC contributions, donating $879,892, $765,500, and $662,830, respectively. Minority Leader Richard Gephardt of Missouri led for the Democrats. His Effective Government Committee contributed $365,568 to Democratic candidates. Leadership '98, a PAC associated with Vice President Al Gore, gave almost $1.2 million—the largest sum contributed by a former member of Congress. Two PACs sponsored by former vice president Dan Quayle, Campaign America and Issues '96, donated $148,143, the next highest amount given by a former member.[43] Needless to say, both Gore and Quayle made these contributions to win member support for their bids for the White House in 2000.

Party-connected contributions were distributed strategically, the vast majority of them going to candidates in competitive contests (see Table 4-5). The major difference between party-connected contributions and money contributed by formal party organizations is that the distribution of party-connected funds favors shoo-in incumbents somewhat more. This difference reflects the fact that individuals who contribute party-connected funds, like party committees, are concerned with maximizing the number of seats under their party's control. However, they also want to do favors for congressional colleagues that they can collect on later, and some of these legislators occupy safe seats.[44] Party-connected contributions demonstrate that parties have become important vehicles for redistributing wealth among congressional candidates.

CAMPAIGN SERVICES

The parties' congressional and senatorial campaign committees provide selected candidates with assistance in specialized campaign activities, such as management, gauging public opinion, issue and opposition research, and communications.[45] They also provide transactional assistance, acting as brokers between candidates and the PACs, individual contributors, political consultants, and powerful incumbents who possess some of the money, political contacts, and campaign expertise that candidates need. The DCCC and the NRCC typically become closely involved in the campaigns of candidates on their watch lists and have little involvement in others. The DSCC and the NRSC offer advice to all of their Senate candidates but focus their attention on those locked in competitive contests.

Campaign Management

Candidates and their campaign organizations can get help from their Hill committees with hiring and training campaign staff, making strategic and tactical decisions, and other management-related activities. The committees maintain directories of campaign managers, fund-raising specialists, media experts, pollsters, voting list vendors, and other political consultants who candidates and managers can use to hire staff and purchase campaign services. Committee officials sometimes recommend particular consultants, especially to House challengers and open-seat candidates, some of whom are involved in their first major campaign.[46]

The Hill committees' field representatives and political staffs in Washington also serve as important sources of strategic advice. Because they follow House and Senate elections nationwide and can draw on experiences from previous election years, the committees are among the few organizations that have the knowledge and institutional memory to advise candidates and their managers on how to deal with some of the dilemmas they encounter. The political staffs of the congressional campaign committees are usually most heavily involved in the planning and tactical decision making of open-seat and challenger candidates. However, they also provide a great deal of advice to House freshmen, members running in heavily redrawn districts, and those in close races.

The six Washington party organizations train candidates and managers in the latest campaign techniques. The DCCC and the NRCC hold training seminars at their headquarters for incumbents that cover such topics as staying in touch with constituents, getting the most political mileage out of franked mail, defending unpopular votes, and PAC fund-raising. The two congressional campaign committees also work with the national committees to host seminars for challengers and open-seat candidates around the country. These focus on more basic subjects, such as giving the "stump" speech, filing campaign finance reports with the FEC, and building coalitions. Even long-term members of the House and Senate find the seminars beneficial as reminders of what they ought to be doing.

Over the course of the 1998 election cycle, the RNC established campaign management "colleges" and held forty-eight "nuts and bolts" training seminars in thirty-five states, serving more than five thousand Republican candidates and activists.[47] The NRCC also held four specialized training seminars in Washington for challengers and open-seat candidates.[48] The NRSC conducted a campaign seminar designed primarily for incumbents, which was attended by senators or political aides from fifteen states, and a training session geared mainly to nonincumbents but open to all Senate candidates, which was attended by representatives from twenty-two campaigns.[49] The Democrats, led by the DNC, held three campaign seminars in Washington and twenty-two in different states, training approximately three thousand campaign operatives in general management, research, communications, fund-raising, and field activities.[50] The DSCC held two training sessions: one for incumbents, attended by all but one senator up for reelection in 1998 and by the staff of all fifteen incumbents' reelection campaigns, and another for all Democratic Senate challengers and open-seat candidates and their campaign staffs.

The most important new lessons delivered at the parties' 1998 training seminars concerned soft money and issue advocacy advertising. Party staff instructed candidates, mainly incumbents, how to defend themselves against party and interest group issue advocacy ads and how to incorporate party-financed issue advocacy and voter mobilization efforts into their campaign strategies. Republican members of Congress responded strongly to these lessons, raising tens of millions in hard and soft money for Operation Breakout and a Senate issue advocacy program.[51] Democratic congressional incumbents also got the message. Even though neither the DCCC nor the DSCC planned a national media campaign like Operation Breakout, Democratic incumbents helped the committees raise $8 million and $6 million in soft money for their issue advocacy efforts, and collected tens of millions of dollars for Democratic state parties. Leading the Democrats in soft money fund-raising were Senate challenger Charles Schumer, who raised an estimated $10 million for the New York State Democratic Party, and Sen. Harry Reid, who collected roughly $6 million for the Democratic Party of Nevada.[52]

Gauging Public Opinion

Many candidates receive significant assistance in gauging public opinion from national party committees. The DNC and RNC disseminate the findings of nationwide polls in newsletters and memoranda that they distribute to members of Congress, party activists, and congressional candidates. The parties' congressional and senatorial campaign committees commission hundreds of district and statewide polls and targeting studies in a given election season. Early on, they use recruitment surveys to show potential candidates the possibilities of waging competitive races and benchmark polls to inform declared candidates of their levels of support and of public opinion on the major issues. They use tracking polls to assist a small group of candidates who are running neck-and-neck with their opponents at the end of the campaign season. Some of these surveys are paid for entirely by a Hill committee and reported to the FEC as in-kind contributions or coordinated expenditures. Most are jointly financed by a committee and the candidates the polls serve.

Parties have significant advantages over individual candidates when it comes to purchasing polls. Parties are able to get polls at discount rates because they contract for so many of them. Parties can also use their extensive connections with polling firms to arrange to "piggyback" questions on polls that are taken for other clients. Benchmark polls, which can be useful weeks after they were taken, give party committees special opportunities to provide candidates with highly useful information at low cost. A party can purchase a poll for roughly $10,000 and give it to a candidate as an in-kind contribution or coordinated expenditure that is valued at a mere fraction of that amount if the party turns it over using a depreciation option allowed by the FEC.[53] The party can also split the costs of a poll evenly with a candidate and claim that it is using the poll for planning purposes, thereby allowing the candidate to receive the full poll for half price.[54] All six Washington party organizations commission national polls to research issues that they expect to occupy a prominent position on the national agenda.

In 1998 the NRCC shared the costs of polling with fourteen House incumbents, thirty-nine challengers, and twenty-five open-seat candidates. The NRCC also played matchmaker for candidates and political action committees sponsored by the American Medical Association, the National Association of Realtors, and the American Hospital Association, arranging for the PACs to take polls for twenty-five GOP candidates who needed them. In addition, the NRCC used tracking polls received from the National Restaurant Association's PAC to advise twelve of its most competitive House candidates. Neither the party nor the PAC gave the poll results to the candidates so the polls did not count as a party or PAC contribution or as a party coordinated expenditure.[55] The NRSC spent $800,000 on polling in twenty-one states, evenly splitting the costs of most of its surveys with its candidates. It usually took one survey for each race in 1997 and two surveys for each in 1998; it did tracking polls in six 1998 races.[56] The DCCC took polls worth $250,000 for thirty-five of its candidates and helped others obtain them from PACs.[57] The DSCC took benchmark polls to obtain an overview of the opinions of voters in sixteen states, trend polls in ten states, and tracking polls at critical junctures in twenty competitive states. Most of the DSCC's polls were used to advise candidates or released to the press, but they were not given to the candidates, so they did not count as in-kind contributions or coordinated expenditures.[58] Officials from all six Washington party organizations agree on the importance of polling. As one political director stated, "It's a good investment to spend $10,000 before deciding whether to spend over a million dollars in a state." [59]

Selected candidates also receive precinct-level targeting studies from the Hill committees. The DSCC and DCCC use geodemographic data provided by the National Committee for an Effective Congress (NCEC) to help their candidates develop targeting strategies. These data are matched with previous election results and current polling figures and used to guide the candidates' direct-mail programs, media purchases, voter mobilization drives, and other campaign efforts.[60] Republican candidates receive similar targeting assistance from the NRCC's and NRSC's political divisions.

Issue and Opposition Research

During the 1980s party organizations in Washington became major centers for political research. The DNC and RNC extended their research activities in several directions, most of which were and continue to be focused on the party rather than directed toward the candidates. The national committees routinely send materials on salient national issues to candidates for Congress, governorships, and state legislatures, to "allied" consultants and interest groups, and to activists at all levels. Party research typically includes statistics, tables, and charts that are drawn from major newspapers, the Associated Press wire service, the

Internet, the Lexis/Nexis computerized political database, and government publications. It weaves factual information with partisan themes and powerful anecdotes to underscore major campaign issues. Some individuals receive this information through the U.S. mail, but most get it by way of "blast-faxes" that the committees transmit daily to thousands during the campaign season. Many journalists and political commentators are also sent issue research—albeit with a partisan spin—by the national committees.

The congressional and senatorial campaign committees also disseminate massive amounts of issue-related materials by mail, fax, and email to candidates, party activists, and partisan political consultants. During the last few Congresses, both parties' House and Senate leaderships distributed talking points, memoranda, pamphlets, and issue handbooks designed to help candidates develop issue positions, write speeches, and prepare for debates. More important than this generic research are the more detailed materials that the Hill committees distribute to individual candidates. Each committee routinely distributes information on the substance and political implications of congressional roll-call votes. Many nonincumbents, who are unable to turn to congressional aides, the Library of Congress, or Washington-based interest groups for information on important issues, use this information to develop policy positions. Challengers also use it to plan attacks on incumbents.

The two House campaign committees assemble highly detailed issue research packages for some candidates involved in competitive races. These packages present hard facts about issues that are important to local voters and talking points that help candidates discuss these issues in a thematic and interesting manner. During the 1998 elections, the DCCC provided individualized research packages to thirty-two challengers and three open-seat candidates. The packages presented detailed information on how Republican House members' votes on legislation concerning health care, gun control, education, the environment, penalties for the tobacco industry, and other major issues would affect different groups of constituents. Included in the packages, among other constituent data, were district-specific estimates of the number of senior citizens and poor people who would be deprived of adequate health care, the number of university hospitals that would lose federal funding and be forced to close, and the number of students whose college loans would be cut under Republican budget proposals.[61]

The NRCC provided similar kinds of detailed research to forty challengers, thirty open-seat contestants, and ten incumbents, many of whom were freshmen in 1998. This research highlighted how Republican-supported tax cuts, anticrime legislation, the constitutional amendment to balance the budget, welfare reform, and other popular GOP proposals would help people living in individual congressional districts.[62] The committee also conducted "vulnerability studies" to help several Republican freshmen and a few other House members respond to attacks it anticipated would be made by their opponents.

The NRSC provided opposition and issue research to twenty Senate candidates.[63] The DSCC did not conduct issue or opposition research, opting instead to advise campaign staffs on how to do it on their own.[64] However, the Democratic Policy Committee, the research arm of Senate Democrats, distributed reports, policy papers, and other issue-related materials that candidates could use when formulating their issue positions.

Campaign Communications

The Hill committees assist selected candidates with campaign communications. The DCCC and the NRCC own television and radio production facilities complete with satellite capabilities, and for much of the 1980s and 1990s they furnished large numbers of candidates with technical and editorial assistance in producing campaign ads. By 1998 recent technological developments made it possible for candidates and media consultants to gain access to high-quality, inexpensive recording and editing technology without visiting their party's Washington headquarters. As a result, fewer congressional candidates used the DCCC's and NRCC's production facilities, and the committees' role in media production became more advisory than "hands-on."

Nevertheless, the DCCC continued to give virtually every Democratic House candidate $20,000 in credits that could be redeemed at its Harriman Communications Center in 1998. Seventy-four House incumbents and forty-eight nonincumbents used the center to edit or produce their television or radio ads or beam them from Washington back to their districts. Others used the center's satellite capabilities to appear "live" on television news shows, at fund-raisers, and at events in their districts. Satellite technology is extremely popular with incumbents from western states, who are not able to get back to their districts as frequently as those living on the East Coast or in the Midwest. Some nonincumbents running low-budget campaigns also used one or more of the center's fourteen "generic" or "doughnut" ads in 1998, which they could customize by incorporating text, sound, and voiceovers. All of these resources were made available to candidates at below market rates.

Prior to 1998 roughly five dozen Republican candidates per election season used the NRCC's media center to produce TV and radio ads. The committee played the role of a full-service media vendor for eighteen to two dozen candidates, developing advertising themes, writing scripts, and arranging for advertisements to be aired on local television or radio stations. In 1998 very few

GOP House candidates produced their TV or radio ads at the committee's media center. Only one candidate—Rep. Helen Chenoweth of Idaho—received a full-service media package, and less than half a dozen others received major help. However, the media center did not sit idle. Numerous House members and some nonincumbents taped fund-raising videos at the center and used its satellite capabilities to beam television communications back to their districts to interact with political activists, contributors, and voters.

The DSCC and NRSC have traditionally been less involved than their House counterparts in candidates' campaign communications. Rather than produce television, radio, or direct-mail advertisements, committee staff often comment on ads created by private consultants. They also finance some ads through in-kind contributions and coordinated expenditures.

In addition, the Hill committees take on supporting roles in other aspects of campaign communications by doing work that candidates' campaign committees cannot. They plant stories with the *New York Times, Washington Post,* and other national media. They release negative information about the opposing party's candidates. And, as will be discussed later, the independent expenditures they make and the issue ads they broadcast can have a major impact on the tenor of a congressional campaign. Senatorial and congressional campaign committee research and communication efforts have clearly contributed to the nationalization of American politics.

Fund-Raising

In addition to providing contributions, coordinated expenditures, and campaign services directly to candidates, and steering party-connected contributions to them, the Hill committees help selected candidates raise money from individuals and PACs. To this end, the committees give the candidates strategic advice and fund-raising assistance. They also furnish PACs and other Washington insiders with information that they can use when formulating their contribution strategies and selecting individual candidates for support.

All six national party organizations give candidates tips on how to organize fund-raising committees and events. The Republican Hill committees and the DSCC even furnish some candidates with contributor lists, with the proviso that the candidates surrender their own lists to the committee after the election. Sometimes the parties host high-dollar events in Washington or make arrangements for party leaders to attend events held around the country either in person or via satellite television uplink. The Speaker of the House and other congressional leaders can draw lobbyists, PAC managers, and other big contributors to even the most obscure candidate's fund-raising event. Of course, nothing can draw a crowd of big contributors like an appearance by the president.

The committees also steer large contributions from wealthy individuals, PACs, or members of Congress to needy candidates. It is illegal for the parties to "earmark" checks they receive from individuals or PACs for specific candidates, but committee members and staff can suggest to contributors that they give to one of the candidates on the committee's watch list. Sometimes they reinforce this message by sending out fund-raising letters on behalf of a candidate, sponsoring events that list congressional leaders as the event's hosts, or organizing joint fund-raising events after which the committee and the candidates share the proceeds.[65]

The Hill committees also give candidates the knowledge and tools needed to raise PAC money. The committees help candidates design "PAC kits" they can use to introduce themselves to members of the PAC community.[66] They also distribute lists of PACs that include the name of a contact person at each PAC and indicate how much cash the PAC has on hand, so candidates will neither waste their time soliciting committees that have no money nor take no for an answer when a PAC manager claims poverty but still has funds. Candidates are coached on how to fill out the questionnaires that some PACs use to guide their contributions and how to build coalitions of local PAC contributors so they can raise money from national PACs. All four Hill committees make meeting rooms and telephones available to facilitate PAC fund-raising, which cannot be legally conducted on Capitol grounds.

The committees also help candidates raise money from PACs by manipulating the informational environment in which PACs make their contribution decisions. The committees' PAC directors work to channel the flow of PAC money toward their party's most competitive congressional contenders and away from their opponents. This is an especially difficult task to perform for House challengers and open-seat candidates because they are largely unknown to the PAC community. Some junior House members also need to have attention called to their races. The PAC directors often call on party leaders, committee and subcommittee chairs, or ranking members to attend a candidate's fund-raising event or to telephone a PAC manager on the candidate's behalf.

The Hill committees use several methods to circulate information about House and Senate elections to PACs and other potential contributors. The committees publicize their targeting lists and contribution activities to draw the attention of PACs and wealthy individual contributors. The committees also host receptions, often referred to as "meet and greets," at their headquarters and national conventions to give candidates, especially nonincumbents, an opportunity to ask PAC managers for contributions. Campaign updates are mailed or faxed to about one thousand of the largest PACs on a weekly basis during the peak of the election season to inform them of targeted candidates' electoral prospects, financial needs, poll results, endorsements, campaign highlights, and revelations about problems experienced by their opponents. Streams of communications are also sent to the editors of the *Cook Political Report,* the *Rothenberg Political Report,* and other political newsletters that handicap congressional races. A favorable write-up in one of these can help a nonincumbent raise more PAC money.

The Hill committees also hold briefings to discuss their opportunity races and to inform PAC managers about their candidates' progress. These are important forums for networking among campaign finance elites. They give PAC managers the opportunity to ask Hill committee staffers questions about specific campaigns and provide them with the chance to discuss contribution strategies among themselves.

The campaign committees' PAC directors and party leaders spend a tremendous amount of time making telephone calls on behalf of their most competitive and financially needy candidates. Some of these calls are made to PAC managers who are recognized leaders of PAC networks. The DCCC and DSCC, for example, work closely with the NCEC and the AFL-CIO's COPE; their GOP counterparts work closely with the Business-Industry Political Action Committee (BIPAC). The committees encourage these "lead" PACs to endorse the party's top contestants and to communicate their support to other PACs in their networks.

One of the more controversial ways that the Hill committees raise money for needy candidates is by "leveraging" it. Campaign committee staff organize functions and clubs that promise PAC managers, lobbyists, and others access to congressional leaders in return for large contributions. Following the Republican takeover of Congress, Majority Whip Tom DeLay, R-Texas, greeted lobbyists with a list that categorized the four hundred largest PACs as "Friendly" or "Unfriendly," depending on the proportion of their contributions that went to Republicans in the 1994 elections, to hammer home the message that groups that wanted access to Republican leaders would be expected to give most of their PAC money to GOP candidates and party committees in the future.[67] He continued delivering this message during the 1998 elections.

The Hill committees also use "buddy systems" to match financially needy but promising nonincumbents and freshmen with committee chairs and other powerful incumbents for fund-raising purposes. These senior incumbents offer their partners contributions, provide advice on campaign-related topics, and use their influence to persuade PAC managers and individuals who have made large contributions to their campaigns to contribute to their "buddy."[68] The buddy system's impact on fund-raising is hard to estimate, but during the 1996 elections 150 Republican House members from safe seats were believed to have raised $50,000 each, either for colleagues who were in jeopardy or competitive nonincumbents.[69] As suggested by the number of incumbents who made contributions from their campaign accounts and leadership PACs to other House candidates, even more members of Congress were involved in redistributing the wealth during the 1998 elections.

The Hill committees are important intermediaries in the fund-raising process because they help needy challengers, open-seat candidates, and incumbents raise money from other PACs, other candidates, and individuals who make large contributions. The committees have created symbiotic relationships with some PACs, resulting in parties' becoming important brokers between candidates and contributors.[70] The relationships are based largely on honest and reliable exchanges of information about the prospects of individual candidates. Hill committee officials and PAC managers recognize that accurate information is the key to this relationship and to the ability of both groups to help candidates.

Party communications to PACs are somewhat controversial because they can harm some individual candidates' fund-raising prospects. Candidates who receive their Hill committee's endorsement derive significant fund-raising advantages from such communications, but nonincumbents who do not are usually unable to collect significant funds from PACs. Some PAC managers justify refusing a contribution request because a nonincumbent was not included on a Hill committee's watch list. Hill committee fund-raising efforts can create both winners and losers in congressional elections.

Grass-Roots Activities

Not all of the campaign assistance that House and Senate candidates get from parties comes from Washington, and not all of it is given by the parties' congressional and senatorial campaign committees. Some state and local party committees give candidates assistance in a few of the aspects of campaigning discussed above, but these committees tend to be less influential than the Hill committees in areas requiring technical expertise, in-depth research, or connections with Washington PACs and political consultants.[71] State and local party committees do, however, provide congressional candidates with substantial help in grass-roots campaigning. Most state committees help fund and organize registration and get-out-the-vote drives, set up telephone banks, and send campaign literature to voters.[72] Many local parties conduct these same activities as well as canvass door-to-door, distribute posters and lawn signs, put up billboards, and engage in other types of campaign field work.[73]

Some of this activity is organized and paid for by the state and local party organizations themselves; however, a significant portion of it is funded by party committees in Washington under the guise of the coordinated campaign—a cooperative party-building and voter mobilization program that is funded mainly by national party organizations. Most of the money that national party organizations spend in coordinated campaigns is targeted to states and localities that are critical to their presidential, senatorial, or congressional candidates' success.[74] Expenditures on voter list development, targeting, direct mail, and telephone banks enable party organizations in the nation's capital to influence locally executed grass-roots activities that benefit the entire party ticket.[75]

The Democratic national, congressional, and senatorial campaign committees spent a record $40 million on coordinated campaigns in 1996. This included hard and soft money used in state and local party-building programs for direct-mail expenses, to purchase voter lists, and to set up telephone banks. According to Don Fowler, DNC's national chairman at the time, that committee alone spent approximately $20 million to contact roughly 14.3 million people through direct mail and 11 million through telemarketing calls.[76] The DNC also spent about $5 million to mobilize racial and ethnic minorities, producing generic advertisements that used ethnic radio, television, and newspaper outlets to deliver a pro-Democratic message to African Americans, Hispanics, and Asian Americans, sometimes in languages other than English.[77]

Lacking a presidential election campaign around which to organize a fully national coordinated effort, the Democrats spent considerably less on voter mobilization in 1998 than they did in 1996. The DNC, hampered by debts incurred in the 1996 elections, spent an estimated $3 million on the coordinated campaign, the DCCC spent approximately $2.4 million, and the DSCC spent $2.6 million.[78]

The national Democrats helped states develop geodemographic targeting plans that isolated particular geographic, racial, ethnic, religious, and occupation groups for voter contacts. They also played a key role in making those contacts. The DNC spearheaded an innovative telephone bank operation that left telephone messages from President Clinton, First Lady Hillary Rodham Clinton, Vice President Gore, Secretary of Energy Bill Richardson, and civil rights leader Jesse Jackson urging Democratic identifiers to vote. Each leader's message was sent to those groups that would be most responsive to his or her appeals. The first lady's message was delivered to urban and suburban women and men living in Democratic-leaning areas, Richardson's was targeted to voters in New Mexico, with whom he was popular as a result of his service in the House, and Jackson's was directed at African American voters.

Republican spending on voter mobilization was impressive in 1998, despite the fact that it declined from the record $48.3 million that the party spent in 1996. As part of their Victory '98 program, the RNC, NRCC, NRSC, and Republican Governors Association transferred approximately $25.7 million to GOP state party organizations for grass-roots activities and related programs. These resources enabled the party to deliver 26.5 million pieces of targeted political mail, send 18 million absentee ballot requests, and make 34 million get-out-the-vote telephone calls.[79]

INDEPENDENT EXPENDITURES AND ISSUE ADVOCACY

Political parties first made independent expenditures and issue advocacy ads in significant numbers during the 1996 elections. These activities are sometimes referred to as "outside campaigning" because they are made by organizations other than candidate campaign committees and mainly by groups that are located in Washington, D.C., rather than in a candidate's district or state. Despite the fact that these activities are conducted by outside groups, they can have a big impact on congressional elections.

Independent expenditures are advertisements made by parties or PACs that *expressly* call for the election or defeat of a federal candidate. They must be made with hard money and without the candidate's knowledge or consent. Television and radio are the media most often employed for these ads, but sometimes direct mail is used. Unlike candidate ads, independent expenditures that appear on television or radio do not qualify for lowest unit rate charges. Independent expenditures used to attack an opposing party's candidate are generally more aggressive than are candidate ads.

Democratic party committees spent slightly less on independent expenditures in 1998 than in 1996, preferring to spend a combination of hard and soft money on issue advocacy advertisements. Party independent expenditures in both years were predominantly intended to influence Senate races. During the 1998 general elections the DSCC and Democratic state party committees spent $650,342 in independent expenditures to advocate the elections of Sen. Barbara Boxer of California and open-seat candidate Scott Baesler of Kentucky. They also spent $800,000 to urge voters to defeat both Baesler's opponent, Jim Bunning, and Senate challenger Mark Neumann, who ran against Sen. Russell Feingold of Wisconsin. The anti-Neumann expenditures were controversial because Feingold had pledged to discourage outside groups from campaigning on his behalf and had to call on the DSCC to pull the ads, which the committee eventually did. State Democratic party committees spent an additional $254,558 in connection with one House race in California and another in Indiana.

The Republicans spent almost thirty-eight times less on independent expenditures in 1998 than they did in 1996, instead focusing huge amounts on issue ads. The NRSC hired the John Gotta Company to spend $316,156 in independent expenditures on direct mail and telephone calls to mobilize voters in support of the failed reelection bid of Sen. Lauch Faircloth of North Carolina. State and local party committees made less than $5,200 in independent expenditures in a House race in Michigan and in House and Senate races in Connecticut.

The DNC, DCCC, RNC, and NRCC made no independent expenditures in the 1996 or 1998 election. They preferred issue advocacy ads to independent expenditures because the former could be partially financed with soft money.[80]

Parties (and some interest groups) use issue advocacy advertisements to encourage citizens to support or oppose public policies or to praise or criticize specific federal candidates. Like independent expenditures, they differ from candidate ads in that they do not qualify for lowest unit rate charges. Unlike independent expenditures, they can be made using soft money and *cannot expressly* advocate the election or defeat of a candidate. Whether issue advocacy ads can be coordinated with a candidate's campaign is under challenge in the courts, but some coordination did occur in 1996 and 1998. Most of the party money used to finance issue advocacy campaigns originates at the national level and is transferred to party committees in states that are hosting competitive elections. The content and timing of most issue advocacy ads are determined by one of the Hill committees.

Most issue advocacy ads resemble candidate-sponsored ads, and it is often difficult to distinguish between them. The major difference between candidate ads and party issue ads is that the latter are more negative and more likely to focus on the opposing candidate. Negative party issue ads enable candidates to avoid taking responsibility for election mudslinging. They also enable parties and interest groups to influence the campaign agenda in congressional races, forcing candidates to discuss issues they might otherwise wish to avoid. As a result, some candidates find themselves campaigning on a political agenda set by a party organization rather than by themselves or their opponents.[81] Issue advocacy has become an important weapon in the arsenals that party committees use to help their candidates contest elections.

The House Republicans' Operation Breakout was the most highly publicized issue advocacy campaign of 1998. Then-NRCC chairman John Linder,

R-Ga., described Operation Breakout as "an aggressive, unprecedented effort to reshape the political environment and get on offense—and put Democrats and their allies on defense." He explained its four overriding objectives: "Set up fall legislative battles with Democrats. Drive the political debate onto GOP turf. Preempt opposition attacks, such as big labor and Democrat party ads. Create a positive environment for Republicans so we can achieve dramatic success." Another goal was to keep the GOP's core supporters energized so that they would turn out in what was expected to be and materialized as a low turnout election.[82]

Operation Breakout was a $21 million combined media campaign that relied on television, radio, cable TV, direct mail, and newspaper advertisements to influence fifty-eight competitive House elections in thirty-six states.[83] Consistent with the House Republicans' moderately aggressive strategy, the party spent 48 percent of the media portion of the campaign to help its hopeful challengers defeat Democratic incumbents and another 18 percent to improve the odds of its open-seat prospects. It committed only 28 percent to shoring up House incumbents.[84]

The first wave of issue ads, disseminated October 1–10, consisted primarily of a generic spot that highlighted congressional Republicans' accomplishments. In the incumbent version the narrator asks, "So what has the Republican Congress done?" and answers, "How about a $500 per-child tax credit? Or health insurance that goes with you when you get a better job? Republicans like [a candidate's name is recited] are reaching out to find solutions to the problems families face. Call Congressman [the candidate's name is repeated]. Tell him to keep working for our families." The nonincumbent version is the same except the closing "Republicans like [candidate's name] agree with these solutions" is substituted for the last two lines of the incumbent ad. In addition to this spot, the NRCC broadcast tailored ads in fifteen districts that attacked Democrats on taxes and other "position" or "wedge" issues that favor Republicans.[85]

The second wave, disseminated October 11–22, consisted of ads that drew unflattering contrasts between Democratic and Republican House contestants on issues such as abortion, taxes, and crime. One issue ad, intended to harm the prospects of Democratic challenger Roxanne Qualls of Ohio, portrayed her as favoring partial-birth abortions, which Qualls actually opposes.[86]

The final, most expensive, and most controversial wave of issue ads cost about $10 million, went on the air October 28, and ran until a few days before the election. Three thirty-second ads, broadcast in thirty-two congressional districts, most in the South, attacked President Clinton for his affair with Monica Lewinsky. In one of the ads the narrator states, "In every election, there is a big question to think about. This year the question is: Should we make the Democrats more powerful? Should we reward the Democratic plans for big government? More big spending? And should we reward not telling the truth? This is the question of this election. Reward Bill Clinton. Or, vote Republican." In a second ad the GOP presents footage of Clinton's infamous finger-wagging denial of his affair with Lewinsky. In the final ad, designed to influence suburban voters, one woman tells another, "For seven months, he lied to us." Another thirty-two House districts, most in the suburbs, were saturated with milder ads that contrasted Republican challengers with their Democratic opponents.[87]

Post-election commentary on Operation Breakout suggests that it was not particularly helpful to the Republicans. GOP and Democratic Party operatives largely agree that many of the ads had only a limited influence because they were not adequately tailored to individual districts in which they were aired. The operatives also agreed that the anti-Clinton ads did little to increase Republican support among moralistic voters, which had already committed to vote for Republican candidates. The ads instead mobilized Democratic voters who felt that GOP attacks on the president had been too partisan and too relentless.[88] This unforeseen result became more consequential when the major television networks and the national press covered the ads in news stories, widening the ads' impact to include districts in which the Republicans did not intend for them to be shown. Ed Brookover and Tom Cole, the respective political directors of the NRCC and RNC, believed that the concept of a nationally focused issue advocacy campaign was not flawed. Rather, the fact that the Republican Congress had few legislative achievements to highlight in their issue advocacy ads, and had substituted anti-Clinton material instead, prevented the ads from producing their desired results.[89]

Neither the NRSC nor the two Democratic Hill committees conducted an issue advocacy campaign that was as expensive or as centrally directed as the one carried out by the NRCC. These committees aired issue ads that were customized to suit conditions in specific races rather than communicate a national message. The NRSC spent $7.3 million on issue advocacy in connection with the Kentucky, Nevada, North Carolina, South Carolina, and Wisconsin Senate elections.[90] The DSCC spent about $8 million in eleven closely contested Senate elections.[91] The DCCC spent $6 million in twenty-five House races.[92]

The DCCC distributed its funds in accordance with its modified defensive strategy. It spent 41 percent of its budget for televised issue advocacy ads to help its incumbents in jeopardy and 35 percent to improve the chances of its open-seat prospects. It spent the remaining 24 percent to boost the candidacies of Democratic hopeful challengers who sought to unseat GOP House members.[93]

Since 1996 the parties have used issue advocacy ads to influence the national political agenda and the agendas in individual House and Senate contests. One high-powered Republican operative who was responsible for his Hill committee's issue advocacy and independent expenditure ads compared his role to that of a chef who prepares a meal. The expenditures allowed the committee "to set the place settings and let others select from what was already on their plate." Once the party had set the agenda with issues and themes that worked to the advantage of their candidate, the operative explained, "the candidate could select what he preferred from among them and force them down the opponent's throat."[94] Party spending is especially important in states that have late primaries because candidates often emerge from them with little cash with which to try to set the agenda and only seven or eight weeks to woo general election voters.

Party issue advocacy and independent expenditure ads are also important late in the election. They can supplement a candidate's advertisements or attack an opponent who is unprepared and lacking the funds needed to respond. The ads also have the benefit of limiting the media time that might otherwise be purchased by an opponent. Another advantage of airing attack ads against an opposing party's candidates, including safe incumbents, is that the ads can encourage the candidates to spend more time at home and less time traveling the country raising money for challengers and needy colleagues. Finally, the effect of issue advocacy and independent expenditure ads is usually magnified many times over because they routinely receive free media coverage. However, as House Republicans learned in 1998, such coverage can backfire, harming rather than helping candidates.

THE IMPACT OF PARTY CAMPAIGNING

How valuable do House and Senate candidates find the campaign services they receive from party organizations? When asked to rate the importance of campaign assistance from local, state, and national party organizations, PACs, unions, and other groups in aspects of campaigning requiring professional expertise or in-depth research, candidates and campaign aides involved in recent House elections ranked their party's Hill committee first. With respect to campaign management, about one-third of all House candidates and campaign aides consider their party's congressional campaign committee to be at least moderately helpful.[95] Roughly 40 percent gave similar assessments for Hill committee assistance in gauging public opinion. Over half of all House contestants report that committee issue research plays at least a moderately important role in their campaigns, with 20 percent describing it as very important and another 11 percent asserting that it is extremely important. More than 40 percent of the

House contestants, mostly challengers, also rely heavily on their congressional campaign committee for opposition research. About 30 percent of all House campaigns receive significant DCCC or NRCC help in developing their communications. Slightly more candidates and campaign aides find that Hill committees are moderately important to their fund-raising efforts; however, campaigners report receiving greater fund-raising assistance from PACs and other interest groups than from the committees. The DCCC and NRCC are also rated lower than are state and local party organizations and interest groups in grass-roots activities. The lower rating reflects their lack of direct involvement in these aspects of campaigning.

The evaluations by House candidates and campaign aides indicate that most congressional campaign committee help is given to candidates in close races, which reflects the parties' goal of winning as many seats in Congress as possible. The evaluations also show that Hill committee assistance is generally more important to hopeful challengers and open-seat prospects than to incumbents in jeopardy, reflecting the fact that incumbents' electoral difficulties are rarely the result of an inability to raise money, assemble a campaign organization, or communicate with voters.

Nevertheless, the Hill committees go to great lengths to protect incumbents in jeopardy. In 1998 they provided sixteen endangered House incumbents with more than $75,000, close to the legal maximum, in campaign contributions and coordinated expenditures. They also helped to start contributions flowing from members of Congress and their leadership PACs to candidates in close races. All four Hill committees also held special seminars to teach first-term members how to exploit their incumbency for campaign purposes and gave incumbents in marginal seats strategic advice, steered millions of PAC dollars in their direction, and complemented the candidates' efforts with issue advocacy advertisements. A political consultant would have charged a candidate hundreds of thousands of dollars for these services, but the congressional campaign committees' staffs provided this help free to candidates in close races.

One freshman Republican, Rep. William Redmond of New Mexico, received a tremendous amount of help. Redmond was first elected in a special election in May 1997 when he edged out Democratic nominee Eric Serna by roughly three thousand votes. Although Redmond had beaten the Democrat by a 3 percent margin, the results were complicated by the fact that Green Party candidate Carol Miller had siphoned off 17 percent of the vote, most of it from Serna. All three parties made New Mexico's 3rd district a top priority for the 1998 elections. Serna, who had served on the state's Corporate Commission prior to running for the House, was defeated in the Democratic primary, 44 percent to 36 percent, by Thomas Udall, the state's popular attorney general and nephew of former Arizona representative Morris Udall. The Greens renominated Miller.

The Republicans geared up for a difficult race. Republican party committees gave $82,393 in contributions and coordinated expenditures to Redmond, GOP legislators donated $121,423 from their campaign committees, and Republican-sponsored leadership PACs contributed an additional $122,755.[96] NRCC political operatives were very involved in the Redmond campaign. The Republicans also did a great deal of outside campaigning on Redmond's behalf. The three Republican national organizations transferred approximately $2.3 million in hard and soft money to New Mexico to help Redmond, their other House candidates and their gubernatorial candidate, and other competitive state and local contestants. The NRCC, the RNC, and the Republican Party of New Mexico purchased $344,247 worth of issue advocacy ads that praised Redmond or attacked Udall as part of Operation Breakout. These spots were aired more than 1,950 times over network and cable television. The state party sent out several direct-mail pieces that praised Redmond's record on crime, education, health care, and Social Security. The GOP also sent out three comparison direct-mail pieces: the first focused on education, the second on crime, and the third on the environment. The pieces were intended to divide the opposition; they showed Udall in an unfavorable light compared with both Redmond and Miller. The GOP also organized extensive telephone banks, mailed thousands of absentee ballots, and conducted a major get-out-the-vote effort. The telephone banks included recorded calls encouraging Republicans to vote for Redmond and the state's popular GOP senator, Pete Domenici.[97]

The Democrats were just as committed to the race, but they had less money to invest in it. Democratic party committees gave Udall $53,153 in contributions and coordinated expenditures, Democratic legislators donated $29,100, and Democratic leadership PACs donated an additional $121,423.[98] The three Democratic national party organizations transferred more than $1.5 million to New Mexico's state Democratic party to help Udall and other Democrats involved in close elections. Most of this money was spent to mobilize Democratic voters. The Democrats mailed several direct-mail pieces, including one letter from Bill Richardson that was written in both English and Spanish and included an absentee ballot. The Democrats also carried out an extensive phone bank effort in New Mexico that used prerecorded calls from Hillary Clinton and Richardson urging Democratic voters to turn out at the polls. The party spent only $130,000 on a televised issue advocacy ad attacking Redmond; it ran 197 times from October 20 through November 2. Although Udall and his party were greatly outspent, the Democrat managed to win the contest by a ten-point margin.[99]

Most Senate candidates and campaign aides give evaluations of Hill committee assistance that are as favorable as those given by House candidates. The senatorial campaign committees are rated above any other group in every area of campaigning, except providing information about voters, mobilizing voters, and recruiting volunteers. State and local party organizations and interest groups were ranked higher in these areas.[100]

Senate candidates in competitive races receive more campaign resources from their party than from any other group. The open-seat race in Kentucky between former House members Jim Bunning and Scott Baesler demonstrates how important party activity can be in a Senate election. The Republicans provided Bunning with $379,178 in contributions and coordinated expenditures, about $27,000 short of the FEC's limit for the race. GOP legislators contributed an additional $33,622, and Republican leadership PACs donated $114,768.[101] Republican national party organizations transferred more than $2.2 million in hard and soft money to the state GOP. Combined with contributions from the Kentucky Republican Party, GOP spending on Bunning's behalf totaled an estimated $3 million, including more than $1.5 million in issue advocacy ads attacking Baesler. Two controversial but effective Republican ads attacked Baesler for supporting the North American Free Trade Agreement (NAFTA). One ad concluded with a stereotypical Mexican "Muchas gracias, Señor Baesler"; the other used Asian and Mexican stereotypes to convey the same message. Both ads were decried for race baiting, but the GOP had little to lose because the state has very few Hispanic or Asian American voters.[102]

The party also delivered 2.3 million pieces of targeted direct mail. While voters in the western, tobacco-growing part of the state received letters attacking Clinton and the Democrats' antitobacco stances, voters in eastern Kentucky, which had lost many jobs due to factory relocations abroad, received letters attacking Baesler's vote for NAFTA. Senior citizens received personal letters and fliers from Bunning's wife that praised his defense of Social Security. The party also aired issue advocacy ads on the radio and made 557,000 telephone calls to Kentucky voters. Under the direction of Senator McConnell, Kentucky's other senator, the NRSC gave Bunning a great deal of strategic and tactical support. McConnell sent two of his top aides to run Bunning's campaign, arranged a bus tour featuring former Republican senator and presidential candidate Bob Dole and other GOP leaders, and helped the Republican state party conduct a grass-roots campaign to mobilize Republican voters.[103]

The Democrats played a major role in Baesler's bid for the Senate. Democratic party organizations donated about the legal maximum $406,344 in contributions and coordinated expenditures, and Democratic legislators and leadership PACs contributed $19,000 and $34,346. The party made $704,000 in independent expenditures: $529,000 advocating that Kentuckians vote for Baesler and another $175,000 attacking Bunning. Democratic party commit-tees in Washington, D.C., transferred almost $2.9 million to the Kentucky Democratic Party. The DSCC and the state party spent approximately $2,260,000 on televised issue ads and another $28,000 on radio ads. The state Democratic Party also ran a coordinated campaign that used direct mail, tar-geted telephone calls, and door-to-door canvassing to turn out the vote. Demo-cratic leaders participated in a whistle-stop train tour across the state. Despite their best efforts, Baesler and the Democrats lost to Bunning and the GOP by 6,766 votes.[104]

SUMMARY

Political parties, particularly party organizations in Washington, play impor-tant supporting roles in contemporary congressional elections. Their agenda-setting efforts encourage voters to focus on issues that traditionally work to the advantage of their candidates. The Hill committees distribute most of their contributions, coordinated expenditures, and campaign services to candidates in close races. They also help these candidates to attract funding and campaign assistance from other politicians, their leadership PACs, other PACs and inter-est groups, and individual contributors. Local parties assist candidates in mobi-lizing voters in some parts of the country. National party organizations have substantially increased their influence in congressional elections by producing issue advocacy ads and financing state and local party campaign efforts.

Republican party organizations are wealthier than their Democratic coun-terparts. GOP party committees, particularly at the national level, have tradi-tionally played a greater role than Democratic party organizations in congressional elections. The Democrats have increased their involvement in congressional campaigns, but Republican party committees maintain an edge in House elections and an overwhelming advantage in Senate contests. The GOP's overall superiority is likely to persist in the near future.

CHAPTER FIVE

The Interests Campaign

Organized interests, pejoratively referred to as "special" interests, have always been involved in American elections. During the earliest days of the Republic, leaders of agricultural and commercial groups influenced who was on the ballot, the coverage they received in the press, and the voting patterns that determined election outcomes. As the electorate grew and parties and candidates began to spend more money to reach voters, steel magnates, railroad barons, and other captains of industry increased their roles in political campaigns. Labor unions counterorganized with manpower and dollars.[1] Religious and ethnic groups also influenced elections, but their financial and organizational efforts paled next to those of business and labor.

Interest groups continue to flourish at the close of the twentieth century, and several developments have significantly affected their roles in congressional elections. The growth in the number of organizations that located or hired representatives in Washington led to the formation of a community of lobbyists that was, and continues to be, attuned to the rhythms of legislative and election politics. The enactment of the FECA led to the development of the modern political action committee—the form of organizational entity that most interest groups use to carry out the majority of their federal campaign activities. Court decisions and FEC rulings handed down in recent years allow interest groups to use new approaches, including issue advocacy advertising, to spend money in congressional elections.

This chapter covers the growth and development of the PAC community in Washington and the roles that PACs and other groups play in congressional elections. I analyze the motives that underlie PAC strategies and activities, the methods that PACs use to select candidates for support, and the distribution of PAC contributions and independent expenditures. I also examine other forms of interest group activity, including issue advocacy ads and voter mobilization efforts.

THE RISE OF PACS

Although interest groups have been active in campaigns throughout American history, it was not until 1943 that the first political action committee, the Committee on Political Education, was founded by the Congress of Industrial Organizations.[2] A PAC can be best understood as the electoral arm of an organized interest. Interest groups form PACs to give campaign assistance to federal, or in some cases state or local, candidates with the hope of influencing election outcomes, the formation of public policy, or both. Most PACs have a sponsoring, or parent, organization, such as a corporation, labor union, trade association, or other group. However, for "nonconnected" PACs, the PAC itself is the organizing group.

The FECA set the scene for the PAC explosion of the mid-1970s. One of the goals of the act was to dilute the influence of moneyed interests on federal elections. The act limited individuals to a maximum contribution of $1,000 per candidate at each stage of the election—primary, general election, and runoff (if a runoff is required)—for a total of $3,000 (see Table 1-1). It also imposed an aggregate annual limit of $25,000 on an individual's contributions to all federal candidates, federal party committees, and PACs (see Table 1-2). It barred corporations, labor unions, trade associations, cooperatives, and other organized groups from giving contributions directly to candidates for federal office.

By limiting the total contributions that a candidate could collect from any one source, the FECA encouraged candidates to solicit smaller donations from a broader array of interests and individuals. The act also encouraged many interest groups to establish PACs. Although the FECA never mentioned the term *political action committee,* it allowed for "a multicandidate committee" that raises money from at least fifty donors and spends it on at least five candidates for federal office, to contribute a maximum of $5,000 per candidate at each stage of the election.[3] The low ceilings the law established for individual contributions to candidates and the $5,000-per-year limit it set for individual contributions to any one PAC have the combined effect of making PAC contributions a popular vehicle among wealthy individuals who wish to influence congressional elections.

In November 1975, in an advisory opinion written for Sun Oil Company, the FEC counseled the company that it could pay the overhead and solicitation costs of its PAC, thereby freeing the PAC to spend all the funds it collected

FIGURE 5-1

The Growth in the Number of Registered PACs, 1974–1998

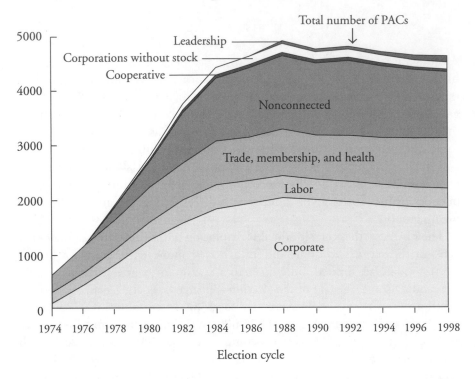

Sources: Joseph E. Cantor, *Political Action Committees: Their Evolution, Growth, and Implications for the Political System* (Washington, D.C.: Congressional Research Service of the Library of Congress, 1984), 88; various Federal Election Commission press releases.

from donors on federal elections.[4] The Sun PAC decision clarified a gray area in the law and, in the process, made PACs a much more attractive vehicle for collecting and disbursing funds. The advisory ruling contributed to an explosion in the number of PACs that lasted from the mid-1970s to the mid-1980s.

The Supreme Court's ruling in *Buckley v. Valeo* allowed PACs to make unlimited independent expenditures (made without the knowledge or consent of a candidate or his or her campaign organization) in congressional and presidential elections.[5] Both the FEC advisory opinion and the Supreme Court decision created new opportunities for organized groups to participate in politics. The advisory opinion was especially important, encouraging a wide range of political leaders, business entrepreneurs, and others to form new PACs.

FIGURE 5-2

The Growth of PAC Contributions in Congressional Elections, 1974–1998

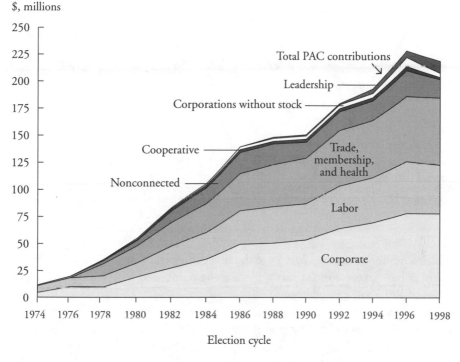

Sources: Joseph E. Cantor, *Political Action Committees: Their Evolution, Growth, and Implications for the Political System* (Washington, D.C.: Congressional Research Service of the Library of Congress, 1984), 88; various Federal Election Commission press releases.

Between 1974 and the 1998 elections, the PAC community grew from more than 600 to 4,599 committees (see Figure 5-1). Most of the growth occurred in the business sector, with corporate PACs growing in number from 89 in 1974 to 1,821 in 1998. Labor unions, many of which already had PACs in 1974, created the fewest new PACs, increasing the number from 201 to 353. The centralization of the labor movement into a relatively small number of unions greatly limited the growth of labor PACs. In addition, three new species of political action committee—the nonconnected PAC (mostly ideological and issue-oriented groups), and PACs whose sponsors are either cooperatives or corporations without stock, such as the Southern Minnesota Sugar Cooperative and the Aircraft Owners and Pilots Association—emerged on the scene in

TABLE 5-1

The Concentration of PAC Contributions in the 1998 Congressional
Elections

	PACs' total contributions					
	Over $250,000	$100,001–$250,000	$50,001–$100,000	$5,001–$50,000	$1–$5,000	$0
Percentage of all PACs	4	6	7	28	20	35
(N)	(185)	(287)	(329)	(1,273)	(921)	(1,604)
Percentage of all PAC contributions	57	20	11	12	1	0
($, millions)	(124.7)	(44.4)	(23.7)	(25.4)	(1.8)	(0)

Source: Compiled from Federal Election Commission, "FEC Releases Information on PAC Activity for 1997–98," press release, June 8, 1999. Some percentages do not add to 100 because of rounding.

1977. The nonconnected PACs are the most important of these. By 1998 their number had grown to 1,213; in contrast, the combined total for the two other types of PAC had reached only 178.[6]

Leadership PACs, briefly covered in Chapter 4, are the most recently formed type of PAC. Sponsored by politicians and closely tied to the parties, these PACs have traditionally been categorized as nonconnected PACs. They remained scarce until the late 1980s because few members of Congress could raise the money to form them. During the 1990s an increasing number of politicians, including some relatively junior members of the House, began to sponsor them. Their numbers reached 58 in 1994, 86 in 1996, and 113 in 1998.

The growth in the number of PACs was accompanied by a tremendous increase in their activity. PAC contributions to congressional candidates grew from $12.5 million in 1974 to almost $220 million in 1998, including about $206.8 million to House and Senate candidates who competed in the 1998 elections. Corporate and other business-related PACs accounted for most of that growth (see Figure 5-2). In 1998 corporate PACs accounted for over 35 percent of all PAC contributions to congressional candidates, followed by trade association PACs, which accounted for 28 percent. Union PACs gave just under 21 percent of all contributions received by congressional candidates, leadership PACs contributed 5 percent, and nonconnected PACs (excluding leadership PACs) gave 8 percent. PACs sponsored by cooperatives and corporations without stock contributed the final 3 percent.

A very small group of PACs is responsible for most PAC activity. A mere 185

PACs, just under 4 percent of the entire PAC community, contributed roughly $124.7 million during the 1998 elections, representing approximately 57 percent of all PAC money given in those contests (see Table 5-1). Each of these committees, which are clearly the "all stars" of the PAC community, gave over $250,000 to federal candidates. These include PACs sponsored by such corporations, trade associations, and unions as United Parcel Service, the National Association of Realtors, and the United Auto Workers, as well as such nonconnected PACs as Voters for Choice/Friends of Family Planning and the Adam Smith Political Action Committee.

Another 6 percent of all PACs are "major players," each having contributed between $100,001 and $250,000 to congressional candidates during the 1998 elections. These committees, which include the American Express PAC, the American Insurance Association PAC, the Association of Flight Attendants' "Flight PAC," the National Right to Life PAC, and Washington PAC (WASHPAC, a pro-Israel group), accounted for just over 20 percent of all PAC contributions. The all stars and major players are particularly influential because their wealth allows them to contribute to virtually every candidate whose election is of importance to them.

The "players" are those PACs that have the resources to give a significant contribution to many but not all of the candidates they wish to support. They comprise 7 percent of all PACs, and include the Coors Employees' PAC, the Association for Manufacturing Technology Machine's "ToolPAC," the International Longshoremen's and Warehousemen's Union PAC, and the Dallas Entrepreneurial PAC. Each of the players contributed between $50,001 and $100,000 during the 1998 elections, accounting for roughly 11 percent of all PAC contributions.

The contributions of the next group of PACs, which might be labeled the "junior varsity," are clearly constrained by their size. These PACs each contributed between $5,001 and $50,000. They constitute 28 percent of the PAC community and gave almost 12 percent of all PAC contributions. Their donations tend to be significantly smaller than those of the larger PACs. The managers of these PACs, such as the PHH Group PAC, the Distilled Spirits Council PAC, the International Union of Police Association PAC, and Republicans for Choice PAC, commonly have to answer requests for contributions by stating that they support the candidate and would like to give a contribution but do not have the money.

Members of the next group, the "little league," each gave between $1 and $5,000, accounting for just under 1 percent of all PAC contributions during the 1998 elections. They include the Bacardi-Martini Corporation PAC, American Sleep Disorders Association PAC, and the Association of American

Publishers (AAP) PAC. These committees, which make up about 20 percent of the PAC community, play a marginal role in the funding of congressional elections.

Finally, 1,604 PACs gave no money in the 1998 elections. Of these, 900 are, for all practical purposes, defunct.[7] Although they registered with the FEC, they spent no money to collect contributions, pay off debts, or cover the costs of committee administration during the 1998 election cycle.

STRATEGY, DECISION MAKING, AND TARGETING

PAC goals and strategies are more diverse than are those of the two major parties, reflecting the fact that parties are consumed with electing candidates and PACs have other goals, such as promoting issues and influencing the policy process. Some PACs follow "ideological" strategies designed to increase the number of legislators who share their broad political perspective or positions on specific, often emotionally charged issues such as abortion. These PACs are similar to political parties in that they consider congressional elections as opportunities to alter the composition of Congress and view the electoral process as their primary vehicle for changing or reinforcing the direction of public policy.[8] Nonconnected PACs have traditionally been categorized as ideological committees.

Ideological PACs give most of their contributions to candidates in close elections, where the PACs have the biggest chance of affecting an election outcome. However, some of these committees make contributions and independent expenditures in connection with uncompetitive contests in order to attract attention to either themselves, their issues, or politicians who share their views. Gaining visibility for themselves and their causes is important because it helps these PACs raise money.

PACs following ideological strategies traditionally have not given much money to members of Congress for the sake of gaining access to the legislative process. The issues these PACs support are often linked to values so fundamental that legislators would not be expected to change their views in response to a contribution or visit by a lobbyist. Prior to giving a contribution, many of these PACs, and some others, require candidates to complete questionnaires that elicit their views on certain issues.

Other types of PACs pursue "access" strategies designed to provide the group with the ability to gain at least an audience with members of Congress.[9] These PACs, which include some corporate and trade association committees, view elections pragmatically. For them, an election is a prime opportunity to shore up relations with members of Congress who work on legislation that is of importance to their parent organization. Elections give these PACs the opportunity to create goodwill with powerful legislators or at least minimize the enmity of legislators who disagree with them. Elections thus lay the groundwork for later lobbying efforts.

A PAC that follows an access strategy is likely to contribute most of its money to incumbents. Members of the House and Senate who chair committees or subcommittees, occupy party leadership positions, or are policy entrepreneurs with influence over legislation are likely to receive large contributions regardless of the competitiveness of their contests.[10] In fact, many access-oriented PACs make contributions to legislators who do not even have opponents. Giving to incumbents enables these PACs to accomplish their goal of ensuring access while meeting organizational imperatives such as backing a large number of winners and contributing to candidates who represent districts that contain many of the PAC's supporters.

Access-oriented PACs also give significant sums to candidates for open seats. Most of these candidates have good chances of winning but need large amounts of money to run competitive campaigns. Giving an open-seat prospect a large contribution is useful to an access-oriented PAC because it can create goodwill, laying the groundwork for productive relations with a future member of Congress.

Access-oriented PACs tend to ignore challengers because most of them are likely to lose. Giving a challenger a contribution is often considered a waste of money and could lead to serious repercussions from an incumbent. Moreover, backing challengers has a high probability of reducing a PAC's win-loss record and could lead to criticism of the PAC's manager. The managers of access-oriented PACs that decided not to support challenger or open-seat candidates know that should these candidates win, they could make amends later by helping them retire their campaign debts.

PACs that use access strategies rarely make independent expenditures to help or attack candidates because of the publicity these expenditures can generate. Independent expenditures could harm a corporation, for example, if they anger congressional incumbents, upset some of the PAC's donors, or call undue attention to the group. Such publicity could lead to charges that a group is trying to buy influence and could hinder the achievement of its goals.

The largest group of PACs practice "mixed" strategies. It includes many trade association and labor union PACs. They give contributions to some candidates because those candidates share the PAC's views, and they give to others because they wish to improve their access to legislators who work on policies the group deems important. Contributions motivated by the former reason are usually distributed to candidates in competitive contests. Contributions informed by the latter motive are given to incumbents who are in a position to influence legislation that is important to the PAC.

In some cases the two motives clash; for example, when a highly qualified challenger who represents the PAC's views runs a competitive race against an incumbent in a position of power. In these situations PACs usually support the incumbent, but sometimes they contribute to both candidates. PACs that follow mixed strategies and PACs that follow pure access strategies are less likely than ideological PACs to make independent expenditures.

PAC Strategy and the Political Environment

PACs, like most other groups and individuals involved in politics, are strategic actors that respond to their environment in ways that enable them to pursue their goals.[11] During the 1970s most PACs used ideological strategies that followed partisan lines. They backed candidates who supported the positions adhered to by their organizational sponsors. Business-oriented PACs, including corporate and trade committees, largely supported Republican candidates. Labor organizations, which were and continue to be the most consistently partisan of all PACs, regularly gave 90 percent of their contributions to Democrats. In time, many business-oriented committees shifted from ideological to access or mixed strategies. These PACs, with the encouragement of former DCCC chair Tony Coelho, redirected their support from Republican House challengers to incumbents, many of whom were Democrats, out of recognition of the Democratic Party's decades-long control of Congress.[12]

Perhaps the clearest strategic response by PACs takes place after partisan control of one or both chambers of Congress changes hands. When control of the Senate switched from the Democrats to the Republicans in 1981 and back to the Democrats in 1987, many access-seeking PACs switched their contributions to Senate candidates, mainly incumbents, who belonged to the new majority party. Similarly, following the 1994 GOP takeover of both the House and the Senate, these PACs gave most of their funds to Republicans, once again reversing their previous contribution patterns.[13]

Because of their desire to influence the composition of Congress, ideologically oriented PACs are the most likely to capitalize on the conditions peculiar to a specific election. A PAC that uses an access-seeking strategy, such as a corporate or trade committee, is less affected by a particular electoral setting, unless changing conditions are almost certain to influence its parent group's ability to meet with key legislators and their staffs. The strategic changes in PAC behavior that occurred in the early 1980s were the result of committees learning how to get the most legislative influence for their dollars and the increasing aggressiveness of incumbent fund-raising.[14] Those that occurred following the 1994 elections were a response to the change in partisan control of Congress.

Making strategic adjustments in anticipation of political change is more difficult. The manager of an access-oriented PAC who believes that a member of Congress is likely to go from having little to major influence in a policy area, for instance, may have difficulty persuading the PAC's board of directors to raise the member's contribution from a token sum to a substantial donation. The manager's prospects of convincing the board that the PAC should totally revamp its strategy because partisan control of Congress might change are slim. For example, many corporate and trade PACs, whose support of a pro-business agenda suggests they would want to support Republicans who have real prospects for victory, did not support Republican challengers during the 1994 elections. Some of the managers of these PACs may have been attuned to the fact that a confluence of anti-Washington sentiments, strong Republican challengers, and vulnerable Democratic incumbents enhanced the challengers' prospects, but their PAC's decision-making process made it impossible for them to change its contribution patterns in anticipation of the Republicans' stunning success.

PAC Decision Making

The decision-making processes that PACs use to select individual candidates are affected by a PAC's overall strategy, wealth, organizational structure, and location.[15] Ideological PACs spend more time searching for promising challengers to support than do PACs that use access-seeking or mixed strategies. Ideological committees are also more likely than other PACs to support nonincumbents in congressional primaries. Wealthy PACs tend to spend more time searching for promising nonincumbents simply because they can afford to fund more candidates.[16] Federated PACs whose organizational affiliates are spread across the country typically have to respond to the wishes of these constituents when making contributions.[17] Nonconnected PACs, leadership PACs, and PACs that are sponsored by a single corporation or cooperative, in contrast, are less constrained by the need to please a diverse and far-flung constituency. Committees located in the nation's capital have more information available to them about the relative competitiveness of individual races because they can plug into more communications networks than can PACs located in the hinterlands.[18]

The decision-making processes of PACs vary according to the PACs' organizational capacities. The Realtors PAC (RPAC), a large institutionalized committee with headquarters in Washington, was formed in 1969.[19] This federated

PAC, which is sponsored by the National Association of Realtors (NAR), receives its money from PACs sponsored by the NAR's eighteen hundred local affiliates and state associations located in all fifty states plus the District of Columbia, Guam, Puerto Rico, and the Virgin Islands. Realtors give donations to RPAC and to these affiliated PACs, each of which passes 30 percent of its revenues to the national PAC. In 1998 RPAC distributed almost $2.5 million in contributions, more than any other political action committee.

The Realtors PAC employs a mixed strategy to advance the goals of the real estate industry. As do most other institutionalized PACs, it has explicit criteria for selecting candidates for support and uses a complex decision-making procedure. Party, incumbency, and electoral competitiveness have a major impact on RPAC contributions. Incumbents, who are typically given preference over challengers, are evaluated on a number of criteria to assess their policy proclivities, level of activism on behalf of real estate issues, and local realtor support. Members who cosponsor priority NAR legislation, give a speech on behalf of NAR legislation on the House or Senate floor, or write letters to their colleagues in support of such legislation are top priorities. The same is true of those who use their congressional authority to compel the president or independent regulatory agencies to respond to real estate industry concerns, vote for key NAR issues in committee or on the floor, or assist constituents with real estate–related matters. Leaders of both parties and members who belong to committees that deal with real estate issues are also targeted for contributions.

Nonincumbents who have previously held elective office, and thus have a record on real estate issues, are judged for contributions using similar criteria. Most are also interviewed by RPAC representatives, usually local or state NAR members, and asked to complete an RPAC questionnaire to help the PAC further discern the candidate's political philosophy, background, and campaign skills. Nonincumbents who have not previously held office must be interviewed by RPAC representatives and complete a questionnaire to be eligible for a contribution. Finally, when considering both incumbents and nonincumbents for contributions, the PAC considers the competitiveness of the race, the amount of cash in a candidate's campaign account, and the number and partisanship of realtors who live in the district.

RPAC's contribution decisions are made in several ways. The PAC's staff and trustees and the NAR's political representatives and lobbyists deliberate using the preceding criteria to make one centralized set of contribution decisions. The PAC's In-State Reception Program constitutes a second, decentralized decision-making process. Under the program, realtors who want to attend a fundraising event held by one of their state's incumbents can make an RPAC contribution of up to $1,000, so long as the donation is approved by the chair of RPAC's state affiliate. The process for contributions to open-seat candidates is similar, except that the candidate must be personally interviewed and approved by state RPAC officials. The In-State Reception Program has a similar but more stringent process for challenger contributions because most challengers have poor prospects of success and NAR officials are concerned about angering incumbents. The state PAC's request for a contribution must be formally approved or rejected by national RPAC trustees, and the contribution is limited to a maximum of $1,000.

Other programs allow RPAC to further increase realtors' contact with legislators and to concentrate its resources in close races. The Special Recognition Fund is used to make additional contributions to party leaders, candidates who serve on committees with jurisdiction over real estate–related matters, and staunch supporters of real estate interests who are involved in competitive contests. The Washington Reception Program Fund allows NAR lobbyists to attend fund-raising events held in the nation's capital and RPAC to host receptions for congressional candidates. RPAC stopped making independent expenditures after the 1992 elections.

Like many interest groups, RPAC's and the NAR's election activities extend beyond making campaign contributions. RPAC and its parent organization mobilize realtors to support their preferred candidates, distribute educational and advocacy mailings in close contests, use telephone banks to conduct voter identification and get-out-the-vote efforts, and occasionally send professional organizers to carry out grass-roots activities designed to help their preferred candidates. These efforts are financed with soft money.

The decision-making process of the Realtors PAC is similar to that of other institutionalized committees, such as AT&T's PAC, the American Medical Association's PAC (AMPAC), and the League of Conservation Voters' (LCV) PAC.[20] It relies on a combination of factual information, local opinion, and national perspective to determine which candidates to support. The requirement that all recommendations receive formal approval is also typical, as is the ability to conduct research on individual elections in-house. The PAC's lack of participation as either a source or a user of the information available in Washington communications networks is unusual for a PAC located in the nation's capital, but its size, federated structure, and tremendous resources enable it to make decisions with information it has collected independently of other committees.

At the opposite end of the spectrum from the Realtors PAC are the noninstitutionalized PACs. WASHPAC is a nonconnected committee that was founded in 1980 by Morris J. Amitay, formerly the executive director of the American Israel Public Affairs Committee (AIPAC), to promote a secure Israel and strong American-Israeli relations.[21] WASHPAC spent $137,650 in congressional elections in 1998, contributing the vast majority of its money to incumbents. The PHH Group PAC, another noninstitutionalized PAC, is sponsored by a small, publicly held corporation that rents commercial vehicles and relocates business personnel. The PAC in 1998 contributed $7,500 to congressional candidates, all of whom were incumbents.[22]

These two PACs—and thousands of other noninstitutionalized committees—are essentially one-person operations with one-person decision-making processes. Noninstitutionalized PACs rely primarily on personal contacts with candidates and other Washington insiders for the political information that guides their contribution decisions. Amitay, who started WASHPAC as a hobby, peruses candidates' speeches and press releases and incumbents' voting records and letters to constituents to gauge their support for Israel. He exchanges information about the competitiveness of different elections when meeting with other pro-Israel political activists. For the PHH Group PAC, collecting the information needed to make contribution decisions is a simple task because the committee routinely contributes all of its funds to incumbents who are in a position to influence legislation that affects the company's income. The manager of PHH Group PAC also considers communications from the Mortgage Bankers Association's MorPAC and scorecards from industry trade organizations when deciding how to allocate contributions.[23] Both PAC managers are open to the suggestions of individuals who give donations to their committees, but they generally do not make contributions to candidates solely on the basis of donor suggestions.

Noninstitutionalized PACs and multitudes of other one-person organizations use informal decision-making processes. Their lack of formal rules and procedures allows their managers great flexibility in choosing candidates for support. Their limited staff resources force the PAC managers to turn to others for election-related information. These PACs are in a better position than more institutionalized committees to adjust their initial strategies in response to changing electoral conditions. Of course, in the case of very small committees, such as the AAP PAC, which contributed only $750 in 1998, this is true only as long as their money holds out.

Between the institutionalized PACs and the small, one-person organizations are semi-institutionalized committees that possess some of the characteristics of the PACs in the other two groups. These PACs include Powell, Goldstein, Frazer, and Murphy ("POGO") PAC, sponsored by a law firm with offices in both Washington, D.C., and Atlanta, Georgia. Semi-institutionalized PACs usually have staffs of two to four people, which are large enough to allow for a functional division of labor and to require the adoption of decision rules but small enough to render them dependent on outside research when making contribution decisions. For instance, POGO PAC, which has consistently pursued a modified access strategy, has a legal counselor, a treasurer, a PAC administrator, and a moderately active board of directors.[24] It contributed $87,242 during the 1998 elections, an amount sufficient to give the PAC and its law firm a presence in national and Georgia politics.

PACs with semi-institutionalized organizations typically rely on their staffs to process requests for contributions, but they look to others for political intelligence. POGO PAC gets most of its information from its parent firm's partners, associates, and clients, some of whom speak to party officials, members of other law firms and PACs, and other politically active individuals in the Washington and Atlanta metropolitan areas. The firm's members submit a short proposal for each contribution they would like the PAC to make. Then, the PAC's board, consisting of a small group of partners in Washington and Atlanta, votes on the request. Like most other semi-institutionalized committees, POGO PAC gives its board a significant role in decision making, but neither the staff nor the board becomes involved in time-consuming strategic planning sessions or searches for potential recipients of contributions.[25] These PACs do not give their officers as much flexibility as do the managers of one-person committees, but these officials have more freedom than is accorded the officers of institutionalized PACs.

Lead PACs constitute a final group of committees. These PACs, which include the NCEC, COPE, and BIPAC, are as complex organizationally as the institutionalized PACs.[26] They are every bit as thorough in their research and decision making as are the institutionalized committees and are motivated by ideological or policy goals. They differ from other committees in that they carry out research and select candidates for support with an eye toward influencing the decisions of other PACs. Much of the research conducted by lead PACs is oriented toward assessing the electability of individual candidates. Like the Hill committees, these PACs spend much time, money, and energy disseminating information about specific campaigns to other PACs. They occupy central positions in the networks of PACs, lobbyists, and individual contributors in the Washington fund-raising community.

CONTRIBUTIONS

PACs contributed a total of $203.6 million to major-party candidates in the 1998 congressional elections. Corporate PACs accounted for the most PAC contributions, followed by trade groups, labor committees, nonconnected PACs,

TABLE 5-2

PAC Contributions in the 1998 Congressional Elections (in thousands)

	House		Senate		
	Democrats	Republicans	Democrats	Republicans	Total
Corporate	$16,047	$33,794	$6,910	$13,963	$70,714
Trade, membership, and health	17,385	28,332	4,640	7,892	58,249
Cooperative	851	945	233	185	2,214
Corporations without stock	1,258	1,576	485	591	3,910
Labor	33,022	3,115	5,425	606	42,168
Leadership	2,600	5,996	375	1,741	10,712
Nonconnected	4,843	5,745	2,673	2,334	15,595
All PACs	$76,006	$79,503	$20,741	$27,312	$203,562

Source: Compiled from Federal Election Commission data.

Note: Figures are for PAC contributions to all major-party candidates, including candidates in primaries, runoffs, and uncontested races.

and leadership PACs. Corporations without stock and cooperatives contributed the least, giving less than $6.2 million (see Table 5-2).

Incumbents have laid claim to the lion's share of PAC money since the PAC boom of the 1970s. Since the mid-1980s, business-related PACs have been among the most incumbent-oriented committees, adhering more closely to an access-oriented strategy than do labor or ideological PACs. In 1998 corporate PACs made 87 percent of their House contributions to incumbents involved in major-party contested races (see Table 5-3), distributing 53 percent of them to shoo-ins. These committees donated little to House challengers and made a mere 8 percent of their House contributions to open-seat candidates. Corporate PACs made only 45 percent of their House contributions to candidates in competitive races, reflecting their goal of maintaining good relations with current members and their lack of concern with changing the composition of Congress.

Corporate PACs also pursue access-oriented goals when they contribute to Senate candidates. In 1998 they distributed 73 percent of their Senate contributions to incumbents, 12 percent to challengers, and 14 percent to open-seat candidates (see Table 5-4). Similarly, trade association PACs were generous to House and Senate incumbents and dedicated few resources to challengers and open-seat contests.

TABLE 5-3

The Allocation of PAC Contributions to House Candidates in the 1998 Elections

	Corporate	Trade, membership, and health	Labor	Leadership	Non-connected
Democrats					
Incumbents					
In jeopardy	13%	15%	27%	9%	16%
Shoo-ins	18	18	36	7	18
Challengers					
Hopefuls	1	2	13	6	6
Likely losers	—	—	4	1	1
Open-seat candidates					
Prospects	1	3	10	6	6
Mismatched	—	1	3	1	1
Republicans					
Incumbents					
In jeopardy	21%	19%	2%	21%	16%
Shoo-ins	35	30	6	8	20
Challengers					
Hopefuls	3	4	—	20	7
Likely losers	1	1	—	3	2
Open-seat candidates					
Prospects	6	6	—	17	7
Mismatched	1	1	—	2	1
Total House contributions ($, thousands)	$39,923	$37,943	$32,454	$8,221	$8,992

Source: Compiled from Federal Election Commission data.

Notes: Figures are for major-party candidates in contested general elections. Dashes = less than 0.5 percent. The categories and numbers of candidates are the same as those in Table 4-3. Some columns do not add to 100 percent because of rounding.

Labor PACs have consistently pursued highly partisan, mixed strategies. They contribute the vast majority of their money to Democrats. In 1998 labor contributions to House Democrats favored candidates in competitive races, but labor PACs distributed 36 percent of their funds to Democratic shoo-ins. Labor committees gave 55 percent of their Senate contributions to Democratic candidates in close races and only 29 percent to Democratic shoo-ins. Labor

TABLE 5-4

The Allocation of PAC Contributions to Senate Candidates in the 1998
Elections

	Corporate	Trade, membership, and health	Labor	Leadership	Non-connected
Democrats					
Incumbents					
In jeopardy	8%	10%	31%	7%	25%
Shoo-ins	19	19	29	3	18
Challengers					
Hopefuls	1	1	12	3	3
Likely losers	—	—	2	1	1
Open-seat candidates					
Prospects	3	5	12	3	4
Mismatched	2	2	4	1	2
Republicans					
Incumbents					
In jeopardy	19%	18%	1%	19%	13%
Shoo-ins	27	25	8	21	20
Challengers					
Hopefuls	11	10	—	22	7
Likely losers	—	1	—	5	—
Open-seat candidates					
Prospects	7	6	—	11	5
Mismatched	2	2	—	4	1
Total Senate contributions ($, thousands)	$20,646	$12,394	$5,827	$2,103	$4,954

Source: Compiled from Federal Election Commission data.

Notes: Figures are for major-party candidates in contested general elections. Dashes = less than 0.5 percent. The categories and numbers of candidates are the same as those in Table 4-3. Some columns do not add to 100 percent because of rounding.

contributions to candidates in both chambers appear to have been motivated by both access-oriented and election-oriented goals.

The flow of leadership PAC contributions follows roughly the same pattern as that of party-connected contributions, which include contributions by candidates, members of Congress not up for reelection, and congressional retirees.

Most 1998 leadership PAC money flowed to candidates in close races and to incumbents, who are likely to be in a position to help the donor with some political or legislative business in the future.

Nonconnected PACs, which have traditionally followed the ideological strategy of spending most of their money in close races, used mixed strategies in 1998. They made 58 percent of their House contributions and 57 percent of their Senate donations to candidates in close races, as compared with 68 percent and 84 percent in 1996.[27] Nonconnected PAC contributions in challenger and open-seat contests followed the familiar ideology-focused pattern of favoring candidates in close races. Nevertheless, these PACs' contributions to incumbents departed from the previous trend: liberal PACs contributed more money to House incumbent shoo-ins than to House incumbents in jeopardy, and conservative PACs contributed more money to safe incumbents in both chambers than to incumbents holding marginal seats.

Several factors contributed to the change in these PACs' giving patterns. The instability of the political environment in 1998—driven by the possibility of a change in partisan control of the House and the potential for the emergence of a filibuster-proof Senate—affected most incumbents. As a result, some safe representatives and senators pressured nonconnected PACs for contributions to bolster their own political survival. Other safe lawmakers took advantage of the political climate to pressure ideologically sympathetic PACs to contribute to their campaigns and later donated the money to their party's congressional campaign committee, their colleagues, or nonincumbents.

Some nonconnected PACs responded to lawmakers' requests for contributions for both policy and ideological reasons. They contributed to some safe incumbents because they were not as confident as usual of their ability to judge the political environment and discern whether these incumbents were indeed safe, and they recognized that a great deal was at stake in terms of controlling Congress. Some nonconnected PACs also contributed to safe incumbents for access. They wanted to ensure that their priority issues would remain visible on these members' and Congress's legislative agendas. The Conservative Victory Fund, for example, contributed 42 percent of its funds to safe incumbents, including 8 percent who faced no Democratic opposition in the general election.

CAMPAIGN SERVICES

Although most of the journalistic reporting on PACs has focused on contributions and independent expenditures, some PACs also carry out activities that have traditionally been conducted by political parties.[28] Some PACs (mainly ideological committees), including various PACs on both sides of the abortion rights issue, recruit candidates to run for Congress.[29] Others provide candidates with in-kind contributions of polls, campaign ads, issue research, fundraising assistance, and strategic advice. AMPAC, the Realtors PAC, and COPE, for example, contribute polls to some candidates.[30] The National Federation of Independent Business's SAFE Trust PAC, whose name stands for Save American Free Enterprise, hosts campaign training schools and produces media advertisements for many of the candidates it supports.[31] The LCV PAC is a centralized committee that coordinates its activities with the efforts of several state leagues of conservation voters. It helps congressional, state, and local candidates frame environmental issues; endorses pro-environment candidates; and publishes the "Dirty Dozen," a list of the members of Congress who the PAC says have the worst environmental records, and the "EarthList," which names candidates it considers major protectors of the environment. It also carries out issue advocacy campaigns, mobilizes pro-environment voters, makes campaign contributions, helps pro-environment candidates raise money, and makes independent expenditures against its opponents.[32] The NCEC provides Democratic House and Senate candidates and party committees with precinct-level demographic profiles, targeting assistance, and technical advice.[33] These and other PACs furnish campaign assistance in lieu of cash contributions because they want to influence how candidates' campaigns are run or leave a more enduring impression than one can get from simply handing over a check.

One of the most important forms of assistance that a PAC can give to a candidate, particularly a nonincumbent, is help with fund-raising. Lead PACs, such as BIPAC, COPE, and the NCEC, brief other PACs about the campaigns on their watch lists, using techniques similar to those used by the Hill committees. Even some smaller PACs, such as the Federal Managers Association PAC (representing federal employees), help congressional candidates raise money by cosponsoring fund-raising events or serving on candidates' fund-raising committees.[34] The maturation of the Washington PAC community has led to the development of several networks of PACs, or PAC "families," which assist each other in selecting candidates for support.[35]

EMILY's List, whose name stands for "Early Money Is Like Yeast" and whose motto is "It makes the dough rise," is an example of a PAC that gives candidates fund-raising assistance. This nonconnected committee supports pro-choice Democratic women candidates, helping them raise money in the early, critical stage of the election. EMILY's List requires its members to donate $100 to the PAC and to make minimum contributions of $100 to each of two candidates whom the PAC has designated for support. Members are instructed to write these checks to the candidates and then send them to the PAC, which in turn forwards the checks to the candidates with a letter explaining the PAC's role in collecting the money. Under this procedure, commonly referred to as "bundling," the PAC acts as a clearinghouse for individual campaign contributions. Bundling enables a PAC to direct more money to candidates than it is legally allowed to contribute. Bundling works well with individuals who wish to have a candidate acknowledge both their and the group's political support. Groups that bundle, and EMILY's List in particular, have played a major role in persuading individuals who have not previously made congressional contributions to become regular donors.[36]

EMILY's list made $233,721 in contributions, including $10,870 in in-kind donations, and $115,050 in independent expenditures during the 1998 elections. This activity was important, but it pales next to the $7.5 million in contributions it bundled from its 50,000 members to women Democratic candidates, including almost $2.3 million for House and $3.4 million for Senate contenders. EMILY's List also spent roughly $3 million on about eight million pieces of mail and more than two million telephone calls to 3.4 million women in twenty-six states.[37]

Organized interests besides PACs also provide candidates with help in congressional elections. Think tanks, such as the Heritage Foundation, provide issue research. Labor unions and church-based organizations in African American and ethnic communities have long histories of political activism and have made decisive contributions to Democratic candidates' field activities. Business leaders have traditionally assisted Republicans. AIPAC provides information about candidates to PACs that support Israel. Despite the fact that it carries out activities similar to those of lead PACs and the Hill committees, AIPAC gives no cash contributions to congressional candidates. Environmental groups and the Christian Coalition are relative newcomers to electoral politics, but their voter guides and voter mobilization efforts have played important roles in recent congressional elections.

Another group that provides information to PACs is Tactical Resources in American Democracy Management Services, more commonly known as Triad Management. Triad pushed the limits on the provision of campaign services to congressional candidates in 1996 when it began advising tax-exempt organizations on how to effectively spend soft money on issue advocacy ads. A conservative for-profit group that is closely tied to the Republican Party, Triad evaluates hundreds of GOP candidates. Then, for a fee, it advises its clients—conservative individuals and organizations—about how they can effectively participate in congressional elections. Like many political organizations, it offers instruction on how to make campaign contributions to candidates and PACs, which candidates and PACs share their views, and where their donations are likely to have the biggest impact on the election. The group's role in funneling money to candidates and PACs is not controversial, but it has been investigated for allegedly coordinating tax-exempt organizations' issue advocacy campaigns with congressional campaigns, a highly questionable practice that could be in violation of the FECA and federal tax law.[38]

INDEPENDENT EXPENDITURES AND ISSUE ADVOCACY

Independent expenditures usually take the form of direct communications from a PAC to voters that explicitly call for the election or defeat of one or more candidates. Issue advocacy ads by interest groups can be intended to harm or help a candidate's prospects, but they cannot expressly advocate a candidate's election or defeat. As noted earlier, independent expenditure efforts must be made with hard money and reported to the FEC, whereas issue advocacy ads can be financed with either hard or soft money. Because they are not subject to federal laws requiring public disclosure, it is impossible to learn precisely how much money interest groups spend on issue advocacy in a given election year, or the source of that money. Nevertheless, most estimates suggest that the amounts spent on issue advocacy and independent expenditures are impressive. The most visible expenditures of both kinds take the form of television, radio, and newspaper advertisements that are directed toward the general public.

Virtually all—98 percent—of the almost $9.3 million in independent expenditures made in the 1998 congressional elections were undertaken by nonconnected, trade, and labor PACs. Independent expenditures are consistent with the ideological or mixed strategies that these PACs follow. Moreover, because nonconnected PACs do not have organizational sponsors, and because labor and trade PACs are established to advance the political views of organizations that frequently have tens of thousands of members, these committees rarely worry about the retribution of an angry member of Congress or the negative publicity that might result from an independent expenditure. Unlike corporate PACs, these PACs are relatively safe from either outcome because they lack a single sponsor whose interests can be directly harmed.

PACs allocated about $5.8 million in independent expenditures in the 1998 primaries and general elections to advocate the election of individual House candidates and another $667,000 calling for their defeat. They spent an additional $2.1 million advocating the election of Senate candidates and $781,000 calling for their defeat.[39] Most independent expenditures are made in connection with closely contested elections. In 1998 PACs spent slightly over $4.5 million on House incumbents in jeopardy, hopeful challengers, and open-seat

TABLE 5-5

PAC Independent Expenditures in the 1998 House Elections

	Democrats		Republicans	
	For	Against	For	Against
Incumbents				
In jeopardy	$866,803	$121,415	$1,238,494	$347,557
Shoo-ins	11,522	67,786	739,151	32,424
Challengers				
Hopefuls	77,689	0	260,505	33,254
Likely losers	431	0	35,290	0
Open-seat candidates				
Prospects	517,587	13,150	956,227	50,293
Mismatched	77,070	0	27,710	0
Total	$1,551,102	$202,351	$3,257,377	$463,528

Source: Compiled from Federal Election Commission data.

Notes: Figures are for major-party candidates in contested general elections. The categories and numbers of candidates are the same as those in Table 4-3.

prospects (see Table 5-5). PACs spent only about $991,000 in uncompetitive House races. Incumbent-challenger contests were the focus of most PAC independent expenditures and, on balance, these favored challengers. The overall partisan balance of PAC independent expenditures had a Republican tilt.

The race in Pennsylvania's 13th congressional district featured the heaviest and most one-sided independent spending. The American Medical Association's PAC and the United Seniors PAC spent $639,645 and $1,334, respectively, to help Republican House member Jon Fox defend his seat against Democratic challenger Joseph Hoeffel, who benefited from a lone $35 independent expenditure by Planned Parenthood's PAC. Hoeffel, nevertheless, won the race by 5 percent of the vote. In contrast, another representative, John Hostettler, R-Ind., faced a barrage of $190,351 in adverse PAC spending by the League of Conservation Voters and counted only $19,647 in his favor, mostly from socially conservative groups. Yet he won by 6 percent of the vote.

PAC independent expenditures in Senate contests are similar to those for the House in that virtually all of the activity—a total of over $2.7 million in 1998—takes place in competitive races (see Table 5-6). Other similarities can be seen in the intention to influence the outcomes of incumbent-challenger races and

TABLE 5-6
PAC Independent Expenditures in the 1998 Senate Elections

	Democrats		Republicans	
	For	Against	For	Against
Incumbents				
In jeopardy	$542,381	$96,756	$595,281	$87,347
Shoo-ins	552	0	22,109	0
Challengers				
Hopefuls	29,314	8,831	481,263	597,345
Likely losers	395	0	16,242	0
Open-seat candidates				
Prospects	0	5,083	266,893	0
Mismatched	0	0	0	0
Total	$572,642	$110,670	$1,381,788	$684,692

Source: Compiled from Federal Election Commission data.

Notes: Figures are for major-party candidates in contested general elections. The categories and numbers of candidates are the same as those in Table 4-3.

the overall tilt in favor of incumbents. The 1998 record for independent expenditures in a Senate contest was set in the Nevada race between Democratic senator Harry Reid and Rep. John Ensign, his Republican challenger. Although the LCV PAC spent $311,169 to defeat Ensign, the National Rifle Association (NRA) PAC and the American Right to Life PAC spent $81,247 and $237, respectively, to help him. Reid benefited from $77,595 in positive independent expenditures from a variety of PACs and faced $2,365 in negative expenditures by the Conservative Victory Fund. Independent spending could have made a difference in the outcome of the race, which was decided in Reid's favor by a mere 428 votes.

The 1998 elections also set new records for interest group issue advocacy. It is estimated that interest groups spent between $170 million and $200 million on TV ads that directly mentioned the name or featured the likeness of a congressional candidate. They spent another $30 million to $40 million on ads that aimed to set a campaign agenda that favored one party's candidates.[40] Roughly three-quarters of the funds that interest groups spent to televise issue ads in House races were intended to affect the outcomes of competitive general elections. Groups allocated these funds in support of both parties' nonincumbents virtually equally, spending 32 percent to help challengers and 18 percent to help open-seat contestants. Groups spent an additional 12 and 15 percent, respectively, in support of Democratic and Republican incumbents. Americans for Limited Terms (ALT) and a few other groups used the remaining one-fourth to help unsuccessful primary candidates, to chastise safe incumbents who disagreed with their policy positions, and to publicize those positions in Washington, D.C.[41] Other issue advocacy expenditures took the form of direct mail, advertisements in trade magazines, or telephone calls to designated groups of voters.

The most extensive and widely discussed interest group–sponsored issue advocacy campaigns in 1996 and 1998 were carried out by the AFL-CIO. In 1996, under its new President John Sweeney, the AFL-CIO and affiliated unions spent $35 million in a highly successful campaign to mobilize union voters and their families in support of Democratic candidates. About $25 million was spent on mass media advertising, and the remainder was spent on voter mobilization.[42] In 1998 the AFL-CIO reversed its tactics, devoting more resources to the ground war and fewer to the air war. It also concentrated its resources on closer races. Whereas the union spent between $18 million and $19 million on voter mobilization efforts, it spent only $5 million on television and radio advertising. Its GOTV activities included 9.5 million pieces of direct mail and 5.5 million telephone calls to urge union members and their families to vote for Democrats. The union also hired three hundred activists to work with local union members to recruit tens of thousands of volunteers to visit work sites and make house calls on behalf of Democratic candidates. In addition, it made special efforts to mobilize black and Hispanic turnout in Chicago and throughout the South, enlisting the help of Jesse Jackson.[43]

The AFL-CIO's campaign was declared a success by labor and business leaders and the leaders of both parties. The result was record turnout and support for Democratic candidates. An estimated thirteen million union members went to the polls, and they registered a 71 percent preference for Democratic candidates, up from 68 percent in 1996 and from 60 percent in 1994, when the Republicans took control of Congress.[44] Labor's efforts were believed to have contributed to several Democratic victories, including Sen. Russell Feingold's 2 percent win over Mark Neumann in Wisconsin, Reid's victory over Ensign in Nevada, and Rep. Lane Evans's 3 percent win over Mark Baker in Illinois.

Various elements of the business community have responded to the AFL-CIO's recent campaign efforts, perhaps none more so than the National Federation of Independent Business (NFIB). During the 1996 elections the NFIB spent $1.1 million on internal communications and training sessions and organized the Coalition–Americans Working for Real Change. The Coalition spent $5 million to counter the AFL-CIO's massive issue advocacy campaign.[45] In 1998 the NFIB spent almost $290,000 on internal communications, and the Coalition spent over $1 million on televised issue advocacy ads.[46]

Noneconomic groups also carry out issue advocacy campaigns. The Sierra Club and the NRA are among the many noneconomic groups that spent money outside of the federal campaign finance system to influence the outcomes of congressional elections in 1998. Like the AFL-CIO and NFIB, these groups used voter guides, television and radio ads, internal communications to their members, and grass-roots activities to influence the campaign agenda in many races.[47] The Christian Coalition has a well-established lead over all other groups in the distribution of voter guides. Its efforts helped GOP candidates win many close contests, including several in the South.[48] The Christian Coalition helped the Republicans win control of Congress in 1994 and maintain control in the following two elections. In 1998 alone the group spent $3.1 million to distribute 36 million guides using church-based networks throughout the nation.

Some groups, such as U.S. Term Limits (USTL) and Americans for Limited Terms, use issue advocacy to promote political reform nationwide and influence individual congressional elections. These groups believe that long-term congressional incumbents are at the root of most of the problems with government. Part of their coordinated strategy consists of sponsoring initiatives and referenda and waging highly publicized issue-focused advocacy campaigns to enact term limits.[49] Another part of their strategy is to use carrots and sticks to get members of Congress and congressional candidates to limit their terms. Those who sign USTL's pledge receive endorsements from both groups, their support in op-ed articles, streams of press releases praising them for taking the pledge, and hundreds of thousands of dollars worth of issue advocacy ads heralding them as outstanding citizen-legislators or potential citizen-legislators. Those who do not sign the pledge face a barrage of negative press releases, unfavorable write-ups in op-ed pieces, and issue ads attacking them for being career politicians.

During the 1998 elections the ALT spent $8.5 million on issue advocacy ads praising or attacking candidates on term limits in fourteen House primaries and fifteen general election campaigns. USTL aired issue advocacy ads in two House races.[50] Following the elections, USTL ginned up its publicity machine to pressure legislators to honor their pledges.[51] Beginning in spring 1998, it sent out press releases and op-ed articles praising the nine representatives "who kept their word" to retire prior to the 2000 elections, attacking those who decided not to retire "for adding to public distrust of our leaders," and imploring those who had yet to decide to "do the right thing, and keep their word." Three candidates who opted to run for reelection despite their pledges were subjected to negative issue ads beginning more than eighteen months before election day 2000: Reps. Martin Meehan, D-Mass., George Nethercutt, R-Wash., and Scott McInnis, R-Colo.[52]

Other initiative campaigns that had both a direct and an indirect impact on individual congressional elections included the "paycheck protection" campaigns that business leaders initiated in several states during the 1990s. These campaigns sought to require that unions obtain written permission from each union member before they could use the member's union dues for political purposes. Their goal was to weaken the unions and thereby deprive Democratic candidates of a major source of campaign support. Not surprisingly, the paycheck protection initiatives met with fierce resistance. The unions responded by organizing their rank and file members. The unions' mobilization efforts had a spillover effect that ironically benefited many Democratic candidates, including Nevada Democrats Reid and Shelley Berkley, who won by slim margins.

Not all groups that carry out initiatives and referenda intend to influence the outcomes of individual congressional elections. Nevertheless, their efforts sometimes have that effect. A notable example is the 1994 campaign in California for proposition 187, which attempted to deny nonemergency medical care, public education, and other social services to illegal immigrants. Backed by Gov. Pete Wilson and other California Republicans, the initiative passed by a margin of 18 percentage points.[53] Although it was later declared unconstitutional, the initiative succeeded in mobilizing Asians, Hispanics, and other ethnic voters to participate in elections. Some of these newly enfranchised voters played an important role in Democrat Loretta Sanchez's defeat of Robert Dornan in 1996 and 1998 and in Barbara Boxer's reelection to the Senate in 1998.

Some of the groups that carry on issue advocacy campaigns are tax-exempt organizations that are not supposed to engage in partisan political activity. A few appear to be little more than fronts for more partisan organizations, including party committees. These groups collect funds from interest groups, party committees, and the individuals that parties and other groups refer to them. Their tax-exempt status enables the groups' contributors to deduct their donations from their federal taxes and enables the groups to avoid disclosing the sources of their funds to the FEC.[54] Two groups affiliated with Triad Management, Citizens for Reform and Citizens for the Republic Education Fund, spent $2.6 million on issue ads in 1996. In 1998 they spent millions more in Senate contests in Arkansas, Kentucky, South Carolina, South Dakota, Washington, and Wisconsin and in numerous competitive House races in the South and elsewhere.[55] Other tax-exempt groups that appear to have engaged in political activities are Project '98, the union-sponsored coalition that mobilized labor voters; Americans for Tax Reform, which mobilized conservative pro-Republican voters; and GOPAC, which was used by former Speaker Newt Gingrich to recruit Republican candidates and disseminate a pro-GOP message. Tax-exempt groups have become a tool for skirting federal campaign finance and tax laws. They have no political accountability, disseminate primarily negative communications, and have been known to impart misleading information to voters.

THE IMPACT OF INTEREST GROUP ACTIVITY

Congressional candidates and their campaign aides generally evaluate the help their campaigns get directly from PACs and other interest groups less favorably than the assistance they get from party committees.[56] They indicate that PACs and other groups play bigger roles in the campaigns of Democrats than in those of Republicans. Democratic candidates, for example, report receiving significantly more help than their GOP counterparts with mobilizing voters and recruiting volunteers from labor unions and other partisan groups. Senate candidates and campaign aides of both parties find PACs and other groups to be helpful in fund-raising but not as helpful as the DSCC or NRSC. House campaigners, however, appraise the fund-raising assistance of organized interests somewhat more favorably than the help they get from the DCCC or NRCC. Of course, interest group election efforts, like party efforts, are targeted to selected races. The information provided by both House and Senate campaigners indicates that interest group activity tends to be more heavily focused on competitive contests and more important to the election efforts of hopeful challengers and open-seat prospects than to those of incumbents. This is largely due to the fact that incumbents begin the election with high levels of name recognition and huge war chests, and nonincumbents do not.

Interest groups were active in many competitive 1998 House races. Their involvement was perhaps best exemplified by the Redmond-Udall race in New Mexico. PACs contributed $588,147 to Redmond and $303,493 to Udall. PACs also made $52,646 in independent expenditures in favor of Redmond, $35 to help Udall, $109,270 in opposition to Redmond, and none in opposition to Udall. Not surprisingly, PACs ignored Green Party nominee Miller.

A host of conservative associations, business groups, right-to-life groups, and organizations championing family values lined up in favor of Redmond. The NRA played a big role in the race. Its PAC, the NRA Political Victory Fund, contributed $9,900 to Redmond's campaign and made $57,037 in independent expenditures in support of him. Its Institute for Legislative Action spent almost $5,700 to communicate a pro-Redmond message to NRA members. The NRA also broadcast issue ads on the radio that featured NRA president Charlton Heston supporting Redmond and New Mexico's other two House members. Variations of these generic ads were broadcast across the nation to help pro-gun, mostly Republican, congressional candidates.[57]

The Association of Builders and Contractors spent almost $8,500 on radio ads pointing out that Redmond helped create jobs in New Mexico by keeping taxes low and business friendly. The Coalition produced direct mail that praised the incumbent's record on taxes, education, Social Security, and health care. The National Association of Manufacturers produced a pro-Redmond television ad that cost about $3,300, ran 310 times, mostly on cable TV, and praised him for working to lower taxes and for supporting families. The San Juan County Right-to-Life Committee spent $7,450 on pro-life ads. The Christian Coalition also blanketed local churches with voter guides that championed Redmond's position on abortion and family values—a tactic that it has used around the country for several election seasons.[58]

Udall benefited from a great deal of support from labor unions. COPE spent $20,316 to communicate a pro-Udall message to union members. It televised two pro-Udall issue advocacy ads that were aired 427 times. The first ad focused on Republican proposed tax cuts that would be paid for by raiding the Social Security Trust Fund. The second focused on health maintenance organizations (HMOs). The national union also sent direct mail that compared the two candidates on education and health care. The New Mexico branch of the AFL-CIO also sent out several pieces of direct mail that highlighted Udall's pro-union positions on these two issues, and the United Auto Workers Union used direct mail to attack Redmond on senior citizens issues.[59]

Environmental groups were also very active in the race. The LCV branded Redmond one of its "dirty dozen" and spent more than $151,200 in independent expenditures against him. It spent almost $130,000 on a TV issue ad that attacked Redmond's position on the environment. It also disseminated its pro-Udall, anti-Redmond views using telephone banks, direct mail, and more personalized, grass-roots activities. The Sierra Club sponsored a grass-roots literature drop, sent direct mail to twenty-five thousand local environmentalists, and sponsored a press conference in front of the state capitol building to discuss the candidates' stands on environmental issues.[60] Other groups that supported Udall included Planned Parenthood, People for the American Way, and the National Organization of Women.

Interest group efforts in Kentucky showed that groups can have a significant impact in Senate elections. Most of the group activity in the Bunning-Baesler race favored Bunning. Bunning raised almost $1.4 million in PAC contributions, and PACs made $250,753 in independent expenditures to help him while spending $5,083 to oppose Baesler. Although Baesler received $722,303 in PAC contributions, PACs themselves made no independent expenditures in support of him or against Bunning. Some groups distributed internal communications to their members and carried out more broadly targeted issue advocacy campaigns on television, radio, and through direct mail and telephone banks. A number of groups also distributed voter guides and carried out other grass-roots voter mobilization activities.

Several conservative groups took major steps to help Bunning. The NRA's Institute for Legislative Action spent $32,341 on internal communications in support of him. The NRA also spent approximately $140,000 on issue advocacy ads broadcast over the radio and on direct mail that praised Bunning and attacked Baesler. The radio ads, featuring Charlton Heston, were similar to the ads that the organization had run for the Redmond-Udall race and elsewhere around the country.[61]

Several pro-life and family values groups also got involved in the race. The National Right to Life Association (NRLA) contributed $4,000 in cash to Bunning, gave $3,690 in election services to his campaign, and made $58,553 in independent expenditures to help him. The NRLA also ran a major issue advertising campaign during the race: it spent almost $33,300 on radio ads, sent 300,000 pieces of direct mail, and paid for 150,000 telephone calls attacking Baesler. Among its target voters were African American Christians, who were urged to support Bunning because of his pro-life position. Most of the group's communications inaccurately portrayed Baesler as supporting "abortion on demand—even as a form of birth control." (The candidate actually favored parental consent for abortions for minors and bans on so-called partial-birth abortion.) The Campaign for Working Families, headed by Gary Bauer, a candidate for the Republican presidential nomination in 2000, contributed $10,000 in cash to the Bunning campaign and made independent expenditures of $40,000 on radio ads. The Christian Coalition distributed 500,000 voter guides to churches that compared the candidates' stances on abortion. The Family Trust Foundation of Kentucky also distributed thousands of voter guides focusing on Bunning's pro-life position to churches, grocery stores, and post offices.[62]

Two groups provided significant support for Baesler. The first group, the AFL-CIO, contributed $9,000 to his campaign and spent $131,385 on direct mail and telephone banks to communicate favorable information about him and to mobilize its members. COPE also spent more that $150,000 on state-wide televised issue ads that attacked GOP policies and urged citizens to vote. It spent additional funds on radio ads in selected parts of the state, including $15,000 in the Louisville area. Further attempts were made to mobilize other likely Democratic voters.[63]

The second group, Campaign for America, which is dedicated to overhauling campaign finance laws, sought to help Baesler because of his successful efforts to force a vote on campaign finance reform in the House during the

105th Congress. Financed almost exclusively by millionaire Jerome Kolberg, this group spent more than $325,000 on television ads that attacked Bunning. Ironically, they focused only indirectly on campaign finance reform. Instead, they mainly attacked Bunning's conservative voting record, especially his opposition to reforming HMOs. Some of these ads contended that Bunning switched his position after receiving large contributions from insurance PACs.[64]

It is impossible to tell whether interest group–sponsored issue advocacy ads and other activities, party efforts, or the candidates' campaigns determined the outcomes of the Bunning-Baesler race, the Redmond-Udall contest, or any of the other hotly contested 1998 congressional elections. In the absence of legal change, interest group-sponsored issue advocacy will probably become more important in setting the political agenda, touting the strengths and weaknesses of candidates, and mobilizing voters. Interest group and party spending in these areas will probably not do away with candidate-centered congressional elections, but in some races they may result in election agendas being set by organizations other than candidates' campaign committees. Also, it may become more common for Washington-based interest groups and party committees to outspend the candidates themselves in competitive House and Senate races.

SUMMARY

Interest groups, like parties, play important supporting roles in congressional elections. Most interest group activity takes the form of PAC contributions to candidates, but some PACs also distribute campaign services and make independent expenditures. In addition, some labor unions, business organizations, and issue-oriented and ideological groups provide congressional campaigns with volunteers, carry out voter mobilization drives, and use issue ads to influence the political agenda or affect individual candidates' election prospects. Because some interest groups view elections as opportunities to lay the groundwork for lobbying members of Congress, as well as vehicles for changing the membership of the legislative branch, they distribute some resources to House and Senate members in safe seats and others to incumbents, challengers, and open-seat candidates in close elections. More businesses than labor unions participate in congressional elections, and business groups typically spend more money in them than do their labor counterparts.

CHAPTER SIX

The Campaign for Resources

Vice President Hubert Humphrey described fund-raising as a "disgusting, degrading, demeaning experience."[1] This is a sentiment with which few politicians would disagree. Yet, spending money on political campaigns predates the Constitution. In 1757 George Washington purchased twenty-eight gallons of rum, fifty gallons of spiked punch, forty-six gallons of beer, thirty-four gallons of wine, and a couple of gallons of hard cider to help shore up his political base and pry loose the support of enough uncommitted voters to get elected to the Virginia House of Burgesses.[2] Population growth, technological advancements, suburbanization, and the other changes associated with the emergence of a modern mass democracy in the United States have driven up the costs of campaigning since Washington launched his political career. By the end of the millennium, candidates for Congress and other political offices will have spent billions of dollars to get elected.

As shown in previous chapters, the FECA restructured the campaign finance system by instituting disclosure requirements and regulating campaign contributions and expenditures made in direct connection with federal elections. Most of the FECA's loopholes concern issue advocacy and other soft money expenditures that are carried out by parties and interest groups. Candidate campaign activities continue to be heavily regulated by the FECA.

Raising the funds needed to run for Congress has evolved into a campaign in and of itself. Part of this campaign takes place in the candidate's state or district, but many candidates are dependent on resources that come from party committees and PACs located in and around Washington, D.C., and from wealthy individuals who typically reside in major metropolitan areas.

The campaign for resources begins earlier than the campaign for votes. It requires a candidate to attract the support of sophisticated, goal-oriented groups and individuals who have strong preconceptions about what it takes to win a congressional election. Theoretically, all congressional candidates can turn to the same sources and use the same techniques to gather campaign funds and services. In fact, however, candidates begin and end on uneven playing fields. The level of success that candidates achieve with different kinds of contributors or fund-raising techniques depends largely on whether they are incumbent, challenger, or open-seat candidates. It also depends on the candidates' party affiliation and on whether they are running for the House or the Senate. In this chapter I analyze the fund-raising strategies and successes of different kinds of candidates.

The 1998 House elections fell $25.3 million short of the $472.5 million spending record set in 1996, mainly because about 300 fewer candidates ran for a House seat.[3] Nevertheless, an all-time high of 110 candidates each spent more than $1 million, and 6 spent in excess of $3 million. Speaker Newt Gingrich, whose expenditures reached nearly $7.6 million, spent the most of any House candidate. Democratic challenger Phillip Maloof came in second, spending almost $5.4 million—96 percent of it his own money—in an unsuccessful rematch against Rep. Heather Wilson in New Mexico's 1st district.

Senate spending reached $287.6 million in 1998, a $300,000 increase over its 1996 spending. Fifty-six of the 68 major-party candidates each spent more than $1 million, including 30 who spent more than $3 million and eleven who spent above $6 million. The two biggest spenders were Republican incumbent Alfonse D'Amato of New York, who spent $24.2 million in an unsuccessful reelection campaign against Democrat Charles Schumer, and Republican challenger Peter Fitzgerald of Illinois, who spent nearly $17.7 million to defeat Sen. Carol Moseley-Braun. Still, these candidates fell well short of the record set by former representative Michael Huffington, R-Calif., who spent almost $30 million—nearly $28.4 million of it his own money—in an unsuccessful attempt to win an open seat in the Senate in 1994.

INEQUALITIES IN RESOURCES

Significant inequalities exist in the resources, including money and party coordinated expenditures, that different kinds of candidates are able to raise. The typical House incumbent involved in a two-party contested race raised just under $818,000 in cash and party coordinated expenditures in 1998, which is three times more than the sum raised by the typical House challenger.[4] Open-seat candidates also gathered significant resources, raising an average of almost $809,000.

FIGURE 6-1

Average Campaign Resources Raised in Competitive House Elections
in 1998

$, thousands

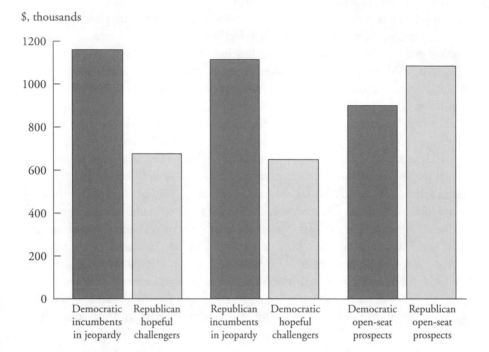

Source: Compiled from Federal Election Commission data.

Notes: Figures include receipts and party-coordinated expenditures for all two-party contests that were decided by margins of 20 percent of the vote or less. The categories and numbers of candidates are the same as
in Table 4-3.

   The resource discrepancies in competitive House races are great. Incumbents in jeopardy raised almost 72 percent more in cash and party coordinated
expenditures than did hopeful challengers during the 1998 elections (see Figure 6-1). Competitive open-seat contests were much more equal in regard to
the amount raised. The resource discrepancies in uncompetitive House contests are even greater than are those in competitive ones. Incumbents, who begin raising funds early (often before they know whom they will face in the
general election), raise much more money than their opponents (see Figure 6-
2). Incumbent shoo-ins raised almost seven times more than likely loser challengers in 1998. The spread among Democratic and Republican open-seat

FIGURE 6-2

Average Campaign Resources Raised in Uncompetitive House Elections in 1998

$, thousands

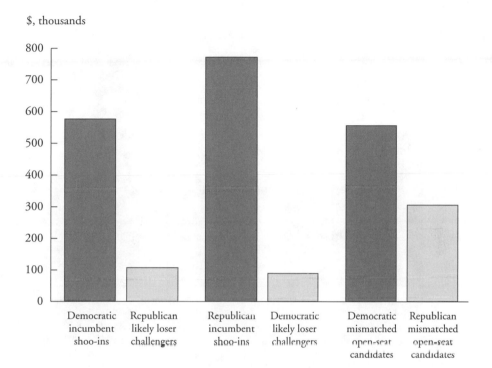

Source: Compiled from Federal Election Commission data.

Notes: Figures include receipts and party-coordinated expenditures for all two-party contests that were decided by margins over 20 percent of the vote. The categories and numbers of candidates are the same as in Table 4-3.

candidates in uncompetitive races is usually much smaller, amounting to less than $251,000.

The typical Senate incumbent raised about $1.8 million more than the typical challenger during the 1998 election (see Figure 6-3). Open-seat Senate contests were fairly well funded, with the average contestant spending just over $2.9 million. The differences in the amounts spent by Democratic and Republican candidates were relatively small, favoring GOP contenders by about $389,000. Finally, electoral competitiveness was important in attracting cam-

FIGURE 6-3

Average Campaign Resources Raised in the 1998 Senate Elections

$, millions

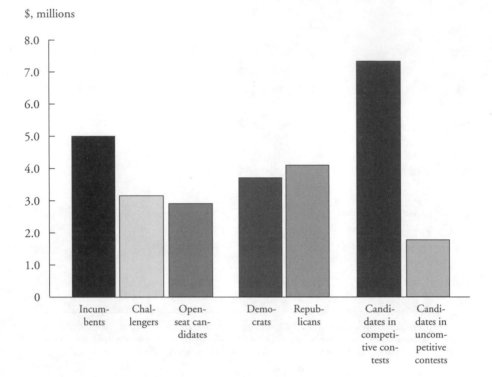

Source: Compiled from Federal Election Commission data.

Notes: Figures include receipts and party-coordinated expenditures for all two-party contested races. N = 68.

paign resources. Senate candidates who defeated their opponents by 20 percent of the two-party vote or less spent four times more than candidates involved in one-sided races.

HOUSE INCUMBENTS

Incumbents raise more money than challengers because they tend to be visible, popular, and willing to exploit the advantages of officeholding. This is reflected both in how incumbents solicit contributions and in whom they turn to for cash. Incumbents rarely hesitate to remind a potential donor that they are in a

FIGURE 6-4

Sources of House Incumbents' Campaign Receipts in the 1998 Elections

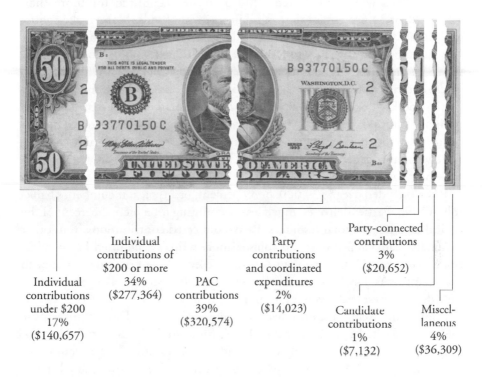

Individual
contributions
under $200
17%
($140,657)

Individual
contributions of
$200 or more
34%
($277,364)

PAC
contributions
39%
($320,574)

Party
contributions
and coordinated
expenditures
2%
($14,023)

Party-connected
contributions
3%
($20,652)

Candidate
contributions
1%
($7,132)

Miscel-
laneous
4%
($36,309)

Source: Compiled from Federal Election Commission data.

Notes: The dollar values in parentheses are averages. Candidate contributions include loans candidates made to their own campaigns. PAC contributions exclude contributions by leadership PACs. Party-connected contributions are made up of contributions from leadership PACs, candidates, retired members, and members of Congress not up for reelection in 1998. Miscellaneous includes interest from savings accounts and revenues from investments. Figures are for major-party candidates in contested general elections. Percentages do not add to 100 percent because of rounding. N = 306.

position to influence public policy and will more than likely still be in that position when the next Congress convenes.

Sources of Funds

Individuals who make contributions of less than $200, many of whom reside in a candidate's state or district, are an important source of funds for House incumbents (see Figure 6-4). In 1998 they accounted for $141,000, or 17 percent, of the average incumbent's campaign war chest.[5] Symbolically, they are often viewed as an indicator of grass-roots support.

Individuals who contributed $200 or more accounted for more than $277,000, or 34 percent, of the typical incumbent's funds. Many make contributions across district or state lines. Individuals living in just one New York City suburb—Greenwich, Connecticut, population 60,000—donated more than $3.1 million to 1998 House and Senate candidates across the United States. These contributions, along with the millions distributed by Washington-based parties and PACs, have helped to form a national market for campaign contributions.[6] Typical House incumbents in two-party contested races relied heavily on this market, raising the vast majority of their PAC money and approximately 23 percent of their individual contributions of $200 or more from outside their states' borders.[7]

PACs provided over $320,000, or 39 percent, of a typical incumbent's bankroll in 1998. Parties delivered much less, accounting for a mere 2 percent of the typical incumbent's total resources. Party-connected contributions from other members, leadership PACs, and congressional retirees accounted for an additional 3 percent. House members contributed even less of their own money to their campaigns. Finally, they raised about $36,000 from miscellaneous sources, including interest and revenues from investments.

Prior to the Republican takeover of Congress in 1994, Democratic House members collected a greater portion of their funds from PACs than did Republicans, who relied more heavily on individual contributors.[8] The Democrats' procedural control of the House gave them greater influence over the substance and scheduling of legislation, which provided them with an overwhelming advantage in raising money from PACs. The 1996 elections witnessed considerable change in this regard. Republican incumbents increased substantially the money they raised from PACs, although they continued to rely more on individuals than did their Democratic counterparts (see Table 6-1). Republican fund-raising followed a similar pattern throughout the 1998 election cycle.

Fund-Raising Activities

Incumbents routinely complain about the time, effort, and indignities associated with raising funds. Their lack of enthusiasm for asking people for money figures prominently in how they raise campaign contributions. A fear of defeat and a disdain for fund-raising have two principal effects: they encourage incumbents to raise large amounts of money and to place the bulk of their fund-raising in the hands of others, mainly professional consultants.

Most incumbents develop permanent fund-raising operations. They hire di-

TABLE 6-1

Sources of Support for House Incumbents in the 1998 Elections

	Democrats		Republicans	
	In jeopardy	Shoo-ins	In jeopardy	Shoo-ins
Individual contributions under $200	$187,100 (16%)	$70,006 (12%)	$220,256 (20%)	$154,004 (20%)
Individual contributions of $200 or more	$354,273 (31%)	$197,044 (34%)	$383,683 (34%)	$275,149 (36%)
PAC contributions	$476,532 (41%)	$271,460 (47%)	$364,536 (33%)	$283,047 (37%)
Party contributions and coordinated expenditures	$35,752 (3%)	$5,977 (1%)	$31,899 (3%)	$4,594 (1%)
Party-connected contributions	$42,302 (4%)	$8,008 (1%)	$52,662 (5%)	$9,297 (1%)
Candidate contributions	$6,115 (1%)	$1,099 (—)	$22,908 (2%)	$6,254 (1%)
Miscellaneous	$46,476 (4%)	$24,895 (4%)	$38,618 (3%)	$42,178 (5%)
(N)	(45)	(105)	(49)	(107)

Source: Compiled from Federal Election Commission data.

Notes: Figures are averages for major-party candidates in contested general elections. Dashes = less than 0.5 percent. Candidate contributions include loans candidates made to their own campaigns. PAC contributions exclude contributions by leadership PACs. Party-connected contributions are made up of contributions from leadership PACs, candidates, retired members, and members of Congress not up for reelection in 1998. Miscellaneous includes interest from savings accounts and revenues from investments. Some columns do not add to 100 percent because of rounding.

rect-mail specialists and PAC finance directors to write direct-mail appeals, update contributor lists, identify and solicit potentially supportive PACs, script telephone solicitations, and organize fund-raising events. These operations enable incumbents to limit their involvement to showing up at events and telephoning potential contributors who insist on having a direct conversation with them prior to making a large contribution.

Incumbents raise small contributions by making appeals through the mail, over the telephone, at fund-raising events, and via the Internet. Direct mail can be a relatively reliable method of fund-raising for an incumbent because solicitations are usually made from lists of previous donors that indicate which appeals garnered earlier contributions.[9] Most direct mail and telephone solicitations generate contributions of less than $100 and are targeted at the candidate's constituents. However, many prominent House members, including Gingrich and Minority Leader Richard Gephardt, have huge direct-mail lists that include hundreds of thousands of individuals who reside across the United States and even a few from abroad. A significant portion of these individuals contribute large sums. In 1998 Gingrich raised almost $652,000 in individual contributions of $200 or more from outside of Georgia, and Gephardt raised almost $2.2 million in individual large contributions from outside Missouri.[10]

The Internet emerged as an important fund-raising tool during the 1998 congressional elections. More than one-third of all House candidates and roughly three-fourths of all Senate candidates had Web sites in 1998; approximately half of them used their sites to solicit funds.[11] Some directed supporters where to send their checks, and others instructed donors how to make contributions online using a credit card.

Some campaigns used email to raise money. They solicited contributions using email addresses purchased from Internet providers and other companies. Email lists of individuals who share a candidate's issue concerns are a potential source of monetary and volunteer support, especially among computer-literate youth. The greatest advantage of email and Internet fund-raising is that the solicitation is delivered for free, compared with the $3 to $4 it costs to send out one first-class solicitation. The trade-off for emails is that they are not always appreciated. Mass distributed emails, often referred to as spam, after the nongourmet tinned meat product, are frequently deleted without having been read. Deleting an unread email is the electronic equivalent of tossing an unopened piece of direct mail into the trash or hanging up on a telemarketer.

Traditional fund-raising events are another popular means for raising small contributions. Cocktail parties, barbecues, and picnics with admission costs ranging from $10 to $50 that are held in the candidate's district are useful ways to raise money. They are also helpful in generating favorable press coverage, energizing political activists, and building goodwill among voters.

Incumbents can ensure the success of local fund-raising events by establishing finance committees that include business executives, labor officials, civic leaders, and political activists who live in their districts. These committees often begin with a dozen or so supporters who host "low-dollar" receptions (where individuals usually contribute from $20 to $100) in their homes and make telephone solicitations on the candidate's behalf. Guests at one event are encouraged to become the sponsors of others. In time, small finance committees can grow into large pyramid-like fund-raising networks, consisting of dozens of finance committees, each of which makes a substantial contribution to the candidate's reelection efforts. Most House and Senate incumbents have fund-raising networks that extend from their district or state to the nation's capital.

Individual large contributions and PAC money are also raised by finance committees, at fund-raising events, and through networks of supporters. Events that feature the president, congressional leaders, sports heroes, or other celebrities help attract individuals and groups who are willing to contribute anywhere from a few hundred dollars to the legal maximum of $1,000 per each stage of the race. Some of these events are held in the candidate's state, but most are held in such political, financial, and entertainment centers as Washington, New York City, and Hollywood.

Traditional fund-raising events can satisfy the goals of a variety of contributors. They give individuals who desire proximity to power, the opportunity to speak with members of Congress and other political elites. Persons and groups that contribute for ideological reasons get the opportunity to voice their specific issue concerns. Individuals and organizations that are motivated by material gain, such as a tax break or federal funding for a project, often perceive these events as opportunities to build a relationship with members of Congress.[12]

In raising individual large contributions House members have advantages over challengers that extend beyond the prestige and political clout that come with incumbency and an ability to rely on an existing group of supporters. Incumbents also benefit from the fact that many wealthy individuals have motives that favor them over challengers. Almost 30 percent of all individuals who contribute $200 or more to a congressional candidate wish to gain access to individuals who will be in a position to influence legislation once the election is over—mainly incumbents. Another 36 percent contribute because they enjoy attending fund-raising events and mixing with incumbents and other elites who attend these events. The final 34 percent contribute for broad ideological reasons or because of their positions on specific, highly charged issues. These donors tend to rally around incumbents who champion their causes.[13]

Moreover, information that parties and PACs mail to their big donors often focuses on incumbents' campaigns, further leading some wealthy individuals to contribute to incumbents in jeopardy rather than to hopeful challengers. The rise of national party organizations, PACs, and other Washington-based cue-givers and the FECA's ceilings on campaign contributions have led to the replacement of one type of fat cat with another. Individuals and groups that directly gave candidates tens or hundreds of thousands of dollars have been replaced by new sets of elites that help candidates raise these sums rather than directly contribute them.[14]

Incumbents consciously use the influence that comes with holding office to raise money from PACs and wealthy individuals who seek political access. Legislators' campaigns first identify potential donors who are most likely to respond favorably to their solicitations. These include PACs that supported the incumbent in a previous race, lobbyists who agree with an incumbent's positions on specific issues, and others who are affected by legislation that the incumbent is in a position to influence. Members of Congress who hold party leadership positions, serve on powerful committees, or are recognized entrepreneurs in certain policy areas can easily raise large amounts of money from many wealthy interest-group-based financial constituencies. It is no coincidence that the four House incumbents who raised more than $900,000 in PAC contributions in 1998 all held leadership positions.[15]

Once an incumbent has identified his or her financial constituency, the next step is to ask for a contribution. The most effective solicitations describe the member's background, legislative goals, accomplishments, sources of influence (including committee assignments, chairmanships, or party leadership positions), the nature of the competition faced, and the amount of money needed. Incumbents frequently assemble this information in the PAC kits they mail to PACs.

Some PACs require a candidate to meet with one of their representatives, who personally delivers a check. A few require incumbents to complete questionnaires on specific issues, but most PACs rely on members' prior roll-call votes or interest group ratings as measures of their policy proclivities. Some PACs, particularly ideological committees, want evidence that a representative or senator is facing serious opposition before giving a contribution. Party leaders and Hill committee staff are sometimes called to bear witness to the competitiveness of an incumbent's race.

Parties are another source of money and campaign services. The most important thing incumbents can do to win party support is demonstrate that they are vulnerable. The Hill committees have most of the information they need to make such a determination, but incumbents can give details on the nature of the threat they face that might not be apparent to a party operative who is unfamiliar with the nuances of a member's seat. The NRCC gives incumbents who request extra party support the opportunity to make their case before a special Incumbent Review Board composed of GOP members. Once a Hill committee has made an incumbent a priority, it will go to great efforts to supply the candidate with money, campaign services, and assistance in collecting resources from others.

The financing of Rep. Ed Royce's 1998 reelection effort in California's 39th congressional district is typical of that of most reelection bids involving safe incumbents. Royce raised $587,551 during the 1998 election season and received $165 in coordinated expenditures from the state GOP, substantially less than the $10,581 received by the typical House incumbent. He collected nearly $130,118 (22 percent of his total resources) in small contributions using campaign newsletters, direct-mail solicitations, and many low-dollar fund-raising events held in the district.[16] He collected another $226,767 (roughly 39 percent) in individual contributions of $200 or more at high-dollar events. Just over 7 percent of these funds were raised from individuals who reside outside of California.[17]

Royce raised $199,282 (34 percent) from PACs (excluding leadership PACs). Corporate, trade, and other business-related committees contributed about 93 percent of these funds. Nonconnected committees accounted for 7 percent of Royce's PAC dollars. The candidate collected no contributions from other members' campaign committees, but he did receive $1,826 (almost 1 percent of his PAC money) from their leadership PACs. He raised no money from labor PACs, which is not unusual for a Republican. Most of his PAC money and large individual donations were raised at events held in the district or in Washington and through solicitations coordinated by the candidate's campaign staff. Finally, the campaign raised $1,000 in contributions from party committees and collected $28,588 from interest in loans and investments (4 percent of its total campaign receipts). Like most congressional incumbents, Royce contributed no money to his own reelection effort.

Royce was successful at capitalizing on his membership on the Banking and Financial Services Committee. The individuals and groups that are affected by the committee's business make up one of the nation's wealthiest interest group constituencies. Royce's campaign collected $109,277 (54 percent of its PAC funds) from finance, insurance, real estate, and miscellaneous business PACs, and it raised another $174,127 in contributions of $200 or more from individuals who work in these economic sectors (77 percent of his total individual large contributions).[18]

With only two-year terms, House incumbents usually begin raising money almost immediately after they are sworn into office. Sometimes they have debts to retire, but often they use money left over from previous campaigns as seed money for the next election. Thirty-five percent of all House incumbents began the 1998 election cycle with more than $100,000 left over from their previous campaigns. Over 62 percent of all successful 1998 incumbents completed their campaigns with more than $100,000 in the bank, including twelve incumbents who had amassed more than $1 million. These funds will provide useful seed money for their reelection campaigns in 2000 or bids for some other office.

Early fund-raising is carried out for strategic reasons. Incumbents build substantial war chests early in the election cycle to try to deter potential challengers.[19] An incumbent who had to spend several hundreds of thousands or even millions of dollars to win by a narrow margin in the last election will have a greater compulsion to raise money early than someone whose previous election was a landslide victory. Once they have raised enough money to reach an initial comfort level, however, incumbents appear to be driven largely by the threat posed by an actual challenger.[20] Incumbents under duress seek to amass huge sums of money regardless of the source, while those who face weak opponents may weigh other considerations, such as developing a "diversified portfolio of contributors."[21]

A typical incumbent's campaign—one waged by a candidate who faces stiff competition in neither the primary nor the general election—will generally engage in heavy fund-raising early and then allow this activity to taper off as it becomes clear that the candidate is not in jeopardy. The 1998 Royce campaign exemplifies this pattern. Between January 1 and December 31, 1997, Royce raised $291,472 (about half of his receipts). All money was raised before Cecy Groom, his general election opponent, had filed for candidacy with the state of California. The following year, Royce continued to raise money at a leisurely pace. Between January 1 and June 30 of 1998, he raised $136,605 (23 percent). In the next three months, he raised another $60,090 (10 percent). During this same three months, Groom raised $60,589, much of which the candidate herself loaned to the campaign. Royce barely responded to Groom's investment. He raised another $96,738 (16 percent)—considerably less than the amount he had collected before Groom declared her candidacy—between October 1 and November 23, the first postelection reporting deadline. After the election he collected $3,096 (less than 1 percent). According to his campaign manager, Royce—who did his own fund-raising—never felt pressured to raise a great deal of money, particularly when it became apparent that Groom's candidacy did not pose a serious challenge.[22]

Royce's 1998 campaign finances demonstrate that a good deal of incumbent fund-raising is challenger-driven. Early money is raised to deter a strong opponent from entering the race. If a strong challenger materializes, then an incumbent's fund-raising activities will usually increase. If none emerges, they will remain steady or slow down.

The 1998 Price campaign also supports the generalization that incumbent fund-raising is challenger-driven. In addition, it shows how an incumbent responds to a strong challenger. The campaign collected almost $1.3 million and more than $24,400 in coordinated expenditures, making it the forty-first-most-expensive House reelection campaign waged that year. It raised $416,995 (33 percent of its total resources) from PACs, excluding leadership PACs, and another $395,294 (31 percent) in individual contributions of $200 or more, over 80 percent of which was collected from individuals living in North Carolina.[23] The campaign collected $335,543 (26 percent) in individual contributions of less than $200. The Democratic Party provided $27,358 in contributions and coordinated expenditures (about 2 percent). Democratic members of Congress and retirees contributed $36,500, and leadership PACs gave another $21,000 (for a total of 3 percent).[24]

Price began to solicit contributions early and aggressively because he recognized that his 1994 defeat and his ten-point victory over an ailing Rep. Fred Heineman in 1996 made him a prime target for a strong Republican challenge. Between January 1 and June 30, 1997, Price's campaign amassed a treasury of $111,719 (roughly 9 percent of its total funds). Between July 1 and December 31 it collected another $125,097 (10 percent). All this money was raised despite the fact that Price had faced only token opposition in the Democratic primary.[25] Thomas Roberg, the only Republican to officially challenge him, did not declare his candidacy until May 20 and by then had yet to raise a penny.

Following Roberg's declaration of candidacy, Price believed he would be in a tough race. He knew Roberg to be an articulate speaker who understood how campaigns are run and was capable of making a large personal investment in his own campaign. Roberg's declaration encouraged the Price campaign to maintain the pace of its fund-raising. By June 30, 1998, the campaign had raised an additional $274,634 (22 percent). Roberg's $227,817 in receipts encouraged the Price campaign to press its fund-raising efforts further. Between July 1 and September 30 Price collected another $428,778 (about 34 percent). The campaign raised $311,019 (25 percent) between October 2 and November 23 and collected just over $3,527 by the end of the year to help close out its debts.

The Price campaign's fund-raising was driven by the threat the candidate had anticipated, which eventually arose. Just as a lack of competition had caused Royce to raise less money than the typical incumbent, stiff competition encouraged Price to set a personal fund-raising record.

HOUSE CHALLENGERS

Challengers have the greatest need for money, but they encounter the most difficulties raising it. The same factors that make it difficult for challengers to win votes also harm their ability to collect campaign contributions. A lack of name recognition, limited campaign experience, a relatively untested organization, and a high probability of defeat discourage most contributors, especially those who give large amounts in pursuit of access, from supporting challengers. The fact that their opponents are established Washington operators who possess political clout does not make challengers' quests for support any easier.

Sources of Funds

Challengers raise less money than incumbents, and their mix of funding sources differs from that of incumbents. House challengers raise a greater portion of their funds from individuals. Challengers competing in the 1998 elections raised an average of about $56,000, or 21 percent of their campaign budgets, in individual contributions of less than $200 (see Figure 6-5). Challengers collected nearly the same portion of their funds as incumbents in the form of individual contributions of $200 or more, but the average $88,705 that they raised was less than one-third the amount raised by a typical incumbent. Moreover, challengers raised only 18 percent of these funds from out of state, a significantly smaller proportion than that collected by incumbents.

Challengers garnered 14 percent of their money from PACs, trailing incumbents by a ratio of more than 1:8. Party money, in contrast, played a greater role in challenger than in incumbent campaigns. Challengers, on average, received almost $3,400 more in party contributions and coordinated expenditures than did incumbents, but they raised almost $9,000 less in party-connected contributions. Finally, challengers dug far deeper into their own pockets than did incumbents. The typical challenger contributed or loaned the campaign almost $52,000—more than seven times the amount contributed or loaned by the typical incumbent.

Democratic challengers, especially Democratic hopefuls, raised substantially more money from PACs than did their Republican counterparts (see Table 6-2). Republican challengers collected more money from individuals who made large contributions. Republican hopefuls received more party support than did Democrats. Democrats, however, invested substantially more in their own campaigns, reflecting the greater career orientation that many Democratic politicians have toward politics.

Fund-Raising Activities

Most competitive challengers start raising early money at home. They begin by donating or loaning their campaigns the initial funds that are needed to solicit contributions from others. They then turn to relatives, friends, professional

FIGURE 6-5

Sources of House Challengers' Campaign Receipts in the 1998 Elections

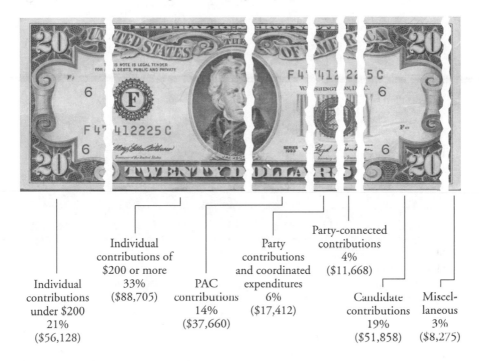

Individual
contributions of
$200 or more
33%
($88,705)

Individual
contributions
under $200
21%
($56,128)

PAC
contributions
14%
($37,660)

Party
contributions
and coordinated
expenditures
6%
($17,412)

Party-connected
contributions
4%
($11,668)

Candidate
contributions
19%
($51,858)

Miscel-
laneous
3%
($8,275)

Source: Compiled from Federal Election Commission data.

Notes: See notes in Figure 6-4. N = 306.

colleagues, local political activists, and virtually every individual whose name is in their Rolodex or on their holiday card list. Some of these people are asked to chair fund-raising committees and host fund-raising events. Candidates who have previously run for office are able to turn to past contributors for support. Competitive challengers frequently obtain lists of contributors from members of their party who have previously run for office or from private vendors. In some cases, challengers receive lists from party committees or PACs; however, most of these organizations mail fund-raising letters on behalf of selected candidates rather than physically turn over their contributor lists.

Only after enjoying some local fund-raising success do most nonincumbents set their sights on Washington. Seed money raised from individuals is especially helpful in attracting funds from PACs, particularly for candidates who have

TABLE 6-2
Sources of Support for House Challengers in the 1998 Elections

	Democrats		Republicans	
	Hopefuls	Likely losers	Hopefuls	Likely losers
Individual contributions under $200	$126,951 (20%)	$18,841 (21%)	$154,039 (23%)	$19,144 (18%)
Individual contributions of $200 or more	$210,044 (32%)	$28,465 (32%)	$227,284 (34%)	$34,076 (32%)
PAC contributions	$116,844 (18%)	$13,404 (15%)	$79,062 (12%)	$7,683 (7%)
Party contributions and coordinated expenditures	$30,433 (5%)	$2,902 (3%)	$59,975 (9%)	$7,879 (7%)
Party-connected contributions	$19,556 (3%)	$819 (1%)	$47,897 (7%)	$3,514 (3%)
Candidate contributions	$131,471 (20%)	$22,375 (25%)	$84,721 (13%)	$30,666 (28%)
Miscellaneous	$12,418 (2%)	$3,270 (4%)	$24,066 (4%)	$4,674 (4%)
(N)	(49)	(107)	(45)	(105)

Source: Compiled from Federal Election Commission data.

Notes: See notes in Table 6-1.

not previously held elective office.[26] The endorsements of local business, labor, party, or civic leaders have a similar effect. If it can be obtained, the assistance of congressional leaders or members of a candidate's state delegation can be very helpful to challengers who hope to raise money from their party's congressional campaign committee, PACs, or individual large contributors.[27] When powerful incumbents organize luncheons, attend "meet-and-greets," and appear at fund-raising events for nonincumbents, contributors usually respond favorably. Unfortunately for most challengers, their long odds of success make it difficult for them to enlist the help of incumbents. House members prefer to focus their efforts on candidates who have strong electoral prospects and may someday be in a position to return the favor by supporting the member's leadership aspirations or legislative goals in Congress.

A knowledge of how party leaders and PAC managers make contribution decisions can improve challengers' fund-raising prospects. Political experience and a professional campaign staff are often helpful in this regard.[28] Candidates who put together feasible campaign plans, hire reputable consultants, and can present polling figures indicating that they enjoy a reasonable level of name recognition can usually attract the attention of party officials, PAC managers, individuals who make large contributions, and the inside-the-beltway journalists who handicap elections. Political amateurs who wage largely volunteer efforts, in contrast, usually cannot.

During the 1998 congressional elections, House challengers in two-party contested races who had previously held elective office raised, on average, $33,500 from party committees and $28,900 in party-connected contributions from other candidates, retired members of Congress, and leadership PACs. Unelected politicians raised an average of $19,100 from party committees and $10,800 in party-connected dollars, whereas political amateurs raised an average of only $11,300 and $6,200 from these sources. Challengers who fielded professional campaign organizations raised an average of $37,300 in party contributions and coordinated expenditures and $27,800 in party-connected contributions, amounting to eighteen times more than was raised from these sources by challengers who relied largely on volunteers.[29] Roberg, who had substantial nonelective political experience and ran a professional campaign, raised $9,500 from the NRCC and the RNC and $63,000 in coordinated expenditures from the NRCC—close to the legal maximum in party support. He also raised $9,281 in party-connected contributions. Groom, who in contrast ran a largely volunteer effort, received a generic television ad valued at $15,700 as a coordinated expenditure from the DCCC and no party-connected donations.

One way in which challengers can increase their chances of success in raising money from PACs is for them to identify the few committees that are likely to give them support. For Democrats, these committees include labor groups. Challengers can improve their prospects of attracting labor PAC money by showing they have strong ties to the labor community, have previously supported labor issues in the state legislature, or support labor's current goals.[30] Competitive Democratic challengers who were able to make this case in 1998 did quite well with the labor community, raising an average of $231,750 from labor PACs.

Challengers of both parties may be able to attract support from PACs, particularly ideological committees, by convincing PAC managers that they are committed to the group's cause. A history of personal support for that cause is useful. Challengers, and in fact most nonincumbents, typically demonstrate this support by pointing to roll-call votes they cast in the state legislature, to the backing of PAC donors or affiliated PACs located in their state or district, or to the support of Washington-based organizations that share some of the PAC's views. Nonincumbents who make a PAC's issues among the central elements of their campaign message and communicate this information in their PAC kits enhance their odds of winning a committee's backing. Properly completing a PAC's questionnaire or having a successful interview with a PAC manager is extremely important.

Political experience and professional expertise also can help a nonincumbent raise PAC money. In 1998 challengers who had previously held office raised an average of $123,100 from PACs, roughly $64,300 more than did the typical unelected politician and $92,600 more than did the typical amateur. Challengers who fielded professional campaign organizations raised, on average, approximately $75,000 more than did those who relied mostly on volunteers.

Ideological causes were in the forefront of many candidates' PAC fund-raising strategies during the last few decades. Women challengers were able to capitalize on their gender and attract large amounts of money and campaign assistance from EMILY's List, the WISH List (the Republican counterpart of EMILY's List), and other pro-women's groups.[31] Challengers who take a stand on either side of the abortion issue are frequently able to raise money from PACs that share their positions. By taking a side on such emotionally laden issues as handgun control or support for Israel some challengers are able to attract the support of ideological PACs.

A perception of competitiveness is critical to challenger fund-raising, and a scandal involving an incumbent can help a challenger become competitive. The 1992 elections were the last to include a large number of legislators implicated in some form of scandal. Clearly not every incumbent who was reported to have bounced a check at the House bank had to worry about being accused of committing a major ethical transgression, but any House member who wrote twenty-five or more bad checks or was the subject of some other highly publicized investigation had good reason to show concern. These incumbents typically drew strong opponents who raised an average of $33,000 more than did challengers who did not run against an incumbent implicated in a scandal, including nearly $5,000 more from parties and almost $10,000 more from PACs.

Groom's and Roberg's experiences demonstrated the effect that perceptions of competitiveness have on challenger fund-raising. Almost from the beginning, Groom's campaign to unseat Royce was in trouble. Her win over Charlie Ara by a 0.4 percent margin in the open primary gave her the right to appear on the ballot as the Democratic nominee, but Royce's commanding first place finish in the primary overshadowed her victory. Royce won more than 67 percent of the vote, whereas Groom finished second with less than 15 percent. Groom began collecting money about a year after Royce, which is typical in most incumbent-challenger races. Between April 1, 1998, when the Groom campaign first began raising money, and June 30, 1998, it collected $60,589 (45 percent of its receipts), two-thirds of which was loaned by the candidate herself. The campaign then raised $39,115 (29 percent) between July 1 and September 30 and another $33,515 (25 percent) between October 1 and November 23.[32] Groom's loans to the campaign again accounted for two-thirds of the total. The campaign raised no money after November 23, despite the fact it owed the candidate $56,801.

Groom's fund-raising troubles typify those of most House challengers, including virtually all likely-loser challengers, who lose by large margins. The candidate got a late start fund-raising and had no professional operation to solicit contributions for her. She had difficulty raising PAC money—collecting only $2,000, which came entirely from the American Federation of State, County, and Municipal Employees' PAC. She also had a hard time collecting from individual donors and raised only $2,500 in out-of-state contributions.[33] She sought to compensate for her shortcomings as a fund-raiser by investing heavily in her own campaign.

The Roberg campaign exemplifies the fund-raising dynamics of a challenger who is capable of waging a competitive campaign. As a result of his chairing the Wake County Republican Party and his involvement in GOP politics, Roberg had established the basis for a fund-raising network in his home state of North Carolina. His campaign fund-raising is typical of that of most hopeful challengers in that he used a variety of techniques to solicit money from a broad array of individuals and groups. Experience, a professional organization, an effective strategy, and personal wealth enabled Roberg to raise $472,008 in contributions, plus $63,000 in party coordinated expenditures, in his race against Price. Roberg raised $29,600 from PACs (excluding leadership PACs), $144,905 in individual contributions of $200 or more, $86,844 in small contributions, and $9,281 in party-connected contributions.[34] Roberg raised more than 97 percent of his large individual contributions in North Carolina.[35] He loaned his campaign $180,000.

The Roberg campaign, unlike the Groom organization, began collecting money for the 1998 contest within eight months of the 1996 election. The candidate loaned his campaign $50,000 in seed money, and its initial solicitations were successful. Its coffers held $81,498 (roughly 17 percent of its funds) by December 31, 1997, and it collected an additional $140,619 (30 percent) between January 1 and June 30, 1998. The campaign raised an additional $142,515 (30 percent) by September 30, and it picked up another $104,876 (22 percent) in the remaining three weeks before election day. After his defeat, Roberg raised $2,500 (less than 1 percent) to help retire his campaign debts.

The initial competitiveness of the race helped Roberg attract the support of party committees, PACs, and individuals who were drawn by the opportunity of recapturing the district from the Democrats. Unfortunately for Roberg, Price's supporters also responded to the competitiveness of the race, enabling the incumbent to raise $2.39 in contributions and coordinated expenditures for every $1.00 the challenger collected. The dynamics of the race were similar to those in many close incumbent-challenger contests: a hopeful challenger raised enough funds to run a competitive campaign, but the incumbent collected many times more money to retain the seat.

CANDIDATES FOR OPEN HOUSE SEATS

Candidates for open seats possess few of the fund-raising advantages of incumbents but also lack the liabilities of challengers. Open-seat candidates rely on many of the same fund-raising strategies as challengers but usually have considerably more success. Because most open-seat contests are competitive, they receive a great deal of attention from parties, PACs, and other informed contributors. This attention places open-seat candidates in a position to convince Washington insiders that their campaigns are worthy of support.

Sources of Funds

The campaign receipts of open-seat candidates resemble those of both incumbents and challengers. Open-seat candidates raise about the same amount of money as do incumbents. Like challengers, however, they usually collect fewer individual contributions from out of state (approximately 17 percent in 1998) and more of their funds from parties and party-connected sources (about 5 percent from each) (see Figure 6-6). The typical open-seat candidate's PAC receipts lie between those collected by incumbents and those amassed by challengers. Open-seat candidates contribute more of their own money than do either incumbents or challengers.

Republican open-seat candidates collected more PAC money in 1998 than

FIGURE 6-6

Sources of House Open-Seat Candidates' Campaign Receipts in the 1998
Elections

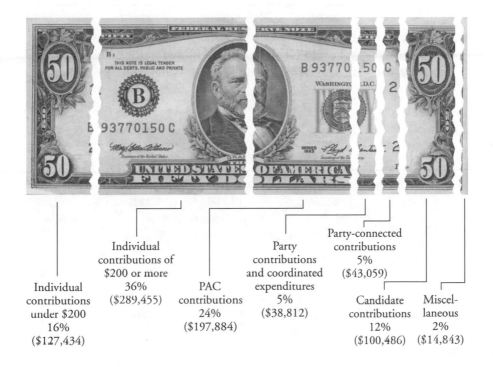

| Individual contributions under $200 16% ($127,434) | Individual contributions of $200 or more 36% ($289,455) | PAC contributions 24% ($197,884) | Party contributions and coordinated expenditures 5% ($38,812) | Party-connected contributions 5% ($43,059) | Candidate contributions 12% ($100,486) | Miscellaneous 2% ($14,843) |

Source: Compiled from Federal Election Commission data.

Notes: See notes in Figure 6-4. N = 68.

they had in elections held before the 1994 Republican takeover of Congress.
Republican candidates relied more on party and party-connected support than
did their Democratic counterparts (see Table 6-3). GOP open-seat candidates
also bankrolled larger portions of their own campaigns.

Fund-Raising Activities

Open-seat candidates can help their cause by informing potential contributors
of the experience and organizational assets they bring to the race, but these
factors have less effect than do others, such as the partisan makeup of the dis-

TABLE 6-3

Sources of Support for House Open-Seat Candidates in the 1998 Elections

	Democrats		Republicans	
	Prospects	Mismatched	Prospects	Mismatched
Individual contributions under $200	$171,487 (19%)	$134,086 (24%)	$119,969 (11%)	$44,282 (14%)
Individual contributions of $200 or more	$331,762 (37%)	$237,617 (42%)	$357,714 (33%)	$110,108 (36%)
PAC contributions	$237,932 (26%)	$132,030 (24%)	$243,901 (22%)	$83,783 (27%)
Party contributions and coordinated expenditures	$48,226 (5%)	$1,191 (—)	$64,736 (6%)	$2,543 (1%)
Party-connected contributions	$41,288 (5%)	$6,166 (1%)	$75,482 (7%)	$15,862 (5%)
Candidate contributions	$52,424 (6%)	$38,739 (7%)	$204,420 (19%)	$45,410 (15%)
Miscellaneous	$16,805 (2%)	$10,514 (2%)	$18,990 (2%)	$6,397 (2%)
(N)	(23)	(11)	(23)	(11)

Source: Compiled from Federal Election Commission data.

Notes: See notes in Table 6-1.

trict, on the fund-raising abilities of open-seat candidates. Unelected politicians raised the most party money in 1998, averaging about $42,400, $2,600 more than that collected by the typical elected official and approximately $8,400 more than that raised by the typical amateur. Elected politicians, however, raised the most party-connected contributions, averaging $47,100, roughly $300 more than that raised by the typical unelected official and $1,500 more than that garnered by the typical amateur. Mounting a professional campaign also helps open-seat candidates attract more party support. In 1998 open-seat candidates who waged professional campaigns raised an average of $44,400 in party money and $46,900 in party-connected contributions, as contrasted with the $140 and $925 raised by candidates who relied mainly on campaign volunteers. Open-seat contestants who have political experience and have assembled professional campaign organizations are better able to meet the campaign objectives that Hill committee staffers set. As a result, they are among the top recipients of party money, campaign services, and fund-raising assistance. Getting the endorsement of their state's congressional delegation and other incumbents can also help an open-seat contestant attract party funds.

Winning support from PACs can be a little more challenging. Although open-seat candidates use the same techniques as challengers to identify interest group constituencies and to campaign for PAC support, they usually have greater success. Because their odds of victory are better, open-seat candidates have an easier time gaining an audience with PAC managers and are able to raise more PAC money. Similarly, open-seat candidates point to the same kinds of information as do challengers to make the case that their campaigns will be competitive. Experienced open-seat contestants and those who wage professional campaigns collect more PAC money than do amateurs. In 1998 open-seat candidates who had previously held elective office raised, on average, almost $234,200, nearly $2,600 more than did the typical unelected politician and almost $115,700 more than did the typical amateur. Open-seat candidates who assembled professional campaign organizations collected $197,000 more in PAC money than did those who relied largely on volunteers.

The fund-raising experiences of Democrat Tammy Baldwin and Republican Jo Musser in Wisconsin's 2nd district mirror those of most open-seat candidates in competitive races. Both candidates had contested primaries and both built up considerable war chests. Baldwin raised about $1.5 million and received an additional $47,789 in Democratic Party coordinated expenditures. She collected roughly $260,478 (17 percent of her resources) from PACs (excluding leadership PACs), using her position as a state representative to leverage significant PAC dollars.[36] Labor committees gave Baldwin $153,200. PACs sponsored by trade associations, corporations, and corporations without stock gave her an additional $50,477, $9,500, and $2,500, respectively.[37] Liberal nonconnected committees gave Baldwin an additional $44,801. PACs that focus on women's issues contributed $23,744, including $10,317 from EMILY's List and $9,910 from the National Organization for Women. PACs that represent human rights issues donated $25,075, including $10,325 from the Gay and Lesbian Victory Fund and $10,000 from the Human Rights

Campaign. Baldwin's PAC fund-raising experiences show that, like ethnic, racial, and religious communities, gender-related communities will mobilize to support their own.

Musser had not served in the state legislature, but her position as state insurance commissioner and the Republicans' control of Congress made her an appealing candidate to many contributors. She raised $875,220 in cash and an additional $63,422 in coordinated expenditures. Musser collected $232,878 (almost 25 percent of her money) from PACs, receiving $205,516 from business-related committees and $24,862 from conservative nonconnected PACs that agreed with her probusiness views and wanted to help the Republicans keep control of the House.[38] PACs advocating women's issues were not as heavily involved in Musser's campaign as in her opponent's, but they did offer some assistance. WISH List, which seeks to elect pro-choice Republican women to Congress, gave her $7,413, the Republican Pro-Choice PAC donated $2,000, and the Republicans for Choice PAC gave $500. The Women's National Political Caucus donated another $500, while Value in Electing Women PAC contributed $4,750. The Log Cabin Republicans gave Musser $2,500 in response to her liberal views on gay rights. Finally, she collected $2,500 from organized labor, a respectable amount for a Republican nonincumbent.

Both candidates raised significant sums through the mail and at low-dollar receptions. Baldwin collected about $630,115 (41 percent of her campaign's funds) and Musser about $81,302 (9 percent) in contributions of less than $200. Baldwin raised $578,735 (about 37 percent) in individual contributions of $200 or more, including $291,234 from contributors who were not residents of Wisconsin.[39] Musser raised nearly $174,886 (18 percent) in individual large contributions, of which approximately $30,925 came from out of state.

Musser, however, received $7,249 more in party support than did Baldwin. The Republican collected $12,798 in party contributions, including $3,200 from local Republican party committees and nearly $63,422 in NRCC coordinated expenditures. Baldwin got $21,000 in contributions, including $5,000 from the state's 2nd district Democratic party committee, and about $42,789 in coordinated expenditures, most of which were given by the Democratic Party of Wisconsin. Musser raised an additional $8,601 from Republican members of Congress and retirees and $63,313 from GOP-sponsored leadership PACs. Baldwin collected $31,649 from Democratic legislators and retirees and $40,447 from leadership PACs. Contributions from formal party organizations and party politicians and their PACs accounted for 16 percent of Musser's and 5 percent of Baldwin's total resources.[40] Leaders of both parties clearly viewed this race as important and succeeded in rallying their colleagues to donate funds.

The two candidates played very different roles in the financing of their campaigns. Because Baldwin was able to collect large amounts of money from others and did not have tremendous personal wealth to draw from, she invested only $3,341 in her campaign, all but $1,000 of which was a loan. Musser, on the other hand, had the resources and the need to invest significant personal funds in the race. She loaned her campaign $300,026 (32 percent of her receipts), investing all but 7 percent of it in her bid to win the hotly contested GOP primary.

The fact that the district had been occupied by Scott Klug, a Republican, for eight years and by Robert Kastenmeier, a Democrat, for thirty-two years before that injected a degree of uncertainty into the district's future once the seat became open. The district attracted a great deal of attention from prospective candidates, party committees, PACs, and other contributors. This attention enabled both Baldwin and Musser to raise large amounts of money. Between January 1 and December 31 of 1997, Baldwin collected $251,699 (16 percent of her receipts). She had amassed an additional $310,291 (20 percent) by June 30, 1998. Between July 1 and September 30, the period that included Wisconsin's September 8 primary, Baldwin raised another $342,048 (27 percent). Once the primary was over, her fund-raising soared. She collected an additional $653,834 (52 percent) between October 1 and November 30.

Musser began fund-raising six months after Baldwin had started. She made an initial investment of $55,000, a loan to her campaign, and collected an additional $65,239 between January 1 and June 30, 1998 (a combined 14 percent of her receipts). Between July 1 and September 30, she loaned her campaign another $234,026 and collected $117,899 from individuals and PACs (a combined 40 percent). After she had won the nomination, Musser was able to raise considerable funds from individuals, PACs, and the Republican Party. Between October 1 and November 30, she collected $392,056 and loaned her campaign $11,000 (totaling 46 percent). Both Musser's and Baldwin's late fund-raising spurts reflected the uncertainty surrounding their race. Prodigious eleventh-hour fund-raising is common in competitive open-seat contests.

SENATE CAMPAIGNS

The differences in the campaigns that Senate and House candidates wage for resources reflect the broader differences that exist between House and Senate elections. Candidates for the Senate need more money and start requesting support earlier. They often meet with party officials, PAC managers, wealthy individuals, and other sources of money or fund-raising assistance three years before they plan to run. Most Senate candidates also attempt to raise money on

FIGURE 6-7

Sources of Senate Candidates' Campaign Receipts in the 1998 Elections

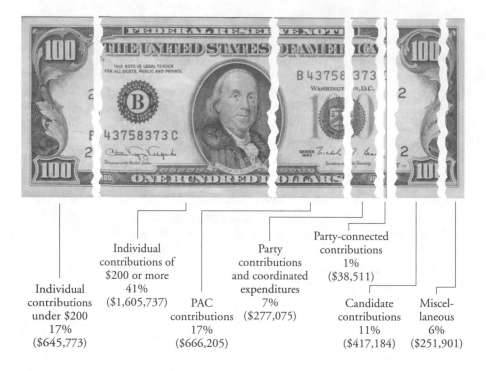

Source: Compiled from Federal Election Commission data.

Notes: See notes in Figure 6-4. N = 68.

a more national scale than do House contestants. The monumental size of the task requires Senate candidates to rely more on others for fund-raising assistance. Nonincumbent Senate candidates are more likely than their House counterparts to hire professional consultants to manage their direct-mail and event-based individual and PAC solicitation programs.

Senate candidates raised on average more than $1.6 million in individual large contributions in 1998—41 percent of their campaign resources (see Figure 6-7). Individual small contributions and donations from PACs each accounted for 17 percent, and party contributions and coordinated expenditures for 7 percent. Party-connected contributions accounted for a mere 1 percent, reflecting the fact that there are fewer senators than House members to contribute to one another. The candidates themselves provided roughly 11 percent of the money spent directly in Senate campaigns. Compared with candidates for the House, candidates for the upper chamber rely more heavily on individuals and formal party organizations and less on PACs and their colleagues to build up their war chests.

Party affiliation affects fund-raising for the upper chamber of Congress less than it does for the lower chamber. Republican Senate candidates raised more PAC money in the 1998 elections than did the Democrats (see Table 6-4). This reversal of the patterns exhibited in previous elections was caused by the GOP's winning the majority in 1994. Republicans also were willing to spend more personal assets than were their Democratic opponents.

There are important similarities and differences among incumbent, challenger, and open-seat candidates. Senate incumbents raise more money from every source except personal funds than do challengers, and they raise more from every source but party-connected money than do open-seat candidates. However, the proportion of funds collected from each source by incumbents and open-seat contestants is almost identical. Challengers rely substantially less on PAC dollars and depend more on their own resources than do the other candidates, reflecting the fact that many access-oriented PACs shy away from supporting challengers.

Incumbency provides members of the Senate with fund-raising advantages. Senators, like House members, often begin their quest for reelection with significant sums left over from their previous campaigns and start raising funds early. Thirteen senators each had more than $600,000 left over after their 1998 campaigns, and seven had in excess of $1 million. Nine of the twenty-eight senators seeking reelection in 2000 had raised over $1 million by December 31, 1998. Sen. Bill Frist, R-Tenn., led the pack, having raised more than $4.3 million.

Senators, like House members, are able to raise these large sums early because they have a great deal of political clout, which few challengers possess. For example, Sen. Richard Shelby, R-Ala., was able to use his chairmanships of the Select Intelligence Committee and the Transportation Subcommittee of the Appropriations Committee as well as his membership on the Banking, Housing, and Urban Affairs Committee to raise $136,750 from defense PACs, $144,628 from transportation PACs, and $386,845 from insurance, real estate, and miscellaneous business PACs for his 1998 reelection campaign (more than 54 percent of his total PAC dollars). He also raised $878,100 from individuals employed in these industries, which represented more than 50 percent of the individual contributions he raised in amounts of $200 or more.[41]

A final difference between House and Senate elections concerns how candi-

TABLE 6-4
Sources of Support for Senate Candidates in the 1998 Elections

	Party		Status			Competitiveness	
	Democrats	Republicans	Incumbents	Challengers	Open-seat candidates	Competitive	Uncompetitive
Individual contributions under $200	$702,818 (19%)	$588,729 (14%)	$871,216 (17%)	$509,118 (16%)	$388,289 (13%)	$1,319,658 (18%)	$228,607 (13%)
Individual contributions of $200 or more	$1,456,816 (39%)	$1,754,659 (43%)	$2,263,150 (45%)	$1,046,010 (33%)	$1,322,450 (45%)	$2,849,689 (39%)	$835,672 (47%)
PAC contributions	$589,179 (16%)	$743,231 (18%)	$1,146,916 (23%)	$187,618 (6%)	$660,046 (23%)	$892,562 (12%)	$526,079 (30%)
Party contributions and coordinated expenditures	$283,895 (8%)	$270,256 (7%)	$324,499 (6%)	$240,582 (8%)	$245,377 (8%)	$662,862 (9%)	$38,255 (2%)
Party-connected contributions	$17,917 (—)	$59,104 (1%)	$45,369 (1%)	$27,260 (1%)	$51,251 (2%)	$68,865 (1%)	$19,720 (1%)
Candidate contributions	$329,979 (9%)	$504,388 (12%)	$76,260 (2%)	$882,585 (28%)	$56,197 (2%)	$1,043,524 (14%)	$29,449 (2%)
Miscellaneous	$327,372 (9%)	$176,429 (4%)	$263,923 (5%)	$262,807 (8%)	$185,407 (6%)	$499,468 (7%)	$98,645 (6%)
(N)	(34)	(34)	(29)	(29)	(10)	(26)	(42)

Source: Compiled from Federal Election Commission data.

Notes: See notes in Table 6-1.

dates obtain support from their Hill committees. All four Hill committees rely on members of Congress to help them raise funds, but candidate assistance in fund-raising is also an informal criterion for senatorial campaign committee support. The DSCC and NRSC have special accounts for elections in different regions. The DSCC also has the Democratic Women's Council to provide support to women candidates for the Senate. These accounts give Senate candidates incentives to participate in fund raising events held for their region—and for women, in the case of female candidates—making it possible for the senatorial campaign committees to meet, or come close to meeting, the high ceilings that the FECA sets for coordinated expenditures in Senate elections.

SUMMARY

The campaign for resources is an important aspect of contemporary congressional elections. It requires candidates and campaign strategists to identify groups of sympathetic potential donors and fashion a pitch that will appeal to them. The campaign for resources is usually a campaign among unequals. Incumbent campaigns typically begin the election season with more money in the bank than do challengers, who usually start fund-raising much later. The levels of skill and resources that incumbents and challengers bring to bear on the fund-raising process, including their prospects for success and political clout, also differ markedly. As a result, incumbents raise more money than challengers, and incumbents raise proportionately more funds from PACs and individuals interested in directly influencing the legislative process. Candidates for open seats typically raise about the same amount as do incumbents, and open-seat candidates are more likely to wage campaigns that are financially competitive with that of their opponent. Nonincumbents who have significant political experience or who have assembled professional campaign organizations typically raise more money, especially from parties, members of Congress, other party leaders, and PACs than do amateur candidates who assemble unprofessional campaign organizations.

CHAPTER SEVEN

Campaign Strategy

The campaign for votes involves voter targeting, communications, and mobilization. During the heyday of the parties, party organizations formulated and executed campaign strategies. Party leaders, candidates, and activists talked with neighbors to learn about their concerns, disseminated campaign communications that addressed those concerns, and turned out the vote on election day. The predisposition of voters to support their party's candidates tended to be strong and was occasionally reinforced with government jobs, contracts, and other forms of patronage. Contemporary campaigns also involve targeting, communicating with, and mobilizing voters. Successful candidates craft a message with broad appeal, set the agenda that defines voters' choices, and get their supporters to the polls on election day. In the years in which a presidential election is held, that contest dominates the news and greatly influences most people's thinking about politics. Candidates who stake out positions that correspond to the national political agenda have an advantage over those who do not.

In this chapter I focus on how voters decide to cast their ballots in congressional elections and on the strategies and tactics that campaigns use to affect those decisions. The primary topics are voting behavior, strategy, targeting, and message.

VOTING BEHAVIOR

Traditional democratic theory holds that citizens should make informed choices when voting in elections. It contends that they should be knowledgeable about the candidates, be aware of the major issues, and take the time to discern which candidate is more likely to represent their views and govern in the nation's best interests. The weight of the evidence, however, suggests that the vast majority of voters in congressional elections fall short of these expectations.[1]

Most voters make their congressional voting decisions on the basis of relatively little information. In a typical House contest between an incumbent and a challenger, for example, only about 12 percent of all voters can recall the names of the two major-party candidates. In open-seat House contests, about 37 percent of all voters can remember both candidates' names.[2] Voters tend to possess more information about contestants in Senate elections: roughly 35 percent can recall the names of both candidates in contests involving an incumbent and a challenger, and about two-thirds can identify both candidates in open-seat races.[3]

When put to the less-stringent test of merely recognizing House candidates' names, roughly two-thirds of all voters recognize the names of both major-party contestants in incumbent-challenger races, and almost 70 percent recognize the names of both candidates in open-seat contests.[4] The levels of name recognition are higher in Senate contests: roughly 76 percent recognize the names of both the incumbent and challenger, and more than 90 percent recognize the names of candidates in open-seat races.[5] Thus, the name recognition test, which demands roughly the same, minimal amount of knowledge from voters as does actually casting a ballot, shows that a substantial portion of the electorate lacks the information needed to make what scholars refer to as "an informed vote choice."

The inability to recall or recognize the candidates' names is indicative of the overall lack of substantive information in congressional elections. Most House election campaigns are low-key affairs that do not convey much information about the candidates' ideological orientations or policy positions.[6] Information on House challengers, most of whom wage underfunded campaigns, is usually scarce. Campaign communications, voters' assessments of the issues, and candidates' qualifications become important only in hard-fought contests.[7]

Incumbency and Voter Information

By and large, the candidates who suffer most from voter disinterest are House challengers. Whereas more than 90 percent of all voters recognize their House member's name, only about 60 percent usually recognize the name of the challenger. Incumbents tend to be viewed favorably. About 54 percent of those voters who recognize their representative's name indicate they like something about that person; roughly one-third percent mention something they dislike. The corresponding figures for House challengers are 35 percent and 32 percent.[8] As the high reelection rates for House members indicate, the name recognition and voter approval ratings of most incumbents are difficult for opponents to overcome. Only those challengers who can overcome their "invisibility problem" and create a favorable image stand a chance of winning.

Senate challengers tend to be less handicapped by voter inattentiveness. They enjoy better name recognition because of their political experience, skill, and superior campaign organizations, and the newsworthiness of their campaigns attracts media attention and voter interest. Voters learn more about the ideological orientations and issue positions of Senate challengers than of their House counterparts.[9] Even though the name recognition of Senate challengers is lower than the near-universal recognition enjoyed by Senate incumbents, it is high enough to make the typical incumbent-challenger race competitive. This helps explain why there is more electoral turnover in the upper than in the lower chamber of Congress.

The inequalities in candidate information that characterize most incumbent-challenger races generally do not exist in open-seat contests. The major-party candidates in an open-seat race for a marginal seat begin the campaign with similar opportunities to increase their name recognition and convey their messages to voters. The greater competitiveness of these contests results in more extensive press coverage, which in turn helps both candidates become better known to voters. Thus, more voters make informed choices in open-seat races than in incumbent-challenger contests.

Voting Decisions

Given their lack of knowledge of the candidates and issues, how do most voters make a decision on election day? Only those voters who know something about the background, political qualifications, party affiliation, and issue stances of both candidates are in a position to sift through the information, weigh the benefits of voting for one candidate over another, and cast their ballots in accordance with classical democratic theory.[10] Nevertheless, voters who fall short of the level of awareness idealized by democratic theory may respond to the campaign information that candidates and the media disseminate. Competitive, high-intensity elections that fill the airwaves, newspapers, and voters' mailboxes with campaign information provide some voters, especially those with an interest in politics, with enough information to form summary judgments about the candidates. And these voters often tend to rely on those judgments when deciding which candidate to support.[11]

In the absence of spirited, high-intensity elections, most voters use "voting cues"—shortcuts that enable them to cast a ballot without engaging in a lengthy decision-making process. The most frequently used voting cue is incumbency.

Knowing only an incumbent's name is sufficient for an individual to cast an adequately informed vote, some scholars argue. Reasoning that the incumbent should be held accountable for the government's performance, the state of the economy, the nation's foreign involvements, or other issues, these voters quickly determine whether to support the status quo and vote for the incumbent or to advocate change and cast their ballot for the challenger.[12]

Other voters pin the responsibility for the state of the nation on the president. When these voters are satisfied with how things are being run in Washington, they support the congressional candidate who belongs to the president's party. When they are dissatisfied with the state of the nation's affairs, as in 1994, they vote for the candidate whose party does not occupy the White House. The connection between presidential and congressional voting, which began increasing in the early 1990s, can help a congressional candidate when a popular president is running for reelection, but belonging to the president's party usually has more harmful than beneficial effects in midterm elections.[13] The 1998 elections were an important exception to this rule. The party cue, like the incumbency cue, enables voters to make retrospective voting choices without having much knowledge about the candidates or their positions on the issues. Under conditions of unified government, party cues are stronger because voters can more readily assign credit or blame for the state of the nation to the party that controls both the executive and legislative branches.[14] The power-sharing arrangements of divided government, in contrast, obscure political responsibility because they enable politicians to blame others in power.

The party cue also enables voters to speculate about a candidate's ideological orientation and issue positions. Republicans are generally identified as more conservative than Democrats and are associated with free-market economics, deregulation, lower taxes, family values, hawkish foreign policy, and the wealthier elements of society. Most Republicans profess to be for limited government, and some campaign as though they are antigovernment. Democrats are often viewed as the party of government. They are associated with greater economic intervention, environmental protection, education, a more dovish foreign policy, and protecting the interests of senior citizens, minorities, the poor, and working people. Some voters project the parties' images to candidates and use these projections to guide their congressional voting decisions.[15] Others habitually support a party's nominees regardless of their credentials, issue positions, or opponents.

Partisanship and incumbency can affect the voting decisions of individuals who possess even less political information than do those individuals described above. The voting behavior of individuals who go to the polls out of a sense of civic responsibility or out of habit and who lack much interest in or knowledge about politics can in many ways be equated with the behavior of shoppers at a supermarket. Individuals in both situations select a product—either a consumer good or a congressional candidate—with little relevant information. Except for first-time shoppers and newly enfranchised voters, these individuals have made similar selections before. Previous decisions and established preferences often strongly influence their current decisions. Shoppers, lacking a good reason to try a new product, such as a sale or a two-for-one giveaway, are likely to purchase the same brand-name product that they previously purchased. Voters are likely to cast a ballot for the candidates or party that they supported in previous elections.[16] If a voter recognizes one candidate's name, which is almost always the incumbent's, that candidate usually gets the individual's vote. If the voter recognizes neither candidate but tends to be favorably predisposed toward one party, then most often the person votes for that party's candidate. Situations in which voters have little information, then, usually work to the advantage of incumbents and of candidates who belong to the district's or state's dominant party.

However, if the recognized candidate or favored party is associated with scandal or a domestic or foreign policy failure, many relatively uninformed voters, as well as some who are informed, break old habits and cast their ballots against that candidate or party. During the elections held in the 1990s, for example, many challengers, with the support of Washington-based party committees and interest groups, sought to make control of Congress itself a major campaign issue. This strategy is credited with enabling the Republicans to take over Congress and end forty uninterrupted years of Democratic control of the House. Attacking Congress contributed to the electoral success of challengers of both parties throughout most of the 1990s.

VOTERS AND CAMPAIGN STRATEGY

Candidates and political consultants generally do not plan election campaigns on the basis of abstract political theories, but they do draw on a body of knowledge about how people make their voting decisions. Politicians' notions about voting behavior have some ideas in common with the findings of scholarly research. Among these are the following: (1) most voters have only limited information about the candidates, their ideologies, and the issues; (2) voters are generally more familiar with and favorably predisposed toward incumbents than they are toward challengers; and (3) voters tend to cast their ballots in ways that reflect their party identification or previous voting behavior. Candidates and consultants also believe that a campaign sharply focused on issues can be used to motivate supporters to show up at the polls and to win the support of undecided voters. They try to set the campaign agenda so that the issues that politically informed voters use as a basis for casting their ballots are the most attractive issues for their candidate.

Politicians' beliefs account for some of the differences that exist among the campaigns waged by incumbents, challengers, and open-seat candidates as well as many of the differences that exist between House and Senate campaigns. Generally, members of Congress use strategies that capitalize on the advantages of incumbency. They discuss the services and the federal projects they have delivered to their constituencies.[17] They focus on elements of their public persona that have helped make them popular with constituents and draw on strategies they have used successfully in previous campaigns.[18]

Some incumbents capitalize on their advantages in name recognition and voter approval by virtually ignoring their opponents. They deluge the district with direct mail, radio advertisements, television commercials, yard signs, or other communications that make no mention of their opponent in order to minimize the attention the challenger gets from the local media and voters. An alternative strategy is to take advantage of a challenger's relative invisibility by attacking his or her experience, qualifications, or positions on the issues early in the campaign. Incumbents who succeed in defining their opponents leave them in the unenviable position of being invisible to most voters and negatively perceived by others. The Royce campaign pursued the former strategy, treating Democratic challenger Cecy Groom as if her candidacy would have no impact on the outcome of their 1998 California House race.[19] The Price campaign in North Carolina followed the latter approach, tying its opponent, Thomas Roberg, to the GOP leadership in Washington and attacking him for "parroting the Gingrich strategy of distortion and half truth." The strategy Price used was popular in both 1996 and 1998 with Democratic incumbents and non-incumbents in the House and Senate alike.[20]

House challengers are in the least enviable position of any candidates. Not only are they less well known and less experienced, but they are also without the campaign resources of their opponents. In order to win, challengers need to force their way into voters' consciousness and to project a message that will give voters a reason to cast a ballot for a little-known quantity.

Many challengers make the election a referendum on some negative aspect of the incumbent's performance. They portray the incumbent as incompetent, corrupt, an extreme ideologue, or out of touch with the district. They magnify the impact of any unpopular policy or scandal with which the incumbent can be associated. Challengers often try to link the current officeholder to unpopular policies or trends and to tout themselves as agents of change, often using negative or comparative ads to do so.

Lacking the advantages of an incumbent or the disadvantages of a challenger, both candidates in an open-seat race face the challenge of making themselves familiar to voters and becoming associated with themes and issues that will attract electoral support. They also both have the opportunity to define their opponents. Some open-seat candidates seek to define themselves and their opponents on the basis of issues. Others, particularly those running in districts that favor their party, emphasize partisan or ideological cues.

GAUGING PUBLIC OPINION

Campaigns use many different instruments to take the public's pulse. Election returns from previous contests are analyzed to locate pockets of potential strength or weakness. Geodemographic analysis enables campaigns to identify individuals who voted in previous elections and to classify them according to their gender, age, ethnicity, race, religion, occupation, and economic background. By combining geodemographic information with polling data and election returns, candidates are able to identify potential supporters and to formulate messages that will appeal to them.

Polls are among the most commonly used means of gauging public opinion. Virtually every Senate campaign and roughly three-quarters of all House campaigns take at least one poll to learn about voters. Benchmark polls, which are taken early in the election season, inform candidates about the issue positions, partisanship, and initial voting preferences of people living in their state or district. House campaigns commonly commission benchmarks a year prior to the election, and Senate candidates have been known to commission them as early as three years before election day.[21] Benchmark polls also measure the levels of name recognition and support that the candidates and their opponents or prospective opponents enjoy. They help campaigns learn about the kinds of candidates voters prefer, the types of messages that are likely to attract support, and to whom specific campaign advertisements should be directed.

Campaigns also use benchmark polls to generate support. Challenger and open-seat candidates disseminate favorable benchmarks to attract press coverage and the support of campaign volunteers and contributors. Incumbents typically publicize benchmarks to discourage potential challengers. When poll results show a member of Congress to be in trouble, however, the incumbent quietly uses them to convince parties, PACs, and other potential contributors that he or she needs extra help to win.

Trend polls are taken intermittently throughout the campaign season to discover changes in voters' attitudes. Some senators use them to chart their public approval throughout their six-year terms. These polls are more narrowly focused than benchmarks. They feature detailed questions designed to reveal whether a campaign has been successful in getting voters to associate their candidate with a specific issue or theme. Trend polls help campaigns determine whether they have been gaining or losing ground with different segments of the electorate. They can reassure a campaign that its strategy is working or indicate that a change in message is needed.

Just as trend and benchmark polls present "snapshots" of public opinion, tracking polls provide campaigns with a "motion picture" overview. Tracking polls typically take samples of 150 to 200 voters to discuss their reactions to a few key advertisements, issue statements, or campaign events. Each night a different group of voters is interviewed. The interviews are pooled and used to calculate "rolling averages" based on the responses from the three most recent nights. Changes in rolling averages can be used to reformulate a campaign's final appeals. Because tracking polls are expensive, most House campaigns wait until the last three weeks of the campaign to use them.

Candidates may supplement their polling with focus groups. Focus groups usually consist of one to two dozen participants and a professional facilitator, who meet for two to three hours. The participants are selected not to be a scientifically representative sample but to represent segments of the population whose support the campaign needs to reinforce or attract. Campaigns use focus groups to learn how voters can be expected to respond to different messages or to pretest actual campaign advertisements. Some high-priced consultants, such as Wirthlin Worldwide, a prominent Republican firm, employ computerized audience response techniques to obtain a precise record of how focus group participants react to specific portions of campaign advertisements.[22] These techniques enable an analyst to plot a line that represents the participants' reactions onto the ad itself, pinpointing exactly which portions participants liked or disliked. Focus group research is useful in fine-tuning the visuals and narratives in television communications.

Finally, candidates learn about public opinion through a variety of approaches that do not require the services of public opinion experts. Newspaper, magazine, radio, and television news stories provide information about voters' positions on major issues. Exchanges with local party leaders, journalists, political activists, and voters can also help candidates get a sense of the public mood.

When asked about the significance of different forms of information, House candidates and campaign aides typically rank direct contact with voters first, indicating that they consider it to be very important to extremely important (see Table 7-1). Voter contact is followed by public opinion polls, which are generally considered to be moderately helpful to very helpful in learning about

TABLE 7-1

Campaigners' Perceptions of the Importance of Different Sources
of Information for Gauging Public Opinion in House Campaigns

		Incumbents		Challengers		Open-seat candidates	
	All	In jeopardy	Shoo-ins	Hope-fuls	Likely losers	Pros-pects	Mis-matched
Candidate contact with voters	4.37	4.23	4.41	4.44	4.44	4.16	4.59
Public opinion surveys	3.53	4.23	3.54	3.68	2.88	3.96	3.09
Newspaper, radio, TV	3.05	2.69	3.13	3.08	3.27	2.86	3.17
Local party activists	2.63	2.78	2.74	2.69	2.41	2.45	2.80
Mail from voters	2.45	2.65	3.43	2.19	1.99	2.00	2.29
National party publications	2.28	1.83	1.96	2.39	2.75	2.12	2.65
National party leaders	2.14	1.80	1.94	2.31	2.32	2.20	2.30
(N)	(325)	(48)	(70)	(52)	(82)	(49)	(24)

Source: The 1992 Congressional Campaign Study.

Notes: Candidates and campaign aides were asked to assess the importance of each source on the following scale: 1 = not important or not used; 2 = slightly important; 3 = moderately important; 4 = very important; 5 = extremely important. The values listed are the arithmetic means of the scores. Figures are for major-party candidates in contested general elections, excluding a small number of atypical races.

voters' opinions. News stories come next, followed by discussions with local party activists and mail from voters. Although they play a bigger role than PACs and other interest groups, national party officials and the materials they publish are less important than local information sources.

Incumbents and candidates for open seats make greater use of surveys than do challengers. Candidates in competitive contests of all types make greater use of them than do those in lopsided races. Challengers and open-seat candidates in one-sided contests often cannot afford to buy polls and must rely heavily on news reports, party publications, and the advice of national party leaders. Incumbents, who are often sensitized to issues by the constituent mail that floods their offices, consider letters to be a more significant indicator of public sentiment than does any other group of candidates. Incumbents in safe seats show a greater preference than others for learning about public opinion through the mail and other forms of unmediated voter contact.

VOTER TARGETING

Campaigns are not designed to reach everyone. Targeting involves categorizing different groups of voters, identifying their political preferences, and designing appeals to which they are likely to respond. It is the foundation of virtually every aspect of campaign strategy. Candidates and campaign managers consider many factors when devising targeting strategies, including the underlying partisan and candidate loyalties of the groups that reside in the district, the size and turnout levels of those groups, and the kinds of issues and appeals that will attract their support.[23] Using this information, they formulate a strategy designed to build a winning coalition.

Partisanship is the number one consideration in the voter targeting of most campaigns. It subsumes all other factors. Roughly 42 percent of all campaigns focus on individuals who identify with their party and independent voters (see Table 7-2). Only about 5 percent of all campaigns primarily target voters who identify with the opposing party. Price, who was locked in a tough race with Roberg, sought to mobilize Democrats and win the support of independents, sometimes called "persuadable" or "swing" voters—some of whom were added to the district as a result of the court-ordered redistricting that took place in the midst of the primary season.[24] Roberg focused on Republicans, independents, and "Jesse-crats, "conservative Democrats who routinely vote for North Carolina's senior senator, Jesse Helms.[25]

Constance Morella, a Republican who has represented Maryland's strongly Democratic-leaning 8th district since 1986, by contrast, is typical of most long-term incumbents in that she has built a measure of bipartisan support over the years. Like many incumbents, she routinely sends out letters to congratulate constituents who recently registered to vote in her district. Unlike most other incumbents, however, she often sends letters of congratulation to voters who have registered in the opposing party, in this case as Democrats.[26]

Challengers in uncompetitive races are the most likely to target voters who identify with the opposing party. Many of these candidates recognize that the one-sidedness of their districts makes it impossible for them to compete without winning the support of some of the opposing party's supporters. Some likely-loser challengers do not even have the resources needed to carry out even a basic party-oriented targeting strategy. Lacking a poll or a precinct-by-precinct breakdown of where Republican, Democratic, and independent vot-

TABLE 7-2

The Partisan Component of Targeting Strategies in House Campaigns

	All	Incumbents		Challengers		Open-seat candidates	
		In jeopardy	Shoo-ins	Hope-fuls	Likely losers	Pros-pects	Mis-matched
Own party	12%	4%	13%	16%	12%	14%	33%
Opposing party	5	4	4	—	11	—	—
Independents	2	—	2	2	1	4	—
Both parties	4	4	6	7	1	—	—
Own party and independents	28	35	27	33	25	21	—
Opposing party and independents	5	4	2	2	8	4	22
All voters	44	49	45	38	41	51	44
Did not target	1	—	—	3	1	4	—
(N)	(313)	(49)	(82)	(58)	(91)	(29)	(9)

Source: The 1998 Congressional Campaign Study.

Notes: Figures are for major-party candidates in contested general elections. Dashes = less than 0.5 percent. Some columns do not add to 100 percent because of rounding.

ers reside, some amateurs resort to unorthodox strategies, such as focusing on precincts that had the highest turnout levels in the previous election.

Other factors that campaigns consider when designing targeting strategies include demography and issues. Sixty-two percent of all House campaigns target demographic, geographic, or occupational groups: 53 percent concentrate on specific ethnic, racial, religious, gender, or age groups; 4 percent focus on counties, suburbs, cities, or other geographic locations; and 5 percent target union members, blue-collar workers, small-business owners, or voters involved in particular industries.[27] Issues and political attitudes, including voting intentions and partisanship, play a central role in the targeting strategies of roughly 36 percent of all campaigns.

Group-oriented and issue/attitudinal-oriented targeting strategies each offer campaigns some distinct advantages. The group-oriented, or geodemographic, approach is based on the idea that there are identifiable segments of the population whose support the campaign needs to attract and that specific communications can be tailored to win that support. Just as soliciting money from a readily identifiable fund-raising constituency is important in the campaign for resources, communicating a message to identifiable groups of supporters and undecided voters is important in the campaign for votes. Campaigns that use group-based targeting strategies emphasize different aspects of their message, depending on the intended audience for a particular campaign advertisement. By tailoring their messages to attract the votes of specific population groups, these campaigns hope to build a winning coalition. During the 1990s, many campaigns stressed the effect of the economy on children and families in literature that was mailed to women, whereas they emphasized tax cuts and economic growth issues in literature that was mailed to business executives and upper-class and upper-middle-class voters.

Candidates focus on many groups, reflecting the diverse segments of the population represented by the two major parties, especially the Democrats.[28] More Democrats than Republicans target senior citizens, and Democratic candidates target women more than any other segment of the population. The 1998 contest between Price and Roberg gives some insights into the dynamics of geodemographic targeting. The race was held in a central North Carolina district that includes many rural communities as well as Durham, Chapel Hill, parts of Raleigh, and other portions of the more urban and suburban "Research Triangle." Price's overall strategy was to win by big margins in Democratic-leaning Chatham, Durham, and Orange Counties, break even in the parts of the district in Wake County, and minimize his losses in northern parts of Raleigh and in Cary and other upwardly mobile, politically volatile suburbs. Price made special outreach efforts in Durham County, which had been added to the district, and in Wake County, which had always been difficult terrain for Democrats. Special attention was also given to turning out women, African Americans, and suburbanites who had recently moved to the district.[29] Roberg targeted Republicans, moderate Democrats, Wake County residents, suburbanites, homeowners, and what he labeled "upscale voters."[30] An overlap in targets is typical of a close election because both campaigns go after the same swing voters.

The issue/attitudinal strategy is based on the premise that issues and ideas should drive the campaign. Campaigns that target on the basis of specific policies or a broad ideology, such as conservatism or progressivism, hope to win the support of single-issue or ideological voters who favor these positions. In many cases, one or two specific issues are emphasized in order to attract the support of swing voters whose ballots a candidate believes will be a deciding factor in the election outcome. Some candidates targeted pro-life or pro-choice voters in the 1990s, believing their ballots would be decisive. Others targeted pro-environment or anti–gun control voters. Republicans who employed these strategies focused primarily on voters who were concerned about the deficit, taxes, the size of government, government regulation, and crime. Democrats who employed them focused on voters who cared about public education, jobs, the environment, health care, and the protections and services that government provides for the elderly, children, and underprivileged groups.

Targeting strategies that are based on issues or voter attitudes more readily lend themselves to the communication of a coherent campaign message than do group-oriented strategies. They are especially effective at mobilizing single-issue voters and political activists who have strong ideological predispositions. Yet they run the risk of alienating moderate voters who agree with the candidate on most policy matters but disagree on the issues the campaign has chosen to emphasize. Campaigns waged by policy amateurs and ideologues are the most likely to suffer from this problem. Often these candidates become boxed in by their own message, are labeled "ultra-liberals" or "right wingers" by their opponents, and ultimately lose.

Incumbents target demographic, geographic, and occupational groups more than do challengers and open-seat candidates. Most incumbents have a detailed knowledge of the voting blocs that supported them in the past and target constituents who belong to them. Many challengers, especially those unable to mount competitive campaigns, do not have this information. Lacking good voter files, and recognizing they need to peel away some of their opponents' supporters, they target on the basis of issues.[31]

THE MESSAGE

The message delivered by a candidate gives substance to a campaign and helps to shape the political agenda, mobilize backers, and win votes. In a well-run campaign, the same coherent message pervades every aspect of the candidate's communications—from paid television advertisements to impromptu remarks. Campaign messages can be an essential ingredient to victory in close elections because they activate supporters and strongly influence the decisions of persuadable voters.

Campaign messages rely heavily on imagery. The most successful campaigns weave the candidate's persona and policy stances into thematic messages.[32] These form the core of the image the candidate seeks to project. According to Joel Bradshaw, president of the Democratic consulting firm Campaign Design Group, good campaign messages are clear and easy to communicate, short, convey a sense of emotional urgency, reflect voters' perceptions of political reality, establish clear differences between the candidate and the opponent, and are credible.[33]

The precise mix of personal characteristics, issues, and broad themes that candidates project depends on their political views, the groups they target, and the messages they anticipate their opponents will communicate. Good strategic positioning results in the transmission of a message that most voters will find appealing; when both candidates achieve this result an election becomes what strategists refer to as a "battle for the middle ground."[34] In designing a message, campaign decision makers consider a variety of factors, which Fred Hartwig of Peter Hart and Associates refers to as "the Seven P's of Strategy": performance, professional experience, positioning, partisanship, populism, progressivism, and positivity.[35] Ladonna Lee, a leading Republican political strategist, emphasizes the importance of consistency. The different components of the message must add up to a coherent public image.[36]

Campaigns endeavor to create a favorable image for their candidates by identifying them with decency, loyalty, honesty, hard work, and other cherished values.[37] Campaign communications interweave anecdotes about a candidate's personal accomplishments, professional success, family, or ability to overcome humble origins to portray him or her as the living embodiment of the American dream—someone whom voters should be proud to have represent them in Washington. Campaigns frequently emphasize elements of their candidate's persona that point to an opponent's weakness. Veterans who run against draft dodgers, for example, commonly emphasize their war records.

Incumbents frequently convey image-oriented messages. They seek to reinforce or expand their base of support by concentrating on those aspects of their persona that make them popular with constituents.[38] Their messages convey images of competent, caring individuals who work tirelessly in Washington to improve the lives of the folks they represent back home. Incumbents' campaign communications often describe how they have helped constituents resolve problems, brought federal programs and projects to the district, and introduced or cosponsored popular legislation. Some discuss their efforts to prevent a military base or factory from closing. Those whose districts have experienced the ravages of floods, earthquakes, riots, or other disasters almost always highlight their roles in bringing federal relief to victims.

Many challengers and open-seat contestants also seek to portray themselves as caring, hard-working, and experienced. Nonincumbents who have previously held elective office frequently contrast their accomplishments with those of their opponent. During the elections held in the early and mid-1990s, many challengers who were state legislators blamed their opponents for contributing to the federal deficit while pointing to their own budget-cutting efforts.

Political amateurs usually discuss their successes in the private sector, seeking to make a virtue of their lack of political experience. Many blame the "mess in Washington" on the "career politicians" and discuss how someone who has succeeded in the private sector is needed to make government work for the people again. Still, a challenger who focuses on experience rarely wins. As one consultant explained, "By virtue of their being the current officeholder, an incumbent can 'out-experience' a challenger to death."

Issues

Most House candidates and campaign aides maintain that the bulk of their messages focus on policy concerns rather than the candidate's personality—a claim that has been borne out by examinations of their campaign materials.[39] Roughly 56 percent of all House campaigns make issues the primary focus of their message; 24 percent, mostly incumbent campaigns, emphasize candidate imagery (see Table 7-3). Candidates in competitive contests run the most issue-oriented campaigns, reflecting the fact that they view their policy stances as a way to attract the support of undecided voters. Challengers run the most opposition-oriented campaigns. They point to incumbents' ethical lapses, congressional roll-call votes that are out of sync with constituents' views, or federal policies that have harmed local voters or the national interest. About 17 percent of all challengers try to make their opponent or their opponent's actions in office a defining campaign issue. A few incumbents holding marginal seats respond in kind by pointing to unpopular aspects of their challenger's background or issue positions. Sixteen percent of open-seat candidates in close contests also make their opponent the central focus of their message.

Almost all candidates take policy stands that identify them with "valence" issues, such as a strong economy, job creation, domestic tranquility, and international security, which are universally viewed in a favorable light. Some make these the centerpiece of their campaign. They either ignore or soft-pedal "positional" issues (sometimes referred to as "wedge" issues), which have two or more sides.[40] When both candidates campaign mainly on valence issues, the dialogue can be likened to a debate between the nearly identical Tweedledee and Tweedledum.

When candidates communicate dissimilar stands on positional issues, however, political debate becomes more meaningful. Issues such as the economy, taxes, gun control, crime, abortion, and civil rights have for several years had the potential to draw the attention of voters and affect elections. Scandals, health care, environmental issues, and social entitlement programs also have the ability to influence elections.

Challengers are especially likely to benefit from emphasizing positional issues. By stressing points of disagreement between themselves and the incumbent, challengers can help their images crystallize, attract media attention, and strip away some of their opponent's support.[41] Incumbents may not derive the same electoral benefits from running on positional issues because they are usu-

TABLE 7-3

The Major Focus of Advertising in House Campaigns

	All	Incumbents		Challengers		Open-seat candidates	
		In jeopardy	Shoo-ins	Hope-fuls	Likely losers	Pros-pects	Mis-matched
Candidate's image	24%	22%	39%	11%	18%	16%	50%
Candidate's issue positions	56	70	49	60	52	64	39
Opponent's image	3	2	1	3	5	4	—
Opponent's issue positions	8	5	1	18	9	12	—
Other	9	—	9	9	16	4	11
(N)	(312)	(49)	(81)	(58)	(91)	(24)	(9)

Source: The 1998 Congressional Campaign Study.

Notes: Figures are for major-party candidates in contested general elections. Dashes = less than 0.5 percent. Some columns do not add to 100 percent because of rounding.

ally evaluated in personal terms.[42] Candidates who campaign on positional issues hope to attract the support of single-issue or ideological voters or to overcome some weakness in their image. Some liberal Democrats emphasize crime to project "tougher" images. Some conservative Republicans discuss health care to show their compassionate side. Both groups of candidates seek to convince centrist voters that they share their concerns.

Candidates try to anticipate the issues their opponents will emphasize before taking a strong policy stance. Candidates who run against police officers rarely mount "law-and-order" campaigns because of the obvious disparities in credibility that they and their opponents have on crime-related issues. During virtually all of his elections, Price emphasized education, capitalizing on his background as a college professor. He also campaigned on health care, especially women's health issues.[43] Roberg focused most of his early media on Clinton's ethical lapses. He acknowledged that doing so was a strategic mistake, one that he later tried to correct.[44]

Candidates who learn that their opponent is vulnerable on a salient issue generally try to make it a major focus of the campaign in order to win the support of independents or pry voters from their opponent's camp. Democrats and some moderate Republicans lure women's votes by making abortion rights a major part of their campaign platforms. In 1992 and 1996, Democrats who adopted this position got the added benefit of being able to coordinate their message with the Clinton-Gore campaign. Divisions within the Republican Party made abortion an issue to avoid for many GOP candidates. Women who run against men are the most likely to campaign as pro-choice and discuss women's concerns, but some male candidates also stake out pro–abortion rights positions to attract the support of women and liberal voters.[45]

Economic issues—whether they be inflation, unemployment, taxes, jobs, the federal budget, or the national deficit—have been the number one concern of voters in most elections since the Great Depression. Virtually every candidate in the 1980s and 1990s made some aspect of the economy part of their campaign. Democratic candidates often discuss the economy as a fairness issue. In 1992 many Democrats followed the Clinton-Gore campaign's lead in pointing to the increased tax burdens that Reagan-Bush policies placed on the middle class and the tax breaks they gave to wealthy Americans. In 1996 and 1998 many Democratic candidates again adopted the Clinton-Gore campaign's message. They claimed credit for the nation's booming economy and for creating new jobs. They also chastised Republicans for proposing to cut popular social safety net programs in order to give a tax break to the rich.

Republican candidates usually focus on economic growth and the deficit. Throughout the 1980s and early 1990s they sought to blame the economic woes of the country on wasteful government subsidies, excessive regulation, and profligate pork-barrel spending approved by the Democratic-controlled Congress. Their message gained supporters in 1994, as Republican candidates proclaimed that tax cuts were the crown jewel of their vaunted Contract with America.[46] Later in the decade the Republican argument for tax cuts and a balanced budget amendment lost much of its persuasiveness as a result of the nation's improved economy.

Political reform was also an important issue for both Republicans and Democrats in the 1990s, reflecting the anti–Washington establishment mood of the country. Many House challengers concentrated on term limits, campaign finance reform, and "reinventing government," often contrasting their reform positions with their opponent's vote for a congressional pay raise and dependence on PAC contributions. Incumbents address political reform differently. Some seek to defend Congress, while others try to impress upon voters that they are part of the solution and not the problem. One House member said he "neutralized" the reform issue by arguing that he "was constructively working to improve government from the inside, while [his opponent] was content to merely lob stones from a distance."[47] Another popular incumbent strategy is to campaign for reelection to Congress by attacking the institution itself.[48] The Republicans' success in making political corruption a campaign issue in 1994 and their lengthy investigations of the Clinton administration and Democratic fund-raising activities in 1996, combined with repeated calls by members of both parties for revamping the campaign finance system, suggest reform will play a prominent role in future congressional elections.

Most candidates prefer themselves to be the ones whom voters associate with valence issues, not their opponents, but candidates can also find it profitable to take strong stands on positional issues. This is especially true when their policy stances on these issues are welcomed by voters in their district or occupy a prominent place on the national agenda. The 1998 national campaign agenda was not dominated by any great policy debate, as were the 1994 contests. Democratic and Republican congressional candidates took opposing positions on many national issues, including education, health care, and tax cuts. Members of both parties sought to set a campaign agenda that worked to their advantage.

Education was the dominant issue in most candidates' campaign communications, followed by Social Security and taxes. Jobs and the economy were ranked fourth, reflecting the nation's overall prosperity (see Table 7-4). Health care and moral/ethical issues, including family values, also formed the major focus of many candidates' campaign agendas. Crime and drugs and the Clinton/Lewinsky scandal were the centerpiece of substantially fewer candidates' campaigns.

The biggest partisan differences in campaign platforms involved taxes, health care, education, and morality. Almost one-fifth of all Democratic candidates made improving the nation's health care system the centerpiece of their campaigns, whereas only 6 percent of all Republicans did. Approximately one-third of all Democrats focused on education, whereas only one-fifth of all Republicans sought to make it a major campaign issue. Republican candidates were more inclined to campaign on tax cuts and moral issues than were their Democratic counterparts. GOP candidates were also slightly more likely than Democrats to focus on the economy.

Other differences in campaign messages depended on whether the candidate had served in the 105th Congress, and therefore could be held accountable for its performance. Fewer incumbents of both parties focused on health care than did challengers, reflecting Congress's failure to pass health care reform. Fewer Republican incumbents than GOP challengers campaigned on tax cuts because the GOP-controlled Congress's record on the issue fell short of some of the party's promises.

Finally, fewer incumbents of both parties campaigned on the Clinton/Lewinsky scandal. Having responded to the issue in constituent mail, at town meetings, on the House floor, and in the media, most members found it to be

TABLE 7-4

Percentage of House Candidates Whose Campaign Ads Focused
on Selected Issues

	All	Democrats			Republicans		
		Incumbents	Challengers	Open-seat candidates	Incumbents	Challengers	Open-seat candidates
Education	26	42	18	45	15	27	15
Taxes	14	7	6	5	16	23	23
Clinton/Lewinsky	3	2	6	—	—	5	—
Social Security	20	28	18	20	20	16	23
Health care	11	7	24	25	3	6	15
Morals and ethics	10	—	9	5	16	12	8
Crime/drugs	3	4	2	—	7	1	—
Jobs and the economy	12	7	15	—	20	10	15
Miscellaneous	2	4	3	—	3	—	—
(N)	(313)	(57)	(67)	(20)	(74)	(82)	(13)

Source: Compiled from *Time*/Congressional Quarterly 1998 Congressional Candidate Survey.

Notes: Figures represent the percentage of candidates whose campaign ads focused primarily on the indicated issue position. Figures are for major-party candidates in contested general elections. Dashes = less than 0.5 percent.

fraught with political landmines and avoided it. Some challengers considered the issue more promising. A small group of Republican challengers believed they could score points with conservatives by pillorying their Democratic opponents for belonging to the same party as Clinton. Roberg and Dan Page, who was challenging Democratic representative Robert Etheridge in North Carolina's 2nd district, used this tactic, as did Republican Walter Massey, who challenged Democratic incumbent Bart Gordon in Tennessee's 6th district. None was successful. An equally small group of Democratic challengers anticipated that they could score points by blaming their opponents for supporting Independent Counsel Kenneth Starr and his investigation. Democratic challenger Rush Holt of New Jersey was given an opening to use the scandal in his campaign when his opponent, freshman representative Michael Pappas, took to the House floor to sing a tune, set to the melody of "Twinkle, Twinkle, Little Star," that praised Kenneth Starr for his investigation of the president. Holt turned a videotaped recording of his opponent's performance into a humorous television ad that is believed to have contributed to his 5,307-vote victory.

Differences between the perspectives of incumbents and nonincumbents can blunt some of the partisanship of congressional elections and are a hurdle that must be overcome for elections to become fully nationalized. Local political culture can also lead candidates of the same party to campaign on different issues. One-third of all 1998 Democratic candidates from the Northeast made Social Security the major focus of their campaign ads, as opposed to roughly 25 percent of all midwestern and western Democrats and only 11 percent of all southern Democrats. Southern Democratic candidates were the most likely to focus on education and moral issues and the least likely to discuss health care. Education also divided the Republicans: western candidates focused on it more than the rest. Midwestern Republican candidates were much more likely to make tax cuts the major focus of their campaign ads than were GOP candidates as a whole. Southern and western Republicans also campaigned more on moral issues than did their northeastern and midwestern counterparts. Northeastern and western candidates from both parties focused the most on jobs and the economy. They were likely hoping to tap into the job insecurities of voters living in the Rust Belt. Regional differences on these issues show that geography still matters in congressional campaign politics. Locally reinforced ideological divisions pose considerable obstacles to the nationalization of congressional elections.[49]

Partisanship, Populism, and Progressivism

Candidates who run in districts that are made up overwhelmingly of people who identify with their party normally emphasize partisan themes and messages. They frequently mention their party in speeches and campaign literature. They also run "authorization lines" at the end of their television or radio advertisements stating, "This ad was paid for by 'Candidate X,' Democrat [or Republican] for Congress." Campaigns that are run in "hostile" or divided districts typically use nonpartisan strategies, avoiding any mention of party affiliation.

Progressive strategies have become increasingly popular with Democrats who run as agents of change. These candidates avoid the term *liberal* because voters associate it with government regulations and high taxes, which are unpopular.[50] They instead choose to call themselves progressives or "new" Democrats.

Many candidates of both parties use populist strategies. Republican populists, like Republican Majority Leader Richard Armey of Texas, rail against the government, taxes, and special interests in Washington. Democratic populists also champion the cause of ordinary Americans. Rather than oppose big government, however, these candidates run against big business. For example, Byron Dorgan, who was elected North Dakota's at-large representative in 1980 and its junior senator in 1992, earned his populist credentials when, as state tax commissioner, he sued out-of-state corporations doing business in North Dakota to force them to pay taxes there.[51]

Negative Campaigning

Negative campaigning has always been and will probably always be a part of American elections. Just as positive campaigning attempts to build up a candidate, negative campaigning endeavors to tear down an opponent. Negative campaigning is a legitimate form of campaign communication that has the potential to enhance the electoral process. Campaign ads that question a candidate's qualifications or point to unpopular, wasteful, or unethical practices bring a measure of accountability to the political system.[52] Still, much negative campaigning amounts to little more than character assassination and mudslinging that turns off voters and discourages them from participating in elections.[53] From the point of view of the candidates this is unimportant. What matters is that more of their supporters than their opponent's show up at the polls.

Negative campaigning is used by one or both candidates in almost three-quarters of all House contests and virtually every Senate election. As elections get closer, the probability that they feature negative ads goes up.[54] The sense of urgency that pervades a close contest encourages the contestants to figuratively tar and feather each other because it is easier to discredit an opponent than to build loyalty.[55]

Attack ads can be an important component of challenger campaigns because they can help break voters of the habit of casting their ballots for the incumbent. However, some incumbents have made negative advertising a central element of their strategies in recent years, using early attacks to define their challengers for voters before the challengers can define themselves.[56] Because of their competitiveness, open-seat campaigns tend to be the most negative of all.

The most effective negative ads are grounded in fact, document their sources, focus on some aspect of the opponent's policy views rather than personality, use ridicule, are delivered by a surrogate, and avoid discussing the plight of unfortunate citizens.[57] Many negative ads feature actors depicting incumbents voting themselves pay raises or attending lavish parties with lobbyists. Some show opponents flip-flopping on the issues. Ridicule is a powerful weapon in politics because it is difficult for people to vote for a candidate at whom they have just laughed. Campaign attacks that do not adhere to the preceding guidelines tend to be less effective and can backfire, making the candidate who levies the charges look dishonest or mean-spirited. This lesson was lost on several unsuccessful

Republican challengers, including Roberg, Page, and Massey, who attacked their opponents for the Clinton/Lewinsky scandal.

Opposition research provides the foundation for negative campaigning. Campaigns begin with a thorough examination of an opponent's personal and professional background. Current members of Congress are qualified to serve in the House or Senate by virtue of their incumbency, although the elections held between 1992 and 1996 poignantly demonstrated that incumbency can be used as a weapon against them. The backgrounds of challengers and open-seat candidates are usually more open to question, especially if the candidates have no political experience or have pursued a career that most constituents would view with skepticism. Junk bond traders and dog catchers, for example, are at risk of being attacked as unqualified because of their professions.

The candidate's public record is the next thing that is usually explored. Challengers often study their opponent's attendance records, roll-call votes, and floor speeches. Incumbents and open-seat candidates usually study their opponent's political record. If an opponent has never held office, then a campaign will usually turn to newspaper or trade magazine accounts of speeches made to civic organizations, trade associations, or other groups.

Virtually all campaigns search for activities that can be construed as illegal or unethical. Federal indictments for influence peddling, the Keating Five scandal in the Senate, and the banking and Post Office scandals in the House provided many challengers with grist for the attack portions of their campaigns in the 1990s. Sometimes proximity to scandal can threaten an incumbent who has not been shown to have done any wrong. The chair of the House ethics committee, Rep. Nancy Johnson, R-Conn., learned this lesson in 1996 when Democratic challenger Charlotte Koskoff charged her with perpetrating a cover-up for Speaker Gingrich and came within 1,587 votes of defeating her.

Similarly, most contestants routinely search for unethical business transactions, evidence of tax dodging, and other questionable activities that could be used to discredit their opponents. Sometimes ex-spouses, estranged children, former friends, colleagues, and neighbors are interviewed to find examples of improper behavior or character flaws. Other times, investigations of military records, drivers' licenses, and campaign finance reports reveal that an opponent has lied about his or her service in the armed forces, is vulnerable to charges of having lived in the state or district for only a few years, or can be charged with being a tool of some wealthy special interest.

Most opposition research is tedious. Researchers scour the *Congressional Record,* search records of the floor proceedings of state legislatures, look through newspapers, surf the World Wide Web, and turn to other public sources to show that a candidate is out of touch with the district, has flip-flopped on an issue, has taken an inordinate number of government-financed trips, or has committed some other questionable act. Opposition researchers often pore over campaign finance reports so a candidate can claim that an opponent is too beholden to PACs and wealthy individuals from out of state to represent the views of constituents.

The widespread use of negative advertising has encouraged most campaigns to search for their own candidate's weaknesses. As one campaign manager explained, "We need to be prepared for the worst. We have to spend a lot of time looking at the things our opponent may try to pin on us."[58] Campaigns investigate their own candidates in anticipation of attacks they expect to be levied against them.

Some campaigns discuss a potential liability with members of the press before an opponent has had a chance to raise it. Preemption is an effective tactic for "inoculating" a candidate against an attack. Another approach is to hire one of the consulting firms that stakes its reputation on its ability to prepare a televised response to an attack in less than one day. A few well-financed Senate and House contenders have gone so far as to record television commercials that present responses to particular charges before their opponent makes them. Anticipating that Roberg might attack him for voting against a constitutional amendment to ban flag burning, the Price campaign took the precaution of recording an ad featuring a Korean War veteran praising the congressman for his patriotism. Roberg made the attack and, although they were prepared to respond, Price campaign officials opted not to use their ad. Still, they were comforted by the fact that the ad was ready and could have been used had their opponent's attack damaged the congressman's reputation.[59]

Many of the most effective negative campaigns run in the 1980s blamed incumbents for fostering economic stagnation, supporting tax increases, causing government gridlock and corruption, or losing touch with their districts. In the early and middle 1990s many challengers added congressional pay raises, political scandal, congressional perks, and the acceptance of PAC contributions to that list. Some personalized their attacks by counting the number of checks a member bounced at the House bank or the number of junkets he or she had taken at taxpayer or corporate expense. In 1994 many Republican House challengers attacked Democratic incumbents for being part of a corrupt, unresponsive Washington establishment. By linking their opponents to President Clinton, who had a low standing in the polls, the Republicans were able to defeat many senior House Democrats. Two years later, many Democratic candidates attacked Republican incumbents for voting to pass legislation that would pay for tax breaks for upper-income citizens by diminishing funding for future

Medicare benefits and other programs that enjoy broad support. The Democrats defeated many House Republican freshmen by comparing their congressional voting records with Gingrich's and exhorting voters to elect a member of Congress who would represent their views, not those of some politician from Georgia.[60] Not many incumbents were defeated in the 1998 congressional elections, but negative advertising played a role in the defeat of virtually all of those who were. One of the lessons to be drawn from the congressional elections of the 1990s is that, if used properly, negative campaigning can be a potent weapon.

SUMMARY

The campaign for votes, like the campaign for resources, requires candidates and strategists to identify groups of supporters and potential supporters and communicate to them a message they will find appealing. Campaign strategists recognize that most voters have little interest in politics, possess little information about congressional candidates, are more familiar with incumbents than with challengers, know more about candidates for the Senate than about those for the House, and tend to cast their ballots for candidates whom they have previously supported or who share their party identification.

Candidates and their advisers consider these factors when plotting strategies. Most campaigns use voting histories, census data, polls, and geodemographic analysis to target voters. They consider the partisan advantages associated with specific policy stances, the positions likely to be staked out by the opponent, the opinions of the blocs of supporters they need to mobilize, and the views of undecided voters they need to win. Most candidates make issues a major component of their message, but incumbents have a greater tendency to focus on imagery and their performance in office. Most candidates also seek to hold their opponent accountable for what they perceive to be weaknesses in their record. However, competitive elections usually feature the most negative campaigns.

CHAPTER EIGHT

Campaign Communications

Campaign communications range from sophisticated television advertisements and Internet Web sites to old-fashioned knocking on doors. The resources at a candidate's disposal, the types of media available, and the competitiveness of the election are the factors that most strongly influence how campaigns reach voters. In this chapter I examine the techniques that campaigns use to disseminate their messages and get their supporters to the polls.

Campaign communications are meant to accomplish six objectives: to improve a candidate's name recognition, project a favorable image, set the campaign agenda, exploit the issues, undermine the opponent's credibility and support, and defend the candidate against attacks. These objectives, of course, are designed to advance the campaign's broader goals of shoring up and expanding its bases of support and getting its supporters sufficiently interested in the election to vote.

Campaign communications usually proceed through four short phases that begin in late summer and continue until election day. In the first, often called the biography phase, candidates introduce themselves to voters by highlighting their experience and personal backgrounds. Next, candidates use issues to attract the support of uncommitted voters, energize their supporters, and further define themselves to the public.

The attack phase often begins after one candidate learns that he or she is slipping in the polls or failing to advance on an opponent. At this time, candidates contrast themselves with their opponent, point to inconsistencies between an opponent's rhetoric and actions, try to exploit unpopular positions that the opponent has taken, or just plain sling mud at one another. In the final weeks of the campaign, most successful candidates pull their message together by reminding voters who they are, why they are running, and why they are more worthy of being elected than their opponent. At this final, or summation, phase they commonly emphasize phrases and symbols that were presented earlier in the campaign.

TELEVISION ADVERTISING

Virtually every household in the United States possesses at least one television set, and the average adult watches between three and one-half and four hours of television per day.[1] About three-fourths of all voters maintain that television is their most important source of information about elections.[2] These factors make television an important vehicle for campaign communications.

Television is the best medium for conveying image-related information to a mass audience. It is also extremely useful in setting the campaign agenda and associating a candidate with popular issues.[3] Television ads enable candidates to transmit action-oriented visuals that demonstrate such desirable qualities as leadership. Images of candidates meeting with voters or attending groundbreaking ceremonies convey more powerfully than do written or verbal statements the message that these individuals are actively involved in community affairs and have close ties to voters. Images also have a stronger emotional impact than words. As Republican strategist Robert Teeter explains, "80 or 90 percent of what people retain from a TV ad is visual. . . . If you have the visual right, you have the commercial right. If you don't, it almost doesn't matter what you're saying."[4] Television advertisements have the added advantage of enabling the campaign to control its message. Unlike interactive modes of communication, such as debates and speeches, paid advertisements do not allow an opponent or disgruntled voter to interrupt. Message control makes TV a potent weapon for increasing name recognition.[5]

Roughly nine of ten Senate campaigns and 70 percent of all House campaigns use television, and these numbers would be higher if the costs were not so high.[6] Campaigns must pay the same rates as commercial advertisers for nonpreemptible advertising slots. These are most often prohibitively expensive, especially during prime time. Democratic representative José Serrano or Thomas Bayley Jr., his Republican opponent, would have had to spend $35,000 to broadcast one thirty-second prime-time advertisement to reach voters living in New York's 16th congressional district during the 1998 election. The cost of broadcasting an ad to this South Bronx district is exorbitant because the district is in a media market that spans the entire New York metropolitan area. Candidates in Texas's 11th district, which includes Waco, in contrast, paid only $1,200 to air a thirty-second prime-time television ad that blanketed virtually the entire district.[7]

Some campaigns save money by forgoing the certainty that their ads will be broadcast during prime time. Those who purchase preemptible broadcast time pay considerably less for TV but run the risk of their ads being aired at some less desirable time. That is a gamble few campaigns take. Some campaigns, including many in major metropolitan areas, save money and improve targeting by substituting cable TV for broadcast stations.[8]

High costs and the mismatch between media markets and the boundaries of congressional districts discourage House candidates in the highly urbanized areas of the Middle Atlantic, West Coast, and southern New England from using television advertising. The distribution of media markets and relatively low advertising rates in most southwestern states and many rural areas, however, enable many House candidates to use television extensively.[9] Senate candidates tend to make greater use of television than do candidates for the House because the configuration of state borders and media markets make television a relatively cost-efficient communications medium in statewide contests. The greater funding levels of Senate campaigns and the expectation that Senate candidates will rely on television also contribute to its greater use in contests for the upper chamber.

Televised campaign advertisements have come a long way since the days when candidates appeared as talking heads that spouted their political experiences and issue positions. Six trends define the evolution of the modern television campaign commercial. They are a movement toward greater emphasis on imagery, the use of action-oriented themes and pictures, the employment of emotionally laden messages, a decrease in the length of ads, an increase in negative advertising, and a reduction in the amount of time required to create an ad.[10] Gimmicky, ten- and fifteen-second spots punctuated by twenty or so words have recently become popular with congressional candidates and other political groups. An ability to counterattack within twenty-four hours has become a major selling point for many media firms. The broadcasting of campaign advertisements under the guise of issue ads by parties and interest groups is the latest development in the use of television in elections.

During the biography stage of the campaign, incumbents' ads typically depict them as experienced leaders who know and care about their constituents. Challengers and candidates for open seats also try to present themselves as capable and honorable by pointing to their accomplishments in politics, family life, or the private sector. All candidates broadcast advertisements that repeatedly mention and display their names, and usually end their commercials with the line "Vote for [candidate's name] for Congress."

Candidates who have led remarkable lives, have long histories of public service, or have overcome humble origins often broadcast what are called "minidocudramas" to showcase their war record, community activism, or road to professional success. The sixty-second biographical ad designed by Alfano Productions for Republican representative J. C. Watts's 1996 reelection campaign in Oklahoma's 4th district highlights Watts's modest background and meteoric political career. The ad shows Watts speaking to an enthusiastic crowd at the 1996 Republican National Convention. Watts's voice can be heard over the din of cheering and applauding delegates:

> I have a special message for the kids in your house tonight: Young people, America needs you, whether your dream is to be a doctor, a teacher, an engineer, or, yes, even a congressman. If you can dream it, you can do it.

The accompanying visuals are close-ups of an African-American girl, an Asian-American boy, and many white children reciting the pledge of allegiance and playing in a park. The ad later features a casually dressed Watts walking out of a school with a group of young white children. One child is holding an American flag that waves across Watts's chest. The visual is accompanied by Watts's voice-over:

> Never in the wildest dreams of Buddy and Helen Watts did they ever think that the fifth child born to them of six children, in the poor rural community of Eufaula, Oklahoma . . .

Here Watts is shown talking to a white farmer in a field as they walk toward a tractor. The voice-over continues:

> . . . would some day grow up to be called "congressman." But friends, after all, this is America. God bless you!

Watts's biographical spot was intended to accomplish more than just highlighting his American success story. Its visuals of school children were designed to inoculate him against charges of being anti-education, which Democratic candidates typically make against Republicans. And its presentation of mainly white children and a white farmer was designed to increase the level of comfort that the district's 84 percent white population had with being represented by an African American. Watts believed that the ad was effective and used it in both his 1996 and his 1998 reelection campaigns.

Few candidates have careers as impressive as that of Congressman Watts, and few minority representatives are from districts that are so heavily dominated by white voters. Yet many would-be members of Congress use television to make the point that they are resourceful leaders whose personal experiences make them fit to serve in the House or Senate.

Some incumbents, and a few nonincumbents with political experience, use "community action" spots to show the impact of their efforts on behalf of constituents. In 1998 Rep. Charles Stenholm, a conservative Democrat from west Texas, broadcast a TV ad showcasing his efforts to maintain funding for the Dyess Air Force Base in Abilene, Texas, which employs 5,000 military and 450 civilian residents.[11] Stenholm is shown speaking directly to the camera and meeting with constituents as newspaper clips about the defense project are superimposed on the screen. The ad closes with Stenholm stating, "I've always believed in doing what's right for the people of the 17th district, regardless of what the president says or leaders of my own party are saying. And that will never change." In addition to reminding voters that he protected their interests, the commercial helped Stenholm to distance himself from Clinton, whose moral indiscretions added to his already low standing in the district (the president received only 39 percent of the district's vote in 1996), and from congressional leaders, whom most of Stenholm's constituents consider too liberal.

"Feel good" ads are virtually devoid of substance and are designed to appeal to the electorate's sense of community pride or nationalism. They feature visuals of a candidate marching in parades, on horseback in the countryside, or involved in some other popular local activity. "Passing the torch" ads manipulate symbols to show that the candidate is the right person for the job. The most effective of these spots in recent years was broadcast in 1992 by a presidential rather than a congressional candidate. It featured a teenage Bill Clinton shaking hands with President John F. Kennedy on the grounds of the White House.

During the issue phase, campaign ads communicate candidates' policy stances on valence or positional issues.[12] The television and radio ads that Rep. Maurice Hinchey, D-N.Y., used in this phase of his 1998 race against Republican challenger William Walker focused on traditional Democratic issues, such as improving health care, protecting Social Security, creating jobs to boost the local economy, fostering better and safer schools, and fighting to protect children from drugs, alcohol, and tobacco. The ads were designed to shore-up support among senior citizens, women, middle-class voters, and blue-collar workers and to appeal to small business owners—a swing group that has formed part of Hinchey's reelection constituency over the years. Walker's issue ads focused primarily on cutting taxes and reducing government regulations, two popular traditional GOP issues. Although most voters have only a limited interest in any single issue, ads that focus on positional issues can help candidates pick up crucial support among single-issue voters or emphasize certain elements of their image.[13]

In the attack phase of the campaign, candidates use televised advertisements that often feature fancy graphics to point to their opponent's shortcomings. Television is ideally suited to comparative ads because it enables candidates to present pictures of themselves and their opponent side-by-side and to roll lists of issues down the screen showing themselves on the popular and the opponent on the unpopular sides of salient policies. Sometimes the opponent's head is reduced in size, "phased out," or distorted to keep voters' attention and to subtly imply that faulty issue positions are only one of an opponent's weaknesses. Television is also an effective medium for portraying inconsistencies in an opponent's positions. Advertisements that feature images of the opponent somersaulting back and forth across the screen or debating him or herself are useful in highlighting inconsistencies among an opponent's speeches, campaign positions, or congressional roll-call votes.

Television can also be used to deliver the message that an incumbent has failed to represent constituents' views in Congress. In 1998 Rep. Mark Neumann, who was challenging incumbent senator Russell Feingold, used humor to paint his opponent as a big spender who was out of touch with Wisconsin voters. One of his ads showed a scientist in a white lab coat and boots sneaking up behind cows to collect their flatulence in a jar. The ad, which features rude noises emanating from the cow's back end, jabs at Feingold for backing an environmental measure to limit greenhouse gases that included $23 million for cow gas research. In the ad Neumann states, "This smelled like government waste so I wrote a bill that killed the funding for this ridiculous program." Another Neumann ad features what appear to be monkeys with thick Russian accents complaining that Neumann wants to stop spending U.S. tax dollars on Russian space monkey experiments, a program the viewer is told that Feingold supports.

Challengers often use televised ads to criticize other aspects of an incumbent's job performance. Some present pictures of empty desks with voice-overs decrying poor attendance records. Pictures of airplanes or beaches are used to make the case that legislators have been vacationing at the public's or some interest group's expense rather than performing their jobs in Washington. Video footage of lavish parties staged in fancy ballrooms make great backdrops for challenger ads claiming that an incumbent has spent so much time partying with lobbyists in Washington that he or she has lost touch with the concerns of ordinary constituents.

One attack ad often begets another, and television is ideal for alternative, often theatrical, strategies. An ad in which a candidate criticizes an opponent for dragging the race into the mud can effectively answer negative charges while enhancing a candidate's image of sincerity as he or she appears to take the high road. Humorous or serious ads can disarm an opponents' attacks. In 1998 Feingold, who had become well-known in Wisconsin for his humorous low-budget ads in 1992, used serious ads to defend himself against attacks by Neumann, the Republican Party, and conservative interest groups. In one spot he looks directly into the camera and complains that his opponents are misrepresenting his views on abortion rights, states what they are, and points out that they are the same as those held by the majority of Wisconsin voters. In another ad he sits at a table holding some documents and discusses a series of attack ads that have distorted his record. Feingold states:

> I've taken some tough votes in the Senate. Still, I never thought I'd have to defend votes I didn't take, but the ads backing my opponent don't tell the truth. The cow gas program: I never supported it. . . . And Russian space monkeys? I led the charge against that program! But the ads backing my opponent don't tell the truth. What's going on here? Isn't it time for more, not less, honesty in government?

As he rebuts each ad the camera presents a close-up of a corresponding document. The first consists of letters to the editor printed under the headline "Neumann's Ads Aim to Deceive Voters." The second is an article clipped from *The Capitol Times* (a major Wisconsin newspaper) with the headline "Ad udderly ridiculous." The third is a newspaper article titled, "GOP's Anti-Feingold Ad Omits the Context Behind the Votes." The final document is a press release on U.S. Senate stationery reporting that Feingold and his colleague Sen. Robert Smith, R-N.H., lauded NASA's decision to end U.S. participation in the "space monkeys" program. Because Smith is a conservative Republican, the press release gave Feingold extra "cover" on the issue.

In the summation stage of the campaign, eleventh-hour television blitzes are used to solidify a candidate's message in the minds of voters. Key phrases and visuals from earlier commercials are repeated as candidates who are ahead shore up support and those running behind appeal to undecided voters.

RADIO ADVERTISING

Radio is an extremely popular medium for congressional campaign communications. More than 90 percent of all House candidates and virtually every Senate contestant purchase radio ads.[14] Inexpensive to record and broadcast, radio commercials are ideal for building a candidate's name identification. Another advantage is that some candidates—whether they are intimidated by the television camera, not telegenic, novices to the spotlight, or products of the pretelevision era—perform better on radio. For many incumbents, taping radio commercials is an easy extension of the radio shows they regularly send back to stations in their districts. Like television, radio is an excellent vehicle for emotion-laden messages.[15]

Radio allows candidates to target voters with great precision. Radio stations broadcast to smaller, more homogeneous audiences than does television, enabling campaigns to tailor their messages to different segments of the population. Campaigns can reach Hispanic voters in the Southwest, Florida, or the inner cities of the Northeast by advertising on Spanish-language stations. "Golden oldies" stations, which feature music from the 1960s and 1970s, are ideal for reaching middle-aged voters. Radio talk programs, such as the *Rush Limbaugh Show,* are excellent vehicles for reaching voters who are committed to particular ideologies. Commuting hours furnish near-captive audiences of suburbanites who travel to work.

NEWSPAPER ADVERTISING

Newspaper advertisements dominated campaign communications for much of American history but fell in importance with the decline of the partisan press in the late 1800s.[16] Congressional campaigns still purchase newspaper ads, but they are not as widely used as radio and many other media. Seventy percent of all House and 80 percent of all Senate campaigns purchase ads in local or statewide newspapers.[17]

Newspapers as a campaign medium have some advantages but many shortcomings. Their major advantages are that they provide plenty of opportunities to deliver a detailed message, and because readers are educated voters they are likely to vote. Newspapers' major downsides are that they do not lend themselves to emotional appeals and do not communicate images or convey emotion as well as does television. They also cannot be used to deliver a personalized message. Moreover, only a few congressional districts and states have large enough minority communities to sustain independent newspapers that can be used to target communications to these groups. The effectiveness of campaign advertisements that appear in newspapers is also somewhat limited.[18]

If such shortcomings exist, why do most campaigns place ads in newspapers? One reason is that they are inexpensive. Newspaper advertisements cost less than ads transmitted via television, radio, mail, or virtually any other medium. Newspaper ads can also be useful in announcing the times and locations of campaign events, and this can help attract coverage by other media. Finally, some candidates and campaign aides believe that purchasing advertising space from a local newspaper can help them secure the paper's endorsement.

DIRECT-MAIL ADVERTISING

Mail can be used to raise money, convey a message, or encourage people to vote, but the key to success in all three areas is a good mailing list. A good fund-raising list is made up of previous donors or persons who have a history of contributing to like-minded candidates; a good advertising list includes supporters and persuadable voters; and a good voter mobilization list includes only the candidate's supporters.

Direct mail (sometimes referred to as persuasion mail) is one of the most widely used methods of campaign advertising in congressional elections. More than nine out of ten House candidates and nearly all Senate candidates use it.[19] Mail is a one-way communications tool that offers significant advantages in message control and delivery. Precise targeting is its main advantage. Campaigns can purchase lists that include such information as a voter's name, address, gender, age, race or ethnicity, employment status, party registration, voting history, and estimated income.[20] This information enables campaigns to tailor the candidate profiles, issue positions, and photographs they include in their mailings to appeal to specific segments of the population. This ability makes mail an excellent medium for staking out positional issues and for campaigning in heterogeneous states or districts. Campaigns waged in highly diverse areas, such as New York's 12th district, which is 58 percent Hispanic and includes most of Chinatown, often use the mail to campaign in more than one language.

Another advantage of mail is that it is relatively inexpensive. Letters that are produced using personal computers and laser printers can be mailed to voters for little more than the price of a first-class stamp. Campaigns can also take advantage of post office discounts for presorted mailings. Finally, mail campaigns often fly under the radar screen for a while. So long as an adversary does not detect them, his or her campaign will not respond.

Nevertheless, direct mail is not without its disadvantages, including the fact that it is often tossed out as junk mail. Another disadvantage is that it rests principally on the power of the printed word. Whereas television and radio enable campaigns to embellish their messages with visual images or sound effects, mail depends primarily on written copy to hold voters' attention and get a message across. This makes it a less effective medium for communicating image-related information.

Direct-mail experts rely on many different techniques to combat the weaknesses of their medium. Personalized salutations, graphs, and pictures are often used to capture and hold voters' attention. Other gimmicks include the use of postscripts that are designed to look as though they were handwritten.

Direct mail is an especially powerful medium for challengers and candidates who have strong ideological positions because it is ideal for negative advertising or making appeals that stir voters' emotions. Yet mail also offers some advantages to incumbents. Many members of Congress send out letters early in the election to reinforce voter support without mounting a highly visible campaign.[21] These mailings often include messages reinforcing those that incumbents communicate in congressionally franked mass mailings to constituents, which are prohibited ninety days before a primary or general election for House members and sixty days before an election for senators.[22]

Direct mail plays a prominent role in many congressional elections. Democrat Loretta Sanchez made it a central element of her communication efforts when she defeated nine-term California GOP incumbent Robert Dornan in 1996 and in their rematch in 1998. Because the 46th district is located in the prohibitively expensive Los Angeles media market, Sanchez used highly targeted mail campaigns to get out her message.[23] She spent roughly 40 percent of her 1996 budget and 25 percent of her 1998 budget (which was almost three times larger) to send dozens of separate mailings to selected voters. Her campaign targeted Democrats and independent voters who had a history of voting, young Republican women, Hispanics, and newly registered Democratic and independent voters. The objective of the campaign was to maximize voter turnout among these groups, which formed the core of her electoral coalition. Members of Sanchez's campaign team believe that direct mail was critical in producing their candidate's razor-thin victory margin in 1996 and that it played a significant role in enabling her to defeat Dornan by a margin of 17 percent of the vote in 1998.[24]

THE INTERNET

The Internet has become a popular communications medium in congressional elections. Web sites are relatively inexpensive to create, are easy to maintain, can convey a great deal of information quickly and with little effort, and because of their interactive nature are useful for getting voters involved in the election. Congressional campaign Web sites usually include the candidate's biography and issue positions, favorable breaking news, a calendar of events, a directory that provides headquarters and staffing information, an area to facilitate voter involvement in the campaign, and negative information on the opposition.[25]

The best Web sites complement the candidate's campaign. They provide a place for voters to collect information that is available elsewhere, but to do so in a more convenient and reliable way than telephoning campaign headquarters, scouring newspapers, or contacting local political activists. Campaigns save money and effort, and avoid mistakes, when they direct voter, donor, and press inquiries to their Web site. Good campaign Web sites have attractive home pages that immediately tell voters about the candidate, are updated regularly, and display icons that direct them to other areas of the site. They provide online areas that permit individuals to volunteer for campaign activities, make a contribution, or sign up on the campaign's email list, which in itself is a valuable communications tool. These data are usually integrated into the campaign's computerized volunteer and finance databases. Some Web sites encourage activists to write op-ed articles, send letters to the editor, or call radio talk shows by providing the names, addresses, and telephone numbers of local media outlets. Some also provide voters with directions to their polling place. More Senate candidates than House candidates, more nonincumbents than incumbents, and more candidates in competitive races than those in one-sided contests use the Internet to communicate with voters.[26]

The Web site Brian Baird, D-Wash., used to help publicize the poor attendance record his Republican opponent, Don Benton, compiled while serving in the Washington State legislature shows how important the Internet can be to a candidate's campaign communications. Baird had two Web sites in 1998: a traditional site, www.brianbaird.com, and an issue-specific site, www.missedvotes.com. Five weeks before the election, the Baird campaign began airing a humorous television attack ad that pointed out that Benton had missed four hundred votes while serving in the legislature. "Missedvotes.com" was printed at the bottom of the ad. Although this Web site did not get a substantial number of "hits," it had a remarkable impact on the media's coverage of the ad and the campaign. Initial stories about the ad indicated that Benton had *allegedly* missed four hundred votes. A few days later, after several reporters visited the Web site, the word *allegedly* disappeared from their news stories. When Benton responded by arguing that he missed only unimportant votes, the campaign again referred reporters to the Web site, which enabled them to sort the votes by subject and to determine that many of the votes were, in fact, important. Members of the Baird organization believe that Benton's poor voting record was one of the reasons they won the endorsement of the *Columbian* and other local newspapers. These endorsements helped Baird defeat Benton by 9 percent of the vote.[27]

FREE MEDIA

One of the major goals of any campaign is to generate free, or "earned," media—radio, television, newspaper, or magazine coverage that candidates receive when news editors consider their activities newsworthy. Earned media has other advantages besides free advertising. Because it is delivered by a neutral observer, it has greater credibility than campaign-generated communications.[28] The major disadvantage of free media is that campaigns cannot control what news correspondents report. Misstatements and blunders are more likely to appear in the news than are issues raised in major policy speeches.

News coverage of congressional elections consists of stories based on press releases issued by campaigns; stories about events, issues, or time that a reporter has spent with a candidate; and analytical or editorial stories about a candidate or campaign.[29] Most analysis focuses on the "horse-race" aspect of the election. Those stories that get beyond handicapping the race usually discuss candidates' political qualifications, personal characteristics, or campaign organizations. Fewer stories focus on the issues.[30] Coverage by television and radio tends to be shorter, more action-oriented, and less detailed and features less editorializing than does print journalism.

Most journalists strive to cover politics objectively, but this does not mean that all candidates are treated the same. Reporters follow certain norms when pursuing leads and researching and writing their stories—norms that usually work to the advantage of incumbents.[31] Moreover, editorials are largely exempt from the norms of objectivity that apply to news stories. Newspaper owners and their editorial boards do not hesitate to voice their opinions on editorial pages. Radio and television stations also air programs that feature pundits discussing the virtues and foibles of specific candidates. Most readers have come to expect newspaper editors and political talk show hosts to endorse specific candidates shortly before the election. Media endorsements and campaign coverage can have a significant impact on elections.

Attracting Coverage

Attracting media coverage requires planning and aggressiveness. Besides issuing streams of press releases, campaign offices distribute copies of the candidate's schedule to correspondents, invite them to campaign events, and make special efforts to grant interviews. Candidates also submit themselves to interrogations by panels of newspaper editors with the goal of generating good press coverage or winning an endorsement.

Successful campaigns carefully play to the needs of different news media.

Press releases that feature strong leads, have news value, provide relevant facts, and contain enough background information for an entire story are faxed to print reporters.[32] Advance notice of major campaign events, including information about predicted crowd size, acoustics, and visual backdrops, is given to television and radio correspondents with the hope that the event will be one of the few they cover.[33] Interpretive information is provided to all journalists, regardless of the media they work in, to try to generate campaign stories with a favorable news spin. News organizations routinely report stories based on materials distributed by campaigns; because few news organizations have adequate resources to research or even verify this information, most free press is uncritical.

Newspapers and radio stations are more likely than television stations to give candidates free media coverage. Television stations devote little time to covering congressional elections, particularly House races. Television news shows occasionally discuss the horse-race aspect of campaigns, cover small portions of campaign debates, or analyze controversial campaign ads, but few are willing to give candidates air time to discuss issues. Radio stations are more generous with air time. Many invite candidates to participate in call-in talk shows and public forums. Newspapers usually give the most detailed campaign coverage. Small, understaffed newspapers frequently print portions of candidates' press releases and debate transcripts verbatim.

Senate candidates attract more free media than do House candidates. Incumbents and open-seat contestants usually get more—and more favorable—press coverage than do challengers, regardless of whether they are running for the House or the Senate. Inequities in campaign coverage are due to the professional norms that guide news journalists and to the inequalities that exist among candidates and campaign organizations. The preoccupation of journalists with candidates' personalities, qualifications, campaign organizations, and probable success are to the advantage of incumbents because they are almost always better known, more qualified, in possession of more professional organizations, and more likely to win than their opponents.[34]

Press coverage in House contests between an incumbent and a challenger is so unequal that veteran Democratic political adviser Anita Dunn believes "the local press is the unindicted co-conspirator in the alleged 'permanent incumbency.'" As Dunn explains, "A vicious circle develops for challengers—if early on, they don't have money, standing in the polls, endorsements, and the backing of political insiders, they—and the race—are written off, not covered, which means the likelihood of a competitive race developing is almost nonexistent."[35]

The coverage that challengers to Maryland Republican Connie Morella receive in the *Washington Post* (the major newspaper covering her seat) demonstrates this point. Morella's 1996 opponent, Don Mooers, was mentioned in a total of twenty-one election stories, and all of them implied he had little chance of winning. In "Lots of Foes, Little Hope," the *Post* quoted one of Mooers's opponents in the Democratic primary as saying, "Heaven help whoever gets the nomination. They're going to need it."[36] The *Post's* general election coverage continued to belittle Mooers's prospects, describing him as involved in "an up-hill struggle against a skilled politician who is experienced, popular and well-financed—three attributes he still is cultivating."[37] A story published a week before the election featured a likeness of Morella flattening six previous Democratic opponents and about to flatten Mooers. The caption above the picture reads, "Caught under the Morella steamroller."[38]

In 1998 Morella faced a more formidable opponent, Ralph Neas. Neas, former director of the Legislative Conference on Civil Rights, handily defeated six largely unknown opponents in the Democratic primary, raised $811,902, and put together an impressive campaign organization in his bid to oust Morella. Yet Neas received little more coverage in the *Post* than did previous Democratic nominees, and most of it was buried in the weekly section that covers Montgomery County politics, rather than in the paper's main news section. Neas had few complaints about the tone of the *Post's* coverage, but he maintained that there was too little coverage and that it came too late.[39] The *Post's* policy of not reporting on challengers until they are actually nominated resulted in the paper's ignoring Neas's campaign until after the state's September 15th primary. That delay allowed for a total of just six weeks of press coverage, not enough for a challenger to gain the visibility needed to become a viable candidate. Although the *Post* is a nonpartisan newspaper, its policy for covering challengers functions as an incumbent retention program when combined with primaries that take place late in the election season. Many congressional challengers are greatly disadvantaged because their local newspaper has the same policy as the *Post's*.

Although many challengers can usually count on getting only four stories—the announcement of their candidacy, coverage of their primary victory, a candidate profile, and the announcement of their defeat—it is still worth pursuing free media coverage. Those few challengers who are able to make the case to journalists that they have the capacity to mount a strong campaign are able to attract significant media coverage, often enough to become known among local voters. Challengers who have held elective office or had significant unelective political experience, assembled professional campaign organizations, and raised substantial funds are in a better position to make this case than are those who have not. They typically receive extra press coverage, which in turn helps them raise more money, hire additional help, become more competitive, and attract even greater attention from the media.[40] A similar set of relationships exists for open-seat candidates, except that it is usually easier for them to make the case that they are involved in a close contest.

Scandal can also help candidates attract more media coverage. Even under-dogs are taken more seriously when their opponents have been accused of break-ing the law or ethical misconduct. California Republican Gary Miller, who defeated Rep. Jay Kim in 1998, is an example of an experienced challenger who took advantage of the heightened media exposure that resulted from scandal. Miller's exhortation to "kick a criminal out of Congress" helped him garner substantial press coverage.[41]

Campaign Debates

Debates are among the few campaign activities that receive extensive press cov-erage and can place a challenger on equal footing with an incumbent. The decision to participate in a debate is a strategic one. Front-runners, who are usually incumbents, generally prefer to avoid debating because they understand that debates have the potential to do them more harm than good. Nevertheless, incumbents recognize that the public expects them to debate; most do so to avoid being blasted for shirking their civic responsibility. Candidates who are running behind, usually challengers, have the most to gain from debating. They prefer to engage in as many debates as possible and to hold them when they will attract the most media coverage.

Before debates are scheduled, the candidates or their representatives negoti-ate certain matters in regard to them. In addition to the number and timing of debates, candidates must agree on whether independent or minor-party candi-dates will participate, on the format that will be used, and on where the debate or debates will be held. All these factors can influence who, if anyone, is consid-ered the winner. Negotiations about debates can become heated but are almost always successfully resolved. Well over 90 percent of all House and Senate con-testants debate their opponents.[42] Those few who refuse usually enjoy insur-mountable leads or lack verbal agility. For example, Sen. Strom Thurmond, R-S.C., who turned ninety-three during the early days of his 1996 reelection campaign, was precisely in this situation and opted not to debate his opponent, Elliot Close, a quick-witted Democrat. Whether or not the candidates debate is one of the few questions in congressional elections that is usually decided in favor of challengers and candidates who are running behind. The Thurmond-Close race was an exception to the rule.

Media Bias

House challengers and incumbents disagree over the nature of the coverage the media give to House campaigns (see Table 8-1).[43] Challengers, particularly those

TABLE 8-1

Campaigners' Perceptions of the Media Coverage in House Campaigns

	All	Incumbents		Challengers		Open-seat candidates	
		In jeopardy	Shoo-ins	Hope-fuls	Likely losers	Pros-pects	Mis-matched
Favored your campaign	2%	4%	4%	2%	—	—	—
Favored your opponent's campaign	38	20	10	52	71	25	11
Equally fair	60	76	86	47	29	75	89
(N)	(312)	(49)	(81)	(58)	(91)	(24)	(9)

Source: The 1998 Congressional Campaign Study.

Notes: Figures are for major-party candidates in contested general elections. Column for hopeful challengers does not add to 100 percent because of rounding.

in uncompetitive contests, are the most likely to perceive an incumbent bias, reflecting the one-sided nature of press coverage in elections for safe seats. To some extent these perceptions are a product of the norms that guide the distribution of media endorsements—which favor incumbents by a margin of six to one.[44]

Some partisan differences also exist in the perception of media coverage. More Democratic campaigners than Republicans maintain that the press gives fair coverage to both campaigns, reflecting a widely shared opinion among Republican politicians and voters that the media corps is made up of members of a liberal establishment. Nevertheless, the fact that almost two of five campaigners from both parties believe that the media are biased against them highlights the adversarial relationship that exists between politicians and the press.[45]

FIELD WORK

Field work involves voter registration and get-out-the-vote drives, literature drops, and the distribution of yard signs and bumper stickers. It also includes candidate appearances at town meetings and in parades, speeches to Rotary Clubs and other civic groups, door-to-door campaigning, and other grass-roots activities. Field work is an important means of campaign communication and voter mobilization.

Field activities were the key to campaigning during the golden age of parties, and they continue to play a role in modern congressional elections. Sophisticated targeting plans, similar to those used in direct mail and mass telephone calling, guide many field activities. Field work remains one of the most labor intensive, volunteer-dependent aspects of congressional elections.[46] Candidates, their supporters, and local party workers knock on doors to learn whether citizens intend to vote, whom they support, and if they have any specific concerns they would like the candidate to address. Supporters and potential supporters who express an interest in an issue, need to register to vote, need help in getting to the polls, or are willing to work in the campaign typically receive follow-up calls.

Person-to-person communication is a highly effective means of political persuasion, especially when it takes place directly between the candidate and a voter. It also provides a campaign with useful feedback. Candidates routinely draw on conversations with individuals they meet along the campaign trail to develop anecdotes that humanize issues.

Field activities are relatively inexpensive because volunteers carry out much of the actual labor. Local party activists, union members, and other volunteers are often called on to deliver campaign literature, register voters, or drive them to the polls. The development of the coordinated campaign has allowed many congressional candidates to rely in part on party organizations to carry out their field work.[47] Forty percent of all House campaigns report that local party committees played a moderately important to extremely important role in their registration and get-out-the-vote drives, and over half of the campaigns maintain that local parties were a moderately important to extremely important source of campaign volunteers.[48]

THE IMPORTANCE OF DIFFERENT COMMUNICATIONS TECHNIQUES

Congressional campaigns disseminate their messages through a variety of media, each having its advantages and disadvantages. Door-to-door campaigning is inexpensive but time consuming. Television advertising requires little commitment of the candidate's time, but it is rarely cheap. Radio advertising and direct mail require accurate targeting to be effective.

Most campaigners believe that television is the best medium for disseminating their messages (see Table 8-2). Those involved in close contests rely on television the most. Incumbents find television more important than challengers do, reflecting the fact that more incumbents can afford to broadcast television commercials. But it is open-seat candidates who most consistently evaluate

TABLE 8-2

Campaigners' Perceptions of the Importance of Different Communications Techniques in House Campaigns

Perception	All	Incumbents		Challengers		Open-seat candidates	
		In jeopardy	Shoo-ins	Hope-fuls	Likely losers	Pros-pects	Mis-matched
Television (paid or free)	4.18	4.34	4.01	4.13	3.81	4.71	4.54
Radio (paid or free)	3.76	3.78	3.70	3.70	3.73	3.86	3.88
Newsletters and direct mail	3.68	3.72	3.80	3.76	3.33	3.88	3.86
Press releases and free media	3.67	3.57	3.76	3.94	3.62	3.34	3.83
Literature drops	3.50	3.27	3.26	3.54	3.72	3.40	4.00
Speeches and rallies	3.46	3.00	3.44	3.26	3.78	3.31	4.04
Candidate visits to shopping centers, factories, etc.	3.10	2.93	3.41	3.27	2.95	2.68	3.52
Door-to-door canvassing	3.10	2.63	2.93	3.55	3.06	3.14	3.61
Debates	3.06	2.70	2.70	2.98	3.17	3.48	3.77
Newspaper ads	3.00	3.09	2.87	3.16	2.97	2.90	3.04
Billboards and buttons	2.62	2.13	2.72	2.83	2.62	2.41	3.30
Surrogate campaigning	2.54	2.13	2.44	2.73	2.73	2.42	2.91
(N)	(325)	(47)	(70)	(54)	(81)	(49)	(24)

Source: The 1992 Congressional Campaign Study.

Notes: Candidates and campaign aides were asked to assess the importance of each technique on the following scale: 1 = not important or not used; 2 = slightly important; 3 = moderately important; 4 = very important; 5 = extremely important. The values listed are the arithmetic means of the scores. Figures are for major-party candidates in contested general elections, excluding a small number of atypical races.

television as extremely important, if not essential, to their campaigns. As shown in Chapter 6, the overwhelming majority of open-seat candidates can afford the high cost of broadcast time, and their races are usually competitive enough to warrant purchasing it.

Most House candidates and campaign aides also assess radio, direct mail, and free media as very important. Campaign literature and speeches are rated slightly lower, except by likely loser challengers and mismatched open-seat candidates, but both are still thought to be moderately important to very important ways of reaching voters. Nonincumbents in uncompetitive races tend to rely more heavily on campaign literature and speeches, reflecting their inability to purchase more expensive media and the overall low-key nature of their campaigns.

Campaigns use candidate visits to shopping malls and workplaces, door-to-door canvasses, campaign debates, and newspaper advertisements to help get out their message, but most see these as only moderately important communication techniques. Neighborhood canvasses, billboards, surrogate campaigning, and other grass-roots activities are viewed less favorably by incumbents because they can use television, direct mail, and other, more expensive forms of campaign advertising. Incumbents in jeopardy, who are often involved in the most expensive campaigns, place the lowest value on grass-roots campaign activities.

District characteristics and campaign strategy also affect media usage patterns. Television is a more important communications medium for House campaigns in rural districts than it is for those conducted in urban and suburban settings, due to cost considerations and the mismatch between media markets and House seats in metropolitan areas (see Table 8-3). Greater population density allows campaigns waged in urban and suburban districts to make greater use of field activities, including distributing campaign literature and canvassing door-to-door, than can campaigns waged in rural areas. Campaigns that target individuals who live in particular neighborhoods, work in certain occupations, or belong to specific segments of the population (such as women, the elderly, or members of an ethnic group) make greater use of direct mail than do campaigns that focus their efforts on less easily identifiable groups, such as single-issue voters.

SUMMARY

Campaign communications are the centerpiece of any bid for elective office. Congressional candidates disseminate their messages using a variety of media. Television and radio allow candidates to powerfully convey emotional messages. Direct mail and the Internet are less expensive and enable campaigns to disseminate highly targeted, customized messages. Free media coverage is highly

TABLE 8-3

The Impact of Geography and Targeting Strategies on the Importance
of Different Communications Techniques in House Campaigns

	District geography			Targeting strategy	
	Urban	Rural	Suburban or mixed	Geodemo-graphic	Issue- or attitude-based
Television (paid or free)	4.17	4.50	4.13	4.25	4.12
Radio (paid or free)	3.77	3.72	3.76	3.78	3.75
Newsletters and direct mail	3.80	3.60	3.58	3.90	3.49
Press releases and free media	3.54	3.88	3.80	3.81	3.59
Literature drops	3.64	3.04	3.40	3.62	3.43
Speeches and rallies	3.46	3.48	3.44	3.47	3.44
Candidate visits to shopping centers, factories, etc.	3.02	3.25	3.22	3.12	3.08
Door-to-door canvassing	3.25	2.89	3.17	3.08	3.11
Debates	3.07	3.12	3.03	3.14	3.00
Newspaper ads	2.99	3.32	2.94	2.99	3.00
Billboards and buttons	2.71	2.68	2.50	2.69	2.57
Surrogate campaigning	2.54	2.40	2.57	2.60	2.50
(N)	(172)	(25)	(125)	(113)	(209)

Source: The 1992 Congressional Campaign Study.

Notes: Districts are defined as urban (or rural) if 60 percent or more of the population lives in an urban (or rural) area; all others are classified as suburban or mixed. Targeting strategies are defined as geodemographic if campaigns focused on voters in specific geographic locations or demographic or occupational groups; targeting strategies are defined as issue- or attitude-based if they focused on issues, voters' party affiliations, persuadable voters, Perot supporters, or miscellaneous factors. Candidates and campaign aides were asked to assess the importance of each technique on the following scale: 1 = not important or not used; 2 = slightly important; 3 = moderately important; 4 = very important; 5 = extremely important. The values listed are the arithmetic means of the scores. Figures are for major-party candidates in contested general elections, excluding a small number of atypical races.

sought after, but it can be difficult for some candidates to attract, and it affords campaigns less control over their message than do other means of communication. Old-fashioned person-to-person contacts between candidates, campaign and local party activists, other volunteers, and voters are among the most effective means of communications.

Of course, the specific media mix that a campaign uses depends on the size of its war chest, the match between the district's boundaries and local media markets, and the talents and preferences of the individual candidate and the campaign's consultants. As is the case in most aspects of congressional elections, incumbents enjoy tremendous advantages when it comes to communicating with voters.

CHAPTER NINE

Candidates, Campaigns, and Electoral Success

During the golden age of parties, party loyalties dominated the voting decisions of the vast majority of citizens and were the primary determinants of the outcomes of most congressional elections. The decline of voter partisanship in the 1960s and 1970s paved the way for incumbency to have a greater effect on election outcomes.[1] Incumbent success rates routinely exceeded 90 percent, as members of Congress began to make better use of the resources that the institution put at their disposal.[2] Although challenger victories were rare, the types of campaign mounted by individual candidates, especially open-seat contestants, could determine the difference between victory and defeat.

The election of 1994 was unusual in that it was one of the few recent contests in which one party was able to nationalize congressional elections at the expense of another. In the 1998 election the Republican Party focused a great deal of attention on President Clinton's ethical lapses, but that contest largely represented a return to normalcy in that incumbency, money, district partisanship, and other factors pertaining to individual candidates and their campaigns were the major determinants of congressional election outcomes.

What separates winners from losers in contemporary congressional elections? How great an impact do candidate characteristics, political conditions, campaign strategy, campaign effort, party and interest group activities, and media coverage have on the percentage of the votes that House candidates receive? Do these factors affect incumbents, challengers, and open-seat contestants equally, or do these candidates need to do different things to win elections? This chapter addresses these questions. It also contains a discussion of the differences in the opinions of winners and losers over what determines the outcomes of elections.

HOUSE INCUMBENT CAMPAIGNS

Incumbency is highly important in regard to the kinds of campaigns that candidates mount, and it is the most important determinant of congressional election outcomes.[3] Virtually all House incumbents begin the general election campaign with higher name recognition and voter approval levels, greater political experience, more money, and better campaign organizations than do their opponents. Incumbents also benefit from the fact that most constituents and political elites in Washington expect them to win and act accordingly. For the most part, voters cast ballots, volunteers donate time, contributors give money, and news correspondents provide coverage in ways that favor incumbents. Most strategic politicians also behave in ways that contribute to high incumbent success rates. These individuals usually wait until a seat becomes open rather than take on a sitting incumbent and risking a loss that could harm their political careers.

The big leads that most incumbents enjoy at the beginning of the election season make defending those leads the major objective of their campaigns. Incumbent campaigns tend to focus more on reinforcing and mobilizing existing bases of support than on winning new ones. As the campaign manager for Connie Morella, a shoo-in House member, explained:

> Our candidate has a great personal story and a strong record. . . . Our goals were to remind voters of her commitment to the district and how she has served as an independent voice that represents them in Congress. We targeted federal employees and retirees, women's groups, teachers, the high-tech sector, Republicans, and independents . . . the same groups that supported us before.[4]

The overwhelming advantages that members of Congress possess make incumbency an accurate predictor of election outcomes in more than nine out of ten House and three-quarters of all Senate races in which incumbents seek reelection.

Of course, not every incumbent is a shoo-in, and a few challengers have realistic chances of winning. First-term House members and incumbents who are implicated in a scandal, have cast a series of roll-call votes that are out of sync with constituents, or possess other liabilities need to mount more aggressive campaigns. They must begin campaigning early to maintain their popularity among supporters, to remind voters of their accomplishments in office, and to set the campaign agenda. They also must be prepared to counter the campaigns of the strong challengers who are nominated to run against them and the outside campaigns waged by party committees and interest groups who

TABLE 9-1

Significant Predictors of House Incumbents' Vote Shares

	Percent
Base vote	64.38
Partisan bias (per one-point advantage in party registration)	+0.14
Incumbent spending on campaign communications (per $100,000)	−1.17
Challenger spending on campaign communications (per $100,000)	−0.32
Media advantage favored the incumbent	+1.79
Party and interest group outside campaign communications to help the challenger (per $100,000)	−2.73
N = 117	

Sources: The 1998 Congressional Campaign Study, Federal Election Commission, Campaign Media Analysis Group, and other sources.

Notes: The figures were generated using ordinary least squares regression to analyze data for major-party candidates in contested general elections. Complete regression statistics are presented in the Appendix (http://herrnson.cqpress.com).

support those challengers. Many incumbents in jeopardy face experienced challengers, some of whom amass the financial and organizational resources needed to mount a serious campaign. A few of these challengers in each election are able to capitalize on their opponent's weaknesses and win.

Because most incumbents have established strongholds on their seats, there is little they can do to increase their victory margins. Incumbents as a group, whether Democrat or Republican, Caucasian or African American, old or young, male or female, have tremendously favorable odds of getting reelected. Few variables—indeed only the five identified in Table 9-1—have a significant direct effect on the percentages of the vote that incumbents win.

Such factors as gender, age, race, and occupation, which are so influential in separating House candidates from the general population, typically have no impact on the votes received by incumbents.[5] Primary challenges from within their own party, which cost Jay Kim the GOP nomination in 1998, rarely harm the reelection prospects of incumbents who defeat their primary opponents. Moreover, incumbents' targeting strategies, issue stances, and communications expenditures do not significantly increase their shares of the vote in the general election. Outside campaigns, which include party and interest group independent expenditures and televised issue advocacy ads, also rarely spell the difference between success and defeat in incumbent-challenger races.

The first figure in Table 9-1, labeled the base vote, represents the percentage of the vote that a House incumbent in a typical two-party contested race would have received if all the other factors were set to zero.[6] A hypothetical incumbent who runs for reelection in a district that has equal numbers of registered Democratic and Republican voters, faces a challenger who spends no money, is not favored by the media, and is not the subject of positive or negative party or interest group independent expenditures or issue advocacy ads would win about 64 percent of the vote.

Certain districts and states lend themselves to the election of particular kinds of candidates. Districts populated mainly by Democratic voters (often urban districts that are home to many lower-middle-class, poor, or minority voters) typically elect Democrats; those populated by Republican voters (frequently suburban and more affluent districts) usually elect Republicans. The partisan bias of the district (the difference between the percentage of registered voters who belong to a candidate's party and the percentage of registered voters who belong to the opponent's party) has a positive impact on incumbents' electoral prospects.[7] As the second figure in the table indicates, for every 1 percent increase in the partisan advantage that incumbents enjoy among registered voters, they receive an additional 0.14 percent of the vote (controlling for the other factors in the table). A Democratic incumbent who represents a one-sided district with seventy-five registered Democratic voters for every twenty-five registered Republicans typically wins 7 percent (a fifty-point advantage in party registration multiplied by 0.14) more of the vote than a Democratic incumbent who holds a seat that is evenly split between Democratic and Republican voters. Partisan bias is an important source of incumbency advantage because most House members represent districts that are populated primarily by members of their party.

Those few House members who represent districts in which the balance of voter registration does not favor their party may be in danger of losing reelection. This was the case in the campaign between GOP incumbent William Redmond and Democratic challenger Thomas Udall in New Mexico's 3rd congressional district. As noted in Chapter 4, Redmond won the seat with a three-point victory in a low-turnout, three-way special election held after seven-term Democratic representative Bill Richardson joined the Clinton administration. Green Party candidate Carol Miller's amassing 17 percent of the vote, most of it drawn from Democratic nominee Eric Serna, was largely responsible for Redmond's victory. Redmond's May 1997 election gave him only one and a half years to prepare for reelection. He tried to expand his base of support by continuing Richardson's tradition of frequently holding town meetings around the district. He sought appointment to the House National Security Committee so that he could advance legislation promoting the interests of military personnel stationed at Cannon Air Force Base and those of the businesses that have contracts with it. His memberships on the Veterans' Affairs and Banking and Financial Institutions Committees enabled him to advance the views of realtors, other business owners, and the many military retirees who live in the district. Redmond also fought for constituents who believed that the federal government should compensate landowners whose property values have been reduced as a result of federal regulations. Despite his best efforts, Redmond was unable to hold the seat in 1998. The Democrats' two-to-one voter registration advantage in the district proved an insurmountable obstacle when Democrats and environmentalists turned out in heavy numbers to support Udall.[8]

Because most House members begin the general election campaign well known and liked by their constituents, few elements of incumbent campaigning have much influence on election outcomes. The targeting approaches that incumbents use and the themes and issues they stress do not significantly affect their vote margins.[9] Nor do the dollars incumbents spend on direct-mail, television, radio, and newspaper advertising, field work, or other communications make a significant contribution to the percentage of the votes they win.[10]

Following the usual pattern, incumbent spending in 1998 increased in direct response to the closeness of the race.[11] Shoo-ins such as Ed Royce, who ran against underfunded challengers, undertook fairly modest reelection efforts by incumbents' standards, assembling relatively small organizations and spending moderate sums of money. Those who were pitted against well-funded challengers, however, followed the examples of Redmond and David Price and mounted extensive campaigns.

Although the communications expenditures and other campaign activities of incumbents are not positively related to higher vote margins, they are not inconsequential. A more accurate interpretation is that incumbent campaigning generally works to reinforce rather than to expand a candidate's existing base of support. Incumbents who are in the most trouble—because they represent marginal districts, have been implicated in a scandal, failed to keep in touch with voters, or cast too many legislative votes that were out of line with constituents' views—usually spend the most. Most of these candidates either succeed in reinforcing their electoral bases or watch their shares of the vote dip slightly from that of previous years. Others watch their victory margins become perilously low. The high-powered campaigns these incumbents wage might make the difference between winning and losing. In a few cases, probably no amount of incumbent spending would make a difference. Scandal, poor performance, and other factors simply put reelection beyond the reach of a few House members. Regardless of whether an incumbent in a close race wins or loses, that individual would undoubtedly have done worse absent an extensive campaign effort.

House challengers' expenditures, however, do reduce incumbents' vote shares somewhat. The typical challenger spent roughly $190,000 on voter contact in 1998, shaving about 0.6 percent more off the typical incumbent's vote share than did a challenger who spent no money or just a few thousand dollars. Strong challengers who ran against weak incumbents were able to raise and spend substantially more. Hopeful challengers committed an average of $410,000 to campaign communications, which drove down the votes won by the typical incumbent in jeopardy by more than 1 percent. Individual challengers who spent even more generally drew greater numbers of votes away from incumbents, although the impact of campaign spending may diminish in the most expensive races.[12]

Attracting free media coverage can help an incumbent's reelection efforts. Incumbent campaigns that receive more free media than do their opponents or are the sole beneficiaries of media endorsements are likely to benefit in the polls.[13] In 1998 85 percent of all incumbents in major-party contested races enjoyed at least one of these advantages. They won almost 2 percent more of the vote, on average, than did incumbents who did not enjoy such positive relations with the fourth estate. The efforts that House candidates and their press secretaries make to cultivate relationships with news correspondents are clearly worthwhile.

These generalizations hold for the vast majority of incumbent campaigns waged in 1998 as well as for most of those held throughout the 1990s. However, a relatively small but important group of incumbent-challenger races illustrated the power of outside campaigning. These contests drew considerable party and interest group independent expenditures and issue advocacy spending.[14] As explained in Chapters 4 and 5, this spending has the potential to change the dynamics of campaigns because it forces candidates to compete with outside groups, as well as with each other, when trying to set the election agenda and influence the campaign debate.

Outside campaigning by parties and interest groups does more harm than good for House incumbents. Independent expenditures by parties and interest groups do not significantly improve incumbents' already high prospects of reelection, nor do the televised issue ads that, like the communications broadcast by the candidates themselves, are intended to boost incumbents' vote shares.[15] By contrast, outside campaigning intended to improve the prospects of challengers produces its intended result. For every $100,000 in outside money that parties and interest groups spent to help a 1998 House challenger, the incumbent lost about 2.7 percent of the vote. Parties and interest groups spent roughly

$360,000 in North Carolina's 4th district race, including $270,000 to help Roberg, the Republican challenger. Although Price won the race by almost 16 percent of the vote, his victory margin would probably have been about 7 points larger if the Republican Party and GOP-leaning groups had not invested in the race. The election in New Mexico's 3rd district provides a more dramatic example of the impact of outside campaigning. Party committees and groups spent approximately $1.4 million on the race, including about $541,000 in independent expenditures and issue advocacy ads to help Udall. This level of outside spending to help the challenger is associated with a 15-point decrease in an incumbent's vote share and helped Udall to defeat Redmond.

In some instances, outside campaigning by parties and groups overwhelms the election efforts of candidates. For incumbents, it neutralizes the benefits that those who attract the most media coverage and endorsements would otherwise receive, but it also reduces the negative effects of challenger spending. This result is largely due to the fact that outside campaigning, and the extensive free media coverage it often receives, can distract voters from the communications disseminated by the candidates and from the coverage the candidates pick up in the traditional media. Even independent expenditures and issue advocacy ads intended to help a challenger can cloud voters' perceptions of the race if they are "off message"—that is, if they communicate information that is not consistent with the imagery and issue stances that the challenger's campaign is struggling to project.

HOUSE CHALLENGER CAMPAIGNS

Most challengers begin the general election at a disadvantage. Lacking a broad base of support, these candidates must build one. Challengers need to mount aggressive campaigns in order to become visible, build name recognition, give voters reasons to support them, and overcome the initial advantages of their opponents. Most challenger campaigns must also communicate messages that will not only attract uncommitted voters but also persuade some voters to abandon their proincumbent loyalties in favor of the challenger. The typical House challenger is in a position similar to that of a novice athlete pitted against a world-class sprinter. The incumbent has experience, talent, professional handlers, funding, equipment, and crowd support. The challenger has few, if any, of these assets and has a monumental task to accomplish in a limited amount of time. Not surprisingly, most challengers end up eating their opponents' dust. Still, not every novice athlete or every congressional challenger is destined to suffer the agony of defeat. A strong challenger, who is able to assemble the

TABLE 9-2

Significant Predictors of House Challengers' Vote Shares

	Percent
Base vote	26.05
Partisan bias (per one-point advantage in party registration)	+0.18
Contested primary	+1.55
Opposed a first-term incumbent	+5.07
Opposed an incumbent implicated in a scandal	+4.03
Challenger spending on campaign communications (per $100,000)	+0.34
Incumbent spending on campaign communications (per $100,000)	+0.33
Targeted party members and independents	+4.26
Democrat ran on Democratic issues	+3.36
Republican ran on Republican issues	+3.38
Media advantage favored the challenger	+3.08
Party and interest group outside campaign communications to help the challenger (per $100,000)	+1.48
Party and interest group outside campaign communications to help the incumbent (per $100,000)	+1.19
N = 139	

Sources: The 1998 Congressional Campaign Study, Federal Election Commission, Campaign Media Analysis Group, and other sources.

Note: See notes in Table 9-1.

money and campaign organization needed to devise and carry out a good game plan, may be able to win if the incumbent stumbles.

Even though the vast majority of challengers ultimately lose, the experience and resources that they bring to their races can have an impact on their ability to win votes. In short, challenger campaigning matters. The figures in Table 9-2 reveal that challengers' primary campaigns, targeting strategies, issue positions, election expenditures, and media relations affect their vote shares in a meaningful way. The same is true of the competition they face and the outside campaign efforts of parties and interest groups. These generalizations hold regardless of a challenger's age, race, gender, or occupation.

A hypothetical House challenger will finish with just over 26 percent of the vote—far from victory—under the following circumstances. First, the candidate runs in a district that is evenly split between registered Republicans and Democrats, tries to defeat a scandal-free incumbent who has served more than one full term in the House, and is handed a major-party nomination without a primary fight. Second, the candidate uses an unorthodox or haphazard approach to voter targeting, campaigns on issues that are favorably associated with the opposing party, runs in a race bereft of all candidate campaign spending, and does not receive favorable media coverage. Third, the race does not attract significant outside party or interest group campaign activity.

Challengers who run under more favorable circumstances fare better. In most cases the partisan composition of the district works to the advantage of the incumbent, but a few challengers are fortunate enough to run in districts that include more members of their party than those of the incumbent's party. Challengers who run in districts in which the balance of registered voters favors their party by 10 percent win roughly 2 percent more votes than do those who run in neutral districts. Those few challengers who run in districts that favor their party by 20 percent win between 3 and 4 percent more votes than do others.

Political experience and campaign professionalism have indirect effects on a challenger's ability to win votes. As explained in Chapters 2 and 3, challengers with officeholding or significant nonelective political experience are more likely than are political amateurs to run when their odds of winning are greatest, to capture their parties' nomination, and to assemble organizations that draw on the expertise of salaried professionals and political consultants. Moreover, political experience and campaign professionalism help challengers to raise money, as Chapter 6 demonstrated. They also help challengers attract free media coverage, as well as favorable independent expenditures and issue advocacy spending by party committees and interest groups, as shown in Chapters 4 and 5. Challenger campaigns that are staffed with experienced political operatives are also presumably better at targeting, message development, communications, and grass-roots activities than are those staffed by amateurs.[16]

Contested primaries, which only rarely have negative consequences in general elections for the incumbents who survive them, have a positive impact on the prospects of House challengers who emerge from them victorious. It should be recalled from Chapter 2 that opposing-incumbent primaries are often hotly contested when an incumbent is perceived to be vulnerable and are usually won by strategic candidates who know how to wage strong campaigns. The organizational effort, campaign activities, and media coverage associated with contested primaries provide the winners with larger bases of support and higher levels of name recognition than they would have enjoyed had the primary not been contested. The momentum that House challengers get from contested primaries, and the incumbent weaknesses that give rise to those primaries in the first place, lead to stronger performances in general elections. In 1998 those challengers who had to defeat one or more opponents in a primary received between 1 and 2 percent more of the general election vote than did challengers who were merely handed their party's nomination.

Challengers who take on first-term representatives or incumbents embroiled in scandal—usually Congress's most endangered members—fare better than do others who face more experienced incumbents or opponents not tainted by alleged wrongdoing. In 1998 challengers to House freshmen typically added about 5 percent to their vote shares. Those who ran against incumbents associated with scandal—such as Rep. Corrine Brown, D-Fla., who was the subject of a House ethics committee investigation for allegedly using her congressional office for personal gain, and who engaged in a number of other questionable activities—collected, on average, an extra 4 percent of the vote.[17] This result reflected the facts that challengers to vulnerable House members tend to be highly strategic and are frequently more qualified than most other challengers. Of course, it also was partly caused by the incumbent's own mistakes.

House challengers who target members of their political base and persuadable voters win over 4 percent more votes than those who target members of their opponent's political base or who focus on all voters equally.[18] Challengers who campaign on issues that are favorably associated with their party win more votes than those who focus on issues that are associated with the opposing party.[19] Democratic challengers, such as Udall, who campaigned on issues that voters associated favorably with the Democratic Party, including Social Security, education, health care reform, or jobs and the economy, attracted an average of about 3 percent more votes than did Democratic challengers who campaigned on issues that voters identify with the GOP.[20] Similarly, Republican challengers, like Roberg, who built their messages around tax cuts, moral and ethical issues, crime and drug prevention, and other traditional GOP issues also increased their vote margins by an average of about 3 percent over Republican challengers who ran on Democratic issues. Conversely, challengers who campaigned on issues favorably associated with the opposing party did not receive this three-point boost.

The importance of running on popular partisan issues cannot be overstated. The few challengers who are able to set the campaign agenda, incorporate their issues stances into a compelling message, and muster the wherewithal to communicate that message have significant advantages over others. In accomplishing these tasks they make it possible for politically engaged citizens to cast an informed vote.[21] Voters who are attuned to a challenger's campaign message and share the challenger's issue priorities are 20 percent more likely to vote for that candidate than are voters who do not share those priorities.[22]

Careful issue selection and message development are critical to a successful challenger campaign.

The 15 percent or so of all House challengers who are endorsed by the local press or receive the largest share of free media coverage typically win over 3 percent more of the vote than do the approximately 85 percent who are not treated so favorably by the media. The combined effects of good campaign targeting, message selection, and press relations—three hallmarks of a strong nonincumbent campaign—help boost challengers' vote margins by roughly 10 percent.

Another factor that has a significant impact on the vote shares received by challengers is campaign spending. For every $100,000 that 1998 House challengers spent on television, radio, newspaper, or direct-mail advertising or on campaign field work, they won an additional 0.34 percent of the vote.[23] As noted above, 1998 challengers spent an average of $190,000 on campaign communications, garnering the typical challenger an additional 0.6 percent of the ballot. Incumbent spending on campaign communications, largely a reaction to the closeness of the race and the efforts of strong challengers and their supporters, is also positively related to challengers' vote shares. Large communications expenditures by both candidates are strongly associated with closely decided incumbent-challenger races. Udall and Redmond spent approximately $1.2 million and $800,000, respectively, on campaign communications in a race that was won by 10 percent of the vote. Cecy Groom spent only about $55,000 to communicate with voters in her twenty-nine-point loss to Ed Royce, who spent about $365,000 in their California House race. The fact that the typical House challenger spent less than $200,000 on campaign communications in 1998 helps to explain why so few of them won that year and why challengers generally fare poorly.

How best to allocate scarce financial resources is a constant concern for strategists in challenger campaigns. Are radio or television commercials more effective than newspaper ads? How effective is direct mail at influencing voters compared with less precisely tailored and less well-targeted forms of advertising? Is it worthwhile to invest money in get-out-the-vote drives, handbills, or grass-roots activities commonly referred to as campaign field work?

Radio and direct mail, which can be targeted to specific voting blocs, are among the most cost-effective campaign activities.[24] For every $10,000 a challenger campaign spends on radio, it gains an average of about 1 percent of the vote. The typical challenger campaign spent about $20,000 on radio in 1998, helping it to win between 1 and 2 percent of the vote. Direct mail provides a somewhat lower return, yielding 0.12 points per $10,000. Challengers spent an average of $33,000 on direct mail, which is associated with a net pickup of 0.4 points in the polls.

Television commercials are less targeted, are considerably more expensive, and bring somewhat lower returns per dollar than do the preceding activities. The typical House challenger campaign spent $85,000 on television ads in 1998, which was associated with an increase of about 1 percent of the vote. Of course, campaigns that spent more on television, such as Roberg's and Udall's, attracted considerably more votes.

Newspaper advertisements, purchased by about half of all 1998 challenger campaigns, are typically a low-priority, low-budget item. The typical challenger spent about $5,000 on newspaper ads. This expenditure helped the candidate increase his or her vote share by a little more than one-half of 1 percent.

Field work is both a labor-intensive and a capital-intensive form of electioneering. It differs from direct mail and radio in that, if done properly, it requires both skillful targeting and a corps of committed campaign workers. Thus, the money that the typical challenger spends on field work does not perfectly describe the candidate's field operations. Still, contact between candidates and voters, and other field activities that are often coordinated by specialized consultants and carried out by volunteer workers, have a very positive impact on challengers' vote shares.

Finally, the outside campaign efforts of parties and interest groups work to the advantage of the challengers they are intended to help. For every $100,000 of outside spending for a 1998 House challenger, that candidate usually garnered an additional 1.5 percent of the vote. Outside campaigning that was intended to improve the prospects of extremely vulnerable House members resembled incumbent spending in that it was positively associated with challengers' vote shares. Despite the advantages that they derived from outside campaigns, many challengers were ambivalent about them. They did not appreciate having their campaign messages overwhelmed by the torrent of outside money that flowed into their districts. In some cases, party and interest group independent and issue advocacy spending combined to drown out the messages disseminated by these candidates.[25]

In sum, most House challengers lose because the odds are so heavily stacked against them. Those few who run in favorable or competitive districts, compete against a vulnerable incumbent, target their base and persuadable voters, campaign on issues that the public identifies favorably with their party, assemble the resources needed to communicate with voters, and spend their money wisely win more votes than those who do not. The same is true of those who curry favor with the media and benefit from party and interest group independent and issue advocacy expenditures. Despite doing all of these things correctly, these challengers rarely win enough votes to defeat an incumbent. The preelection activities that incumbents undertake to cultivate the support of constituents and their success in warding off talented and well-funded challengers are critical in determining the outcome of most incumbent-challenger races.

Nevertheless, politics is a game that is often played at the margins. Not all House incumbents begin the general election as shoo-ins and go on to win. The few incumbents who hold competitive seats, cast unpopular votes on salient issues, draw a strong major-party opponent, or are targeted for defeat by the opposing party and independent-spending interest groups often find themselves in a precarious position. Many of these incumbents spend huge sums of money, sometimes to no avail. If the challengers who run against these incumbents are able to apply the lessons they learned while working in politics and assemble the money and organizational resources needed to wage a strong campaign, they can put their opponents on the defensive. Challengers have some chance of winning if they run against first-term House members or members running under the cloud of scandal, set the campaign agenda, carefully target groups of actual and potential supporters, tailor their messages to appeal to these voters, and communicate their messages through paid advertisements, free media, and strong field operations. Those challengers who can attract considerable outside spending by parties and interest groups have even better odds. A victory by a challenger is typically the result of both incumbent failure and a strong challenger campaign. Numerous House members were anxious about their reelection prospects before the 1998 campaign. Some of these legislators retired. Of those who sought reelection, ninety-four House incumbents were considered somewhat at risk at some point during the 1998 election season. Challengers succeeded in defeating only six of them.

HOUSE OPEN-SEAT CAMPAIGNS

Elections for House open seats are usually won by far smaller margins than are incumbent-challenger races. Once a seat becomes open, several factors come into play. The partisanship of the district and the skills and resources that candidates and their organizations bring to the campaign have a greater influence on elections when there is no incumbent who can draw on voters' personal loyalties. Because voters lack strong personal loyalties to either candidate, factors outside the control of campaigns, such as national political trends, redistricting, and the mass media, can also have an important effect on open-seat elections. The factors that significantly affect the outcome of open-seat House races are listed in Table 9-3.

TABLE 9-3

Significant Predictors of Open-Seat Candidates' Vote Shares

	Percent
Base vote	47.55
Partisan bias (per one-point advantage in party registration)	+0.32
Candidate spending on campaign communications (per $100,000)	+0.77
Opponent spending on campaign communications (per $100,000)	−0.78
Media advantage favored the candidate	+5.59
N = 32	

Sources: The 1998 Congressional Campaign Study, Federal Election Commission, Campaign Media Analysis Group, and other sources.

Note: See notes in Table 9-1.

The partisan bias of open seats is important. Candidates who run for open seats in districts where the balance of voter registration favors their party do much better than others. Those who run for open seats in districts where the balance of party registration favors their party by 10 percent end up winning, on average, an additional 3 percent of the vote.

Candidates in open-seat elections stand to make large gains in name recognition and voter support through their campaign communications. In contrast to candidates in incumbent-challenger races, those in open-seat elections benefit virtually equally from spending on voter outreach. Open-seat candidates typically win about 0.77 percent above the base vote of 47.55 for every $100,000 they spend on campaign communications. Given that the open-seat candidates in competitive races spent an average of $541,000 on campaign communications, money can be a determining factor in these elections. Many things influenced the outcome of the 1998 open-seat race in Wisconsin's 2nd district, and money was certainly one of them. Tammy Baldwin's estimated $873,000 to $1.5 million spending advantage over Jo Musser gave the Democrat a big advantage in the battles that took place in the airwaves and on the ground. The candidates' spending differentials contributed significantly to Baldwin's 5.8 percent victory margin.

The mass media also play an important role in open-seat House races. Experienced politicians who have strong campaign organizations and run for open seats in districts that are made up mostly of voters who belong to their party usually receive better treatment from the media than do their opponents. Open-seat candidates who attract more media coverage than do their opponents and win the endorsements of the local press typically pick up almost 6 percent of the vote on top of their base. This preferential treatment also brings some indirect benefits. An open-seat candidate who is labeled the front-runner by the media early in a race usually raises more money, is able to spend more on campaign communications, achieves higher levels of name recognition, and gathers more momentum than does his or her opponent.

The amounts that open-seat campaigns spend on various forms of campaign communications are positively related to the number of votes they receive, but the precise effects of these communications are difficult to evaluate because relatively few open-seat contests take place in a given election year. It is possible, however, to make some generalizations about the relative importance of the techniques open-seat candidates use to get out their message. Open-seat candidates spend substantial portions of their campaign budgets on TV, direct mail, field work, and radio. Of these communications devices, TV and direct mail have the greatest electoral impact.[26]

One way in which open-seat contests differ from incumbent-challenger races is that the candidates' communications are only rarely overshadowed by party and interest group outside campaigning. The overall quality of open-seat contestants, the electoral and financial competitiveness of their campaigns, and the relatively high level of media attention they receive allows candidates' messages to be heard over the din of the independent expenditures and issue advocacy ads that are disseminated by other groups.

SENATE CAMPAIGNS

The small number of Senate elections that occur in a given election year and the differences in the size and politics of the states in which they take place make it difficult to generalize about Senate campaigns. Nevertheless, a few broad statements are possible. Not surprisingly, chief among them is that incumbents possess substantial advantages over challengers. The advantages that incumbency conveys in Senate elections are similar to those it bestows in House elections. Most Senate incumbents enjoy fund-raising advantages, higher levels of name recognition, and more political experience—particularly in running a statewide campaign—than do their opponents.

Yet, the advantages that senators enjoy are not as great as those that House members have over their opponents. Most Senate challengers and open-seat candidates have previously served in the House, as governor, or in some other public capacity and are more formidable opponents than are their House counterparts. Their previous political experience helps Senate challengers assemble the financial and organizational resources and attract the media coverage that are needed to run a competitive campaign.[27]

One of the most important differences between Senate and House contests is the effect of incumbent expenditures on election outcomes. Although increased challenger spending has a negative effect on incumbents' margins in both Senate and House elections, it is only in Senate races that spending by incumbents is positively related to the number of votes they receive. Incumbent expenditures on campaign communications are not as important as are challenger expenditures, but the amounts spent by both sides are influential in determining the victor in Senate elections.[28]

This difference between House and Senate contests is due to two major factors. First, because Senate challengers are usually better qualified, Senate elections tend to be closer than House contests. Second, senators tend to have weaker bonds with their constituents than do representatives; senators' larger constituencies prevent them from establishing the kinds of personal ties that House members have with voters.[29] Senators' six-year terms and greater responsibilities in Washington also discourage them from meeting as frequently with constituents as do House members. The greater diversity of their constituencies also means that senators are more likely to offend some voters when carrying out their legislative activities. As a result of these differences, campaign spending, and campaigning in general, are more likely to affect the electoral prospects of Senate than House incumbents.

Senate elections bear further comparison with House contests. Scandal and the partisan bias of the constituency influence the results of elections for both the upper and lower chambers. Senate campaigns' targeting strategies and issue selection also are believed to be important.[30] Whereas primary challenges have no detrimental effects on the election prospects of House incumbents, they harm those of incumbents in Senate campaigns.[31]

Several 1998 Senate elections illustrate the preceding generalizations. The general election between Sen. Russell Feingold, D-Wis., and Republican representative Mark Neumann highlights the importance of incumbency, issues, voter targeting, and field work. The race featured an experienced challenger who sought to defeat a first-term incumbent in a politically competitive state.[32] Neither candidate had to defeat a primary opponent, and the two campaigned on roughly equal financial footing in the general election. This was somewhat unusual for an incumbent-challenger contest, but the candidates agreed to limit themselves to spending $3.8 million—$1 dollar per Wisconsin voter—and both stuck close to the bargain. Neumann, who was well known in the areas surrounding his southern Wisconsin 1st congressional district, took to the airwaves first to try to overcome his lack of visibility in the rest of the state. Feingold, who was recognized throughout Wisconsin, spent the early days of the campaign building grass-roots organizations that he would later use to turn out the Democratic vote.[33]

Feingold, like most incumbents, used a strategy that focused on mobilizing his base and winning swing voters.[34] He selected as his primary issue campaign finance reform—one he has championed throughout most of his Senate career. This issue has tremendous appeal to Wisconsin's Democrats and progressive independent voters, who were the major targets of his voter contact program. Neumann, like many competitive challengers, sought to shore up his base, win the support of independents, and attract some voters from the opposing party. To mobilize Republicans, he advocated a ban on "partial-birth abortion" and cuts in government spending. He tried to appeal to independents and Democratic senior citizens by discussing Social Security, which traditionally has been positively associated with Democrats.[35]

Like most incumbents, Feingold enjoyed more favorable media coverage than did the challenger. His media advantage grew due to some of the Neumann campaign's tactics. The challenger suffered a spate of bad press when a number of Wisconsin newspapers reported that his "Cow Gas" and "Russian Space Monkey" attack ads were inaccurate.[36]

Party committees and interest groups spent relatively little on independent expenditures and issue advocacy ads because the candidates had pledged to discourage outsiders from spending soft money in the election. Nevertheless, outside campaigning became an important issue in the race when both parties' senatorial campaign committees and several interest groups violated the candidates' agreement on outside spending. Feingold publicly demanded that the DSCC, the AFL-CIO, and the Sierra Club pull their advertisements from the airwaves. His actions helped reinforce his image as a progressive reformer and drive home the point that he was not just another "Washington politician."[37]

The race ultimately was won on the ground. Neumann's campaign exceeded its projected vote total by 150,000 and ran well ahead of its expectations in many parts of the state. However, citizens in liberal Dane County, home of the University of Wisconsin–Madison, turned out to vote in record numbers. Attracted to Feingold's progressive image and encouraged to vote by the GOTV efforts of his and Tammy Baldwin's campaigns, a record 55 percent of Dane County voters showed up at the polls. They gave Feingold 65,000 more votes than they gave Neumann and were the key to his 37,787-point victory.[38]

The contest between three-term Republican Senate incumbent Alfonse D'Amato of New York and Democratic challenger Charles Schumer, a nine-term House member who represented parts of Brooklyn and Queens, further illustrates the importance of a competitive environment, careful issue selection, and voter targeting. It also demonstrates the impact that scandal can have on a Senate election.[39]

Both campaigns were well funded, but the D'Amato campaign outspent Schumer's, $24.2 million to $16.7 million. Both campaigns also benefited from more than $1.5 million in party coordinated expenditures. In addition, the race drew considerable outside spending. D'Amato was the beneficiary of more than $290,000 in favorable PAC independent expenditures, which were only partially offset by the more than $87,000 in PAC attack ads launched against him. PACs committed a mere $2,300 in independent expenditures to attack Schumer and spent nothing on his behalf. National and state party committees and interest groups also spent millions of dollars on issue advocacy.

D'Amato, who cultivated the nickname of "Senator Pothole," tried to attract broad-based support by airing a series of testimonial ads over the radio reminding voters of his efforts to bring federal largess back to the state and of his diligent attention to constituent service. His campaign strategy included reaching beyond traditional Republican constituencies and independent voters. He sought to mobilize conservative Republicans by opposing both gun control and abortion. He appealed to women and Jews, who traditionally vote Democratic, by supporting more research on women's health issues, emphasizing his pro-Israel voting record, and working to get restitution from Swiss banks for Holocaust survivors. Schumer chose Democratic issues that were intended to mobilize his base and win the support of independents. His campaign highlighted his House voting record on education, health care reform, Social Security, and gun control. Schumer's combination of issues and targeting worked; D'Amato's did not. The incumbent ran poorly among the Jews, women, and other Democratic constituencies whose support he had hoped to attract.[40]

The race was one of the most negative contests in the country, with the D'Amato campaign attacking Schumer within twelve hours of his winning his party's nomination. The Schumer campaign responded with ads they had taped in anticipation of the D'Amato campaign's onslaught. The Schumer campaign also ran a thirty-second TV ad that listed D'Amato's alleged involvement in a kickback scandal, his rebuke by the Senate ethics committee, and numerous other questionable activities with which the incumbent had been associated over the course of his political career. One of the D'Amato campaign's televised attack ads severely backfired. The ad claimed that Schumer had missed more House votes in the last twelve months than D'Amato had missed in the last twelve years. The Schumer campaign responded by pointing out that when D'Amato had first run for the Senate in 1980, he had missed almost one thousand votes as a member of the Nassau County Board of Supervisors. The tag line for this and many other Schumer ads—"D'Amato: too many lies for too long"—reinforced D'Amato's image as a shady politician. When the votes were counted, Schumer had defeated the incumbent by more than ten points.[41]

The Bunning-Baesler contest in Kentucky was the nation's most competitive open-seat Senate race in 1998. It shows that primary competition, party campaign assistance, and party and interest group outside campaigning can have major effects on an election. To secure his party's nomination, Baesler had to defeat five primary opponents, including Lieut. Gov. Steve Henry and millionaire Charles Owen, who spent more than $6.8 million. Bunning, on the other hand, easily captured his party's nomination by defeating state senator Barry Matcalf by 48 percent of the vote. The Bunning campaign began the general election with Bunning's party united behind him and with $1.4 million in cash on hand; the Baesler campaign's resources were largely depleted, and the candidate had to build some bridges to those who had supported his opponents.

The Bunning campaign also benefited from the assistance of NRSC chairman Mitch McConnell. It should be recalled from Chapter 4 that McConnell, a fellow Kentuckian, and the NRSC provided a great deal of strategic and fundraising assistance to the Bunning campaign. Parties, PACs, and other interest groups also carried out a significant amount of outside campaigning, most of which favored Bunning. Ultimately, the combined effects of the divisive Democratic primary, the assistance the Bunning campaign received from McConnell and the Republican Party, and the pro-Republican tilt of party and interest group outside campaigning helped the GOP candidate win by a slim 6,766-vote margin. After the election, Baesler commented that Republican Party spending on radio ads, direct mail, and telephone get-out-the-vote efforts had given Bunning a decisive edge. Remarking on disparities in mail alone, he stated, "I suspect the calculations will blow your mind."[42]

CLAIMING CREDIT AND PLACING BLAME

Once the election is over, candidates and their campaign staffs have a chance to reflect on their contests. Their main interest, naturally, is what caused their election to turn out as it did. Winners and losers have very different ideas about what factors influence congressional election outcomes. Some differences are obvious. With the exception of incumbents, losing candidates almost always obsess about money. Virtually all assert that if they had had more funds, they would have reached more voters and received more votes. The three-to-one overall spending advantage that victorious House incumbents had over losing challengers in 1998 supports this point (see Figure 9-1). The 48 percent spend-

FIGURE 9-1

Average Campaign Expenditures of House Winners and Losers in 1998

$, thousands

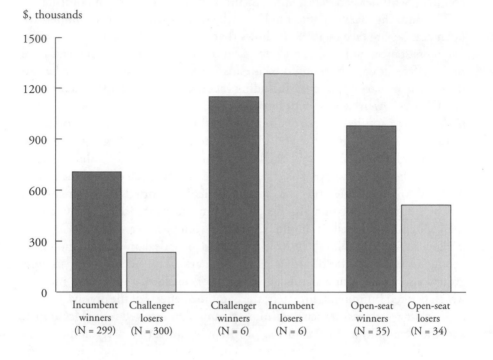

Source: Compiled from Federal Election Commission data.

Note: Figures are for major-party candidates in contested general elections.

ing advantage that successful open-seat candidates had over their opponents is not as large, but it also lends credence to the point that money matters. The fact that the winning House challenger with the lowest total campaign expenditures in 1998, Rep. Mark Green, R-Wis., spent almost $848,000 further suggests that challengers must cross a high spending threshold to be competitive. Indeed, successful challengers in normal two-party races spent an average of $1.1 million in 1998. The patterns of spending in Senate elections reinforce these points (see Figure 9-2).

Once one gets beyond the obvious factor of money, there are differences of opinion about the extent to which other factors influence election outcomes. Successful House candidates have a strong tendency to credit their victories to attributes of the candidate and to factors that were largely under their campaign's

FIGURE 9-2

Average Campaign Expenditures of Senate Winners and Losers in 1998

$, thousands

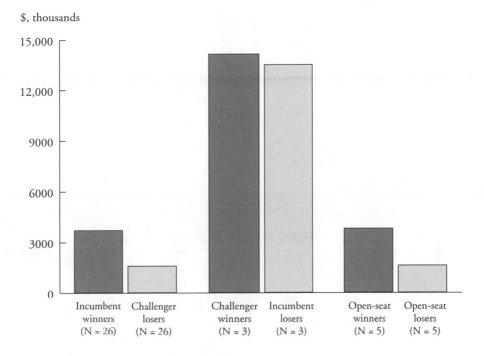

Source: Compiled from Federal Election Commission data.

Note: Figures are for major-party candidates in contested general elections.

control. They believe that the candidate's image was the most important determinant of their election (see Table 9-4). Successful incumbents credit their record in office next, followed by the advantages they derived from incumbency.

The winners of House races rank issues next. Some Democratic winners in 1998 believed they benefited from focusing on Medicare, education, the environment, and other traditional Democratic issues; some successful Republican candidates believed they benefited from concentrating on tax cuts, crime, government waste reduction, President Clinton's personal peccadilloes, and other issues that formed the core of the GOP's communications effort. Even so, relatively few winners from either party believed the election was nationalized. Indeed, if anything, they considered local concerns more important than national issues. Candidates rate the partisan loyalties of voters in their districts as

TABLE 9-4

Winners' and Losers' Opinions of the Determinants
of House Elections

	Winners	Losers
Candidate's image	4.16	3.40
Party loyalty	3.11	3.65
Local issues	3.28	2.43
National issues	3.21	3.00
Debates	1.72	1.85
Newspaper endorsements	2.23	2.25
Negative campaigning	1.86	2.04
Incumbent's record	4.10	2.79
Incumbency advantages	3.51	4.51
Anti-incumbency	1.24	1.59
Political scandal in own race	1.37	1.40
Presidential scandal	1.93	2.33
U.S. Senate election	1.96	2.58
State or local elections	1.96	2.55
(N)	(154)	(159)

Source: The 1998 Congressional Campaign Study.

Notes: Candidates and campaign aides were asked to assess the importance of each factor on the following scale: 1 = not important; 2 = slightly important; 3 = moderately important; 4 = very important; 5 = extremely important. The values listed are arithmetic means of the scores. Figures for impact of incumbent's record, incumbency advantages, and anti-incumbency exclude responses from candidates and campaign aides from open seats. Figures for impact of U.S. Senate election include only responses from candidates whose states hosted Senate elections. Figures are for major-party candidates in contested general elections.

moderately important. Finally, winners believe that newspaper endorsements, other elections, the Clinton/Lewinksy scandal, negative campaigning, and debates were much less important in the outcome of their contests. The winners' opinions reflect a tendency to attribute their victories to their own efforts and the wisdom of voters.[43] These beliefs stand in stark contrast to political science theories that suggest that congressional election outcomes are primarily a function of national conditions and events.[44]

Defeated House candidates have a very different view of what caused their candidacies to end as they did. First and foremost, losing challengers point to the incumbent's perquisites of office, which they believe to have been very important. Next, most losers blame voters' partisanship. They ranked their images third. They also considered national issues to have been moderately important. Losers believe that local issues and debates are less important than these other factors. They prefer to rationalize their defeats by blaming them on factors over which neither they nor their campaigns had any control.[45] The losers' views bear similarities to political science theories that downplay the importance of individual candidates and campaigns.[46]

Senate candidates have a somewhat different view of the causes of their election outcomes than do House contestants. Both the winners and losers in Senate contests emphasize factors that are largely under their control. Contestants generally believe that the images they projected to the voters were the number one determinant of the outcome of their elections. Winners typically maintain that candidate imagery was extremely important, whereas losers believe it was moderately important. Winners are more likely to emphasize the importance of issues, ranking them second only to imagery. Losing challengers, in contrast, believe that the advantages of officeholding are substantially more important. Winning and losing incumbents are equally likely to view incumbency as a two-edged sword, agreeing that the anger that many voters direct at Washington reduces their vote margins.

Senate incumbents place greater emphasis on the importance of their voting records than do Senate challengers, but both sets of candidates acknowledge that job performance was at least a moderately important determinant of the outcome of Senate elections. Both winners and losers also place moderate importance on the partisan loyalties of state voters and the presidential election. Senate candidates attribute less influence to such factors as debates, negative campaigning, local issues, and state and local elections than do House contestants.

SUMMARY

The efforts that candidates make to communicate with voters have an impact on congressional elections, and they are especially important for House challengers and open-seat contestants. Challengers who carefully target their campaign resources, run on issues that voters identify favorably with their party, spend significant sums on campaign advertising and voter mobilization, and attract favorable media coverage can significantly increase the number of votes they receive. House challengers who must defeat an opponent to secure their party's nomination, run in districts that have many members of their party, oppose vulnerable incumbents, and draw significant outside campaigning by their party and supportive interest groups also increase their share of the vote. House incumbents can do little to substantially increase their standing in the polls. The efforts they make to serve their constituents and deter a strong challenger from emerging result in most incumbents beginning and ending their campaigns with commanding leads. Indeed, most House incumbent campaigns, like most incumbent fund-raising, are driven by the threat posed by an opponent and are directed at shoring up the candidate's support. Campaigns for House open-seats are usually very competitive. Candidate communications and media coverage have a decisive impact on these races, even in districts that are inundated by outside campaign advertisements aired by parties and interest groups. Senate elections bear many similarities to House contests; however, they are usually both more expensive and more competitive. Moreover, although contested primaries hurt Senate incumbents and their spending has a positive impact on their vote shares, these factors do not have the same effects on the votes House incumbents garner.

Congressional campaigners have divergent views on what caused their elections to end as they did. Successful campaigners credit their candidates' abilities and their organizations' strategic and tactical efforts for their wins. While House losers focus on incumbents' perks of office, voter partisanship, and other factors outside of their control, Senate losers are somewhat more likely to acknowledge that candidate characteristics and some aspects of their campaigns contributed to their loss.

CHAPTER TEN

Elections and Governance

"The election is over, and now the fun begins." Those were the words of one new House member shortly after being elected to Congress. Others had more sober, if not more realistic, visions of what lay ahead. Although getting elected to Congress is difficult, especially for those who have to topple an incumbent, staying there also requires great effort. The high reelection rates enjoyed by members of Congress are not a guarantee of reelection; they are the result of hard work, the strategic deployment of the resources that Congress makes available to its members, and the campaign dynamics discussed in previous chapters.

This chapter examines the efforts that members of Congress make in order to stay in office and analyzes the resources and strategies they use to shore up their electoral coalitions. Also reviewed is the impact of elections on Congress as a policy-making institution. First, I discuss the goals and activities of members of Congress and their congressional staffs. I then discuss the committees, issue caucuses, party organizations, and other groups that influence congressional activity. Finally, I comment on the policy-making process.

THE PERMANENT CAMPAIGN

As locally elected officials who make national policy, members of Congress almost lead double lives. The main focus of their existence in Washington, D.C., is framing and enacting legislation, overseeing the executive branch, and carrying out other activities of national importance. Attending local functions, ascertaining the needs and preferences of constituents, and explaining their Washington activities are what legislators do at home. Home is where members of Congress acquire their legitimacy to participate in the legislative process. The central elements of legislators' lives both at home and in Washington are representing the voters who elected them, winning federally funded projects for their state or district, and resolving difficulties that constituents encounter when dealing with the federal government. The two aspects of members' professional lives are unified by the fact that much of what representatives do in Washington is concerned with getting reelected, and a good deal of what they do at home directly affects the kinds of policies and interests they seek to advance.[1] In a great many respects, the job of legislator resembles a permanent reelection campaign.

Members of Congress develop home styles that help them to maintain or expand their bases of electoral support. One element of these home styles concerns how legislators present themselves to voters. Members build bonds of trust between themselves and voters by demonstrating that they are capable of handling the job, care about their constituents, and are living up to their campaign promises.[2]

A second component of home style is concerned with discussing the Washington side of the job. Members describe, interpret, and justify what they do in the nation's capital to convey the message that they are working relentlessly on their constituents' behalf.[3] Many respond to the low opinion that people have of Congress by trying to separate themselves from the institution in the minds of voters. Members frequently portray themselves as protectors of the national interest locked in combat with powerful lobbyists and feckless colleagues.

Members of Congress and their staffs spend immense amounts of time, energy, and resources advertising the legislator's name among constituents, claiming credit for favorable governmental actions, and taking strong but often symbolic issue positions to please constituents.[4] Their offices provide them with abundant resources for these purposes. House members are annually entitled to $632,355 for staff and receive one or more state or district offices, an average of $195,000 for general office expenses, a postage account of $108,000, a travel budget of up to $67,200, and virtually unlimited long-distance telephone privileges.[5] Members who are assigned to certain committees, occupy committee chairs, or hold party leadership positions receive extra staff, office space, and operating funds. Senators are allowed even greater budgets, reflecting their larger constituencies and the greater responsibilities associated with representing an entire state. Senators' staffs, office space, and budget allocations are determined by their state's population and by their committee assignments.

Although few legislators consume all the resources they are allocated, many come close. The average House member hires approximately fourteen full-time aides; the average senator hires about thirty-four.[6] Among these aides are administrative assistants, legislative assistants, legislative correspondents, computer

operators, schedulers, office managers, caseworkers, press secretaries, receptionists, staff assistants, and interns. Each performs a different set of functions, but
nearly all are somehow related to building political support among constituents. Legislative correspondents, legislative assistants, and computer operators
are highly conscious of the electoral connection when they send franked mail to
constituents or set up their boss's Web site.[7] Caseworkers help constituents resolve problems with the federal bureaucracy, knowing that their performance
can directly affect the reelection prospects of the legislator for whom they work.
Receptionists, staff assistants, and schedulers are well aware that the tours they
arrange for visitors to Washington contribute to the support their member
maintains in the district. Those who forget that constituents come first are
quickly reminded of this by the member's administrative assistant, who is responsible for making sure that the office runs smoothly and frequently serves as
the member's chief political adviser.

The most reelection-oriented staffers tend to be congressional press secretaries. Most members of Congress have at least one press secretary, and some have
two or three deputy press assistants.[8] The press secretary is the chief public
relations officer in a congressional office. Press secretaries write newsletters and
press releases and are heavily involved in crafting the targeted mass mailings
that legislators send to constituents. They also produce copy for radio and television spots, which they arrange to have aired over local stations. Press secretaries help to organize town meetings, arrange interviews with the local
correspondents, and disseminate to the news media transcripts and videotapes
of their boss's floor and committee speeches. A good press secretary is often able
to arrange for local media outlets to print or air a legislator's remarks verbatim
or with minimal editing.[9]

The election of highly media-conscious members in the mid-1970s, increased
television coverage of politics, the opening of Congress to greater media scru-
tiny, the growth in the size of the congressional press corps, and the availability
of new communications technologies led to the emergence of the press secretary as a key congressional aide. These changes created both pressures and opportunities to increase the public relations side of congressional offices.[10]
Members of Congress, who work in a resource rich institution, responded by
allowing themselves to hire specialized staff who could help them advance their
political careers.

Congress has also allowed its members to exploit new computer technologies to firm up their relations with voters. Legislative aides use computerized
databases to target large volumes of mail to specific audiences. Constituents
who write or telephone their legislator about an issue are routinely entered into
a computerized list that records their name, address, and the reason for their

contact. They are then sent periodic communications that update them on what their legislator is doing in this area. Constituents who contact members' offices via electronic mail or by accessing their Internet Web sites often receive emails in return.

Subsidized House and Senate recording studios and party-owned recording facilities also help legislators reach out to voters. Many members use the studios to record radio shows and television briefings or to edit floor speeches that they deliver to local media outlets. Some make use of satellite technology to hold live "town meetings" with constituents located on the other side of the country.

A DECENTRALIZED CONGRESS

The candidate-centered nature of congressional elections provides the foundation for a highly individualized, fragmented style of legislative politics. Members are largely self-recruited, are nominated and elected principally as a result of their own efforts, and know they bear the principal responsibility for ensuring they get reelected. Local party organizations, Washington-based party committees, PACs, and other groups and individuals may have helped them raise money and win votes, but politicians arrive in Congress with the belief that they owe their tenure to their own efforts.

Reelection Constituencies

Legislators' first loyalties are to their constituents, and most staff their offices, decide which committee assignments to pursue, and choose areas of policy expertise with an eye toward maintaining voter support. Campaign contributors, including those who live outside a legislator's district or state, form another important constituency. Local elites and interest groups that provide campaign support or political advice routinely receive access to members of Congress, further encouraging legislators to respond to forces outside of the institution rather than within.[11] Other personal goals, including advancing specific policies, accruing more power in the legislature, or positioning themselves to run for higher office, also have a decentralizing effect on the legislative process.[12] Much of the work done to advance these goals—policy research, disseminating press releases, bill drafting, attending committee meetings, bureaucratic oversight, and meeting with constituents, campaign contributors, and lobbyists—is borne by staffers who owe their jobs and their loyalties to individual legislators more than to the institution.[13] This, in turn, makes their bosses less dependent on congressional leaders and encourages members to march to their own drums.

Congressional Committees

The dispersal of legislative authority among nineteen standing committees and eighty-four subcommittees in the House, sixteen standing committees and sixty-nine subcommittees in the Senate, four joint committees, and a small number of select committees in each chamber adds to the centrifugal tendencies that originate from candidate-centered elections. Each committee and subcommittee is authorized to act within a defined jurisdiction. A chair and ranking member, who are among the majority and minority parties' senior policy experts, head each committee and subcommittee. Each also has its own professional staff, office, and budget to help it carry out its business.

The committee system originally was designed to enable Congress to function more efficiently. It allows Congress to investigate simultaneously a multitude of issues and to oversee a range of executive branch agencies. Although committees and subcommittees are Congress's main bodies for making national policy, much of what they do revolves around local issues, the distribution of federal grants and programs, and the reelection of individual legislators. Most legislators serve on at least one committee or subcommittee with jurisdiction over policies of importance to their constituents. Members use their committee assignments to develop expertise in policy areas, to actively promote their constituents' interests, to build reputations as champions of popular issues, and to attract political support.

Congressional committees can be categorized according to the objectives they enable members to pursue: reelection, prestige, and policy.[14] "Reelection committees," such as the House Transportation and Infrastructure Committee and the Senate Environment and Public Works Committee, enable their members to work directly on the policy areas that are most important to constituents. Reelection committees usually rank high among the assignments sought by new members of Congress. More than half of all first-term House members seek appointment to one or more of them.[15]

"Prestige committees" give their members influence over legislative activities that are of extraordinary importance to their congressional colleagues. The House and Senate Appropriations Committees are the ultimate prestige, or power, committees. They are responsible for funding federal agencies and programs and have the ability to initiate, expand, contract, or discontinue the flow of federal money to projects located across the country. This gives their members the power to affect the lives of those who are the beneficiaries of these programs and the ability to influence the reelection prospects of legislators who represent them. The House Ways and Means and Senate Finance Committees' jurisdiction over tax-related matters, and particularly their ability to give tax breaks to various interests, give members of these panels sway with their colleagues. Members of prestige committees can help their constituents by acting directly or, by wielding their clout with other legislators, indirectly. Membership on one of the appropriating or tax-writing committees is particularly helpful when it comes to raising campaign funds from individuals and PACs associated with a wide array of economic interests.

In contrast with reelection and prestige committees, "policy committees," such as those that deal with criminal justice, education, or labor issues, are sought by legislators who have a strong interest in a particular policy area. These committees are among the most divisive because they are responsible for some highly charged issues, such as education, health insurance, and welfare reform, and many members use them to stake out conservative or liberal stands. Ambitious legislators who seek a career beyond Congress often use policy committees as platforms for developing a national reputation on salient issues.

Thus the committee system gives expression to the differing goals and viewpoints of representatives, senators, and their constituents. By so doing, it decentralizes Congress.

Congressional Caucuses

Congressional caucuses—informal groups of members who share legislative interests—have a similar but less powerful effect on Congress. Even though caucuses were prohibited from having their own congressional staffs and office space when the House adopted its rules for the 104th Congress, they continue to function as competing policy centers, alternative suppliers of information, and additional sources of legislative decision-making cues.[16] Groups such as the Congressional Black Caucus and the Congressional Women's Caucus are recognized as advocates for specific segments of the population. The Northeast-Midwest Senate Coalition, Western States Senate Coalition, and other geographically based groups seek to increase the clout of legislators from particular regions. The Steel, Auto, and Textile Caucuses have ties to outside industries and work to promote their interests in Congress. Although they do not hold any formal legislative powers, caucuses further add to the fragmentation of Congress.

Interest Groups

Privately funded interest groups, which form an important part of the political environment with which Congress interacts, also have decentralizing effects on the legislative process. Like caucuses, interest groups are sources of influence that compete with congressional leaders for the loyalty of legislators on certain issues. Roughly eighty thousand people work for trade associations, legal firms, and consulting agencies in the Washington area.[17] Not all these people are lobbyists, but in one way or another they work to advance the political interests of some group, and Congress is their number one target.[18]

Interest groups work to influence the legislative process in many ways. Some groups advertise on television, on radio, in newspapers, or through the mail to influence the political agenda or stimulate grass-roots support for or opposition to specific pieces of legislation. Their efforts often resemble election campaigns. The advertisements purchased by the American Association of Health Plans against the "patients' bill of rights" legislation in 1998 exemplify such efforts, as do the advertising campaigns waged by unions and other groups in support of or in opposition to the minimum wage bill in 1996.

Most interest groups also advocate their positions in less visible ways, designed to play to the legislative and electoral needs of individual members of Congress. Representatives of interest groups testify at committee hearings and meet with legislators at their offices and informally at social events. Lobbyists use a variety of forums to provide members and their staffs with technical information, impact statements of how congressional activity (or inactivity) can affect their constituents, and insights into where other legislators stand on the issues. Sometimes they go so far as to draft a bill or help design a strategy to promote its enactment.[19]

Many groups supplement these "insider" techniques with approaches that focus more directly on the electoral connection. Trade and business groups ask local association members to contact their legislators. Unions, churches, and other groups with large memberships frequently organize telephone and letter-writing campaigns. These communications show members of Congress that important blocs of voters and their advocates are watching how they vote on specific pieces of legislation.[20] The recent increase in interest group–sponsored issue advocacy advertising in connection with the legislative process and elections has resulted in some groups contributing to the permanent campaigns that consume a significant portion of the professional lives of most members of Congress.

Interest groups, congressional subcommittee members, and executive-branch officials form collegial decision-making groups, which are frequently referred to as "iron triangles," "issue networks," or "policy subgovernments."[21] These issue experts often focus on the minutiae of arcane, highly specialized areas of public policy. Because they form small governments within a government, they further contribute to the decentralization of Congress.

POLITICAL PARTIES AS CENTRALIZING AGENTS

Unlike the structural, organizational, and political factors that work to decentralize Congress, political parties act as a glue—albeit sometimes a weak one—to bond members together. They socialize new members, distribute committee assignments, set the legislative agenda, disseminate information, and carry out other tasks that are essential to Congress's law-making, oversight, and representative functions. Although they are not the central actors in elections, party committees do help individual candidates develop their campaign messages. Party campaign efforts on behalf of individual candidates and election agenda-setting efforts encourage legislators to vote for bills that are at the core of their party's agenda when Congress is in session.[22] Party issue advocacy that takes place outside of the campaign season is meant to increase or reduce support for specific bills or damage the reputations of members who voted against them. Issue advocacy ads, such as those that the Republicans aired against Senate Democrats who voted against the balanced budget amendment in 1997 and were up for reelection in 1998, have given party organizations, especially those in the nation's capital, a greater role in the permanent campaign.

The congressional parties' leadership organizations are structured similarly to those of legislative parties in other countries. The Democrats and Republicans are each headed by one leader in each chamber—the Speaker and minority leader in the House and the majority and minority leaders in the Senate. Each party has several other officers and an extensive whip system to facilitate communications between congressional party leaders and rank-and-file legislators. Legislative parties convene caucuses and task forces to help formulate policy positions and legislative strategy. Providing campaign assistance, giving out committee assignments and other perks, setting the congressional agenda, structuring debate, and persuading legislators that specific bills are in the best interests of their constituents and the nation are tools that congressional leaders use to build coalitions.[23]

Nevertheless, party leaders have less control over the policy-making process than do their counterparts in other democracies.[24] The persuasive powers of party leaders are usually insufficient to sway members' votes when party policy positions clash with those of legislators' constituents and campaign supporters. Recognizing the primacy of the electoral connection, party leaders generally tell legislators to respond to constituents rather than "toe the party line" when the latter could endanger their chances of reelection. The efforts of congressional party leaders are probably less of a factor in explaining how party members cast their roll-call votes than are commonalities in political outlook or similarities among legislators' constituents.[25] Party leaders are most able to overcome the forces that fragment Congress when they seek to enact policies that possess widespread bipartisan support or when the majority party possesses many more seats than the opposition and proposes popular legislation that advances its core principles. As the historic 104th Congress showed, a change in party control can also act as a catalyst for party unity. Members of the new House and Senate majorities were aware that their accomplishments as a party would directly influence their individual reelection campaigns and their party's ability to maintain control of Congress.

RESPONSIVENESS, RESPONSIBILITY, AND PUBLIC POLICY

In representative democracies, elections are the principal means of ensuring that governments respond to the will of the people and promote their interests. Voters, through elections, hold public officials accountable for their actions and for the state of the nation as a whole. Elections are a blunt but powerful instrument of control that allow people to inform their individual representatives or the government as a collectivity of how political action or inaction has affected the quality of their lives. Elections are the primary means that democracies use to empower or remove political leaders at all levels of government. Campaigns help to establish standards by which officeholders are judged. Other paths of influence, such as contacting members of Congress and giving campaign contributions, are usually used to advance narrower goals, are more demanding, and are in practice less democratic.

Despite the extensive resources for building and maintaining relationships with constituents that Congress and the rest of the Washington establishment put at the disposal of representatives and senators, members cannot fully insulate themselves or Congress as an institution from the impact of electoral forces. Voters can, and occasionally do, expel large numbers of incumbents, leading to changes in the membership, leadership, operations, and output of Congress. The 1994 elections resulted in a new Republican majority taking control of Congress for the first time in forty years and led to the selection of Newt Gingrich—a relative newcomer to his party's leadership—as House Speaker. The elections also empowered the Republicans to claim a mandate to change some of the ways in which Congress operates and to overturn Democratic programs that originated more than sixty years earlier during the New Deal.

The 1998 midterm elections brought the Gingrich regime to an end and took much of the steam out of the Republicans' program to remake the federal government. The GOP's historic loss of five House seats during the midterm election cost Gingrich the confidence of his Republican House colleagues and led him to resign both the speakership and his House seat. The GOP's focus on the Clinton/Lewinsky scandal, the Starr investigation, and sexual mores during the campaign had an unexpected side effect. It encouraged *Hustler* publisher Larry Flynt to pay for a private ethics investigation that turned the tables on some Republican legislators. The major casualty of that investigation was Republican Speaker-designate Robert Livingston of Louisiana, who after acknowledging having had an extra-marital affair, resigned from the House. Dennis Hastert, a consensus-building Republican from Illinois, rose from relative obscurity to become the new Speaker. In contrast with Gingrich's first session as the House's leader, Hastert's first session was characterized by few legislative accomplishments. The politics surrounding the elections of the 1990s show that voters can shake up the status quo in Washington, inspire change in the direction of government, and set standards for what is considered acceptable behavior by public officials.

Individuals whose public service is contingent on getting reelected often straddle the fuzzy line that demarcates responsiveness and responsibility in government. On some occasions, legislators are highly responsive, functioning as delegates who advance their constituents' views. On others, they take the role of trustee, relying on their own judgment to protect the welfare of their constituents or the nation.[26] Responsible legislators must occasionally vote against their constituents' wishes in order to best serve the interests of the nation.

Election Systems and Public Policy

The type of political system in which elected officials function influences to whom they answer. The United States' candidate-centered system is unique, and it results in a style of governance that contrasts sharply with that of parliamentary systems, which are used to govern the vast majority of democracies. Parliamentary systems feature party-focused elections that tend to hold elected officials accountable to national political majorities.[27] Members of the British Parliament (MPs), for example, perform casework and are attentive to their constituents, but they are inclined to vote for legislation that is fashioned to please national rather than local constituencies. MPs support party initiatives because they know that their prospects for reelection are closely tied to their party's ability to enact its legislative program. The candidate-centered nature of the American system, in contrast, encourages elected officials to be responsive to the desires of constituents and organized groups that support their campaigns, sometimes in opposition to their party's leadership.

The separation of powers reinforces legislators' predispositions to support district voters first and campaign supporters second when making public policy.

Even when one party controls the White House and both chambers of Congress, it may find it difficult to unify legislators because they can disagree with one another without fear of losing control of the government. Members of the majority party in Congress cast roll-call votes secure in the knowledge that they will remain in office for their full two- or six-year terms even if their party suffers a major legislative defeat. In parliamentary systems, majority party members understand that a major policy defeat may be interpreted as a vote of no confidence in their party and may force an election that could turn them out of office in less than a month. The separation of powers also affects the behavior of legislators who are in the minority party. They have little incentive to vote against legislation that could benefit their constituents just because it was sponsored by the majority party, since even a smashing legislative defeat would not force a snap election.

President Clinton's close defeat on "fast track" trade authority legislation in September 1998 demonstrates the difficulties that congressional parties face when they try to overcome the centrifugal forces influencing members of Congress. Fast track was opposed by many congressional Democrats, whose constituents feared that giving the president the authority to negotiate trade agreements—specifically, agreements that Congress must approve or defeat without amendment within ninety days—would result in manufacturing jobs leaving the country. Fast track forced many legislators to choose between remaining loyal to their party's leader and pleasing their constituents. Most members, regardless of seniority, placed their constituents' interests and their own views above those of President Clinton. Among those who opposed fast track were Democratic Minority Leader Richard Gephardt, Minority Whip David Bonior, and Caucus Chair Vic Fazio. These leaders, who were selected by their congressional colleagues to advance core party policies, used the prestige, staff, and other resources of their leadership offices to deny Clinton—the head of their party—trade negotiating authority that had been enjoyed by every occupant of the White House since Gerald Ford.[28]

Democratic leaders were more loyal to Clinton when it came to voting on impeachment. However, even on an issue that could have initiated the process of removing their party's leader from office, constituent demands and individual legislators' own consciences inspired five House Democrats to abandon their party and vote for one or more articles of impeachment. These same forces also resulted in an equal number of House Republicans breaking ranks with their GOP colleagues and voting against one or more impeachment articles. In the Senate Democrats remained loyal to the president, voting unanimously against both articles of impeachment. The Republicans, on the other hand, experienced some division in their ranks: five of fifty-five members of the GOP conference voted against the article of impeachment charging obstruction of justice, and another ten voted against the article stating that the president had committed perjury.

Most acts of Congress are neither as monumental nor as short-term in focus as the impeachment proceedings, and many are not as driven by constituent concerns as was fast track legislation. The separation of powers, bicameralism, federalism, and a fixed-date system of elections make it difficult for legislators to enact longer-term, more nationally focused policies. Members of Congress who believe that their individual images, policy positions, and public records were decisive in their election are less likely than legislators in party-centered democracies to sacrifice the short-term interests of constituents or to compromise on salient issues to enact policies advocated by party leaders. House members, who must run for reelection every two years, respond particularly strongly to parochial concerns.

The effects of parochialism are most apparent in distributive politics, which provide tangible benefits to private individuals or groups. Building coalitions in support of spending on roads, bridges, universities, museums, and other projects is relatively simple in a decentralized legislature such as the U.S. Congress. Bill sponsors can add new programs and projects in order to win enough legislative supporters to pass their plan.[29] A farm advocate who is hoping to subsidize northern sugar beets, for example, might build support for this cause by expanding the number of subsidized crops in a bill to include sugar cane, rice, corn, wheat, and even tobacco, thereby expanding support that began with representatives from Minnesota to include colleagues from Hawaii, Massachusetts, virtually every southern state, and the states of the Midwest.[30] Subsidies for ostrich farmers can be left out because they will not draw many legislative votes, but food stamps can be added to attract the support of legislators from poor urban districts.[31] Trading subsidies for votes is a simple example of logrolling. Other deals are cut over tax breaks, budget votes, and even appointments to the federal judiciary.

Logrolling and other forms of compromise usually do not allow individual legislators to get all the federal "pork" they would like for their constituents. Nevertheless, these compromises enable most legislators to insert enough pork into a bill to claim credit for doing something to help their constituents. A broadly supported distributive bill is an easy candidate for congressional enactment because, like a Christmas tree decorated by a group of friends, everyone can see his or her handiwork in it and find something to admire in the finished product.

Distributive politics are problematic because they are practiced with both eyes focused on short-term gains and little attention to long-range consequences.

Broadening programs that were originally intended to provide benefits to one group to include others usually causes the programs to become ineffectively targeted, watered down, and overly expensive. When large sums are spent to benefit many groups, overall spending is increased, and fewer funds remain available to help the group that was originally targeted for assistance. This does little to promote the original goals of a bill and leads to deficit spending.[32] Pork-barrel spending and logrolling, which are at the heart of distributive politics, have contributed heavily to the national debt of more than $5.6 trillion that the U.S. government reported in the summer of 1999. Distributive politics are a prime example of what happens when independently elected officials seek to promote the interests of their constituents and campaign supporters without giving much thought to the effect of their collective actions on the nation. Recent Congresses, especially those elected since 1994, have taken steps to reduce government spending, generating budget surpluses in 1998 and 1999. However, constant wrangling over tax cuts, military spending, and other federal programs have hindered their attempts at debt reduction.

Policy Gridlock and Political Cycles

Parochialism also leads to a reactive style of government and incremental policy making. Congress is better at making short-term fixes than at developing long-term initiatives. Congressional leaders often find it difficult to develop a vision for the future. During the 1980s House Democrats took steps to outline, publicize, and act on a partisan agenda. Parts of this effort were successful, but much of it was not. Differences in legislators' political philosophies, the diversity of their constituencies, and the limited resources available to party leaders made it difficult to develop and implement a Democratic game plan for the nation's future.[33] House Republicans also tried on several occasions in the 1980s to develop a partisan agenda, but prior to the Contract with America, they, too, enjoyed only limited success.[34]

Under most circumstances election outcomes, constituent demands, interest group pressures, and White House initiatives support the continuation of the status quo or suggest only small changes in public policies. When pressure for change exists, Congress generally initiates limited reform, but only after a period of some delay. On some occasions, however, the federal government does enact comprehensive programs that significantly affect people's lives.

Major policy change is most likely to occur during periods of crisis and is frequently associated with partisan realignments. Realignments traditionally occur when a critical event polarizes voters on a major issue, the two major parties take clear and opposing stands on that issue, and one party succeeds in capturing the White House and large majorities in both the House and Senate. The ascendant party then has an electoral mandate to enact major policy change.[35]

The events leading up to and continuing through Franklin Roosevelt's presidency exemplify federal policy making during a period of crisis. The seeds of Roosevelt's New Deal programs were sewn in the Great Depression of the 1930s. Republicans controlled the White House, the House of Representatives, and the Senate when the stock market crashed in 1929. The Democrats made the Republicans' failure to initiate economic reforms to reverse the depression a major campaign issue. After winning the White House and both chambers of Congress, the Democrats used their mandate to replace laissez-faire economics with Keynesian policies, which relied on government intervention to revive the economy. Other partisan and policy realignments took place during the late 1820s, the Civil War era, and the 1890s.

Some major policy changes have been instituted in the absence of partisan realignments, but most of these were less sweeping than were those that followed critical elections. The civil rights and Great Society programs of the 1960s and the American withdrawal from Vietnam are examples of major policy changes that occurred in the absence of a partisan realignment. Historical perspective is needed before scholars can conclude that the 1994 congressional elections constituted a full-scale realignment in favor of the Republicans, but Democratic hegemony over Congress has clearly ended.[36] Regardless of whether a realignment was constituted in 1994, the GOP was able to use its stunning electoral success to institute major changes in public policy and shift the national policy debate. Under Gingrich's leadership, the GOP-controlled Congress passed legislation reducing federal mandates on the states, cutting federal regulations, and changing the welfare system from a federally mandated program to one run by each state independently with a block grant from the federal government.[37]

The Republicans also shifted the policy debate from how to improve the efficiency and performance of the federal government to how to decrease its scope. For the first time since the New Deal, the subject of reducing entitlement benefits dominated public debate. Politicians, commentators, and policy analysts discussed whether reducing current or future per capita outlays for Social Security, Medicare, Medicaid, and other entitlement programs was an acceptable way to cut the size and cost of government, reduce the federal deficit, and pay for tax cuts. Other debates raged over issues such as a presidential line-item veto, a balanced budget amendment, and term limits. The first of these changes was signed into law but later declared unconstitutional. The latter two have yet to make it to the president's desk.

Republican House leaders also restructured some major aspects of how the House did business. The GOP cut the number of House committees, subcommittees, and committee staffs, enacted term limits for committee chairs and the Speaker, and made other formal changes aimed at strengthening the hands of the majority party leadership. The Republicans eliminated legislative study organizations, which had formerly enhanced the representation of specific—mostly Democratic—constituencies. Republican leaders also bypassed the normal committee process in writing several important pieces of legislation, relying instead on task forces, which facilitate coalition building within the majority party but greatly reduce minority party input.[38]

The 1994 elections and the revolutionary 104th Congress that followed showed that contemporary elections can lead to major policy and institutional change. The influx of a large number of new House members who were committed to the policy proposals outlined in the Contract with America, and the indebtedness that many other Republican legislators felt toward Gingrich for leading the charge to take over the House, set the stage for the changes that followed the GOP takeover. The Clinton administration's temporary abdication of leadership on domestic policy issues immediately following the election enabled Republican leaders to set the political agenda and pass many of their policy proposals in the House. The Senate, which also witnessed the election of a Republican majority, adopted many of the legislative initiatives created by the House but left its unique stamp on the bills that were ultimately signed into law. It also rejected some of the House bills, including the House Republicans' much-heralded balanced budget amendment.

The 1994 elections show that the elections of individual members of Congress can collectively lead to great political change. Elections that result in a shift in partisan control and the swearing in of many new members can help the legislative branch overcome its normal state of decentralization, especially when there is a widespread consensus for change among the American people. These conditions help the majority party in Congress act programmatically. When this occurs, congressional parties in the United States resemble both parliamentary parties in other countries and an idealized system of responsible party government.[39] However, as the final days of the 104th and most of the 105th and 106th sessions of Congress demonstrated, once public support for sweeping change erodes, the centrifugal forces that customarily dominate Congress reassert themselves, and the legislature returns to its normal, incremental mode of policy making. The parochialism of members of Congress, bicameralism, the internal decentralization of the House and the Senate, and other centrifugal forces promote political cycles marked by long periods of incremental policy making followed by short periods of major policy change.

SUMMARY

The candidate-centered congressional election system has a major impact on how Congress functions. The electoral connection encourages members of Congress to develop home styles that result in their building bonds of trust with local voters. Congress, as an institution, provides its members with resources to help them accomplish this objective. The candidate-centered system also finds expression in the highly individualistic legislative behavior exhibited by most representatives and senators and in Congress's decentralized style of operation. Although political parties occasionally overcome the legislature's naturally fragmented state, the centrifugal forces exerted on Congress by constituents, campaign contributors, interest groups, committees, and other organizations within Congress itself cause the institution to return to its normal decentralized operations after short periods of centralization. The result is that national policy making in the United States is characterized by prolonged periods of gradual policy modification followed by brief episodes of sweeping political change.

CHAPTER ELEVEN

Campaign Reform

Congress has come under assault in recent years for its inability to solve some of the nation's most pressing problems, its perceived shortcomings in representing the general public, and its failure to keep its own house in order. Gridlock, deficit spending, scandal, the foibles of its members, and the operations of Congress itself have led many to champion congressional reform.[1] Reformers have called for a variety of changes, ranging from a balanced budget amendment to term limits, which would restructure the political careers of members and would-be members and drastically transform the way in which Congress operates. Campaign reform falls somewhere in between these two extremes. In this chapter I identify aspects of the system that should be considered for reform, present some reform proposals, and discuss the prospects for meaningful reform to be enacted.

THE CASE FOR REFORM

Numerous arguments can be made for reforming Congress: some focus on the outcomes of congressional elections and others on the processes that produce those outcomes. Arguments that fall in the first category, most notably those for term limits, dwell on the fact that incumbents almost always win. They frequently discount or ignore that incumbents' successes are largely the result of legislators' efforts to serve their constituents prior to the election season, the weak competition they encounter once the campaign has begun, and inequalities in the campaign resources available to different kinds of candidates. They also ignore that many incumbents choose to retire rather than face a strong challenge.

Many of those who build their case for reform on the outcomes of congressional elections are willing to embrace fairly radical changes because they are frustrated with their economic situation, rising crime, increased taxes, and reduced government services and because they believe the desires of the average taxpayer are being sacrificed by a government that panders to special interests. Reform movements are often headed by defeated congressional challengers and other frustrated politicians, some of whom have even served in Congress. Some reform efforts draw financial support from private groups that have strong ties to a political party. Despite their lofty rhetoric, which is designed to tap into Americans' traditional ambivalence toward politics and distrust of politicians, the heads of reform groups usually stand to receive some kind of benefit if their objectives are achieved.

Advocates of term limits argue that a regular rotation of public-spirited amateur legislators in and out of Congress would result in the enactment of laws that would solve the nation's most pressing problems. This argument is based on a superficial understanding of the political process and fails to consider the insightful deliberations of the Constitution's framers on the lengths of congressional terms.[2] Term limits might encourage greater rotation among national legislators, but those nonincumbents with the best prospects of getting elected would continue to be experienced politicians and wealthy individuals who have the ability to assemble the organizational and financial resources needed to communicate to voters, not the public-spirited "citizen legislators" that some reformers have in mind. Putting a cap on the number of terms a legislator can serve would also strengthen the congressional and executive branch aides and "inside-the-beltway" lobbyists who are part of the permanent Washington establishment. Turning members of Congress into lame ducks at the end of a fixed number of terms would encourage even the most popular and effective legislators to become more concerned with courting new employers than with responding to constituent interests or governing responsibly. Congressional term limits would also probably reduce electoral competition and incumbent accountability because most strategic nonincumbents who are capable of waging strong campaigns would wait until a seat in Congress became open rather than challenge an incumbent.

The fact that almost 57 percent of all members of the 106th Congress were sworn into office after the 1990 elections makes questionable the premise from which advocates of term limits proceed—that there is not enough turnover in the federal legislature. This is a point that was not lost on members of the House and Senate, who failed to provide the two-thirds votes needed to pass a term limits amendment to the Constitution in both the 104th and 105th Congresses. Ironically, term limits for state legislators, which currently exist in eighteen states, might enhance competition in congressional elections by encouraging state legislators serving their last term to run for Congress.[3]

Term limits are one of many "shot gun" proposals for reform that are advocated by those who have failed to achieve their goals through normal political channels. A balanced budget amendment and many of the initiatives and referenda on state and local ballots are others.[4] These shortcuts and bypasses to regular elections and legislative processes are no substitute for the political will of citizens and their elected representatives. If enacted, they would probably do more harm than good, despite reformers' best intentions.

Reform proposals designed to make congressional elections more competitive have the potential to improve the political system. Rather than altering the principles of republican government, which are the foundation of American democracy, these proposals have the potential to improve the system's capacity to live up to those principles. Real campaign reform must increase the competitiveness of congressional elections, improve the accountability of the electoral process, increase voter participation in midterm and presidential year elections, enhance representation in Congress, and endeavor to increase the legitimacy of the election system in the eyes of citizens.

The first step toward increasing competition in congressional elections is to encourage a larger number of talented candidates to run for office, especially in races against incumbents. The best way to accomplish this goal is to provide all candidates with access to adequate campaign resources. More qualified challengers will run if they know they will be competing on a more level playing field. The fact that most incumbents begin and end both the campaign for resources and the campaign for votes far ahead of their opponents discourages many of the best would-be challengers from running.[5] Others are discouraged by the prospect of having to compete against wealthy opponents who can spend almost unlimited personal funds on campaigning. The advantages associated with incumbency and millionaire candidacies cannot be completely eliminated by campaign reform, but campaign reform should ensure that nonincumbents have access to adequate resources. The promise of resources will encourage better challengers to run and give those who decide to enter the fray a fighting chance.

Merely imposing limits on campaign spending by incumbents, challengers, or open-seat contestants is not the solution. Even though reformers raise the issue of campaign costs more often than they discuss electoral competition, the complaint that campaigns cost too much has little foundation in reality. The amount of money spent on congressional elections has risen in recent years but not inordinately so when one takes into consideration the rate of inflation and the growth in advertising costs imposed by television, radio, and direct-mail companies. The price that candidates pay for political campaigns is minuscule compared with the price that corporations pay to advertise consumer products. The state of American advertising is such that Coca-Cola and other companies, which spend billions of dollars a year repeating the names of products that are already household terms, drown out candidate communications. This is particularly harmful to House challengers. As Will Robinson, a veteran Democratic media consultant, has commented: "Our challengers not only have to compete with an incumbent congressman, they also have to compete with that damned 'Energizer Bunny!' They need more, not less, money."[6]

The resources—not necessarily cash—committed to educating citizens about candidates and issues are critical to the functioning of a representative democracy, and if anything, the sums available to some candidates—mainly nonincumbents—ought to be increased. Increasing election resources would potentially enhance the knowledge that voters have about candidates, issues, and campaigns. And the more information individuals possess about elections, the more likely they are to vote.[7] Spending and contribution limits should be imposed on candidates only in combination with reforms that substitute publicly mandated access to communications resources for private cash.

Another solution in search of a problem is the imposition of limits on the funds that candidates can raise outside of their district or state. The emergence of national fund-raising constituencies reflects both the uneven geographic distribution of wealth in the United States and the uneven distribution of power in Congress. When it comes to congressional fund-raising, candidates go where the money is, and most of the money flows to those who are in positions of power or those who have the best chances of attaining power. Where candidates get their contributions from should not be a major concern because members of Congress, including congressional leaders, remain highly responsive—perhaps too much so—to their constituents despite the fact that they currently reach beyond district or state boundaries when raising money. Furthermore, as national policy makers, members of Congress should pay at least some attention to representatives of organized interests that are affected by congressional action, even if those interests are not located in their states or congressional districts. Interest group representatives may be among the few knowledgeable sources of information that members have about the views of individuals and interests who reside outside of their districts or states.

Ceilings on the amounts that candidates can raise from nonconstituents are not likely to improve representation in Congress, but they will make fund-raising more difficult, particularly for congressional challengers whose ability to collect needed campaign money is usually limited. Moreover, most voters are probably not overly concerned about the contributions that legally flow across state borders. A vigilant media and a reasonably funded opponent can hold a candidate publicly accountable for those contributions.

The real problem of campaign spending, as it relates to electoral competition, is not how much money is spent or whether it originates out of state but who spends it. Congressional elections can be improved by taking steps to broaden the distribution of campaign resources, not reduce them. If ceilings on campaign expenditures are set too low, challengers will have less opportunity to communicate with voters and elections will become less competitive. Critics of spending limits are probably correct in their assertion that legislation limiting the amounts that challengers can spend would be tantamount to an incumbent protection act.[8] Spending limits in open-seat races and incumbent-challenger contests would also work to the advantage of candidates who belong to the majority party in their state or district, thereby deterring competition in those places.

Related to the issue of costs are concerns about who makes large campaign contributions and how they are raised. Complaints that wealthy and well-organized elements of society play too big a role in funding campaigns have been around for a long time and have been addressed by various pieces of legislation.[9] The FECA bans businesses and unions from making contributions directly to candidates and limits individuals to contributions of $1,000 and PACs to contributions of $5,000 per candidate during each phase of the election. The law has not eliminated the role of wealthy individuals and groups in campaign finance. Rather, it has forced candidates to turn to a broader array of financial sources and encouraged some individuals and groups to spend money outside of the federal campaign finance system through independent voter mobilization programs and issue advocacy ads.

An unintended side effect of the FECA has been to increase the amount of time and money that candidates spend chasing contributions. Nearly 40 percent of the members of the House and Senate report spending a moderate to a great deal of time raising money for their next campaign—time that they would prefer to devote to learning about pending legislation, attending floor debates, meeting with constituents, and other important congressional duties.[10] Of course, the demands made by fund-raising on incumbents are minuscule compared with those on challengers and open-seat candidates. Fund-raising imperatives reduce the time that all candidates have to communicate with voters.

A second unanticipated consequence of the law is that it has increased the role of soft money in elections. Soft money is the "black market" economy of campaign finance. Ceilings on individual contributions to federal candidates and the parties' federal campaign accounts have encouraged wealthy individuals to look for alternative ways to spend money in elections. Prohibitions against corporations, trade associations, and unions contributing or spending funds from their treasuries have had similar effects. Members of Congress and other political leaders have encouraged these prospective donors by inviting them to soft money fund-raising events, often with the tacit understanding that the party committees and interest groups that collect the funds will spend them in ways that benefit their campaigns or those of like-minded politicians. The efforts of these members and organizations add to the suspicions of voters who are too unfamiliar with the nuances of campaign finance law to recognize that soft money flows to and is spent by party committees and interest groups rather than candidates. Journalistic reports suggesting that issue advocacy ads and other soft money expenditures influence the outcomes of elections, which are strongly supported by the systematic research in chapter 9, further drive voters' suspicions.

Court decisions and FEC rulings prompted by the efforts of enterprising contributors, politicians, party officials, political consultants, and interest group leaders expanded the activities on which soft money can be spent to include nationally directed voter mobilization programs and issue advocacy ads designed to influence the outcome of federal elections. The closer integration of party and interest group soft money efforts and hard money financed candidate campaigns has resulted in soft money becoming a more attractive vehicle for parties, interest groups, wealthy individual donors, and some candidates. The popularity of soft money has also been increased by the premiums routinely offered to contributors, including private audiences with presidents, cabinet members, and congressional leaders.

Skyrocketing soft money transactions have drastically changed the financing of federal elections, and they pose unique problems. So much soft money flows outside the normal, federally regulated areas of congressional campaign finance that the FECA is more loophole than law. The 1990s witnessed the growth of a national economy of soft money contributions and expenditures that almost rivals in size the campaign finance economy that is regulated by federal law.

Soft money contributions and expenditures, some of which exceed $1 million, greatly increase the influence that wealthy elements of society have on the financing of campaigns. Individuals and groups located in Washington's Capitol Hill community, alone, contributed almost $32.7 million—$30.1 million of it in soft money—over the course of the 1998 elections.[11] Contributors located inside or in areas immediately adjacent to the Washington Beltway contributed more than $90.9 million.[12] Citizens should be concerned when such huge sums of unregulated campaign money are collected in large denominations from such a small area, particularly an area that is home to both the U.S. Capitol and many of the nation's top lobbying firms. Revelations that large amounts of soft money have been raised from noncitizens and foreign corporations and spent by tax-exempt organizations have added new twists to the soft money problem.

Nevertheless, not all soft money is the same. Party soft money is given to and spent by party committees, which are umbrella organizations that represent a broad range of interests. This does not create such strong policy-oriented IOUs between contributors and legislators as those created by narrowly focused interest groups that spend soft money to help only a few candidates. Party leaders and fund-raisers may urge House members and senators to support legislation that is important to the party's financial benefactors, but the argument that "we owe it to a group of wealthy donors to pass this bill" is unlikely to carry much sway with legislators who oppose passage because of constituent interests or their own views. More important is the fact that party committees and candidates are held accountable for their soft money finances because national party soft money transactions are publicized by the FEC. As both parties, but especially the Democrats, learned in the closing weeks of the 1996 elections and throughout the 1998 election season, the odor of tainted money can cost a party votes and hinder future fund-raising efforts.

Soft money raised and spent by interest groups is another matter. Some of these groups, such as those that in 1997 spent $2.3 million on issue advocacy ads featuring Sen. Alfonse D'Amato promoting a New York State environmental bond, carry out political activities designed to advance the careers of one or a small group of politicians.[13] By spending millions of undocumented dollars on activities intended to influence congressional elections, these groups create relationships between candidates and wealthy donors that are hidden from the public.

Some groups make it difficult to discern their true policy agendas by adopting nondescript names, such as Citizens for Reform, Citizens for the Republic Education Fund, the National Policy Forum, and Vote Now '98. Some groups also have strong ties to one of the major parties, as noted in Chapters 4 and 5. Many soft money groups, including those that have strong ties to congressional candidates, party committees, or interest groups, are little more than subterfuges that enable wealthy individuals, organizations, and party committees to skirt federal campaign finance statutes. These groups have little or no public accountability. They should be barred from spending soft money in ways that are intended to affect the outcomes of federal elections or, at the very least, required to report all their election-related activity to the FEC.

A third unintended consequence of the FECA is its contribution to the decline in public trust in Congress. This lessening of confidence manifests itself in attitudes toward the institution, declining levels of voter turnout, feelings of political apathy and alienation, and a disapproval of politics and politicians. The FECA's disclosure requirements greatly improved campaign finance reporting. Yet, public awareness of the role of money in politics has done little to increase citizen confidence in the political system. In fact, it has probably had the opposite effect. More than four of five Americans agree that "the campaign finance system is broken and needs to be replaced" or that "it has problems and needs to be changed."[14] More than three-quarters of all major congressional donors (who gave $200 or more to one or more congressional candidates) share those sentiments, as do 60 percent of all candidates for state legislatures—the major steppingstones to Congress—and 86 percent of all House candidates.[15] The same is true of 77 percent of all House incumbents, who are the major beneficiaries of the current campaign finance system.[16] Many of these citizens, donors, potential candidates, candidates, and members of Congress would probably agree with the statement that Sen. Max Cleland, D-Ga., made before the Senate Governmental Affairs Committee on the opening day of the 1997 campaign finance hearings: "Our democracy has become an auction, not an election."[17]

Some political observers maintain that a fourth unintended consequence of the FECA is its creation of a system of campaign contributions that enables wealthy contributors to have a greater influence than others on elections. In situations where money matters, primarily in close races, reformers are correct in their assertion that those who make large contributions have a greater effect on elections than those who do not. By providing their preferred candidates with some of the money needed to communicate with voters, wealthy individual contributors and PACs, like the hundreds of thousands of professionals and volunteers who work on campaigns, increase their influence on the electoral process.

It is unclear, however, exactly what campaign contributors receive for their efforts. The sums that any one individual or one PAC can legally contribute directly to a candidate—in contrast to soft money transactions involving parties and other groups—are too small to determine the outcomes of elections, given the hundreds of thousands of dollars that are spent in most House contests and the millions of dollars spent in many Senate and some House campaigns. What individuals and groups usually get for their contributions is the opportunity to meet with members of Congress and their staffs, not the power to tell them how to govern.[18] Representatives and senators consider an array of factors when making policy decisions, including the views of constituents, committee chairs, party leaders, other legislators, and executive branch officials.[19] Legislators also strive to keep their roll-call votes consistent with those they have cast on related issues.[20]

Reformers who focus on the role of money underestimate the importance of these other factors. Despite public perceptions, campaign contributions ranging from one to several thousand dollars in most races probably do not seriously skew the representation in Congress. The lobbying efforts that groups make have a greater effect on members' voting decisions than do their campaign contributions.[21] Moreover, these contributions certainly have a smaller effect than do the hundred thousand dollar donations that were common during the pre-FECA era and the multimillion dollar expenditures that have become commonplace in the era of soft money. Public perceptions that individual and PAC contributions can buy votes in Congress are probably inaccurate, but the role of money in politics has undoubtedly contributed to the decline in public support for Congress.

The growing disconnection between the campaign for votes and the campaign for resources is a big part of the problem. During the golden age of parties, when local party activists were among the most important campaign resources, there was an intimate connection between the two campaigns. Elections were neighborhood affairs, and campaigns involved personal contact between candidates, party activists, other volunteers, and voters. Personal contact between voters and campaigners existed before, during, and after the election season. Parties provided ordinary voters and campaigners with ongoing relationships with members of Congress and others involved in the political system. Often these relationships revolved around jobs, contracts, social clubs, and opportunities to improve oneself or one's neighborhood.[22] Such relationships humanized government for voters and built bonds of trust between people and political institutions.

Contemporary campaigns encourage fewer meaningful ties to develop between voters and candidates. Campaigns for votes are more impersonal, consisting of television, radio, and direct-mail ads and the free media they generate. Fleeting contacts occasionally take place between citizens, candidates, and party and campaign activists, but they rarely result in the development of enduring personal relationships. Moreover, campaigns for resources are increasingly focused away from ordinary voters and toward national party organizations, PACs, and wealthy individuals who are in a position to provide the wherewithal needed to mount a contemporary campaign. Corporations, unions, and other organizations that finance issue advocacy advertisements, direct mail campaigns, and mobilization efforts have also become important targets in the campaign for resources.

Many voters believe that the elite "special interests" that spend large sums in elections, rather than individuals who vote in them, possess the strongest and most beneficial relationships with members of Congress and others in government.[23] Because members of Congress and the organizations that elect them have relatively little patronage, few preferments, and hardly any opportunities for social advancement to distribute to their constituents, many voters have come to believe that these "goodies" are being distributed instead to wealthy campaign contributors in Washington and the nation's other financial centers. Transformations in the way that campaigns are conducted at home and in Washington have contributed to the public's belief that the operation of the federal government has changed in ways that favor special interests in Washington over the folks back home.

Low voter turnout is a serious shortcoming of congressional elections that is raised less frequently by reformers than the shortcomings of the FECA and the role of money in politics. Approximately 36 percent of all eligible Americans turned out to vote in 1998.[24] Turnout-related issues are important because the political legitimacy of elected officials who receive the votes of less than half of all eligible voters can be questioned. Congress sought to address this issue in 1993 when it enacted the motor-voter bill, which mandated that Americans be able to sign up to vote when registering their cars or transacting other business with national, state, or local governments. The law resulted in an almost 4 percent increase in voter registration between 1994 and 1998 in the forty-four states covered by the act.[25] More efforts should be taken to encourage people to register to vote and to participate in politics.

The content of campaign messages is another aspect of congressional elections that is rarely discussed by reformers, but 84 percent of the general public is bothered by what politicians say to get elected.[26] Candidates campaign in slogans and sound bites mainly because short communications are cheaper than long ones. Candidates and political consultants also believe that repetition is preferable to detail because their audiences have limited attention spans. Meeting the needs of the journalists who cover campaigns and controlling the flow of campaign information are two other objectives that encourage candidates to disseminate short, symbolic statements. The fact that most voters cast their ballots on the basis of candidate imagery and qualifications rather than on a detailed understanding of the issues further encourages many candidates, particularly incumbents, to campaign on valence issues rather than focus on concrete solutions to major problems. Reforms that provide candidates with free or subsidized postage, radio time, or television time could improve the quality of campaign communications.

The fact that many candidates from the two major parties campaign on similar positions is a complaint raised by radicals and supporters of minor parties, who constitute a small part of the population. They argue that the narrow range of positions is caused by the way elections are financed; Democrats and

Republicans, they say, raise money from similar sources. Although their charge is undeniable, their explanation is wrong. The narrow breadth of dialogue in American elections is caused by candidates and parties responding to the fundamental agreement that exists among most voters on the issues. Ballot access or campaign finance reforms designed to strengthen minor parties or increase their number might slightly influence the nation's political debate, but it is doubtful that these changes would break the consensus that exists on major issues. Moreover, minor parties divide political opposition, which can help unpopular incumbents get reelected and impede majority rule.[27]

Reformers should not be overly optimistic about the effect that campaign reform would have on voters' confidence in their elected representatives, Congress as an institution, or the entire political system. Congress has never been looked upon with much favor by the American public, and changing the way that its members finance their campaigns is unlikely to alter this viewpoint.

RECOMMENDATIONS

Campaign reform should be founded on an understanding that elections are primarily fought between candidates. Candidates and their campaign organizations devise strategies, accumulate and distribute resources, publicize issue positions, communicate images, and carry out grass-roots activities in order to win voter support. Party committees, PACs, and other groups play important supporting roles in the election process—roles that have grown as a result of the weakening of the FECA and, especially, the rise of issue advocacy. Reformers need to appreciate the different goals and resources that individuals and groups bring to elections and need to consider how their proposals will affect these groups.

Campaign reform should be predicated on the assumption that highly participatory, competitive elections are desirable because they are the best way to hold elected officials accountable to voters, enhance representation, and build trust in government. Reform should make congressional elections more competitive by encouraging more qualified candidates to run and by improving the ability of candidates, particularly nonincumbents, to communicate with voters. Campaign reform should also seek to increase the number of people who vote and give campaign contributions. It should attempt to minimize the amount of unregulated money spent to influence federal elections. The recommendations that follow are not a comprehensive reform package but are a series of proposals that would make congressional elections more participatory and more competitive and instill greater public confidence in the political system.

Free or Subsidized Communications

Free or subsidized campaign communications—whether they come in the form of postage, television or radio time, or communications vouchers—would give candidates, particularly challengers, the opportunity to present their messages to the public. The promise of free or heavily discounted communications resources would probably encourage better candidates to run for Congress because it would give them the knowledge that should they win their party's nomination they would be guaranteed access to some of the resources needed to campaign.[28] By encouraging the entry of better candidates and providing those who win a nomination with resources, this reform would lead to more competitive congressional elections.

The availability of resources for communications also might indirectly encourage greater electoral competition. Congressional challengers and open-seat candidates who used these resources effectively would be in a position to attract the attention of local journalists, thereby helping the candidates communicate more effectively with voters and helping voters cast their ballots on the basis of more information. Because campaign communications help stimulate public interest in elections, reforms that ensured both candidates adequate communications resources would probably also increase voter turnout.[29] A perception of greater competitiveness might also encourage some PACs and wealthy individuals to contribute to challengers, although most would likely continue to employ access or mixed strategies, which dictate contributing primarily to incumbents.

Free or subsidized mailings would give candidates opportunities to present targeted, detailed information about their qualifications, issue positions, and political objectives. Giving congressional candidates free postage for three or four first-class mailings—including postage for one or two newsletters of six to ten pages—is a simple reform that would improve the quality of the information that voters receive and increase voter turnout and electoral competitiveness.

Parties should also be offered free postage to mobilize current supporters and attract new ones. Minor parties and their candidates, as well as candidates who run as independents, could be given free postage if they persuaded a threshold number of voters to register under their label prior to the current election or if their candidates had received a minimum number of votes in the previous contest. Minor parties and their candidates and independent candidates could also be reimbursed retroactively for postage if they reached some threshold level of votes in the current election. Extending free postage to candidates and parties is justified by the fact that it would contribute to the education of citizens—the same argument that is used to justify congressionally franked mail and reduced postage for party committees and nonprofit educational groups.

Giving candidates access to radio and television broadcast time would be more complicated because of disparities in rate charges and because congressional districts and media markets often do not match one another.[30] One solution is to require local broadcasters to provide Senate candidates with free television time and to require local radio stations to give free radio time to both House and Senate candidates. Congress could require broadcasters to issue back-to-back, prime-time segments to opposing candidates. Candidates could be issued five-minute blocks of time early in the campaign season, which they could use to air "infomercials" similar to those that Ross Perot popularized during the 1992 presidential election. These time slots would be lengthy enough for candidates to communicate some information about their personal backgrounds, political qualifications, issue positions, and major campaign themes. Later in the campaign season, two- or one-minute time slots could be distributed so that candidates could reinforce the images and campaign themes they introduced earlier. Thirty- or fifteen-second time slots could be made available during the summation stage of the election for candidates to pull together their campaign messages and rally their supporters.

This system of structured, free media time would give candidates the opportunity to communicate positive, substantive messages. It would also encourage voters to compare those messages. The differences in requirements for each chamber reflect the fact that television is an efficient and heavily used medium in virtually all Senate elections but is less practical and less frequently used in House contests, especially those held in major metropolitan areas.

The Democratic and Republican national committees should also be given free blocks of television and radio time so that each can have the opportunity to remind voters of their party's accomplishments, philosophies, and objectives. Giving parties resources they can use to influence the national political agenda during (and after) an election could introduce more collective responsibility into the political system.[31] Minor parties and candidates should be given free broadcast time on terms similar to those for free postage.

Requiring local broadcasters to provide free political advertisements is justifiable because the airwaves are public property and one of the conditions of using them is that broadcasters "serve the public interest, convenience, and necessity."[32] The United States is the only major industrialized democracy that does not require broadcasters to contribute air time to candidates for public office—a distinction that should be eliminated.[33] Cable television operators should also be required to distribute advertising time to House and Senate candidates and parties with the justification that much of what is viewed on cable television passes through the public airwaves or over publicly maintained utility poles.

An alternative to providing candidates and parties with communications resources is government distribution of communications vouchers. This practice would allow campaigners to exercise more freedom in designing their communication strategies. Campaigns that felt the need to allocate more resources to setting the agenda could use their vouchers to purchase mass media ads. Campaigns that wished to focus on mobilizing specific population groups could devote a greater portion of their vouchers to targeted direct mail or telephone calls. One of the trade-offs of the voucher option is that it imposes fewer costs on broadcasters and greater costs on taxpayers. One way to ease the burden on the public treasury would be to require all radio, television, and cable companies to sell candidates and parties prime-time advertising space at highly discounted rates.[34] Another way to lessen the onus of campaign costs on taxpayers would be to require all candidates who accept communications vouchers to turn over any portion of their campaign treasury that remained after the election to a federal election campaign fund that would be used to help provide vouchers in the next election.[35]

The preceding proposals would not provide communications resources to primary candidates or general election contestants from parties lacking widespread political support. This denial would serve as both a cost-saving measure and a way to discourage the declaration of trivial candidacies. Reforms that placed free or subsidized communications resources at the disposal of candidates and parties would potentially reduce the importance of money in politics as well as lower campaign costs and increase the competitiveness of congressional elections.

Contributions and Coordinated Expenditures

The amounts that individuals and groups can contribute to campaigns should be reviewed periodically in light of the roles that each set of contributors plays in the electoral process. The limits on individual contributions to candidates should be raised to $3,600 for the primary and the same amount for the general election to account for inflation and increases in campaign costs that have taken place since the limits were first set in 1974. PAC contributions should be raised to $12,000 for each phase of the election—a sum that reflects inflation and increased campaign costs but takes into consideration public skepticism about PAC money. The aggregate limit for individual contributions to all federal candidates and party committees and PACs that participate in federal elections should be raised from $25,000 to $90,000 per year to match the rate of inflation. This change would increase the amount of hard money that parties spend in federal elections without greatly increasing the influence of wealthy individuals on any one congressional race. These changes, which should be coupled with limits on the contribution of soft money, would encourage wealthy individuals and groups to increase their hard money contributions.

Expenditures by House and Senate candidates' campaign organizations should remain unlimited, unless large communications subsidies are made available to them. Money is essential to communicating with voters under the current cash-based campaign system. Spending limits could reduce the communications that candidates have with citizens, deprive voters of the information they need to cast informed ballots, and increase the influence of interest groups, parties, and the media. Independent expenditures and issue advocacy ads financed by wealthy individuals, parties, PACs, corporations, unions, and other groups are no substitute for the unfiltered communications that candidates disseminate to voters. The same is true of field activities carried out by party committees and news stories published in local newspapers or over the airwaves.

Party coordinated expenditures on behalf of candidates should be increased twofold from current levels to account for increased campaign costs and to allow party organizations to play a bigger role in congressional elections. Increasing the level of party hard money activity in elections could enhance their competitiveness because parties strive to focus most of their resources on close contests, including those of challengers. Greater party expenditures would indirectly affect the competitiveness of some campaigns in that they would help candidates attract resources and attention from other contributors and the press. By enabling parties to pledge more support to potential candidates, this reform could help the parties to encourage strategic politicians who are undecided about entering a race for Congress to decide in favor of running. Reforms that make it easier for parties to raise hard money and increase the amount of hard money they can spend in individual elections should be accompanied by reforms that limit the amounts of soft money that parties and interest groups can spend in those elections.

Candidate Contributions and Incumbent War Chests

The amounts that candidates can contribute to their own campaigns or carry over from previous elections should be limited. If, because of constitutional challenges, limits cannot be imposed, the impact of these resources should be minimized. Personal funds and existing war chests give incumbents and millionaires great advantages in congressional elections, not the least of which is discouraging talented potential opponents from running against them. These funds should be limited by offering candidates who adhere to ceilings of $150,000 access to subsidized campaign resources. In addition, a challenger who faces an incumbent with a huge existing war chest or any candidate who faces an opponent who makes personal contributions to his or her own campaign in excess of $150,000 should be allowed to raise contributions from individuals, parties, and PACs that are twice as large as normally allowed.

Tax Incentives

Tax incentives should be used to broaden the base of campaign contributors and to offset the impact of funds collected from wealthy and well-organized segments of society. Prior to the tax reforms introduced in 1986, individuals were able to claim a tax credit of $50 if they contributed $100 or more to federal candidates. (Couples who contributed $200 could claim a tax credit of $100.) Although a significant number of taxpayers took advantage of these credits, the credits themselves were not sufficient to encourage many citizens to give campaign contributions.[36]

A system of graduated tax credits similar to those used in some other Western democracies might accomplish this goal.[37] Individuals who are eligible to claim a 100 percent tax credit for up to $100 in campaign contributions would be more likely to make them. Credits of 75 percent for the next $100 and 50 percent for the following $100 would encourage further contributions. Tax credits would encourage candidates and parties to pursue small contributions more aggressively and would increase the number of taxpayers who give them. Using taxpayer dollars to increase the number of individuals who give money to federal candidates is an expensive proposition, but it would probably be the most effective way to increase the number of people who participate in the financing of congressional elections. Increasing the base of small contributors is the best way to offset the influence of individuals and groups that make large contributions while maintaining a tie between a candidate's level of popular and financial support.

Soft Money

Soft money contributions and expenditures need to be better regulated. Individuals and groups should be allowed to continue to make soft money contributions, but a ceiling of $75,000 (somewhat less than the proposed hard money limit) should be set on the amounts raised from any one source by party organizations that make expenditures designed to influence federal elections. This ceiling would enable party committees to continue to spend soft money while forcing them to broaden their base of soft money donors. So the public can be more fully apprised of soft money campaign activities, disclosure rules should be changed to require that all funds spent to directly or indirectly influence federal elections, including all soft money, be reported to the FEC. This change would bring party soft money directly under the FECA's regulatory umbrella.

Party soft money expenditures should be limited to party-building efforts, grass-roots efforts, and generic campaign advertising. Voter mobilization and election agenda setting are activities that parties have traditionally financed with soft money. These activities are important for several reasons. First, they contribute to the competitiveness of elections. Second, they register and mobilize new voters, unlike candidate voter mobilization efforts, which mainly target citizens who have a previous voting history.[38] Third, they stimulate local political activism, thereby strengthening state and local party organizations and improving the farm teams from which congressional candidates emerge. Fourth, they help build bridges among elected officials who serve in different branches and levels of government. And fifth, they encourage voters to discern differences between the parties and to reward or punish politicians for their performance in office or the substance of their platforms.

Parties should be prohibited from spending soft money on television, radio, and direct-mail issue advocacy advertisements that include the names or likenesses of federal candidates. These are not traditional party activities. The very fact that an ad makes a direct reference to one or more federal candidates is justification for classifying it as a federal election activity that should be regulated under federal campaign finance law.

Interest group soft money expenditures have become too important in congressional elections to ignore. Barring an outright ban on interest group expenditures intended to influence federal elections, a ceiling should be placed on the amount of soft money that interest groups can spend in a given state, depending on the size of its population. Interest groups, like parties, should also be banned from spending soft money on issue advocacy ads that directly name or present the likeness of a federal candidate. Interest groups that claim tax-exempt status should be prohibited from engaging in any election-related activities; those that do not comply should be stripped of their tax-exempt status.

Given recent Supreme Court rulings, it would take a constitutional amendment to ban election-related interest group soft money expenditures, but Congress ought to attempt to alter the tax code to discourage the formation of the groups that make these expenditures. Privately run, nonparty groups and their backers are currently the least regulated organizations in congressional elections, and they are not subject to the same kind of public accountability or institutional checks as are parties, PACs, and candidates. At a minimum, Congress should require interest groups that engage in any election-related spending to detail the substance of their political activities, including issue advocacy, to both the FEC and the Internal Revenue Service.

The Federal Election Commission

The Federal Election Commission should be strengthened. The commission is currently unable to investigate many of the complaints brought before it, has a backlog of cases that is several years old, and has been criticized for its failure to dispense quickly with frivolous cases and pursue more important ones. Some of these shortcomings are caused by the fact that it is often micromanaged by its oversight committees in Congress and is severely underfunded. Other short-comings are due to the FEC's structure—it has three Democratic and three Republican commissioners—which lends itself to indecision and stalemate.

It is essential that the FEC be restructured so that it operates in a more decisive fashion. Only strong enforcement by the FEC, with backup from the Justice Department and a specially appointed independent counsel on appropriate cases, can discourage unscrupulous politicians from violating the law. Recent failures by the FEC to enforce the law adequately have encouraged members of Congress to spend tens of millions of dollars on partisan investigations. Such investigations, which may be useful for embarrassing political opponents, are an inadequate substitute for the fair and impartial administration of the law.

Voter Turnout Initiatives

Campaign reform should address low voter turnout in elections. Citizen apathy and disenchantment with the political system are probably responsible for some voter abstention, but voter registration laws are believed to depress turnout by about 9 percent.[39] The motor-voter law, enacted in 1993, has eased some barriers to voter registration. Requiring all states to include a check-off box on their income tax forms to enable citizens to register to vote when they file their tax returns could further reduce the barriers to voting.

Measures that make it easier for voters to exercise the franchise should also be considered. Making election day a national holiday is one possibility. Making wider use of mail-in ballots, such as those Oregon used for its 1996 Senate special election, is another. "Early," "countywide," and "mobile" voting procedures should also be considered. Such procedures currently allow voters in Texas to cast their ballots over a seventeen-day period commencing twenty days before an election at any of the numerous locations in the county in which they are registered to vote. These locations include mobile units that are dispatched to parks and other popular locations on weekends. It also might be possible to allow people to vote by telephone or via the Internet. Measures that make it easier to register to vote or cast a ballot will not cause a groundswell in voter turnout, but they should increase it, especially when combined with increased competition and greater efforts by candidates and parties to mobilize voters.[40]

PROSPECTS FOR REFORM

It would not be easy to enact legislation that improves the quality of candidates for Congress, enhances the ability of candidates—especially nonincumbents—to communicate with voters, and enables campaigns to turn out more of their supporters. Campaign reform is a highly charged issue. Candidates and parties often portray themselves as reformers while advocating changes that reflect their own self-interest. Incumbents are preoccupied with protecting elements of the system that benefit them. Challengers are just as vocal about doing away with those advantages, at least until they become incumbents. Republicans advocate an increase in existing limits on party spending, which would enable them to take advantage of their party's superior fund-raising prowess. Democrats are more favorably disposed toward public subsidies coupled with spending limits, which would reduce the Republicans' financial advantages.

Interchamber differences in regard to reform also exist, with some senators advocating the elimination of PAC contributions and House members defending PACs. These differences reflect the greater dependence of members of the lower chamber on PAC funds. Other differences of opinion reflect the demands that campaigning makes on different kinds of candidates from varied districts. Women, African Americans, ethnic minorities, and members of other traditionally underrepresented groups, who depend on national donor networks, have preferences that differ from those of most white male candidates. Candidates' opinions about campaign reform also vary according to the characteristics of their constituencies. Candidates from wealthy urban seats tend to have fund-raising opportunities, spending needs, and views on reform different from those from poor rural states or districts. Of course, not all differences are grounded in personal or partisan advantage. Philosophical differences also divide politicians and parties.

The diversity of views and the complexity of the issue make it difficult to find the common ground needed to pass meaningful campaign reform. The sometimes questionable recommendations and inflammatory public relations campaigns of reform groups have made it difficult for members of Congress to move beyond public posturing and engage in serious reform efforts. Since the late 1970s House members and senators of both parties have introduced comprehensive packages that they knew would never be adopted by their respective chambers, survive a conference committee, and be signed into law by the president. Their efforts have been geared largely to providing political cover for themselves rather than to enacting campaign finance reform.

Members of the 105th Congress introduced 135 campaign finance reform bills, most of which were all but ignored after they were introduced.[41] As of October 1999, members of the 106th Congress had introduced 48. The two bills that received the most serious consideration were House Resolution 417, cosponsored by Reps. Christopher Shays, R-Conn., and Martin Meehan, D-Mass., and Senate Resolution 1593, cosponsored by Sens. John McCain, R-Ariz., and Russell Feingold, D-Wis.[42] Versions of both of these bills had been defeated by earlier Congresses. The Shays-Meehan bill passed in the House by a vote of 252-177. The McCain-Feingold measure took a more tortuous and, ultimately, less successful course. When its sponsors realized that the first version of the bill (S. 26), which had been introduced in the 105th Congress and was similar to the Shays-Meehan measure, had no chance of passage in the Senate, they stripped it of all provisions except those dealing with party soft money and amended it to add disclosure requirements. Despite the bill's bare bones approach, its opponents, led by NRSC chairman Mitch McConnell, R-Ky., and Senate Majority Leader Trent Lott, R-Miss., defeated it with a filibuster. Its supporters, including many long-term congressional aides who specialize in campaign finance issues, believe the House bill passed because members knew its companion bill in the Senate would fail. Both bills attracted a great deal of national attention and provided the foundation for other campaign finance reform legislation that was considered in the 106th Congress.

The Shays-Meehan bill primarily aimed to reduce the flow of soft money in federal elections. Its major soft money provisions would have banned national parties from raising, spending, transferring, or directing the flow of soft money; prevented state and local parties from spending soft money in federal elections or raising federal funds with soft money; and prohibited federal candidates, state officials, or their PACs from raising or spending soft money in connection with federal elections. The provisions on issue advocacy would have required the disclosure of significant issue advocacy spending and expanded the definition of issue advocacy ads to include communications that identify a federal candidate within sixty days of a general election. The provisions on independent expenditures would have tightened the definitions of independent and coordinated spending and prohibited an organization from making both types of expenditures for a single candidate.

The bills' other major provisions would have banned the solicitation or receipt of direct or indirect contributions, including soft money, from foreign nationals in connection with any U.S. election or political party; disallowed party coordinated expenditures for congressional candidates who do not abide by a $50,000 limit on personal and family funds and loans to their own campaigns; and prevented minors from making contributions to candidates or parties.[43]

The sponsors of these bills learned lessons that served them well in the battle over campaign finance legislation. They shunned comprehensive packages in favor of a somewhat narrower approach to reform. Previous bills had included provisions for public funding or free media, spending caps for candidates, bans on leadership PACs, bans on all PACs, requirements for in-state or in-district contributions, or provisions eliminating all contribution limits. Although some of these measures have the potential to improve the financing and conduct of congressional elections, members of Congress have repeatedly balked at supporting comprehensive approaches to campaign finance reform. Nevertheless, it may be that the McCain-Feingold and Shays-Meehan bills still were not focused enough and that an even less aggressive approach to reform is needed. More progress can probably be made if Congress first enacts changes that enjoy widespread support, such as banning foreign contributions, and then works to build bipartisan coalitions on the less consensual issues. Incrementalism offers the additional advantage of enabling Congress to adjust the law to offset the unintended consequences that routinely emerge as the result of regulatory change.

Reform often occurs in response to the public outcry for change that follows a major political scandal. The Federal Election Campaign Act of 1974, the most important piece of campaign finance legislation enacted in American history, was passed after the Watergate scandal focused public attention on the break-in at Democratic National Committee headquarters and the financing of presidential elections. The Keating Five, House Post Office, and House banking scandals and the general frustrations that many Americans vented at the 103rd and 104th Congresses did not generate enough pressure to result in reform. Public disapproval of campaign contributions made by foreign interests fell short of inspiring both the 105th and 106th Congresses to enact campaign finance reform legislation. Feingold's strategy of injecting into Senate debates on legislation favored by interest groups the amounts those groups have contributed to candidates and parties is a novel way to call attention to the role of money in politics, but it is more likely to anger some of his colleagues than to result in reform.[44]

Moreover, a massive overhaul in the campaign finance system will not serve as a panacea for the nation's problems. Campaign finance reform may improve elections, but it will not remedy other shortcomings in the political system. Reform is an ongoing process that requires continuous vigilance. Many politicians, party officials, and interest group leaders discovered avenues for campaign spending that bypassed the contribution and spending limits imposed by the FECA; they or others will undoubtedly find new ways to circumvent future campaign reforms.

CONCLUSION

The rules and norms that govern congressional elections resemble those that structure any activity: they favor some individuals and groups over others. In recent years the number of Americans who believe that the electoral process is out of balance and provides too many advantages to incumbents, interest groups, wealthy individuals, and other "insiders" has grown tremendously. Their views are reflected in the growing distrust that citizens have of government, the sense of powerlessness expressed by many voters, and the public's willingness to follow the leads of insurgent candidates and reformers without scrutinizing their qualifications or objectives. These are signs that the prestige and power of Congress are in danger. They are also signs that meaningful campaign reform is in order.

Campaign reform should make congressional elections more competitive and increase the number of citizens who participate in them, both as voters and as financial contributors. Campaign reform should enable candidates to spend less time campaigning for resources and more time campaigning for votes. Reform should also seek to enhance representation, accountability, and trust in government. The campaign finance reform legislation that has been debated by Congress during the last few years would succeed in accomplishing some, but not all, of these goals.

Without major campaign reform, incumbency will remain the defining element of most congressional elections. Challengers, particularly those who run for the House, will continue to struggle to raise campaign funds and attract the attention of the media and voters. The dialogue that occurs in House incumbent-challenger contests will remain largely one-sided, whereas that in open-seat contests and Senate races will continue to be somewhat more even. Huge sums of soft money that are intended to influence the outcomes of congressional elections will continue to flow outside the federal campaign finance system and, in some cases, overshadow the election activities of candidates. Congress, elections, and other institutions of government will remain targets for attack both by those who have a sincere wish to improve the political process and by those seeking short-term partisan gain.

Elections are the most important avenues of political influence that are afforded to the citizens of a representative democracy. They give voters the opportunity to hold public officials accountable and to reject politicians with whom they disagree. Respect for human rights and political processes that allow for citizen input are what make democratic systems of government superior to others. Yet all systems of government have their imperfections, and some of these are embodied in their electoral processes. There are times when these imperfections are significant enough to warrant major change. Such change should bring the electoral process closer in line with broadly supported notions of liberty, equality, and democracy as well as with the other values that bind the nation. The current state of congressional elections, and campaign finance in particular, demonstrates that change is warranted in the way in which Americans elect those who serve in Congress.

Notes

INTRODUCTION

1. Abraham Lincoln, Gettysburg Address.

1. THE STRATEGIC CONTEXT

1. Thomas A. Kazee, "The Emergence of Congressional Candidates," in *Who Runs for Congress? Ambition, Context, and Candidate Emergence,* ed. Thomas A. Kazee (Washington, D.C.: Congressional Quarterly, 1994), 1–14; L. Sandy Maisel, Linda L. Fowler, Ruth S. Jones, and Walter J. Stone, "Nomination Politics: The Roles of Institutional, Contextual, and Personal Variables," in *The Parties Respond: Changes in the American Party System,* 2d ed., ed. L. Sandy Maisel (Boulder, Colo.: Westview Press, 1994), 145–168.

2. Leon D. Epstein, *Political Parties in Western Democracies* (New York: Praeger, 1967), chap. 8.

3. James G. Gimpel, *Fulfilling the Contract: The First 100 Days* (Boston: Allyn and Bacon, 1996); Robin Kolodny, "The Contract with America in the 104th Congress," in *The State of the Parties,* ed. John C. Green and Daniel M. Shea (Lanham, Md.: Rowman and Littlefield, 1996), 314–327.

4. Kenneth Martis, *The Historical Atlas of U.S. Congressional Districts, 1789–1983* (New York: Free Press, 1982), 5–6.

5. See, for example, Frank J. Sorauf, "Political Parties and Political Action Committees: Two Life Cycles," *Arizona Law Review* 22 (1980): 445–464.

6. Jerrold B. Rusk, "The Effect of the Australian Ballot Reform on Split Ticket Voting: 1876–1908," *American Political Science Review* 64 (1970): 1220–1283.

7. See, for example, V. O. Key, *Politics, Parties, and Pressure Groups* (New York: Thomas Y. Crowell, 1964), 371.

8. Ibid., 389–391.

9. Committee on Political Parties, American Political Science Association, "Toward a More Responsible Two-Party System," *American Political Science Association,* supp. 44 (1950): 21.

10. The FECA's predecessor, enacted in 1971, had little effect on congressional elections. For an overview of the FECA and the campaign finance system that existed prior to it, see Herbert E. Alexander, *Financing Politics: Money, Elections, and Political Reform* (Washington, D.C.: CQ Press, 1992), esp. chaps. 2 and 3. For more recent coverage of the law, see Anthony Corrado, Thomas E. Mann, Daniel

R. Ortiz, Trevor Potter, and Frank J. Sorauf, eds., *Campaign Finance Reform: A Sourcebook* (Washington, D.C.: Brookings Institution, 1997).

11. The only subsidy the FECA gives to the parties is a grant to pay for their presidential nominating conventions. As nonprofit organizations, the parties also receive a discount for bulk postage.

12. Karl-Heinz Nassmacher, "Comparing Party and Campaign Finance in Western Democracies," in *Campaign and Party Finance in North America and Western Europe,* ed. Arthur B. Gunlicks (Boulder, Colo.: Westview Press, 1993), 233–263.

13. Arthur B. Gunlicks, "Introduction," in *Campaign and Party Finance,* 6.

14. Sorauf, "Political Parties and Political Action Committees," 445–464.

15. Paul S. Herrnson, *Party Campaigning in the 1980s* (Cambridge, Mass.: Harvard University Press, 1988), 82.

16. The term *soft money* was coined by Elizabeth Drew in *Politics and Money: The New Road to Corruption* (New York: Macmillan, 1983), esp. 15. See also Herbert E. Alexander and Anthony Corrado, *Financing the 1994 Election* (Armonk, N.Y.: M. E. Sharpe, 1995), chap. 6.; Robert Biersack, "The Nationalization of Party Finance," in *The State of the Parties,* 108–124.

17. Federal Election Commission, "FEC Reports on Political Party Activity for 1997–98," press release, April 9, 1999.

18. Figures compiled from Jeffrey D. Stanger and Douglas G. Rivlin, *Issue Advocacy Advertising During the 1997–1998 Election Cycle* (Philadelphia, Pa.: Annenberg Public Policy Center, 1998), 2.

19. See Anthony Corrado, *Creative Campaigning: PACs and the Presidential Selection Process* (Boulder, Colo.: Westview Press, 1992), 80–84.

20. Charles R. Babcock, "Use of Tax-Exempt Groups Integral to Political Strategy," *Washington Post,* January 7, 1997; Rebecca Carr, "Tax-Exempt Groups Scrutinized as Fundraising Clout Grows," *Congressional Quarterly Weekly Report,* February 22, 1997; and Charles R. Babcock and Ruth Marcus, "For Their Targets, Mystery Groups' Ads Hit Like Attacks from Nowhere," *Washington Post,* March 9, 1997.

21. *FEC v. Massachusetts Citizens for Life, Inc.,* 479 U.S. 248 (1986); *Colorado Republican Federal Campaign Committee v. FEC,* 116 S.Ct. 2309 (1996).

22. As is explained in Chapter 4, the FEC has ruled that a portion of the party money that is spent on issue advocacy must be hard money.

23. Paul S. Herrnson and Diana Dwyre, "Party Issue Advocacy in Congressional Elections," in *The State of the Parties,* 3d ed., ed. John C. Green and Daniel M. Shea (Lanham, Md.: University Press of America, 1999), 86–104.

24. Louis Hartz, *The Liberal Tradition in America* (New York: Harcourt, Brace, 1955).

25. See, for example, Robert A. Dahl, *Democracy in the United States: Promise and Performance* (Chicago: Rand McNally, 1967), 252; Herbert McClosky and John Zaller, *The American Ethos: Public Attitudes toward Democracy* (Cambridge: Harvard University Press, 1984), 62–100.

26. See Rusk, "The Effect of the Australian Ballot."

27. Key, *Politics, Parties, and Pressure Groups,* 342, 386; Nelson W. Polsby, *The Consequences of Party Reform* (Oxford: Oxford University Press, 1983), 72–74; William J. Crotty, *American Parties in Decline* (Boston: Little, Brown, 1984), 277–278.

28. Lee Ann Elliot, "Political Action Committees—Precincts of the '80s," *Arizona Law Review* 22 (1980): 539–554; Kay Lehman Schlozman and John T. Tierney, *Organized Interests and American Democracy* (New York: Harper and Row, 1986), 75–78.

29. John R. Petrocik, *Party Coalitions: Realignments and the Decline of the New Deal Party System* (Chicago: University of Chicago Press, 1981), chaps. 8 and 9; Paul Allen Beck, "A Socialization Theory of Partisan Realignment," in *Controversies in American Voting Behavior,* ed. Richard G. Niemi and Herbert F. Weisberg (Washington, D.C.: CQ Press, 1984), 396–411; Martin P. Wattenberg, *The Decline of American Political Parties, 1952–1988* (Cambridge: Harvard University Press, 1990), chap. 4.

30. Austin Ranney, *Channels of Power: The Impact of Television on American Politics* (New York: Basic Books, 1983), 110; Doris Graber, *Mass Media and American Politics,* 4th ed. (Washington, D.C.: CQ Press, 1993), 250–252.

31. Jack Dennis, "Support for the Party System by the Mass Public," *American Political Science Review* 60 (1966): 605.

32. CBS News/*New York Times* poll, October 1986, cited in Bruce E. Keith, David B. Magleby, Candice J. Nelson, Elizabeth Orr, Mark C. Westlye, and Raymond E. Wolfinger, *The Myth of the Independent Voter* (Berkeley: University of California Press, 1992), 8.

33. This group includes independents who "lean" toward one of the parties. Figures for party identification and voting behavior are compiled from Virginia Sapiro, Stephen J. Rosenstone, and National Election Studies, *American National Election Study, 1998: Post-Election Survey* (Ann Arbor: University of Michigan, 1999).

34. Sorauf, "Political Parties and Political Action Committees," 447.

35. Robert Agranoff, "Introduction/The New Style of Campaigning," in *The New Style in Election Campaigns,* ed. Robert Agranoff (Boston: Holbrook Press, 1972), 3–50; Larry J. Sabato, *The Rise of the Political Consultants: New Ways of Winning Elections* (New York: Basic Books, 1981).

36. See Ranney, *Channels of Power,* 110; and Graber, *Mass Media,* 250.

37. Agranoff, "Introduction/The New Style of Campaigning."

38. Sorauf, "Political Parties and Political Action Committees."

39. Cornelius P. Cotter and John F. Bibby, "Institutional Development and the Thesis of Party Decline," *Political Science Quarterly* 95 (1980): 1–27; David Adamany, "Political Parties in the 1980s," in *Money and Politics in the United States: Financing Elections in the 1980s,* ed. Michael J. Malbin (Washington, D.C.: American Enterprise Institute, 1984), 70–121; Herrnson, *Party Campaigning,* chaps. 3 and 4; Stephen E. Frantzich, *Political Parties in the Technological Age* (New York: Longman, 1989), 81–90, 182–186.

40. Norman J. Ornstein, Thomas E. Mann, and Michael J. Malbin, *Vital Statistics on Congress, 1997–1998* (Washington, D.C.: Congressional Quarterly, 1998), table 2-8 and various issues of *Congressional Quarterly Weekly Report.*

41. Another four House Democrats lost in primaries in 1994.

42. See, for example, Key, *Politics, Parties, and Pressure Groups,* 421.

43. David R. Butler and Bruce Cain, *Congressional Redistricting: Comparative and Theoretical Perspectives* (New York: Macmillan, 1992), 10, 87; Michael Lyons and Peter F. Galdersi, "Incumbency, Reapportionment, and U.S. House Redistricting," *Political Review Quarterly* 49 (1995): 857–873. For another view, see Richard Niemi and Alan I. Abramowitz, "Partisan Redistricting and the 1992 Elections," *Journal of Politics* 56 (1994): 811–817.

44. David R. Mayhew, *Congress: The Electoral Connection* (New Haven, Conn.: Yale University Press, 1974); Morris P. Fiorina, *Congress: Keystone of the Washington Establishment* (New Haven, Conn.: Yale University Press, 1978), 19–21, 41–49, 56–62; Diane E. Yiannakis, "The Grateful Electorate: Casework and Congressional Elections," *American Journal of Political Science* 25 (1981): 568–580; Bruce Cain, John Ferejohn, and Morris Fiorina, *The Personal Vote* (Cambridge: Harvard University Press, 1987), 103–106; Gary C. Jacobson, *The Politics of Congressional Elections,* 4th ed. (New York: Longman, 1997), 28–33; George Serra and Albert Cover, "The Electoral Consequences of Perquisite Use: The Casework Case," *Legislative Studies Quarterly* 17 (1992): 233–246.

45. Harrison W. Fox and Susan Webb Hammond, *Congressional Staffs: The Invisible Force in American Lawmaking* (New York: Free Press, 1977), 88–99, 154–155.

46. Herrnson, *Party Campaigning,* chap. 4; Frank J. Sorauf, *Inside Campaign Finance* (New Haven, Conn.: Yale University Press, 1992), 80–84.

47. Donald Ostdiek, "Congressional Redistricting and District Typologies," *Journal of Politics* 57 (1995): 533–543.

48. Bruce I. Oppenheimer, James A. Stimson, and Richard W. Waterman, "Interpreting U.S. Con-

gressional Elections: The Exposure Thesis," *Legislative Studies Quarterly* 11 (1986): 227–247; James E. Campbell, "The Presidential Surge and Its Midterm Decline in Congressional Elections, 1868–1988," *Journal of Politics* 53 (1991): 478–487.

49. Michael S. Lewis-Beck and Tom W. Rice, *Forecasting Elections* (Washington, D.C.: CQ Press, 1992), chaps. 4–6.

50. Jerome M. Clubb, William H. Flanigan, and Nancy H. Zingale, *Partisan Realignment: Voters, Parties, and Government in American History* (Beverly Hills, Calif.: Sage Publications, 1980), 258–260.

51. On coattail effects see esp. Walter Dean Burnham, "Insulation and Responsiveness in Congressional Elections," *Political Science Quarterly* 90 (1975): 411–435; Randall L. Calvert and John A. Ferejohn, "Coattail Voting in Recent Presidential Elections," *American Political Science Review* 77 (1983): 407–419; Richard Born, "Reassessing the Decline of Presidential Coattails: U.S. House Elections, 1952–1980," *Journal of Politics* 46 (1980): 60–79; James E. Campbell, "Predicting Seat Gains from Presidential Coattails," *American Journal of Political Science* 30 (1986): 397–418; Gary C. Jacobson, *Electoral Origins of Divided Government, 1946–1988* (Boulder, Colo.: Westview Press, 1990), 80–81.

52. Edward R. Tufte, "Determinants of the Outcomes of Midterm Congressional Elections," *American Political Science Review* 69 (1975): 812–826; Lewis-Beck and Rice, *Forecasting Elections,* 60–75.

53. Morris P. Fiorina, *Retrospective Voting in American National Elections* (New Haven, Conn.: Yale University Press, 1981), 165; Eric M. Uslaner and M. Margaret Conway, "The Responsible Electorate: Watergate, the Economy, and Vote Choice in 1974," *American Political Science Review* 79 (1985): 788–803.

54. The Republicans picked up an additional five House and two Senate seats as a result of Democratic incumbents who switched parties following the 1994 election. The Democrats picked up another House seat in 1999, when Michael Forbes of New York switched parties.

55. Gerald Kramer, "Short-Term Fluctuations in U.S. Voting Behavior," *American Political Science Review* 65 (1971): 131–143; Gary C. Jacobson and Samuel Kernell, *Strategy and Choice in Congressional Elections* (New Haven, Conn.: Yale University Press, 1983), chap. 6; Jacobson, "Does the Economy Matter in Midterm Elections?" *American Journal of Political Science* 34 (1990): 400–404. For another interpretation see Robert S. Erikson, "Economic Conditions and the Vote: A Review of the Macro Level Evidence," *American Journal of Political Science* 34 (1990): 373–399.

56. John F. Bibby, *Parties, Politics, and Elections in America* (Chicago: Nelson Hall, 1987), 239–240.

57. Norman Nie and Kristi Andersen, "Mass Belief Systems Revisited: Political Change and Attitude Structure," *Journal of Politics* 36 (1974): 540–591; Crotty, *American Parties in Decline,* 49–50.

58. Richard A. Brody and Benjamin I. Page, "The Assessment of Policy Voting," *American Political Science Review* 66 (1972): 450–458; Norman H. Nie, Sidney Verba, John R. Petrocik, *The Changing American Voter* (New York: Twentieth Century Fund, 1979), esp. chap. 18.

59. *Thornburg v. Gingles,* 478 U.S. 30 (1986).

60. Richard F. Fenno Jr., *Home Style: House Members in Their Districts* (Boston: Little, Brown, 1978), 164–168.

61. The estimate for the savings and loan cleanup is from Barbara Miles and Thomas Woodward, "The Savings and Loan Cleanup: Background and Progress," CRS Issue Brief, Washington, D.C.: Library of Congress, updated March 10, 1994.

62. David B. Magleby, Kelly D. Patterson, and Stephen H. Wirls, "Fear and Loathing of the Modern Congress: The Public Manifestation of Constitutional Design" (paper presented at the annual meeting of the Midwest Political Science Association, Chicago, April 1994), 14–16; see also Gary C. Jacobson, "The 1994 House Elections in Perspective," in *Midterm: The Elections of 1994 in Context,* ed. Philip A. Klinkner (Boulder, Colo.: Westview Press, 1996); and John R. Hibbing and Elizabeth Theiss-Morse, *Congress as Public Enemy: Public Attitudes toward American Political Institutions* (Cambridge: Cambridge University Press, 1995), 31–33, 69–71, 96–100.

63. On the 1994 elections, see the essays in Klinkner, *Midterm.*

64. Gimpel, *Fulfilling the Contract.*

65. See Gary C. Jacobson, "Impeachment Politics in the 1998 Congressional Elections," *Political Science Quarterly* 114 (1999): 3–36.

66. Richard F. Fenno Jr., "If, as Ralph Nader Says, Congress Is 'the Broken Branch,' How Come We Love Our Congressmen So Much?" in *Congress in Change: Evolution and Reform,* ed. Norman J. Ornstein (New York: Praeger, 1975).

67. L. Sandy Maisel and Walter J. Stone, "Candidate Emergence Study: Report to Respondents," January 1998 (Web site: http://sobek.colorado.edu/CES/report_final.html).

68. Marc Fisher, "Who's Running for Congress? Who Cares?" *Washington Post,* October 27, 1998.

69. Twenty percent is an appropriate victory margin given the heightened level of uncertainty in contemporary congressional elections. A narrower margin, such as 15 percent, would have eliminated campaigns that were competitive for part of the election season but were ultimately decided by more than 15 percent of the vote. Slightly changing the boundaries for the competitiveness measure does not significantly change the results. For a fuller discussion of the classification scheme see the appendix to the first edition of this book.

70. Gary C. Jacobson, *The Politics of Congressional Elections,* 23–24.

2. CANDIDATES AND NOMINATIONS

1. E. E. Schattschneider, *Party Government* (New York: Holt, Rinehart, and Winston, 1942), 99–106.

2. Kazee, "The Emergence of Congressional Candidates"; Maisel et al., "Nomination Politics."

3. Joseph A. Schlesinger, *Ambition and Politics: Political Careers in the United States* (Chicago: Rand McNally, 1966), 11–12, 16–19, 198–199; Jacobson and Kernell, *Strategy and Choice in Congressional Elections,* chap. 3; William T. Bianco, "Strategic Decisions on Candidacy in U.S. Congressional Districts," *Legislative Studies Quarterly* 9 (1984): 360–362; Kazee, "The Emergence of Congressional Candidates"; David T. Canon, *Actors, Athletes, and Astronauts: Political Amateurs in the United States* (Chicago: University of Chicago Press, 1990), 76–79.

4. L. Sandy Maisel, Linda L. Fowler, Ruth S. Jones, and Walter J. Stone, "The Naming of Candidates: Recruitment or Emergence?" in *The Parties Respond: Changes in the American Party System,* 1st ed., ed. L. Sandy Maisel (Boulder, Colo.: Westview Press, 1990); Linda L. Fowler and Robert D. McClure, *Political Ambition: Who Decides to Run for Congress* (New Haven, Conn.: Yale University Press, 1989), 231.

5. Gary C. Jacobson and Samuel Kernell, "National Forces in the 1986 U.S. House Elections," *Legislative Studies Quarterly* 15 (1990): 65–87; Canon, *Actors, Athletes, and Astronauts,* 106–108.

6. See, for example, John Alford, Holly Teeters, Daniel S. Ward, and Rick Wilson, "Overdraft: The Political Cost of Congressional Malfeasance," *Journal of Politics* 56 (1994): 788–801.

7. Timothy Groseclose and Keith Krehbiel, "Golden Parachutes, Rubber Checks, and Strategic Retirements from the 102nd House," *American Journal of Political Science* 38 (1994): 75–99; Gary C. Jacobson and Michael Dimock, "Checking Out: The Effects of Bank Overdrafts on the 1992 House Election," *American Journal of Political Science* 38 (1994): 601–624.

8. See n. 3.

9. Mayhew, *Congress;* Fiorina, *Congress.* The value of a congressional allowance is calculated from Roger H. Davidson and Walter J. Oleszek, *Congress and Its Members,* 7th ed. (Washington, D.C.: CQ Press, 2000), 154.

10. See Fenno, *Home Style.*

11. Peverill Squire, "Preemptive Fundraising and Challenger Profile in Senate Elections," *Journal of Politics* 53 (1991): 1150–1164; Janet M. Box-Steffensmeier, "A Dynamic Analysis of the Role of War

Chests in Campaign Strategy," *American Journal of Political Science* 40 (1996): 352–371. But see Jonathan S. Krasno and Donald Philip Green, "Preempting Quality Challengers in House Elections," *Journal of Politics* 50 (1988): 920–936.

12. Sara Fritz and Dwight Morris, *Gold-Plated Politics: Running for Congress in the 1990s* (Washington, D.C.: Congressional Quarterly, 1992), esp. chap. 2.

13. On redistricting, see Richard G. Niemi and Laura R. Winsky, "The Persistence of Partisan Redistricting Effects in Congressional Elections, *Journal of Politics* 54 (1992): 565–571.

14. Stephen E. Frantzich, "De-Recruitment: The Other Side of the Congressional Equation," *Western Political Quarterly* 31 (1978): 105–126; Michael K. Moore and John R. Hibbing, "Is Serving in Congress Fun Again? Voluntary Retirements from the House Since the 1970s," *American Journal of Political Science* 36 (1992): 824–828; Eric M. Uslaner, *The Decline of Comity in Congress* (Ann Arbor: University of Michigan Press, 1993), esp. chap. 2.

15. Frantzich, "De-Recruitment," 105–126; Joseph Cooper and William West, "The Congressional Career in the 1970s," in *Congress Reconsidered*, ed. Lawrence Dodd and Bruce Oppenheimer (Washington, D.C.: CQ Press, 1981); and John R. Hibbing, "Voluntary Retirement from the U.S. House: The Costs of Legislative Service," *Legislative Studies Quarterly* 8 (1982): 57–74.

16. Another prominent Republican whose decision to retire in 1996 was influenced by his failure to gain a leadership position was Rep. Robert Walker, R-Pa., who finished a distant second in his bid to become majority whip.

17. Steven G. Livingston and Sally Friedman, "Reexamining Theories of Congressional Retirement: Evidence from the 1980s," *Legislative Studies Quarterly* 18 (1993): 231–254; John B. Gilmour and Paul Rothstein, "Early Republican Retirement: A Cause of Democratic Dominance in the House of Representatives," *Legislative Studies Quarterly* 18 (1993): 345–365; D. Roderick Kiewiet and Langche Zeng, "An Analysis of Congressional Career Decisions, 1947–1986," *American Political Science Review* (1993): 928–941; Richard L. Hall and Robert P. Van Houweling, "Avarice and Ambition in Congress: Representatives' Decisions to Run or Retire from the U.S. House," *American Political Science Review* 89 (1995): 121–136.

18. For a comprehensive assessment of these factors, see Canon, *Actors, Athletes, and Astronauts,* 103–110.

19. Some of the data used in Figures 2-2 through 2-6 and Tables 2-1 through 2-4 come from various editions of *Who's Who in American Politics* (New Providence, N.J.: Marquis Who's Who); *Who's Who among African Americans* (Detroit: Gale Research); "Election '96: Republican National Convention," *AsianWeek,* August 9–15, 1996; "Election '96: Democratic National Convention," *AsianWeek,* August 23–29, 1996; the Joint Center for Political and Economic Studies; and the National Association of Latino Elected and Appointed Officials.

20. On ambitious, policy, and experience-seeking or hopeless amateurs see Canon, *Actors, Athletes, and Astronauts,* xv, 26–32; and Canon, "Sacrificial Lambs or Strategic Politicians? Political Amateurs in U.S. House Elections," *American Journal of Political Science* 37 (1993): 1119–1141.

21. Jacobson and Kernell, *Strategy and Choice,* 94–96, 102.

22. Ibid., 77–78.

23. On the decision making of quality challengers, see Gary W. Cox and Jonathan N. Katz, "Why Did the Incumbency Advantage in U.S. House Elections Grow?" *American Journal of Political Science* 40 (1996): 478–497.

24. Throughout this chapter seats are categorized according to their status (open or incumbent-occupied) at the beginning of the election cycle. Seats that began the election cycle as incumbent-occupied but featured two nonincumbents in the general election are classified as open from Chapter 3 forward.

25. An exception to this rule occurs in Texas, where an individual can appear on the ballot for two offices simultaneously.

26. Harold D. Lasswell, *Power and Personality* (Boston: W. W. Norton, 1948), 39–41.

27. The generalizations that follow are drawn from responses to question 18 of the 1992 Congressional Campaign Study (see the appendix to the first edition of this book and the book's Web site: http://herrnson.cqpress.com). See also L. Sandy Maisel, *From Obscurity to Oblivion: Running in the Congressional Primary* (Knoxville: University of Tennessee Press, 1982), 31–32; Herrnson, *Party Campaigning,* 86; and Kazee, "The Emergence of Congressional Candidates."

28. Thomas A. Kazee and Mary C. Thornberry, "Where's the Party? Congressional Candidate Recruitment and American Party Organizations," *Western Political Quarterly* 43 (1990): 61–80; Steven H. Haeberle, "Closed Primaries and Party Support in Congress," *American Politics Quarterly* 13 (1985): 341–352.

29. Herrnson, *Party Campaigning,* 51–56.

30. See, for example, Fowler and McClure, *Political Ambition,* 205–207.

31. On WISH List, see Craig A. Rimmerman, "New Kids on the Block: Wish List and the Gay and Lesbian Victory Fund," in *Risky Business? PAC Decisionmaking in Congressional Elections,* ed. Robert Biersack, Paul S. Herrnson, and Clyde Wilcox (Armonk, N.Y.: M. E. Sharpe, 1994), 214–223; Mark J. Rozell, "WISH List: Pro-Choice Women in the Republican Congress," in *After the Revolution: PACs and Lobbies in the New Republican Congress,* ed. Robert Biersack, Paul S. Herrnson, and Clyde Wilcox (Boston: Allyn and Bacon, 1991), 184–191.

32. Phil P. Duncan and Brian Nutting, eds., *CQ's Politics in America 2000: The 106th Congress* (Washington, D.C.: Congressional Quarterly, 1999), 1336–1338.

33. Ibid.

34. Web site of Rep. Larry Combest, "Combest Biography" (Web site: http://www.house.gov/combest/bio.htm).

35. Fenno, *Home Style,* 176–189.

36. See Paul S. Herrnson, "National Party Organizations and the Postreform Congress," in *The Postreform Congress,* ed. Roger H. Davidson (New York: St. Martin's Press, 1992), 48–70.

37. Paul S. Herrnson and Robert M. Tennant, "Running for Congress under the Shadow of the Capitol Dome: The Race for Virginia's Eighth District," in *Who Runs for Congress?* 67–81.

38. Ibid., 73.

39. See, for example, Schlesinger, *Ambition and Politics,* 99; and Canon, *Actors, Athletes, and Astronauts,* 50–53, 56–58; L. Sandy Maisel, Elizabeth J. Irvy, Benjamin D. Ling, and Stephanie G. Pennix, "Re-exploring the Weak-Challenger Hypothesis: The 1994 Candidate Pools," in *Midterm;* L. Sandy Maisel, Walter J. Stone, and Cherie Maestas, "Reassessing the Definition of Quality Candidates" (paper presented at the annual meeting of the Midwest Political Science Association, Chicago, April 1999).

40. Philip P. Duncan and Christine C. Lawrence, eds., *CQ's Politics in America 1996: The 104th Congress* (Washington, D.C.: Congressional Quarterly, 1995), 183.

41. Rick Holguin and Gebe Martinez, "California Elections/Congress: Federal Probe is Central Issue as Four Challenge Kim," *Los Angeles Times,* May 31, 1994.

42. Duncan and Lawrence, *CQ's Politics in America 1996,* 183.

43. David Rosenzweig, "Kim Aide's Felony Conviction Changed to Misdemeanor," *Los Angeles Times,* October 7, 1997.

44. Duncan and Nutting, *CQ's Politics in America 2000,* 195.

45. Marc Birtel, "Changing Demographics Keep Orange County in Play," *CQ Weekly,* May 23, 1998, 1373.

46. Duncan and Nutting, *CQ's Politics in America 2000,* 195.

47. See Herrnson and Tennant, "Running for Congress."

48. Duncan and Nutting, *CQ's Politics in America 2000,* 1425.

49. This case study draws from David T. Canon and Paul S. Herrnson, "Professionalism, Progressivism, and People Power," in *Campaigns & Elections: Contemporary Case Studies,* ed. Michael A. Bailey, Ronald A. Faucheux, Paul S. Herrnson, and Clyde Wilcox (Washington, D.C.: CQ Press, 2000), 83–92.

50. Less than one-third of all individuals between eighteen and twenty-four years of age vote. See, for example, Paul R. Abramson, John H. Aldrich, and David W. Rohde, *Change and Continuity in the 1996 and 1998 Elections* (Washington, D.C.: CQ Press, 1999), 76.

51. Donald R. Matthews, "Legislative Recruitment and Legislative Careers," *Legislative Studies Quarterly* 9 (1984): 551.

52. Amy Keller, "The *Roll Call* Fifty Richest," *Roll Call*, January 18, 1999.

53. R. Darcy, Susan Welch, and Janet Clark, *Women, Elections, and Representation* (New York: Longman, 1987), 93–108.

54. Ibid., 138–140; Robert A. Bernstein, "Why Are There So Few Women in the House?" *Western Political Quarterly* 29 (1986): 155–164; Linda L. Fowler, *Candidates, Congress, and the American Democracy* (Ann Arbor: University of Michigan Press, 1993), 127–136.

55. Barbara Burrell, "Women Candidates in Open-Seat Primaries for the U.S. House: 1968–1990," *Legislative Studies Quarterly* 17 (1992): 493–508.

56. On the impact of religious participation on the development of political and civic skills, see Sidney Verba, Kay Lehman Schlozman, and Henry E. Brady, *Voice and Equality: Civic Voluntarism and American Politics* (Cambridge: Harvard University Press, 1995), 333.

57. On the effect of race on candidate selection, see Fowler, *Candidates, Congress, and the American Democracy,* 136–142.

58. Kevin A. Hill, "Does the Creation of Majority Black Districts Aid Republicans? An Analysis of the 1992 Congressional Elections in Eight Southern States," *Journal of Politics* 57 (1995): 384–401; Charles Cammeron, David Epstein, and Sharyn O'Halloran, "Do Majority-Minority Districts Maximize Substantive Black Representation in Congress?" *American Political Science Review* 90 (1996): 794–812.

59. Former representative Cleo Fields, who chose not to run in 1996 after his district was obliterated, was the only House member who had occupied a majority-minority district and was not re-elected. On racial redistricting, see David T. Canon, Matthew M. Schousen, and Patrick Sellers, "The Supply Side of Congressional Redistricting: Race and Strategic Politicians, 1972–1992," *Journal of Politics* 58 (1996): 846–862.

60. David T. Cannon, *Race, Redistricting, and Representation: The Unintended Consequences of Black Majority Districts* (Chicago: University of Chicago Press, 1999).

61. Amy Keller, "The *Roll Call* Fifty Richest," *Roll Call,* January 20, 1997.

62. Alan Ehrenhalt, *The United States of Ambition: Politicians, Power, and the Pursuit of Office* (New York: Random House, 1991), 225–226.

63. It should be noted that some members of Congress list more than one occupation. Percentages are compiled from Norman J. Ornstein, Thomas E. Mann, and Michael J. Malbin, *Vital Statistics on Congress, 1997–1998* (Washington, D.C.: Congressional Quarterly, 1998), Table 1-11, and various issues of *CQ Weekly.*

64. Compiled from Duncan and Nutting, *CQ's Politics in America 2000.*

65. Some senators had held more than one office. Compiled from Duncan and Nutting, *CQ's Politics in America 2000.*

66. See, for example, David Ian Lublin, "Quality, Not Quantity: Strategic Politicians in U.S. Senate Elections, 1952–1990," *Journal of Politics* 56 (1994): 228–241.

67. This generalization is drawn from responses to question 18 of the 1992 Congressional Campaign Study (see the appendix to the first edition of this book and the book's Web site: http://herrnson.cqpress.com).

3. THE ANATOMY OF A CAMPAIGN

1. See, for example, Edie N. Goldenberg and Michael W. Traugott, *Campaigning for Congress* (Washington, D.C.: CQ Press, 1984), 19–24.

2. Committee on Political Parties, "Toward a More Responsible Two-Party System"; Agranoff, "Introduction," 3–50; Sabato, *The Rise of the Political Consultants.*

3. James A. Thurber, Candice J. Nelson, David A. Dulio, "Political Consulting: A Portrait of the Industry" (paper presented at the annual meeting of the American Political Science Association, Boston, 1998); Bill Hamilton and Dave Beattie, "The Big Metamorphosis: How Campaigns Change Candidates," *Campaigns & Elections,* August 1999, 34–36.

4. The figure is for the 1992 elections. It includes office furniture, supplies, rent, salaries, taxes, bank fees, lawyers, accountants, telephone, automobile, computers, other office equipment, and food but excludes campaign travel. The Campaign Study Group (Web site: http://www.campaignstudygroup. com/spending/92House.htm).

5. Ibid. (Web site: http://www.campaignstudygroup.com/spending/1992House/mo03.htm).

6. There have been important exceptions to this generalization in recent years. See Canon, *Actors, Athletes, and Astronauts,* 3, 36.

7. 1998 Congressional Campaign Study (Web site: http://herrnson.cqpress.com [select "Methodological Appendix"]).

8. This finding supports Fenno's observation that the explanatory power of challenger quality and political experience is largely the result of the quality of the candidates' campaign organizations. See Richard F. Fenno Jr., *Senators on the Campaign Trail: The Politics of Representation* (Norman: University of Oklahoma Press, 1996), 100.

9. David Gilliard, Gilliard, Banning, and Associates, interview, August 12, 1999; Marcia Gilchrest, director of Representative Royce's district office, interview, August 11, 1999.

10. Asuncion "Cecy" R. Groom, candidate for Congress, interview, August 3, 1999.

11. Ibid.

12. Rep. David Price, interview, August 31, 1998.

13. Jean Louise Beard, finance director for the Price campaign, interviews, July 23, 1998, and July 14, 1999; and William Moore, chief of staff of Representative Price's congressional office, interview, July 14, 1999.

14. Ibid.

15. Thomas Roberg, candidate for Congress, interview, July 30, 1999.

16. Ibid.

17. Canon and Herrnson, "Professionalism, Progressivism, and People Power," 83–92.

18. The estimates are for budgetary allocations made during the campaign season. Studies that examine the money collected and spent over the course of an entire two-year House or six-year Senate election cycle report lower expenditures for voter contact and higher expenditures on overhead, research, and other activities that take place before the campaign season. See Fritz and Morris, *Gold-Plated Politics*; Goldenberg and Traugott, *Campaigning for Congress,* 85–92; Stephen Ansolabehere and Alan Gerber, "The Mismeasure of Campaign Spending: Evidence from the 1990 U.S. House Elections," *Journal of Politics* 56 (1994): 1106–1108.

19. Moore interview; Roberg interview.

20. Groom interview; Gilliard interview.

21. The Campaign Study Group (Web site: http://campaignstudygroup.com/spending/ 1998Senate/CALIFORNIA.htm).

22. Ibid.

4. THE PARTIES CAMPAIGN

1. Sorauf, "Political Parties and Political Action Committees," 447.

2. See, for example, Agranoff, "Introduction," 3–50.

3. Sorauf, "Political Parties and Political Action Committees"; Herrnson, *Party Campaigning*, chaps. 2 and 3.

4. Joseph A. Schlesinger, "The New American Political Party," *American Political Science Review* 79 (1985): 1151–1169; Paul S. Herrnson, "Political Leadership and Organizational Change at the National Committees," in *Politics, Professionalism, and Power*, ed. John Green (Lanham, Md.: University Press of America, 1993), 186–202.

5. Herrnson, *Party Campaigning*, chap. 2.

6. Paul S. Herrnson, Kelly D. Patterson, and John J. Pitney Jr., "From Ward Heelers to Public Relations Experts: The Parties' Response to Mass Politics," in *Broken Contract? Changing Relationships between Citizens and Government in the United States*, ed. Stephen C. Craig (Boulder, Colo.: Westview Press, 1996), 251–267.

7. Richard K. Armey, Jennifer Dunn, and Christopher Shays, *It's Long Enough: The Decline of Popular Government under Forty Years of Single Party Control of the U.S. House of Representatives* (Washington, D.C.: Republican Conference, U.S. House of Representatives, 1994). Richard K. Armey, *Under the Clinton Big Top: Policy, Politics, and Public Relations in the President's First Year* (Washington, D.C.: Republican Conference, U.S. House of Representatives, 1993).

8. Gimpel, *Fulfilling the Contract*; Kolodny, "The Contract with America in the 104th Congress."

9. Ceci Connolly and Howard Kurtz, "Gingrich Orchestrated Lewinsky Ads," *Washingon Post*, October 30, 1998.

10. Ed Brookover, political director, NRCC, interview, July 14, 1999.

11. The Republicans originally planned to spend $37 million on Operation Breakout, but they had to scale back the project because they did not meet their fund-raising goals. See Rep. John Linder, R-Ga., chairman, NRCC, "Operation Breakout," memorandum to Republican House members, August 5, 1998.

12. Other surveys, such as the American National Election Study, also show voters having a slight preference for traditional Democratic issues over Republican issues.

13. Even though the reports that candidates filed with the FEC indicate that some received large national committee contributions and coordinated expenditures, this spending is almost always dictated by a congressional or senatorial campaign committee's election strategy. As is explained later in this chapter, national committee spending in congressional elections is often the result of a "money swap."

14. The term *Hill committees* probably originates from the fact that the congressional and senatorial campaign committees were originally located in congressional office space on Capitol Hill.

15. These figures include "hard" dollars, which can be spent directly on individual federal campaigns, and soft money, which can be spent on issue advocacy advertisements, party building, and voter mobilization activities. See Federal Election Commission, "FEC Reports on Party Activity for 1997–98," press release, April 9, 1998.

16. Jim VandeHei, "NRCC Gets $25,000 Check, Sarcasm from Rep. Crane," *Roll Call*, October 8, 1998.

17. Figures compiled from Federal Election Commission data.

18. Prior to the 1992 elections, both the DCCC and the NRCC created redistricting divisions, which will probably be resurrected to help the committees focus on the decennial redrawing of House districts before the 2002 elections.

19. Gary C. Jacobson, "Party Organization and Campaign Resources in 1982," *Political Science Quarterly* 100 (1985–1986): 604–625.

20. Herrnson, "Political Leadership and Organizational Change"; Brooks Jackson, *Honest Graft: Big Money and the American Political Process* (New York: Alfred A. Knopf, 1988), 286–290; Robin Kolodny, *Pursuing Majorities: Congressional Campaign Committees in American Politics* (Norman: University of Oklahoma Press, 1998), 175–195.

21. Jacobson and Kernell, *Strategy and Choice in Congressional Elections,* 39–43, 76–84.

22. The information on committee strategy, decision making, and targeting is from numerous interviews conducted before, during, and after the 1992, 1994, 1996, and 1998 election cycles with several high-ranking officials of the congressional and senatorial campaign committees.

23. On the 1990 election, see Les Frances, "Commentary," in *Machine Politics, Sound Bites, and Nostalgia,* ed. Michael Margolis and John Green (Lanham, Md.: University Press of America), 58; on the 1994 election, see Paul S. Herrnson, "Money and Motives: Spending in House Elections," in *Congress Reconsidered,* 6th ed., ed. Lawrence C. Dodd and Bruce I. Oppenheimer (Washington, D.C.: CQ Press, 1996), 106–107; on the 1992 and 1996 elections, see previous editions of this book.

24. Brookover interview; Scott Douglas, deputy political director, NRCC, interview, October 7, 1998; Karen Johanson, political director, DCCC, interview, July 9, 1999.

25. Paul S. Herrnson, "Campaign Professionalism and Fundraising in Congressional Elections," *Journal of Politics* 54 (1992): 859–870.

26. Robert Biersack and Paul S. Herrnson, "Political Parties and the Year of the Woman," in *The Year of the Woman? Myths and Realities,* ed. Elizabeth Adell Cook, Sue Thomas, and Clyde Wilcox (Boulder, Colo.: Westview Press, 1994), 173–174.

27. Sen. Mitch McConnell, R-Ky., quoted on *Face the Nation,* November 1, 1998.

28. These are considered separate elections under the FECA. Party committees usually give contributions only to general election candidates.

29. The coordinated expenditure limit for states with only one House member was originally set at $20,000 and reached $65,100 in 1998.

30. Herrnson, *Party Campaigning,* 43–44.

31. Anthony Corrado, "The Politics of Cohesion: The Role of the National Party Committees in the 1992 Elections," in *The State of the Parties,* ed. John C. Green and Daniel M. Shea (Lanham, Md.: Rowman and Littlefield, 1996), 79–80; Diana Dwyre, "Spinning Straw into Gold: Soft Money and U.S. House Elections," *Legislative Studies Quarterly* 21 (1996): 411; James A. Barnes, "New Rules for the Money Game," *National Journal,* July 6, 1996.

32. John F. Bibby, "The New Party Machine: Information Technology in State Political Parties," in *The State of the Parties,* ed. John C. Green and Daniel M. Shea (New York: Rowman and Littlefield, 1999), 69–85.

33. Party committees can also give "in-kind" services in lieu of cash contributions; however, they are more likely to use the coordinated expenditure route.

34. Most of the contributions and coordinated expenditures made by state and local parties in connection with the 1998 Senate races were the result of money swaps.

35. John Mercurio, "Linder, Frost Both See Gains," *Roll Call,* July 30, 1998.

36. For data on the 1996 elections, see the second edition of this book, 81–83; for 1994 data, see Herrnson, "Money and Motives"; for 1992 data, see the first edition of this book, 84–86; for 1984 data, see Paul S. Herrnson, "National Party Decision Making, Strategies, and Resource Distribution in Congressional Elections," *Western Political Quarterly* 42 (1998): 301–323; for 1982 data, see Jacobson, "Party Organization and Campaign Resources in 1982," 604–625.

37. Jim VandeHei, "Speaker Predicts Republicans Could Gain Up to 40 Seats in Fall," *Roll Call,* July 16, 1998.

38. Scott Douglas, deputy political director, NRCC, interview, October 10, 1998; Mercurio, "Linder, Frost Both See Gains."

39. Brookover interview; Tom Cole, executive director, RNC, interview, July 13, 1998.

40. Ross K. Baker, *The New Fat Cats: Members of Congress as Political Benefactor* (New York: Twentieth Century Fund, 1989), 31.

41. Herrnson, "Money and Motives," 108–109.

42. A few nonincumbents also made contributions to other congressional candidates.

43. In 1996 Campaign America, sponsored by both Quayle and former Senate Republican majority leader Robert Dole of Kansas, donated $819,681, the largest contribution associated with a leadership PAC.

44. Herrnson, "Money and Motives," 109.

45. The coverage of these topics draws heavily from Herrnson, *Party Campaigning,* chaps. 4 and 5.

46. In some cases, the congressional campaign committees require candidates to use the services of one of their preferred consultants as a precondition for committee support. Although these cases are rare, they can arouse the ire of both candidates and political consultants. See Herrnson, *Party Campaigning,* 56–57; Stephen E. Frantzich, *Political Parties in the Technological Age* (New York: Longman, 1989), 82, 87–88; and Barbara G. Salmore and Stephen A. Salmore, *Candidates, Parties, and Campaigns: Electoral Politics in America,* 2nd ed. (Washington, D.C.: CQ Press, 1989), 240–241.

47. Jim Nicholson, *1998 Chairman's Report to the Members of the Republican National Committee* (Washington, D.C.: Republican National Committee, 1999).

48. Brookover interview.

49. David Hansen, political director, NRSC, August 5, 1999.

50. Johanson interview.

51. Linder, "Operation Breakout"; Tim Curran, "McConnell Asks GOP Senators for $9 Million," *Roll Call,* September 24, 1998.

52. Johanson interview; Joseph Hansen, national field director, DSCC, interview, July 19, 1999; Ceci Connolly and Ruth Marcus, "GOP Launches Aerial Attack," *Washington Post,* October 18, 1998.

53. The allocable costs of the polls vary by their type, size, and when they are released to candidates. FEC regulations specify that candidates must pay 100 percent of the costs if they receive the poll results within 15 days of when the poll was completed, 50 percent if they receive them between 16 and 60 days, and 5 percent if the results are received between 61 and 180 days. After 180 days, a poll can be given to a candidate free of charge. See General Services Administration, *Title 11—Federal Elections,* sec. 2 U.S.C. 106.4, 77–78.

54. An added advantage to this arrangement is that because the party claims that it used the poll for planning purposes, the poll's cost does not count against the party's contribution or coordinated expenditure limits. Brookover interview.

55. Brookover interview.

56. David Hansen interview.

57. Johanson interview.

58. Joseph Hansen interview.

59. Gail Stoltz, political director, DSCC, interview, February 1, 1997.

60. Paul S. Herrnson, "The National Committee for an Effective Congress: Ideology, Partisanship, and Electoral Innovation," in *Risky Business?*

61. Johanson interview.

62. Brookover interview.

63. David Hansen interview.

64. Joseph Hansen interview.

65. Brookover interview.

66. PAC kits typically include information about the candidate's personal background, political experience, campaign staff, support in the district, endorsements, issue positions, and campaign strategy.

67. David Maraniss and Michael Weisskopf, "Speaker and His Directors Make the Cash Flow Right," *Washington Post,* November 27, 1995.

68. Herrnson, *Party Campaigning,* 75.

69. Maraniss and Weisskopf, "Speaker and His Directors."

70. See, for example, Larry J. Sabato, *PAC Power: Inside the World of Political Action Committees* (New York: W. W. Norton, 1984), 144–149; Herrnson, *Party Campaigning*.

71. This generalization is drawn from responses to questions 29, 31, 32, 33, 34, and 36 of the 1992 Congressional Campaign Study. See also Herrnson, *Party Campaigning*, chap. 4.

72. Cornelius P. Cotter, James L. Gibson, John F. Bibby, and Robert J. Huckshorn, *Party Organizations in American Politics* (Pittsburgh: University of Pittsburgh Press, 1989), 20–25.

73. Ibid.; Herrnson, *Party Campaigning*, 102–106; Robert Huckfeldt and John Sprague, "Political Parties and Electoral Mobilization: Political Structure, Social Structure, and the Party Canvass," *American Political Science Review* 86 (1992): 70–86; Gregory A. Caldeira, Samuel C. Patterson, and Gregory A. Markko, "The Mobilization of Voters in Congressional Elections," *Journal of Politics* 47 (1985): 490–509; Michael A. Krassa, "Context and the Canvass: The Mechanisms of Interactions," *Political Behavior* 10 (1988): 233–246; Peter W. Wielhower and Brad Lockerbie, "Party Contacting and Political Participation, 1952–90," *American Journal of Political Science* 38 (1994): 211–229.

74. Exceptions exist: in 1996 NRSC chair Sen. Alfonse D'Amato, R-N.Y., spent nearly $1 million of the committee's funds (mostly soft money) in New York despite the fact that the state had no Senate race. The money was ostensibly used to help state and local Republican candidates and build support for the GOP, but the expenditures were also probably motivated by D'Amato's desire to create a climate that would help his 1998 reelection campaign. See Jonathan D. Salant, "D'Amato: Well Funded, if Not Loved," *Congressional Quarterly Weekly Report*, February 22, 1997; and Marc Humbert, "Democrats Also Piped Money into New York," *Washington Post*, March 9, 1997.

75. See, for example, Noah J. Goodhart, "The New Party Machine: Information Technology in State Political Parties," in *The State of the Parties*, ed. John C. Green and Daniel M. Shea (Lanham, Md.: Rowman and Littlefield, 1999), 125.

76. Don Fowler, national chairman, DNC, interview, February 23, 1997.

77. Todd Glass, deputy press secretary, DNC, interview, January 10, 1997.

78. Joseph Hansen interview; Johanson interview.

79. Nicholson, *1998 Chairman's Report*, 15.

80. Brookover interview; Mary Meade Crawford, press secretary, RNC, interview, January 10, 1997; Rob Engel, political director, DCCC, interview, February 5, 1997.

81. Paul S. Herrnson and Diana Dwyre, "Party Issue Advocacy in Congressional Elections," in *The State of the Parties*, 3rd ed., ed. John C. Green and Daniel M. Shea (Lanham, Md.: University Press of America, 1999), 86–104.

82. Linder, "Operation Breakout."

83. Figures are for candidates in major-party contested races. They were compiled from data collected by CMAG. Data were not available for Senate elections.

84. The remainder was spent in uncompetitive races. See n. 83.

85. Brookover interview; Linder, "Operation Breakout"; Rachel Van Dongen, "Making Their Case a Coast-to-Coast Offensive," *Roll Call*, October 8, 1998.

86. Brookover interview; Thomas B. Edsall, "GOP Spends Millions in Key House Races in Ohio Valley," *Washington Post*, October 31, 1998.

87. Brookover interview; "Clinton Scandal Takes Center Stage in Last Days," *Roll Call*, October 29, 1998.

88. Cole interview; Brookover interview; Rob Engel, political director, DNC, interview, July 13, 1999.

89. Brookover interview; Cole interview.

90. David Hansen interview.

91. Joseph Hansen interview.

92. Johanson interview.

93. See n. 83.

94. Anonymous NRSC official, interview, January 23, 1997.

95. These generalizations are drawn from responses to questions 29 through 36 of the 1992 Congressional Campaign Study.

96. The figures for legislators' contributions include a small number of donations from retired members of Congress.

97. Lonna Rae Atkeson and Anthony C. Coveny, "New Mexico Third District," in *Outside Money: Soft Money & Issue Ads in Competitive 1998 Congressional Elections,* ed. David B. Magleby and Marianne Holt (Provo, Utah: Brigham Young University, 1999).

98. The figures for legislators' contributions include a small number of donations from retired members of Congress.

99. See n. 97.

100. These generalizations are drawn from responses to questions 29 through 36 of the Senate version of the 1992 Congressional Campaign Study and from similar studies of Senate campaigns that were conducted in the 1984 and 1986 election cycles. See Herrnson, *Party Campaigning,* chap. 4.

101. The figures for legislators' contributions include a small number of donations from retired members of Congress.

102. Donald A. Gross and Penny Miller, "Kentucky Senate," in *Outside Money.*

103. Ibid.

104. Ibid.

5. THE INTERESTS CAMPAIGN

1. See, for example, Alexander, *Financing Politics,* 10–17.

2. Although it was referred to as a political action committee from its inception, COPE operated somewhat differently from modern (post-1974) PACs until the enactment of the FECA. See Clyde Wilcox, "Coping with Increasing Business Influence: The AFL-CIO's Committee on Political Education," in *Risky Business?*

3. PACs that do not meet these requirements are subject to the same $1,000 contribution limit as are individuals.

4. FEC Advisory Opinion 1975-23 (December 3, 1975).

5. *Buckley v. Valeo,* 424 U.S. 1 (1976).

6. The number of nonconnected PACs excludes leadership PACs.

7. Removing the 900 defunct PACs from the calculation reduces the number of inactive PACs to 19 percent of the total, but it does not affect the generalization that a small portion of the PAC community accounts for the overwhelming majority of all PAC expenditures.

8. See, for example, Theodore J. Eismeier and Philip H. Pollock III, *Business, Money, and the Rise of Corporate PACs in American Elections* (New York: Quorum Books, 1988), 27–30; J. David Gopoian, "What Makes PACs Tick? An Analysis of the Allocation Patterns of Economic Interest Groups," *American Journal of Political Science* 28 (May 1984): 259–281; Craig Humphries, "Corporations, PACs, and the Strategic Link between Contributions and Lobbying Activities," *Western Political Quarterly* 44 (1991): 353–372; Sorauf, *Inside Campaign Finance,* 64–65, 74–75; and the case studies in *Risky Business?*

9. Laura Langbein, "Money and Access: Some Empirical Evidence," *Journal of Politics* 48 (1986): 1052–1062; Richard Hall and Frank Wayman, "Buying Time: Moneyed Interests and the Mobilization of Bias in Congressional Committees," *American Political Science Review* 84 (1990): 797–820.

10. John Frendreis and Richard Waterman, "PAC Contributions and Legislative Behavior: Senate Voting on Trucking Deregulation," *Social Science Quarterly* 66 (1985): 401–412; Janet M. Grenzke, "PACs and the Congressional Supermarket: The Currency Is Complex," *American Journal of Political Science* 33 (February 1989): 1–24; John Wright, "Contributions, Lobbying, and Committee Voting in the U.S. House of Representatives," *American Political Science Review* 84 (1990): 417–438; Kevin B.

Grier and Michael C. Munger, "Comparing Interest Group PAC Contributions to House and Senate Incumbents, 1980–1986," *Journal of Politics* 55 (August 1993): 615–643; Thomas Romer and James M. Snyder Jr., "An Empirical Investigation of the Dynamics of PAC Contributions," *American Journal of Political Science* 38 (1994): 745–769.

11. Jacobson and Kernell, *Strategy and Choice,* esp. chap. 4.

12. Theodore J. Eismeier and Philip H. Pollock III, "The Tale of Two Elections: PAC Money in 1980 and 1984," *Corruption and Reform* 1 (1986): 189–207; Sorauf, *Inside Campaign Finance,* 67–77; Jackson, *Honest Graft,* 69–70, 77–81, 90–93.

13. Herrnson, "Money and Motives," 122–124; Thomas J. Rudolph, "Corporate and Labor PAC Contributions in House Elections: Measuring the Effects of Majority Party Status," *Journal of Politics* 61 (1999): 195–206; Gary W. Cox and Eric Mager, "How Much is Majority Status in the U.S. Congress Worth?" *American Journal of Political Science* 93 (1999): 299–309.

14. Sorauf, *Inside Campaign Finance,* 61–71.

15. See the case studies in *Risky Business?* and *After the Revolution.*

16. Clyde Wilcox, "Organizational Variables and the Contribution Behavior of Large PACs: A Longitudinal Analysis," *Political Behavior* 11 (1989): 157–173.

17. John Wright, "PACs, Contributions, and Roll Calls: An Organizational Perspective," *American Political Science Review* 79 (1985): 400–414.

18. Sabato, *PAC Power,* 44–49; Robert Biersack, "Introduction," in *Risky Business?*

19. The information on the Realtors PAC is from Anne H. Bedlington, "The Realtors Political Action Committee: Covering All Contingencies," in *After the Revolution,* 170–183.

20. On AT&T's PAC, see Robert E. Mutch, "AT&T PAC: A Pragmatic Giant," in *Risky Business?*; and Mutch, "AT&T PAC: The Perils of Pragmatism," in *After the Revolution.* On AMPAC, see Michael K. Gusmano, "The AMA in the 1990s: Surviving in a Crowded Policy Network," in *After the Revolution.*

21. The information on WASHPAC is from Barbara Levick-Segnatelli, "WASHPAC: One Man Can Make a Difference," in *Risky Business?*

22. On the PHH Group PAC, see Jack E. Rossotti, "How the Little People Choose: PAC Decisionmaking in the PHH Group, Inc., and the National Air Traffic Controllers' Association," in *Risky Business?* 225–227.

23. Rossotti, "How the Little People Choose."

24. Brett Kappel, legal counsel, Powell, Goldstein, Frazer, and Murphy PAC, interview, August 17, 1999.

25. Kappel interview.

26. On lead PACs see the introduction to part I in *Risky Business?* 17–18. On the NCEC, see Herrnson, "The National Committee for an Effective Congress." On COPE, see Wilcox, "Coping with Increasing Business Influence," in *Risky Business?*; and Robin Gerber, "Building to Win, Building to Last: The AFL-CIO COPE Takes on the Republican Congress," in *After the Revolution,* 77–93. On BIPAC, see Candice J. Nelson, "The Business-Industry PAC: Trying to Lead in an Uncertain Climate," in *Risky Business?*; and Candice J. Nelson and Robert Biersack, "BIPAC: Working to Keep a Pro-Business Congress," in *After the Revolution,* 36–46.

27. On the flow of PAC money in the 1996 elections, see the previous edition of this book; for information on the 1994 elections, see Herrnson, "Money and Motives," 110–113; and Herrnson, "Interest Groups, PACs, and Campaigns," in *The Interest Group Connection: Electioneering, Lobbying, and Policymaking in Washington,* ed. Paul S. Herrnson, Clyde Wilcox, and Ronald G. Shaiko (Chatham, N.J.: Chatham House, 1997).

28. Theodore J. Eismeier and Philip H. Pollock III, "Political Action Committees: Varieties of Organization and Strategy," in *Money and Politics in the United States: Financing Elections in the 1980s,* ed. Michael J. Malbin (Washington, D.C.: American Enterprise Institute, 1984), 122–141; Margaret

Ann Latus, "Assessing Ideological PACs: From Outrage to Understanding," in *Money and Politics in the United States,* 150–160; Sabato, *PAC Power,* 93–95.

29. On abortion rights PACs, see, for example, Sue Thomas, "NARAL PAC: Reproductive Choice in the Spotlight," in *Risky Business?*

30. Fowler and McClure, *Political Ambition: Who Decides to Run for Congress,* 205–207.

31. Ronald G. Shaiko and Marc A. Wallace, "From Wall Street to Main Street: The National Federation of Independent Business and the Republican Majority," in *After the Revolution*; James G. Gimpel, "Peddling Influence in the Field: The Direct Campaign Involvement of the Free Congress PAC," in *Risky Business?*

32. Philip A. Mundo, "League of Conservation Voters," in *After the Revolution.*

33. Herrnson, "The National Committee for an Effective Congress."

34. Mark Gable, PAC director, Federal Managers Association PAC, interview, April 25, 1997.

35. See, for example, Sabato, *PAC Power,* 44–49.

36. John C. Green, Paul S. Herrnson, Lynda Powell, and Clyde Wilcox, *Individual Congressional Campaign Contributors: Wealthy, Conservative—and Reform-Minded,* June 9, 1999 (Web site: http://www.georgetown.edu/wilcox/donors.htm).

37. Stephanie Kahn, communications director, EMILY's List, interview, August 9, 1999 (Web site: http://www.emilyslist.org/el-about/index.html).

38. Rebecca Carr, "Questions Arise About Role of Tax-Exempt Groups in '96," *Congressional Quarterly Weekly Report,* October 4, 1997.

39. Federal Election Commission, "FEC Releases Information on PAC Activity for 1997–1998," press release, June 8, 1999.

40. Figures compiled from Jeffrey D. Stanger and Douglas G. Rivlin, "Issue Advocacy Advertising During the 1997–1998 Election Cycle" (Philadelphia: Annenberg Public Policy Center, 1998). (Web sites: http://appcpenn.org/ and http://appcpenn.org/issueads/profiles.)

41. Figures compiled from CMAG data.

42. Gerber, "Building to Win, Building to Last." See also Gary C. Jacobson, "The Effect of the AFL-CIO's Voter Education Campaigns on the 1996 House Elections," *Journal of Politics* 61 (1999): 185–194.

43. Aaron Bernstein and Richard S. Dunham, "Laboring Mightily to Avert a Nightmare in November," *Business Week,* October 19, 1998; Donald Lambro, "AFL-CIO's Election Day Effort Paid Off Big for Democrats," *Washington Times,* November 5, 1998.

44. "Many Union Leaders Happy with Outcome," *Des Moines Register,* November 5, 1998.

45. Shaiko and Wallace, "From Wall Street to Main Street."

46. Jill Lawrence and Jim Drinkard, "Getting Out the Vote," *USA Today,* October 29, 1998.

47. On the Sierra Club, see David M. Cantor, "The Sierra Club Political Committee: Spreading Some Green in Congressional Elections," in *After the Revolution*; on the National Rifle Association, see Kelly D. Patterson, "Political Firepower: The National Rifle Association," in *After the Revolution.*

48. John C. Green, James L. Guth, and Kevin Hill, "Faith and Election: The Christian Right in Congressional Campaigns, 1978–1988," *Journal of Politics* 55 (1993): 80–91.

49. On initiatives and referenda, see Shaun Bowler, Todd Donovan, and Caroline J. Tolbert, eds., *Citizens as Legislators: Direct Democracy in the United States* (Columbus: Ohio State University Press, 1998); Shaun Bowler and Todd Donovan, *Demanding Choices: Opinion, Voting, and Direct Democracy* (Ann Arbor: University of Michigan Press, 1998); David B. Magleby, *Direct Legislation: Voting on Ballot Propositions in the United States* (Baltimore: Johns Hopkins University Press, 1984); and Thomas E. Cronin, *Direct Democracy: The Politics of Initiative, Referendum, and Recall* (Cambridge: Harvard University Press, 1989).

50. ALT also aired issue advocacy ads in two 1998 special elections. Figures are from Stanger and Rivlin, "Issue Advocacy Advertising."

51. Staise Rumenap, field representative director, U.S. Term Limits, interview, August 12, 1999.

52. "USTL Names Names in Full Page Newspaper Ads," U.S. Term Limits, press release, May 26, 1999.

53. Caroline J. Tolbert and Rodney E. Hero, "Race/Ethnicity and Direct Democracy: The Contextual Basis of Support for Anti-Immigrant and Official English Measures," in *Citizens as Legislators,* 215.

54. Anthony Corrado, *Creative Campaigning: PACs and the Presidential Selection Process* (Boulder, Colo.: Westview Press, 1992), 80–84.

55. Ken Foskett, "Issue Ads Firm Draws a Bead on Bishop," *Atlanta Journal and Constitution,* October 17, 1998.

56. This generalization is drawn from responses to questions 29 through 36 of the 1992 Congressional Campaign Study.

57. The information on campaign contributions, independent expenditures, and internal communications was compiled from FEC data. The information on issue ads is from Atkeson and Coveny, "New Mexico Third District."

58. Ibid.

59. Ibid.

60. Ibid.

61. The information on campaign contributions, independent expenditures, and internal communications was compiled from FEC data. The information on issue ads is from Gross and Miller, "Kentucky Senate."

62. Ibid.

63. Ibid.

64. Ibid.

6. THE CAMPAIGN FOR RESOURCES

1. Quoted in David Adamany and George E. Agree, *Political Money: A Strategy for Campaign Finance in America* (Baltimore: Johns Hopkins University Press, 1975), 8.

2. George Thayer, *Who Shakes the Money Tree? American Campaign Finance Practices from 1789 to the Present* (New York: Simon and Schuster, 1973), 25.

3. Federal Election Commission, "Reports on Political Party Activity for 1997–98," press release, April 9, 1999.

4. The figures for House and Senate campaign contributions and expenditures include spending by all candidates involved in typical major-party contested general elections.

5. The denominator used to calculate the percentages is the candidates' total receipts plus any coordinated spending the parties made on the candidates' behalf. Coordinated expenditures are included because candidates have some control over the activities on which they are spent.

6. Sorauf, *Inside Campaign Finance,* 47.

7. This figure includes only out-of-state contributions of $200 or more because the FEC does not require candidates to collect information about individuals who contribute less than $200 to their campaigns.

8. Herrnson, "Interest Groups, PACs, and Campaigns," in *The Interest Group Connection,* 45–50.

9. On direct-mail fund-raising, see Kenneth R. Godwin, *One Billion Dollars of Influence: The Direct Marketing of Politics* (Chatham, N.J.: Chatham House, 1988).

10. Center for Responsive Politics (Web site: http://www.opensecrets.org/1998elect/dist_instate/98GA06instate.htm).

11. "Characteristics of 1998 Campaign Web Sites," Democracy OnLine Project (Web site: http://democracyonline/numbers); and David A. Dulio, Donald L. Goff, and James A. Thurber, "Untangled

Web: Internet Use During the 1998 Election," *PS: Political Science and Politics* (March 1999): 53–55. See also Elaine Ciulla Kamarck, "Campaigning on the Internet in the Off-Year Elections of 1998," February 1999 (Web site: http://siayset.bilkent.edu.tr/harvard/kamarck.htm).

12. For a discussion of these motives—often referred to as solidary, purposive, and material—see James Q. Wilson, *Political Organizations* (New York: Basic Books, 1973), chap. 6.

13. Green, Herrnson, Powell, and Wilcox, *Individual Congressional Campaign Contributors.*

14. See, for example, Sorauf, *Inside Campaign Finance,* 124–127.

15. They were the minority leader, Richard Gephardt; the DCCC chair, Martin Frost; Speaker Newt Gingrich; and the chair of the Human Resources Subcommittee of the Ways and Means Committee, Nancy Johnson.

16. See n. 5.

17. Center for Responsive Politics (Web site: http://www.opensecrets.org/politicians/sector/H6CA39020.htm).

18. Center for Responsive Politics (Web site: http://www.opensecrets.org/politicians/sector/H4NY19073.htm).

19. Some argue that preemptive fund-raising by incumbents may not discourage quality challengers from running. See Krasno and Green, "Preempting Quality Challengers"; Squire, "Preemptive Fundraising."

20. Gary C. Jacobson, *Money in Congressional Elections* (New Haven, Conn.: Yale University Press, 1980), 113–123; Jonathan S. Krasno, Donald Philip Green, and Jonathan A. Cowden, "The Dynamics of Fundraising in House Elections," *Journal of Politics* 56 (1994): 459–474.

21. Sorauf, *Inside Campaign Finance,* 75.

22. Gilliard interview.

23. Center for Responsive Politics (Web site: http://www.opensecrets.org/politicians/geog/H6NC04037.htm).

24. The remaining 5 percent came from interest on investments and miscellaneous funds.

25. Price won the primary against Ralph McKinney Jr. by a 74 percent vote margin.

26. Robert Biersack, Paul S. Herrnson, and Clyde Wilcox, "Seeds for Success: Early Money in Congressional Elections," *Legislative Studies Quarterly* 18 (1993): 535–553; Krasno, Green, and Cowden, "The Dynamics of Fundraising in House Elections."

27. Herrnson, *Party Campaigning in the 1980s,* 75.

28. Herrnson, "Campaign Professionalism," 859–870.

29. Campaign organizations that employed paid staff or political consultants to perform four or more of the campaign activities listed in Table 3-1 are classified as professional; those that employed three or fewer are classified as amateur.

30. Clyde Wilcox, "Coping with Increasing Business Influence"; Gerber, "Building to Win, Building to Last"; Denise L. Baer and Martha Bailey, "The Nationalization of Education Politics: The National Education Association PAC and the 1992 Elections," in *Risky Business?*

31. The WISH List's name is an acronym for Women in the Senate and House. See Craig A. Rimmerman, "New Kids on the Block"; Rimmerman, "The Gay and Lesbian Victory Fund Comes of Age: Reflections on the 1996 Elections," in *After the Revolution;* and Rozell, "WISH List," in *After the Revolution.*

32. Figures do not add to 100 percent due to rounding.

33. Center for Responsive Politics (Web site: http://www.opensecrets.org/1998elect/dist_instate/98ca39instate.htm).

34. The Roberg campaign also raised $11,878 from miscellaneous sources.

35. Center for Responsive Politics (Web site: http://www.opensecrets.org/1998elect/dist_instate/98NC04instate.htm).

36. See n. 5.

37. Cooperative PACs made no contributions in the race.

38. PAC contribution totals exclude donations by leadership PACs.

39. Figures for out-of-state money are from the Center for Responsive Politics (Web site: http://www.opensecrets.org/1998elect/dist_instate/98WI02instate.htm).

40. Total resources include party-coordinated expenditures and receipts.

41. Center for Responsive Politics (Web site: http://www.opensecrets.org/politicians/sector/S6AL00013.htm).

7. CAMPAIGN STRATEGY

1. Angus Campbell, Philip E. Converse, Warren E. Miller, and Donald E. Stokes, *The American Voter* (New York: John Wiley and Sons, 1960), 541–548; and Donald R. Kinder and David O. Sears, "Public Opinion and Political Action," in *Handbook of Social Psychology,* 3rd ed., ed. Gardner Lindzey and Elliot Aronson (New York: Random House, 1985), 659–741.

2. Figures compiled from Sapiro et al., *American National Election Study, 1998.*

3. Senate figures are not available for 1998 because the ANES did not ask this question that year. See Alan I. Abramowitz and Jeffrey A. Segal, *Senate Elections* (Ann Arbor: University of Michigan Press, 1992), 39; Peverill Squire, "Challenger Quality and Voting Behavior," *Legislative Studies Quarterly* 17 (1992): 247–263.

4. See n. 2.

5. Abramowitz and Segal, *Senate Elections*, 39; Squire, "Challenger Quality."

6. Alan I. Abramowitz, "A Comparison of Voting for U.S. Senator and Representative in 1978," *American Political Science Review* 74 (1980): 633–640. Gerald C. Wright and Michael B. Berkman, "Candidates and Policy in United States Senate Elections," *American Political Science Review* 80 (1986): 567–588; and Mark C. Westlye, *Senate Elections and Campaign Intensity* (Baltimore: Johns Hopkins University Press, 1992), 122–151.

7. Robert D. Brown and James A. Woods, "Toward a Model of Congressional Elections," *Journal of Politics* 53 (1991): 454–473; John R. Zaller, *The Nature and Origins of Mass Opinion* (Cambridge: Cambridge University Press, 1992), chap. 10.

8. See n. 2.

9. Wright and Berkman, "Candidates and Policy in United States Senate Elections," 567–588; and Westlye, *Senate Elections and Campaign Intensity,* chap. 6.

10. See, for example, Raymond E. Wolfinger and Steven J. Rosenstone, *Who Votes?* (New Haven: Yale University Press, 1980), 34–36, 58–60, 102–114.

11. Zaller, *The Nature and Origins of Mass Opinion,* chap. 10; Westlye, *Senate Elections and Campaign Intensity,* esp. chap. 5; Milton Lodge, Marco R. Steenbergen, and Shawn Brau, "The Responsive Voter: Campaign Information and the Dynamics of Candidate Evaluation," *American Political Science Review* 89 (1995): 309–326; Jon K. Dalager, "Voters, Issues, and Elections: Are the Candidates' Messages Getting Through?" *Journal of Politics* 58 (1996): 496–515.

12. See Morris P. Fiorina, *Retrospective Voting in American National Elections* (New Haven: Yale University Press, 1981); Edward R. Tufte, "Determinants of the Outcomes of Midterm Congressional Elections," *American Political Science Review* 69 (1975): 812–826; James E. Campbell, "Explaining Presidential Losses in Midterm Congressional Elections," *Journal of Politics* 47 (1985): 1140–1157; Samuel C. Popkin, *The Reasoning Voter: Communication and Persuasion in Presidential Campaigns* (Chicago: University of Chicago Press, 1991), esp. chaps. 3 and 4.

13. Alan I. Abramowitz, Albert D. Cover, and Helmut Norpoth, "The President's Party in Midterm Elections: Going from Bad to Worse," *American Journal of Political Science* 30 (1986): 562–576; Henry W. Chappell Jr. and Motoshi Susuki, "Aggregate Vote Functions for the U.S. Presidency, Senate, and House," *Journal of Politics* 55 (1993): 207–217; Gary C. Jacobson, "Reversal of Fortune: The

Transformation of U.S. House Elections in the 1990s" (paper presented at the annual meeting of the Midwest Political Science Association, Chicago, April 10–12, 1997). See also the studies cited in n. 12.

14. Fiorina, *Divided Government* (Boston: Allyn and Bacon, 1996), 109–110; Stephen P. Nicholson and Gary M. Segura, "Midterm Elections and Divided Government: An Information-Driven Theory of Electoral Volatility" (paper presented at the annual meeting of the Midwest Political Science Association, Chicago, April 10–12, 1997).

15. Alan I. Abramowitz and Kyle L. Saunders, "Ideological Realignment in the U.S. Electorate," *Journal of Politics* 61 (1998): 634–652.

16. Raymond E. Wolfinger, "Candidates and Parties in Congressional Elections," *American Political Science Review* 74 (1980): 622–629; Barbara Hinckley, "House Re-Elections and Senate Defeats: The Role of the Challenger," *British Journal of Political Science* 10 (1980): 441–460; and Jacobson, *The Politics of Congressional Elections*, 106–108.

17. Mayhew, *Congress.*

18. Fenno, *Home Style,* esp. chaps. 3 and 4.

19. Groom interview; Gilliard interview.

20. Chris Chwastyk, manager, Price campaign, quoted in Rob Christensen, "Roberg Assails Price's Record," *The News and Observer*, July 25, 1998; "NC4: Roberg-Price Contest Heats Up," *The Bulletin's Frontrunner*, July 27, 1998; Paul Fricke, field director, DCCC, personal communication, June 13, 1997.

21. On polls see Salmore and Salmore, *Candidates, Parties, and Campaigns*, 116–119.

22. Bryce Bassett, director of marketing support, the Wirthlin Group, presentation to the Taft Institute Honors Seminar in American Government, June 15, 1993.

23. See, for example, Robert Axelrod, "Where the Votes Come From: An Analysis of Presidential Election Coalitions, 1952–1968," *American Political Science Review* 66 (1972): 11–20.

24. Moore interview.

25. Roberg interview.

26. Manuel Perez-Rivas, "Opponent Tries to Make Party Label Stick to Morella," *Washington Post*, March 7, 1996.

27. These generalizations are drawn from responses to question 4 of the 1998 Congressional Campaign Study.

28. Axelrod, "Where the Votes Come From," 11–20; Henry C. Kenski and Lee Sigelman, "Where the Vote Comes From: Group Components of the 1988 Vote," *Legislative Studies Quarterly* 18 (1993): 367–390.

29. Moore interview.

30. Roberg interview.

31. These generalizations are drawn from further breakdowns of question 4 of the 1998 Congressional Campaign Study.

32. See, for example, Patrick J. Sellers, "Strategy and Background in Congressional Campaigns," *American Journal of Political Science* 92 (1998): 159-171.

33. Joel C. Bradshaw, "Who Will Vote for You and Why: Designing Campaign Strategy and Theme" (paper presented at the Conference on Campaign Management, American University, Washington, D.C., December 10–11, 1992).

34. The logic behind the battle for the middle ground is presented in Anthony Downs, *An Economic Theory of Democracy* (New York: Harper and Row, 1957), chap. 8.

35. Fred Hartwig, vice president, Peter Hart and Associates, presentation to the Taft Institute Honors Seminar in American Government, June 15, 1993.

36. Ladonna Y. Lee, "Strategy," in *Ousting the Ins: Lessons for Congressional Challengers,* ed. Stuart Rothenberg (Washington, D.C.: Free Congress Research and Education Foundation, 1985), 18–19.

37. Kathleen Hall Jamieson, *Dirty Politics: Perception, Distraction, and Democracy* (New York: Oxford University Press, 1992), esp. chap. 2.

38. Fenno, *Home Style,* chaps. 3 and 4.

39. See Peter Clarke and Susan H. Evans, *Covering Campaigns: Journalism and Congressional Elections* (Stanford: Stanford University Press, 1983), 38–45.

40. On the differences between valence issues and position issues, see Donald E. Stokes, "Spatial Models of Party Competition," in *Elections and the Political Order,* ed. Angus Campbell, Philip E. Converse, Warren E. Miller, and Donald E. Stokes (New York: John Wiley and Sons, 1966), 161–169.

41. See, for example, Gary C. Jacobson and Samuel Kernell, "National Forces in the 1986 U.S. House Elections," 72–85.

42. Jacobson, *The Politics of Congressional Elections,* 112–116.

43. Moore interview.

44. Roberg interview.

45. This generalization is drawn from responses to question 13 of the 1992 Congressional Campaign Study. See also Philip Paolino, "Group Salient Issues and Group Representation: Support for Women Candidates in the 1992 Senate Elections," *American Journal of Political Science* 39 (1995): 294–313; Kirsten la Cour Dabelko and Paul S. Herrnson, "Women's and Men's Campaigns for the U.S. House of Representatives," *Political Research Quarterly* 50 (1997): 121–135.

46. Gimpel, *Fulfilling the Contract;* Kolodny, "The Contract with America."

47. Anonymous 1992 House candidate, interview, December 1992.

48. Richard F. Fenno, "If, as Ralph Nader Says, Congress Is 'The Broken Branch,' How Come We Love Our Congressmen So Much?" in *Congress in Change: Evolution and Reform,* ed. Norman J. Ornstein (New York: Praeger, 1975).

49. The generalization is based on breakdowns of question 13 of the 1998 Congressional Campaign Study.

50. Hartwig presentation.

51. Phil Duncan, ed., *Politics in America, 1992: The 102nd Congress* (Washington, D.C.: Congressional Quarterly, 1991), 1133.

52. See, for example, James Innocenzi, "Political Advertising," in *Ousting the Ins,* 53–61; Salmore and Salmore, *Candidates, Parties, and Campaigns,* 159.

53. Stephen Ansolabehere, Shanto Iyengar, Adam Simon, and Nicholas Valentino, "Does Attack Advertising Demobilize the Electorate?" *American Political Science Review* 88 (1994): 829–838; and Stephen Ansolabehere and Shanto Iyengar, *Going Negative: How Attack Ads Shrink and Polarize the Electorate* (New York: Free Press, 1995), esp. chap. 5. For an opposing viewpoint, see Steven Finkel and John G. Geer, "Spot Check: Casting Doubt on the Demobilizing Effect of Attack Advertising," *American Journal of Political Science* 42 (1998): 573–595.

54. These generalizations are drawn from responses to question 11 of the 1998 Congressional Campaign Study and question 28 of the 1992 Congressional Campaign Study.

55. Richard R. Lau, "Negativity in Political Perception," *Political Behavior* 4 (1982): 353–377; and Richard R. Lau, "Two Explanations for Negativity Effects in Political Behavior," *American Journal of Political Science* 29 (1985): 110–138; Jamieson, *Dirty Politics,* 41.

56. Lee, "Strategy," 22.

57. Jamieson, *Dirty Politics,* 103.

58. Anonymous campaign manager for a 1992 House candidate, interview, December 1992.

59. Beard interview.

60. Sunil Ahuja, "Reelection of Freshmen Republicans of the 104th Congress" (paper presented at the annual meeting of the Midwest Political Science Association, Chicago, April 10–12, 1997).

8. CAMPAIGN COMMUNICATIONS

1. Matthew Katz, "Living Without TV: More Time to Get a Life," *Washington Times,* September 17, 1998.

2. Pew Research Center, "Election Pleases Voters Despite Mudslinging," November 1998 (Web site: http://www.people-press.org/nov98que.htm).

3. Darrell M. West, *Air Wars: Television Advertising in Election Campaigns, 1952–1992* (Washington, D.C.: Congressional Quarterly, 1993), esp. chap. 6.

4. Quoted in Frank I. Luntz, *Candidates, Consultants, and Campaigns* (Oxford: Basil Blackwell, 1988), 77.

5. Darrell M. West, "Political Advertising and News Coverage in the 1992 California U.S. Senate Campaigns," *Journal of Politics* 56 (1994): 1053–1075.

6. This generalization is drawn from responses to question 22 of the 1992 Congressional Campaign Study.

7. The figures for New York and Waco are for a prime-time advertisement broadcast during *Monday Night Football.* Figures provided by the Campaign Media Analysis Group.

8. See Joe Ostrow, "Six Reasons to Buy Cable," *Campaigns and Elections,* February 1996, 37.

9. John R. Alford and Keith Henry, "TV Markets and Congressional Elections," *Legislative Studies Quarterly* 9 (1984): 665–675.

10. Luntz, *Candidates, Consultants, and Campaigns,* 76.

11. "Abilene to get B-1 Bomber Squadron," *The Austin American-Statesman;* Duncan and Nutting, eds., *CQ's Politics in America 2000,* 1331.

12. As discussed in chapter 7, whereas *valence issues,* such as a strong economy, have only one side and are universally viewed by voters in a favorable light, *position (or wedge) issues,* which would include either position in the abortion rights debate, divide voters because they have two or more sides.

13. Kim F. Kahn, Patrick J. Kenney, and Tom W. Rice, "Ideological Learning in U.S. Senate Elections" (paper presented at the annual meeting of the American Political Science Association, Washington, D.C., September 2–5, 1993). See also Jay Bryant, "Paid Advertising in Political Campaigns" (paper presented at the Conference on Campaign Management, American University, Washington, D.C., December 10–11, 1992).

14. See n. 6.

15. Luntz, *Candidates, Consultants, and Campaigns,* 108.

16. Frank Luther Mott, *American Journalism: A History of 250 Years, 1690 to 1940* (New York: Macmillan, 1947), 411–430.

17. See n. 6.

18. Luntz, *Candidates, Consultants, and Campaigns,* 109–110.

19. See n. 6.

20. Kenneth R. Godwin, *One Billion Dollars of Influence: The Direct Marketing of Politics* (Chatham, N.J.: Chatham House, 1988), chaps. 1–3; Jonathan Robbin, "Geodemographics: The New Magic," in *Campaigns and Elections,* ed. Larry J. Sabato (Glenview, Ill.: Scott Foresman, 1989), 105–124; and Sabato, "How Direct Mail Works," in *Campaigns and Elections,* 88–89.

21. Salmore and Salmore, *Candidates, Parties, and Campaigns,* 86–87.

22. Mass mailings consist of five hundred or more pieces of the same letter.

23. The campaign did, however, purchase advertising on local cable TV stations, which is considerably cheaper than advertising on the other television stations.

24. Andrew Kennedy, senior vice president, M and R Research, Inc., and direct-mail consultant to the Sanchez campaign, interviews, April 2, 1997, and August 4, 1999.

25. Mike Connel, "Internet Survival Guide: Designing Lively Web Sites," *Campaigns & Elections,* September 1998; Ron Faucheux, "How Campaigns Are Using the Internet: An Exclusive Nationwide Survey," *Campaigns & Elections,* September 1998; Kamarck, "Campaigning on the Internet."

26. Connel, "Internet Survival Guide"; Faucheux, "How Campaigns Are Using the Internet"; Kamarck, "Campaigning on the Internet"; "Characteristics of 1998 Campaign Web Sites," Democracy OnLine Project.

27. Jeff Mize, "Baird Fires Back at Benton in New TV Commercial," *Columbian*, October 9, 1998; Lynn Reed, president of Netpolitics.com, interview, August 6, 1999.

28. Peter Clarke and Susan Evans, *Covering Campaigns: Journalism in Congressional Elections* (Stanford: Stanford University Press, 1983), chap. 6.

29. Xandra Kayden, *Campaign Organization* (Lexington, Mass.: D.C. Heath, 1978), 125.

30. Clarke and Evans, *Covering Campaigns,* 60–62; Doris A. Graber, *Mass Media and American Politics,* 4th ed. (Washington, D.C.: CQ Press, 1993), 262, 268–270.

31. Richard Born, "Assessing the Impact of Institutional and Election Forces on Evaluations of Congressional Incumbents," *Journal of Politics* 53 (1991): 764–799.

32. Sallie G. Randolph, "The Effective Press Release: Key to Free Media," in *Campaigns and Elections,* 26–32.

33. Kayden, *Campaign Organization,* 126.

34. Clarke and Evans, *Covering Campaigns,* 60–62; Goldenberg and Traugott, *Campaigning for Congress,* 127.

35. Anita Dunn, "The Best Campaign Wins: Coverage of Down Ballot Races by Local Press" (paper presented at the Conference on Campaign Management, American University, Washington, D.C., December 10–11, 1992).

36. Manuel Perez-Rivas and Deirdre M. Childress, "Lots of Foes, Little Hope," *Washington Post,* February 29, 1996.

37. Manuel Perez-Rivas, "Opponent Tries to Make Party Label Stick to Morella," *Washington Post,* April 28, 1996.

38. Karl Vick, "Always Up to the Challenge," *Washington Post,* October 27, 1996.

39. Ralph Neas, interview, July 14, 1999.

40. These generalizations are drawn from the following four sources, which together demonstrate that political experience, campaign professionalism, and campaign receipts are positively related to the free media coverage that campaigns receive: (1) candidates' campaign receipts, (2) the political experience measure developed in Chapter 2, (3) the measure of campaign professionalism developed in Chapter 3 (total number of campaign activities performed by paid staff or consultants), and (4) responses to question 9 of the 1998 Congressional Campaign Study and to question 25 of the 1992 Congressional Campaign Study.

41. Marc Birtel, "Changing Demographics Keep Orange County in Play," *CQ Weekly,* May 23, 1998, 1373.

42. See n. 6.

43. See also Clarke and Evans, *Covering Campaigns,* chap. 4.

44. This generalization is drawn from responses to question 10 of the 1998 Congressional Campaign Study and to question 27 of the 1992 Congressional Campaign Study. See also Table 8-3 of the first edition of this book.

45. This generalization is drawn from responses to question 9 of the 1998 Congressional Campaign Study and to question 26 of the 1992 Congressional Campaign Study. See also Table 8-2 of the first edition of this book. On media bias, see Herbert J. Gans, "Are U.S. Journalists Dangerously Liberal?" *Columbia Journalism Review* 24 (1985): 29–33. On politicians and the press, see also Lance W. Bennett, *News: The Politics of Illusion* (New York: Longman, 1983), 76–78; and Ranney, *Channels of Power,* 54–55.

46. See, for example, Will Robinson, "Campaign Field Work" (paper presented at the Conference on Campaign Management, American University, Washington, D.C., December 10–11, 1992); and Robbin, "Geodemographics," 105–124.

47. Paul S. Herrnson, "National Party Organizations and the Postreform Congress," in *The Postreform Congress,* ed. Roger H. Davidson (New York: St. Martin's Press, 1992), 65–66.

48. These generalizations are drawn from responses to questions 30 and 35 of the 1992 Congressional Campaign Study.

9. CANDIDATES, CAMPAIGNS, AND ELECTORAL SUCCESS

1. Larry M. Bartels, "Partisanship and Voting Behavior, 1952–1996," *American Journal of Political Science* 44 (2000): 42–43.

2. Fiorina, *Congress;* John A. Ferejohn, "On the Decline of Competition in Congressional Elections," *American Political Science Review* 71 (1997): 166–177.

3. See Michael Krashinsky and William J. Milne, "Incumbency in U.S. Congressional Elections, 1950–1988," *Legislative Studies Quarterly* 18 (1993); also see the sources cited in Chapter 1, nn. 44-46.

4. William C. Miller Jr., Representative Morella's campaign manager and the chief of staff of her congressional office, interview, March 14, 1997.

5. On the effect of candidate gender on voting behavior see Monika L. McDermott, "Voting Cues in Low-Information Elections: Candidate Gender as a Social Information Variable in Contemporary United States Elections," *American Journal of Political Science* 41 (1997): 270–283.

6. Tables 9-1, 9-2, and 9-3 were created using ordinary least-squares regressions to analyze data from 1998 major-party contested general election campaigns for the House. The full regression equations and an overview of the survey and statistical methods used to conduct the study are presented at this book's Web site (http://herrnson.cqpress.com). The equations are the product of an extensive model-building process that tested the impact of numerous variables using a variety of statistical techniques. Numerous regressions were tested prior to selecting the final equations. The final models were selected for reasons of statistical fit, parsimony, and ease of interpretation. They are statistically robust. The models replicated to the extent possible similar analyses for the 1992, 1994, and 1996 elections to verify that the basic relationships that are presented held across elections.

7. Partisan bias was measured using the respondents' answers to question 2 of the 1998 Congressional Campaign Study.

8. Philip D. Duncan and Christine C. Lawrence, *CQ's Politics in America 1998: The 105th Congress* (Washington, D.C.: CQ Press, 1997), 952-953.

9. These generalizations are similar to those reported in Goldenberg and Traugott, *Campaigning for Congress,* chap. 3.

10. The figures for candidate spending on campaign communications equal the sum of candidate expenditures and party coordinated expenditures made on behalf of the candidate minus candidate contributions to other candidates, and multiplied by the portion of the campaign budget respondents reported spending on campaign communications in question 15 of the 1998 Congressional Campaign Study. These funds exclude money spent on overhead and research, but they include party coordinated expenditures because they are spent on campaign communications and because the candidate and the party each exercise some control over them. They exclude independent expenditures and issue advocacy ads because the candidate has no control over these. On the effect of total candidate campaign spending (including overhead and research) on congressional elections see esp. Jacobson, *Money in Congressional Elections;* Gary C. Jacobson, "The Effects of Campaign Spending in House Elections: New Evidence for Old Arguments," *American Journal of Political Science* 34 (1990): 334–362; Jonathan S. Krasno and Donald Philip Green, "Salvation for the Spendthrift Incumbent," *American Journal of Political Science* 32 (1988): 844–907; Donald Philip Green and Jonathan S. Krasno, "Rebuttal to Jacobson's 'New Evidence for Old Arguments,'" *American Journal of Political Science* 34 (1990): 363–372.

11. Jacobson, *Money in Congressional Elections,* 113–123; Krasno, Green, and Cowden, "The Dynamics of Fundraising in House Elections"; Christopher Kenney and Michael McBurdett, "A Dynamic Model of Congressional Spending on Vote Choice," *American Journal of Political Science* 36 (1992): 923–937.

12. Jacobson, *Money in Congressional Elections,* 38-45; Jacobson, "The Effects of Campaign Spending"; and Green and Krasno, "Salvation for the Spendthrift Incumbent."

13. Media advantage is measured using respondents' answers to questions 10 and 11 of the 1998 Congressional Campaign Study.

14. See the case studies in Magleby, *Outside Money.*

15. Party and interest group outside campaign communications for the candidate are the sum of all monies that a party and interest group spent on independent expenditures and televised issue advocacy ads to help the candidate or harm the opponent. These figures were combined because both forms of spending are outside the candidates' control and both variables were highly correlated.

16. See, for example, Richard F. Fenno Jr., *Senators on the Campaign Trail: The Politics of Representation* (Norman: University of Oklahoma Press, 1996), 100.

17. None of the incumbents who were involved in scandals were first-term legislators. Brown was also the subject of an investigation by the Federal Election Commission and of a heavily covered scandal involving her daughter, who received a $50,000 Lexus from a West African businessman. The House member had allegedly used her influence to keep him out of prison. See Duncan and Nutting, *CQ's Politics in America 2000*, 293. The scandal data were compiled by Jock Friedly of *The Hill.*

18. Targeting is measured using respondents' answers to question 3 of the 1998 Congressional Campaign Study.

19. For more on the concept of issue ownership, see John R. Petrocik, "Issue Ownership in Presidential Elections, with a 1980 Case Study," *American Journal of Political Science* 40 (1996): 825-850; and George Rabinowitz and Stuart McDonald, "A Directional Theory of Voting," *American Political Science Review* 65 (1989): 93-122.

20. The campaign's issue focus was measured using respondents' answers to question 14 of the 1998 Congressional Campaign Study.

21. Paul S. Herrnson and Kelly D. Patterson, "The Impact of Campaign Agendas in Congressional Elections," *Crowded Airwaves: Campaign Advertising in Modern Elections*, ed. James A. Thurber (Washington, D.C.: Brookings Institution, 2000), 96-112.

22. This probability was calculated using a logistic regression equation that predicted whether voters cast their ballots for a challenger. Calculations drew from a data set consisting of responses to the 1998 Congressional Campaign Study and exit surveys by the Voter News Service of voters in candidates' districts. For more information about the methodology, see the Appendix at this book's Web site (http://herrnson.cqpress.com).

23. Communications expenditures exclude money spent on overhead and research. Field work includes get-out-the-vote drives and the distribution of campaign literature, billboards, and signs.

24. The figures for each form of campaign communication expenditure (for radio, direct mail, and so on) are regression coefficients that were generated using separate equations. The equations used the same variables as those that appear in Table 2 for challengers and Table 3 for open-seat candidates, except they substituted the spending on the specific form of expenditure for overall spending on campaign communications. See the Appendix (http://herrnson.cqpress.com) for more details.

25. When outside spending is included in the analysis it reduces the size of some coefficients and renders statistically insignificant the variables for candidate issue selection and incumbent and challenger spending on campaign communications.

26. See n. 24.

27. Jonathan S. Krasno, *Challengers, Competition, and Reelection: Comparing Senate and House Elections* (New Haven, Conn.: Yale University Press, 1994), esp. chaps. 4–7; Peverill Squire and Eric R. A. N. Smith, "A Further Examination of Challenger Quality in Senate Elections," *Legislative Studies Quarterly* 21 (1996): 231–248.

28. Abramowitz and Segal, *Senate Elections*, 109-114; Kim Fridkin Kahn and Patrick J. Kenney, *The Spectacle of U.S. Senate Campaigns* (Princeton, N.J.: Princeton University Press, 1999), 216-223.

29. John R. Hibbing and John R. Alford, "Constituency Population and Representativeness in the United States Senate," *Legislative Studies Quarterly* 15 (1990): 581–598.

30. See, for example, Michael A. Bailey, "So Close and Yet So Far: Two Unpopular Incumbents Meet with Different Fates in California and New York," in *Campaigns & Elections: Contemporary Case Studies*, 43-44.

31. See Westlye, *Senate Elections and Campaign Intensity*, chaps. 7 and 8; Abramowitz and Segal, *Senate Elections*, 109–115.

32. Before the election Wisconsin had a Republican governor and two Democratic senators, and its U.S. House, state assembly, and state senate delegations were closely divided.

33. Clyde Wilcox, "They Did It Their Way: Campaign Finance Principles and the Realities Clash in Wisconsin," in *Campaigns & Elections: Contemporary Case Studies*, 48.

34. On campaign strategy in Senate elections, see Kahn and Kenney, *The Spectacle of U.S. Senate Campaigns*, 12.

35. Wilcox, "They Did It Their Way," 50-52.

36. Ibid.

37. Ibid.

38. Ibid.

39. Before the race New York had a Republican governor, George Pataki, and a senator from each party. The state's House delegation favored the Democrats by a margin of 18 to 13. The state assembly had 98 Democrats and 52 Republicans, while the state senate had 25 Democrats and 36 Republicans.

40. Bailey, "So Close and Yet So Far," 33, 35, 43.

41. Ibid., 39-41.

42. *Courier-Journal*, December 28, 1998. Quoted in Gross and Miller, "Kentucky Senate," 35.

43. See John W. Kingdon, *Candidates for Office: Beliefs and Strategies* (New York: Random House, 1968), chap. 2.

44. See the sources listed in nn. 48-53 and 55 of Chapter 1.

45. See Kingdon, *Candidates for Office*, chap. 2.

46. See n. 42.

10 ELECTIONS AND GOVERNANCE

1. See Davidson and Oleszek, *Congress and Its Members*, esp. chap. 1.

2. Fenno, *Home Style*, 54–61.

3. Ibid., 153.

4. Mayhew, *Congress*, 49–68.

5. The figures are for 1999. See Davidson and Oleszek, *Congress and Its Members*, 154.

6. Ibid., 150-155.

7. Scott Adler, Chariti E. Gent, and Cary B. Overmeyer, "The Home Style Home Page: Legislative Use of the World Wide Web for Constituent Contact," *Legislative Studies Quarterly* 23 (1998): 585–596.

8. Timothy E. Cook, *Making Laws and Making News: Media Strategies in the U.S. House of Representatives* (Washington, D.C.: Brookings Institution, 1989), 71.

9. See, for example, Ben H. Bagdikian, "Congress and the Media: Partners in Propaganda," *Columbia Journalism Review* 12 (1974): 5.

10. Ibid., 2, 3, 37, 90.

11. Langbein, "Money and Access"; Wright, "Contributions, Lobbying, and Committee Voting."

12. Richard F. Fenno Jr., *Congressmen in Committees* (Boston: Little, Brown, 1973), 13.

13. Fox and Hammond, *Congressional Staffs*, 121–124.

14. Fenno, *Congressmen in Committees*, 1–14.

15. Kenneth J. Cooper, "The House Freshmen's First Choice," *Washington Post*, January 5, 1993, A13.

16. Davidson and Oleszek, *Congress and Its Members,* 355–357; Hammond, "Congressional Caucuses in the 104th Congress," *Congress Reconsidered,* 274–292.

17. "80,000 Lobbyists? Probably Not, but Maybe," *New York Times,* May 12, 1993, A13.

18. Kay Lehman Schlozman and John T. Tierney, *Organized Interests and American Democracy* (New York: Harper and Row, 1986), 272.

19. Ibid., 289–310.

20. Linda L. Fowler and Ronald D. Shaiko, "The Grass Roots Connection: Environmental Activists and Senate Roll Calls," *American Journal of Political Science* 31 (1987): 484–510; James G. Gimpel, "Grassroots Organizations and Equilibrium Cycles in Group Mobilization and Access," in *The Interest Group Connection.*

21. See Gordon Adams, *The Iron Triangle* (New York: Council on Economic Priorities, 1981), 175–180; Hugh Heclo, "Issue Networks and the Executive Establishment," in *The New American Political System,* ed. Anthony King (Washington, D.C.: American Enterprise Institute, 1978), 87–124.

22. Paul S. Herrnson and Kelly D. Patterson, "Toward a More Programmatic Democratic Party? Agenda Setting and Coalition Building in the House," *Polity* 27 (1995): 607–628; Paul S. Herrnson and David M. Cantor, "Party Campaign Activity and Party Unity in the U.S. House of Representatives," *Legislative Studies Quarterly* 22 (1997): 393–415.

23. Kelly D. Patterson, *Political Parties and the Maintenance of Liberal Democracy* (New York: Columbia University Press, 1996), chap. 4.

24. See Epstein, *Political Parties in Western Democracies,* 340–348.

25. See, for example, Herbert F. Weisberg, "Evaluating Theories of Congressional Roll Call Voting," *American Journal of Political Science* (1978): 554–577.

26. Hannah Pitkin, *The Concept of Representation* (Berkeley: University of California Press, 1967).

27. Cain, Ferejohn, and Fiorina, *The Personal Vote.*

28. David Hosansky, "How Two Fervent Free-Traders Helped Set Back 'Fast Track,' " *CQ Weekly,* October 3, 1998.

29. R. Douglas Arnold, "The Local Roots of Democracy," in *The New Congress,* ed. Thomas E. Mann and Norman J. Ornstein (Washington, D.C.: American Enterprise Institute, 1981), 250–287.

30. Davidson and Oleszek, *Congress and Its Members,* 278-279.

31. John Ferejohn, "Logrolling in an Institutional Context: A Case Study of Food Stamp Legislation," in *Congress and Policy and Change,* ed. Gerald C. Wright Jr., Leroy N. Rieselbach, and Lawrence C. Dodd (New York: Agathon Press, 1986), 223–253.

32. In recent Congresses legislation was supposed to stay within a set of overall budgetary limits in order to limit growth of the federal deficit. This zero-sum process has frequently required legislators to cut spending in some areas if they wish to increase it in others.

33. Herrnson and Patterson, "Agenda Setting and Coalition Building"; Herrnson and Cantor, "Party Campaign Activity and Party Unity."

34. Herrnson, Patterson, and Pitney, "From Ward Heelers to Public Relations Experts," 251–267.

35. V. O. Key Jr., "A Theory of Critical Elections," *Journal of Politics* 17 (1955): 3–18; Walter Dean Burnham, *Critical Elections and the Mainsprings of American Politics* (New York: W. W. Norton, 1970); Everett Carll Ladd Jr. with Charles D. Hadley, *Transformations of the American Party System* (New York: W. W. Norton, 1978).

36. Alan I. Abramowitz, "The End of the Democratic Era? 1994 and the Future of Congressional Election Research," *Political Research Quarterly* 48 (1995): 873–889; Jacobson, *The Politics of Congressional Elections,* 219–224.

37. Gimpel, *Fulfilling the Contract.*

38. On the evolution of and most recent changes in the legislative process, see Barbara Sinclair, *Unorthodox Lawmaking* (Washington, D.C.: CQ Press, 1997), esp. chaps. 1 and 6.

39. Committee on Political Parties, "Toward a More Responsible Two-Party System"; Leon D. Epstein, *Political Parties in the American Mold* (Madison: University of Wisconsin Press, 1986), 30–38.

11. CAMPAIGN REFORM

1. See, for example, John R. Hibbing and Elizabeth Theiss-Morse, *Congress as Public Enemy: Public Attitudes toward American Institutions* (Cambridge: Cambridge University Press, 1995), 63–71.

2. See, for example, James Madison, "Federalist No. 57," in *The Federalist Papers,* written by Alexander Hamilton, James Madison, and John Jay (New York: New American Library, 1961), 352.

3. For further discussions of the detrimental impact of term limits, see Jeffrey J. Mondak, "Elections as Filters: Term Limits and the Composition of the U.S. House," *Political Research Quarterly* 48 (1995): 701–727. For arguments in favor of and against term limits, see the essays in *Limiting Legislative Terms,* ed. Gerald Benjamin and Michael J. Malbin (Washington, D.C.: CQ Press, 1992).

4. On initiatives and referenda see Bowler, Donovan, and Tolbert, *Citizens as Legislators*; Bowler and Donovan, *Demanding Choices*; Magleby, *Direct Legislation*; and Cronin, *Direct Democracy.*

5. L. Sandy Maisel and Walter J. Stone, "Candidate Emergence Study: Report to Respondents."

6. Will Robinson, Democratic political consultant, interview, February 2, 1993.

7. Lyn Ragsdale and Jerrold G. Rusk, "Candidates, Issues, and Participation in Senate Elections," *Legislative Studies Quarterly* 22 (1995): 305–327.

8. There is much debate over spending limits and other kinds of campaign finance reforms. See Jacobson, *Money in Congressional Elections,* 48–49, 211–214; Jacobson, "The Effects of Campaign Spending"; Krasno and Green, "Salvation for the Spendthrift Incumbent"; Robert A. Jackson, "Voter Mobilization in the 1986 Midterm Election," *Journal of Politics* 55 (1993): 1081–1099; Robert Goidel and Donald A. Gross, "Reconsidering the Myths and Realities of Campaign Finance Reform," *Legislative Studies Quarterly* 21 (1996): 129–147.

9. See, for example, Alexander, *Financing Politics,* 23–26.

10. Joint Committee of Congress, *Organization of Congress,* Final Report, H. Rept. 103-413, 103rd Cong., 1st sess., 1993, 2:231–232, 275–287. Cited in Davidson and Oleszek, *Congress and Its Members,* 133.

11. Figures include contributions by individuals and groups located in the five zip-code areas surrounding the U.S. Capitol only. Compiled from FEC data.

12. Location of contributors determined by zip code. Compiled from FEC data.

13. Ironically, D'Amato's voting record is rarely characterized as pro-environment, and he received a zero rating from the League of Conservation Voters in 1996. See Blaine Harden, "D'Amato Has Reelection Recipe Simmering," *Washington Post,* February 22, 1997.

14. Results from a *Washington Post* poll cited in Eliza Newlin Carney, "Donor Fatigue," *National Journal,* February 22, 1997.

15. On large congressional donors see John C. Green, Paul S. Herrnson, Lyndal Powell, and Clyde Wilcox, *Individual Congressional Campaign Contributors: Wealthy, Conservative, and Reform-Minded* (Web site: http://www.georgetown.edu/wilcox/donors.htm); on state legislative candidates see Ron Faucheux and Paul S. Herrnson, "See How They Run: State Legislative Candidates," *Campaigns & Elections,* August 1999. Compiled from Paul S. Herrnson and Ronald A. Faucheux, The Campaign Assessment and Candidate Outreach Project, mail survey.

16. Compiled from Herrnson and Faucheux, The Campaign Assessment and Candidate Outreach Project.

17. Quoted in "Excerpts from Remarks on First Day of Campaign Finance Hearings," *New York Times,* July 9, 1997.

18. Wright, "PACs, Contributions, and Roll Calls" and "Contributions, Lobbying, and Committee Voting"; Grenzke, "PACs and the Congressional Supermarket." For an alternative viewpoint see John Frendreis and Richard Waterman, "PAC Contributions and Legislative Behavior: Senate Voting and Trucking Deregulation," *Social Science Quarterly* 66 (1985): 401–412.

19. John W. Kingdon, *Congressmen's Voting Decisions* (New York: Harper and Row, 1981).

20. Aage R. Clausen, *How Congressmen Decide* (New York: St. Martin's Press, 1973).

21. Wright, "Contributions, Lobbying, and Committee Voting" and "PACs, Contributions, and Roll Calls."

22. The parties of the golden age, especially the political machines, had shortcomings as well as strong points. Their shortcomings included undemocraticness, corruption, secrecy, and formal and informal barriers to the participation of women and various racial, ethnic, and religious groups. For some lively accounts of these parties see William Riordan, *Plunkitt of Tammany Hall* (New York: E. P. Dutton, 1905) and Mike Royko, *Boss: Richard J. Daley* (New York: E. P. Dutton, 1971).

23. See Hibbing and Theiss-Morse, *Congress as Public Enemy,* esp. chap. 5.

24. Findings of the Center for the Study of the American Electorate cited in Earl Lane, "The Impeachment Trial," *Newsday,* February 14, 1999.

25. Federal Election Commission, "FEC Issues Report on Impact of National Voter Registration Act," July 7, 1999.

26. Conference on Campaign Reform, Committee for the Study of the American Electorate, "Poll Finds Public Sour on Congress, Seeking More Bi-Partisanship on Issues and Reform, Uncertain and Divided on Details of Reform," press release, July 29, 1994.

27. On the roles of minor parties see Steven J. Rosenstone, Roy L. Behr, and Edward H. Lazarus, *Third Parties in America: Citizen Response to Major Party Failure* (Princeton, N.J.: Princeton University Press, 1984); David Gillespie, *Politics at the Periphery: Third Parties in Two-Party America* (Columbia: University of South Carolina Press, 1993); and the essays in *Multiparty Politics in America,* ed. Paul S. Herrnson and John C. Green (Lanham, Md.: Rowman and Littlefield, 1997).

28. L. Sandy Maisel, "Competition in Congressional Elections: Why More Qualified Candidates Do Not Seek Office," in *Rethinking Political Reform,* ed. Ruy A. Teixeira, L. Sandy Maisel, and John J. Pitney Jr. (Washington, D.C.: Progressive Foundation, 1994), 29.

29. Gary W. Cox and Michael C. Munger, "Closeness, Expenditures, and Turnout in the 1982 U.S. House Elections," *American Political Science Review* 83 (1989): 217–231.

30. The idea of giving candidates free television and radio broadcast time has been around for many years. See, for example, Twentieth Century Fund Commission on Campaign Costs, *Voters' Time* (New York: Twentieth Century Fund, 1969); and Campaign Study Group, "Increasing Access to Television for Political Candidates" (Cambridge: Institute of Politics, Harvard University, 1978).

31. Herrnson, *Party Campaigning,* 127.

32. Graber, *Mass Media and American Politics,* 53–55.

33. Larry J. Sabato, *Paying for Elections: The Campaign Finance Thicket* (New York: Twentieth Century Fund, 1989), 31.

34. The law currently requires broadcasters to make preemptive time available at the lowest unit rate; most candidates choose the more expensive nonpreemptible time slots.

35. Subsidized or free communications can also be used to induce certain desirable behaviors in candidates. They could be offered communications subsidies in exchange for participating in campaign debates or abiding by spending limits, for example.

36. See Ruth S. Jones and Warren E. Miller, "Financing Campaigns: Macro Level Innovation and Micro Level Response," *Western Political Quarterly* 38 (1985): 190, 192.

37. For countries and American states that offer citizens the opportunity to obtain tax credits for political contributions, see the case studies in *Campaign and Party Finance in North America and Western Europe.*

38. Marshall Ganz, "Voters in the Cross-Hairs: Elections and Voter Turnout," *The American Prospect,* winter 1994, 4–10; Michael T. Hannahan, "Campaign Strategy and Direct Voter Contact," in *Playing Hardball: Campaigning for the U.S. Congress,* ed. Paul S. Herrnson (Saddle River, N.J.: Prentice Hall, 2000).

39. Raymond E. Wolfinger and Stephen J. Rosenstone, *Who Votes?* (New Haven, Conn.: Yale University Press, 1980), 61–88.

40. J. Eric Oliver, "The Effects of Eligibility Restrictions and Party Activity on Absentee Voting and Voter Turnout," *American Journal of Political Science* 40 (1996): 498–513.

41. Joseph E. Cantor, *Campaign Finance Legislation in the 105th Congress* (Washington, D.C.: Congressional Research Service, Library of Congress, November 5, 1999).

42. Joseph E. Cantor, *Campaign Finance Bills, 106th Congress: Comparison of Shays-Meehan and McCain-Feingold Proposals* (Washington, D.C.: Congressional Research Service, Library of Congress, February 19, 1999); Cantor, *Campaign Finance Bills in the106th Congress: Comparison of Shays-Meehan, as Passed, with McCain-Feingold, as Considered* (Washington, D.C.: Congressional Research Service, Library of Congress, October 27, 1999); and Cantor, *Campaign Financing* (Washington, D.C.: Congressional Research Service, Library of Congress, October 20, 1999).

43. Cantor, *Campaign Financing*.

44. On Feingold's strategy see "Senator Vows to Note Donations in Debates," *New York Times*, June 17, 1999.

Index

Notes Name Index